States and Rulers
in Later Medieval Europe

States and Rulers
in Later Medieval Europe

BERNARD GUENÉE

Translated by
Juliet Vale

Basil Blackwell

First published in French as *L'Occident aux xive and xve siècles* ©
Presses Universitaires de France, 1971. Second enlarged
edition, 1981.

English translation first published 1985

Basil Blackwell Ltd
108 Cowley Road, Oxford OX4 1JF, UK

Basil Blackwell Inc.
432 Park Avenue South, Suite 1505,
New York, NY 10016, USA

British Library Cataloguing in Publication Data
Guenée, Bernard
States and rulers in later medieval Europe.
1. Europe—Politics and government—476–1492
I. Title   II. L'Occident aux XIVe et XVEe
siecles. *English*
320.94   JN7
ISBN 0–631–13673–8

Library of Congress Cataloging in Publication Data
Guenée, Bernard.
States and rulers in later medieval Europe.
Translation of: L'Occident aux XIVe et XVe siècles.
Bibliography: p
Includes index.
1. Europe—Politics and government—476–1492.
2. Europe—Kings and rulers.   I. Title.
JN7.G913   1985   940.1   84–28375
ISBN 0–631–13673–8

Typeset by Freeman Graphic, Tonbridge, Kent.
Printed in Great Britain by Bell & Bain Ltd, Glasgow

Contents

Translator's Note   ix
List of Abbreviations   x
Maps   xii

Introduction: Definitions and Problems
    The concept of the West   1
    'State': etymology and semantics   4
    The diversity of the West   6
    The unity of the West   18

Part 1   Intellectual Attitudes

1   INFORMATION AND PROPAGANDA   25

2   IDEAS AND BELIEFS
    Intellectual training   32
    Sources of political thought   37
    Fundamental assumptions   41
    Prophetic writings   44

3   STATE AND NATION
    The names of people and countries   50
    Nation and language   52
    Nation and country   54
    Nation and religion   56
    Nation and history   58
    Native and foreign   63
    Conclusion   65

4   THE IMAGE OF THE PRINCE
    The necessity of monarchy   66

The legitimacy of the ruler   67
The ideal ruler   69
The ceremonial prince   74

5   KING AND TYRANT
The limits to royal power   81
The punishment of a tyrant   84
The unthinkable sacrilege   86

Part II   The Power of the State

6   THE RESOURCES OF THE STATE
Traditional resources   91
The coinage   92
Indirect taxation: customs dues   96
Indirect taxation: the salt tax   99
Direct taxation   101
Public credit   105
Conclusion   108

7   THE AIMS OF THE STATE: JUSTICE AND FINANCE
Local administration   111
Central administration   120
The rise of the capital   126

8   THE AIMS OF THE STATE: WAR AND DIPLOMACY
War   137
Diplomacy   145

9   THE AIMS OF THE STATE: ECONOMIC POLICY   148

Part III   State and Society

10   THE BIRTH OF THE COUNTRY
The formation of orders or estates   157
The integration of orders or estates   159
The union of orders or estates   170

11   PRINCE AND COUNTRY
Oaths and contracts   171
The origins of representative assemblies   172
The influence of representative assemblies   177
The decline of representative assemblies   185

12   THE COUNTRY: LEGAL THEORY AND REALITY
Aristocratic societies   188
The revolts of the excluded   192

13 SERVANTS OF THE STATE 198

Conclusion 207

Appendix   Historiographical Problems: An Outline of Some
  Debates
    The Empire 209
    The origins of the Swiss Confederation 212
    Nations and national sentiment 216
    States and assemblies of estates 221
    The English Parliament 226
    Civic humanism 230
    The Hussite Revolution 233
    Reformatio Sigismundi 235
    When did the Middle Ages end in England? 237

Bibliography
    Sources 241
    The concept of the West 243
    Etymology and semantics of the later medieval State 243
    The Empire: concept and reality 245
    National studies: The British Isles, France and the
      Low Countries 247
    National studies: Italy and the Iberian peninsula 250
    National studies: Germany, Switzerland, Hungary, Poland
      and Scandinavia 252
    Information and propaganda 254
    Political thought 256
    Prophets and prophecies 260
    State and nation 261
    Nation and history 263
    The image of the prince 264
    King and tyrant 268
    The administration of the State: general studies 268
    The administration of the State: justice 270
    The administration of the State: finance 273
    The administration of the State: Chancery, Council
      and secretaries 281
    The administration of the State: the rise of the capital 283
    War 284
    Diplomacy 287
    Economic policy 288
    Society and the State: general studies 288

Society and the State: nobility and feudalism 289
Society and the State: town and country 292
Society and the State: the Church 294
Representative assemblies: general studies 296
Representative assemblies: the Continent 297
Representative assemblies: the British Isles 300
Revolts of the excluded 302
Servants of the State 306
Civic humanism 309

Index 311

Translator's Note

The bibliographies of the two French editions of this book (1971, 1981) have been supplemented by the author and revised and amalgamated for the English translation. Interruptions to the text in the form of translator's notes have been kept to a minimum: wherever possible terms unfamiliar to the English-speaking reader have been expanded or explained in the text.

Abbreviations

ABSHF   *Annuaire-Bulletin de la Société de l'Histoire de France*
AHR   *American Historical Review*
AFISA   *Annali della Fondazione Italiana per la Storia Amministrativa*
Ann.   *Annales (Economies, Sociétés, Civilisations)*
APAE   *Anciens Pays et Assemblées d'Etats*
BEC   *Bibliothèque de l'Ecole des Chartes*
BIHR   *Bulletin of the Institute of Historical Research*
BJRL   *Bulletin of the John Rylands Library*
BPH   *Bulletin philologique et historique (jusqu'à 1610)* of the Comité des travaux historiques et scientifiques
CH   *Cahiers d'Histoire*
DA   *Deutsches Archiv für Erforschung des Mittelalters*
EHM   *Estudios de Historia Moderna*
EHR   *English Historical Review*
HJ   *Historisches Jahrbuch*
HZ   *Historische Zeitschrift*
JWCI   *Journal of the Warburg and Courtauld Institutes*
MA   *Le Moyen Age*
MAH   *Mélanges d'Archéologie et d'Histoire* published by the Ecole Française de Rome
MIÖG   *Mitteilungen des Instituts für österreichische Geschichtsforschung*
MSHD   *Mémoires de la Société pour l'histoire du droit et des institutions des anciens pays bourguignons, comtois et romands*
NRS   *Nuova Rivista Storica*
PP   *Past and Present*
PTEC   *Positions des thèses de l'Ecole nationale des Chartes*
RBPH   *Revue belge de Philologie et d'Histoire*
RH   *Revue historique*
RHDFE   *Revue historique de droit français et étranger*

RMAL	*Revue du Moyen Age latin*
RQ	*Römische Quartalschrift für christliche Altertumskunde und für Kirchengeschichte*
RSI	*Rivista storica italiana*
SB	*Schweizer Beiträge zur Allgemeinen Geschichte*
SMRH	*Studies in Medieval and Renaissance History*
Spec.	*Speculum*
SZ	*Schweizerische Zeitschrift für Geschichte*
TRHS	*Transactions of the Royal Historical Society*
VSWG	*Vierteljahrschrift für Sozial- und Wirtschaftsgeschichte*
ZGW	*Zeitschrift für Geschichtswissenschaft*
ZHF	*Zeitschrift für historische Forschung*

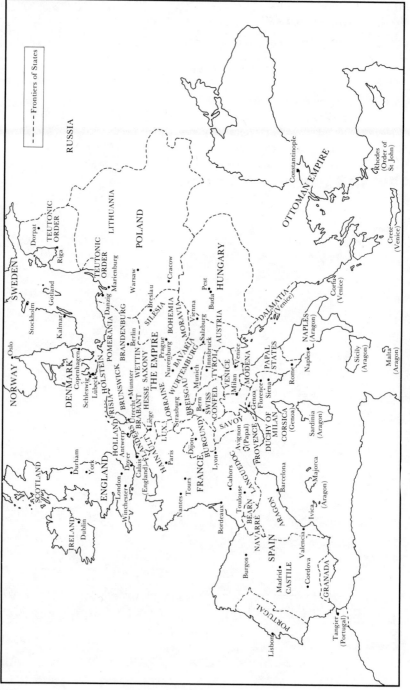

Map 1   The States of the West in the Later Middle Ages

The Burgundian Dominions (before 1477)

Imperial frontier

Frontiers of States

Lancastrian possessions in France (before 1453)

I   Normandy: English 1419–50

II   Paris region: English 1420–36

III Gascony : English to 1453

HOLSTEIN

FRISIA   POMERANIA

HOLLAND

BRUNSWICK   BRANDENBURG

Calais   Berlin

FLANDERS   BRABANT   HESSE

HAINAULT   WETTIN

Rouen   SAXONY

Paris   Rheims   Koblenz   THE EMPIRE   SILESIA   Breslau

I   LUX.

II   Orléans   Metz   Nuremberg   Prague

Tours   Toulon   LORRAINE   WURTEMBERG   BOHEMIA   MORAVIA

Bourges   Strasburg   Tabor

Basel   BREISGAU   BAVARIA   Passau

Augsburg

Poitiers   BURGUNDY   Bern   Zurich   Munich   Innsbruck   Vienna

FRANCE   SWISS   AUSTRIA   Salzburg

Lyon   CONFEDERATION   TYROL   STYRIA

Bordeaux

III   SAVOY   FRIULI

Toulouse   DUCHY   VENICE

LANGUEDOC   OF   MILAN   Venice

BÉARN   Avignon   PROVENCE   Genoa   MODENA   Ferrara

Bologna

Florence   Ancona

Siena   PAPAL STATES

Rome

NAPLES

Map 2   France and the German Empire c.1450

Introduction:
Definitions and Problems

At the end of antiquity the world *Occident* ('West') had already enjoyed a long career, in the course of which it had taken on various meanings. But for a contemporary of Constantine or of St Augustine one thing was clear: the West, domain of the Latin language, was set against the East, home of the Greek language. When Charlemagne accepted the imperial crown in 800 it became necessary to distinguish his Empire from the old Byzantine Empire: people referred – admittedly rarely – to the *Imperium Occidentale* ('Western Empire'). But Charlemagne's entourage was not content with this initial assimilation of the Empire and the West. They diverted other words from their ordinary sense to their master's profit. Charlemagne was called the venerable Pharo of Europe (*Europae veneranda pharus*), emperor and prince of Christendom (*imperator et princeps populi christiani*). As a result, for a brief instant at least, and for a small group of men, 'West' was synonymous with Empire, Europe and Christendom. It was not intended to express anything other than all the countries subject to the Emperor (*omnes imperatori subjectas provincias*). But it was only a fleeting moment. Scholars had not forgotten the purely geographical sense of a Europe whose borders were the Bosphorus and the Don; and the Papacy knew that Christendom (or *Christianitas*: the term was first used by John VIII) extended, if not – as they would have wished – to the entire world, at least well beyond the Carolingian Empire. Moreover, once that Empire had disintegrated, mental horizons did not extend so far; all sense of a wider community disappeared. At the beginning of the tenth century the great concepts of West, Empire, Christendom and Europe had fallen from use.

Soon, however, the peoples of the West became aware once more of the ties that bound them together. Not that the coronation of Otto I in 962 created a common political framework for them. For although in the second half of the twelfth century Frederick Barbarossa certainly said that one God, one Pope and one Emperor sufficed the whole world, and although the theme of universal Empire was common to many dreamers of the fourteenth century, the Saxon and Salian Emperors did not have such wide-ranging ambitions. They did not speak of their Empire until some considerable while after being proclaimed Emperors, and when for the first time, under Conrad II in 1034, the term *Imperium Romanum* appeared with a truly territorial sense, this Empire comprised nothing other than the three kingdoms of Germany, Italy and Burgundy. The Emperor was the most powerful ruler of the West; but the Empire did not by any means extend to all of Western Europe. The peoples of the West would not have allowed it; and the Emperor, moreover, did not claim it. There was no political unity in the West.

The term 'Christendom', to which John VIII had first given a social and geographical sense, was scarcely used in the two centuries that followed. But the First Crusade gave rise to a new awareness, and the word became sharply familiar. From then until the eighteenth century 'Christendom', 'the Christian republic', 'Christian peoples' and 'Christian lands' became expressions of everyday speech. Certainly Christendom was sometimes quite logically extended to all countries occupied by Christians, whether Latin, Greek or oriental. Christendom in the broad sense thus extended beyond Europe. But the oriental churches were so far away and the difference between the Greek and Latin churches so marked and so conscious, especially after the schism of 1054, that Western writers generally used the word 'Christendom' in a narrow sense. In the same way they easily forgot the Latin churches founded by the Crusaders in the Mediterranean, and the expression 'Latinity' – the Latin-speaking world – was most frequently employed in the narrow sense. Consequently, the words 'Christianity' and 'Latinity' usually meant no more to them than the sum of the European countries who recognized the authority of the Pope of Rome and whose liturgical and cultural language was Latin: they were in effect synonyms for 'Occident', the West. For the man of the thirteenth century the unity of the West was religious and cultural.

In contrast with the thoroughly organic religious and cultural community evoked by the words 'West', 'Christendom' and 'Latinity', 'Europe' in the thirteenth century was a word with purely geographical connotations and, moreover, rarely used. But political and cultural developments favoured its rise. Acre fell in 1291 and Rome lost sight of the Christian communities in the East; in 1386 Lithuania was converted to Roman Christianity; the Turks seized Byzantium in 1453, while in 1492 the Moorish kingdom of Grenada fell and Islam was no longer a presence in Western Europe. Slowly, and without ever really filling it, Christianity began to cast itself within the European mould. And because 'Europe' was a classical word and, besides, *Christianitas* would not fit into a hexameter, the humanists preferred to speak of 'Europe'. Certainly for a long while Christendom remained the more common term: Æneas Silvius Piccolomini, the future Pope Pius II, spoke constantly of *christianitas, christianus populus, christiana respublica*; in fifteenth-century France Thomas Basin referred to *christianitas, terrae christianorum*, Chastellain to *sainte crestienté* (sacred Christendom) and Commynes to *chrétienté*. The word 'Europe' scarcely appears in Dante, but is constant in Petrarch. In 1434 Æneas Silvius Piccolomini composed his *De Europa* and in 1458 invented the adjective *europaeus*: that was the beginning of the word's long and successful history. When Christendom was immeasurably extended by the discovery of the New World at the end of the fifteenth century, 'Europe' remained to describe the old community of the West more precisely. In the mid-fifteenth century Europe was still a scholarly word; a century later it was part of everyday speech. About 1450 the *Débat des Hérauts de France et d'Angleterre* spoke only of Christendom; its English riposte, the *Debate* (*c*.1550), spoke only of Europe.

The most scholarly writers did not forget that for early geographers Europe extended as far as the Bosphorus and the Don. But in contemporary usage Europe more frequently possessed a historical rather than a geographical sense. Ultimately, it was no more than a new word for the Christian and Latin communities of the West. Pius II spelt out what many others underlined; he spoke of Europeans, or Christians (*Europei, aut qui nomine christiano censentur*), and added, moreover, that neither the Eastern peoples nor the Greek (that is, the Byzantines) were truly Christian. Furthermore, he stated that, for him, Christendom meant essentially Spain, Gaul, Britain, Germany, Poland, Hungary and Italy. The Europe of the Western peoples was thus still Latin Christendom.

But the slow transition from Christendom to Europe was not purely the fantasy of a classical scholar. It also reflects an awareness of a certain secularization of the Western community. In 1300 the West felt religiously and culturally united. Two centuries later, although religion remained an essential part of that community, the peoples of the West were henceforth more readily distinguished by cultural and political structures. Not that they had created some kind of political unity in the West: Pope and Emperor were no more than names and figureheads (*ficta nomina, picta capita*). But it seemed to them that, in contrast with the oriental despots, all the *princes chrestiens* as Chastellain called them, the *principi occidentali* or the *principi di tutta l'Europa* as Machiavelli put it, were united by a certain solidarity and had a certain attitude and mode of political behaviour in common. At the end of the Middle Ages the West was not simply Christendom or the Latin-speaking world; it was also Europe. The West no longer simply defined itself by Roman religion or Latin culture, but also by political liberty.

The aim of this book is thus to study the structures and fortunes of States which, from Norway to Sicily and from Portugal to Poland, shared the same religious, cultural and political atmosphere, and whose profound unity did not escape the men of the fourteenth and fifteenth centuries who spoke of Christendom, the Latin-speaking world, Europe and the West.

'STATE': ETYMOLOGY AND SEMANTICS

Today all Latin and Germanic languages, and even Czechoslovak (but not the other Slavonic languages), use words deriving from the same Latin word – *status* – to refer to the State. But although *status* and its vernacular derivatives were already in existence at the end of the fifteenth century, they had still not acquired the sense which we commonly give them today. Indeed, it is possible that some authors of the late Empire, such as Tertullian or Orosius, used the word *status* for 'State'; but after that the usage died out. For centuries *status* meant nothing other than 'state' or 'condition'. But from the twelfth century onwards the use of *status* increased and its meaning developed to such an extent that it could be the source in English, for example, of three words with meanings as different as 'status', 'estate' and 'state'.

It was about 1200 that *status* appeared with its social sense, but our concern is rather with its ·political import. From late antiquity and throughout the Middle Ages people spoke of the *status reipublicae* (the republic), *status imperii* (the Empire) and *status regni* (the kingdom). In the second half of the twelfth century people began to refer to the *status regis* (the king, kingship). At the beginning of the thirteenth century in countries such as England or Hungary, where the concept of the crown assumed particular importance, they spoke of the *status coronae*. In all these expressions the word *status* still meant no more than 'condition', 'situation', 'state'.

It was in the second half of the thirteenth century that, as a result of the work of French and Italian theologians and legal writers, *status* began both to be employed in a more precise sense and to be used on its own. *Status regis*, the state of the king, could at first have a private sense and refer to the king's fortune and possessions. But it appears more frequently to have had a public sense, which also proved longer lasting. By *status regis* must be understood the royal function, office and dignity. From this semantic development came the meaning of *status* as the force and power of the prince, who would speak in the fourteenth and fifteenth centuries of maintaining his state and lordship (*estat et seigneurie, stato e signoria*). From the same development came also the meaning of government: in the fourteenth and fifteenth centuries *status*, 'state' and *stato* are frequently synonymous with *potestas, regimen, gubernatio* (power, rule, governance). As for *status reipublicae* or *imperii* or *regni*, the sense of political regime developed quite naturally from them: Bartolus of Sassoferrato knew that from the works of St Thomas Aquinas. Finally, to designate the whole political body, both governors and the governed, the writers of the late Middle Ages seem to have had a particular liking for the endlessly repeated expression, *status regis et regni*, the state of the king and the kingdom.

Thus *status* slowly approached its final sense: at the beginning of the sixteenth century, in the political writings of both Claude de Seyssel and of Machiavelli, *état* and *stato* still hardly ever had a sense other than that of the power of command over men, government, regime. But here and there at the very end of the fifteenth century 'state' was undoubtedly beginning to acquire its present meaning. In sixteenth-century usage that sense appeared everywhere, without the word losing any of its other and manifold social and political meanings. But to attribute to 'state', in a text of before 1500, its present most common meaning of a political body subject to a government and to common laws has every chance of being a gross misinterpretation.

The Middle Ages did not use the word 'state' in this sense. That does not mean to say that the concept of the State escaped them, at least in the fourteenth and fifteenth centuries. Certainly, with the barbarian invasions the word *respublica* disappeared without replacement. For Adalbero, bishop of Laon (*fl. c.*1030), *publica res* meant only the lay order, as opposed to the order of the Church (*ordo ecclesiae*). But with the great intellectual, juridical and political expansion of the twelfth century, medieval thought gradually rediscovered the concept of the State. At that time they used the word *populus*, but *populus*, those who are governed, failed to include the whole body politic of the State. They also used *corona*, but this term overemphasizes the opposite end of the socio-political structure. The word *regnum* was used above all. And the need for a general term was so great that the theorists could use *regnum* in referring to, for example, Bohemia, even though that country had no king. Nevertheless, *regnum* primarily meant kingdom, and many political bodies were not kingdoms. The Scholastics were also to speak very often of *civitates et regna* and Machiavelli after them of *città e régni*. But it is the return of *respublica* which marks the progress of political thought. In the last two centuries of the Middle Ages *respublica*, that which is public, did not necessarily have the precise sense of State, but it might do so. The notion of the State was revived well before 1500.

Were there in fact States in the West in the fourteenth and fifteenth centuries? The theorists of our own day, armed with the knowledge of many centuries of reflection and intervening political developments, have a precise definition of the State, in which the concept of sovereignty in particular is ascribed great importance. They undoubtedly would maintain that the political entities of the period did not accord with their definition and consequently would refuse to allow them the title of State, but we should not be excessively troubled by these refinements of definition. Let us avoid the trap of enclosing 'State' in a definition that is too exact and too modern for our purposes. If it is thought reasonable to admit the existence of a State once the population of a limited area is subject to government, it is in that case self-evident that there were States in the West in the fourteenth and fifteenth centuries whose political structures need to be examined.

THE DIVERSITY OF THE WEST

The West, the Empire and the Papacy

The Empire and the Papacy had long covered the West with a veil of apparent unity. From 1300 the veil was in tatters and allowed the political diversity of the West to become visible. It is nevertheless difficult to assess the significance of these two prestigious powers in the fourteenth and fifteenth centuries. Having recounted its greatness under the Saxons, the Salians and the Hohenstaufen, historians generally take leave of the Empire with the 'Great Interregnum' of 1250 to 1273. Afterwards, according to them, the Empire was merely a name, and the concept of an universal Empire was no more than a rhetorical theme for theorists out of touch with political reality. If we are really to understand the political life of the West at the end of the Middle Ages, they say, we must not be duped by appearances, but leave this spectre behind.

Such an attitude is not unjustified. There was a real collapse of the Empire after the death of Frederick II in 1250. His demise gave added impetus to the movement which, from the tenth and eleventh centuries onward, had been driving the princes of the West to proclaim their sovereignty by taking the title of emperor and adopting his attributes. The gestures of these first 'emperors' were short-lived. Nevertheless, in the twelfth century Roger II of Sicily had his sovereignty recognized by the Papacy and adopted a closed crown like that worn by the Emperors; Galbert of Bruges called Louis VI *imperator Franciae*; John of Salisbury said of Henry I of England that in his own realm he was *rex, legatus apostolicus, patriarcha, imperator*. The Papacy, in conflict with the Empire, encouraged these new ambitions, and the canon lawyers prepared and later justified the famous formula by which, in the decretal *Per venerabilem* of 1202, Innocent III proclaimed that the king of France should not recognize any temporal sovereign ('Cum rex ipse superiorem in temporalibus minime recognoscat'). The civil lawyers followed the example of the canonists. In the thirteenth century they established the sovereignty of their own countries without jeopardizing the principle of the universal Empire: the government of the world, said the Spaniards, had been handed down to the Germans, with the exception of Spain (*excepto regimini Hyspanie*); the Emperor rules over all rulers except, said Guillaume Durant, the king of France (*preter regem Francie*). In the second half of the thirteenth century the combined effort of Sicilian and, especially, French legal writers (such as Marino da Caramanico, Jean de Blanot, Jacques de Révigny, Pierre de Belleperche) perfected the definitive formula: 'rex in regno suo est imperator' (the king is emperor in his own kingdom). In the same period the kings of Aragon, Hungary and Bohemia assumed the orb, symbol of sovereignty proudly held by the Emperors since Charles the Bald. At the beginning of the fourteenth century the theorists, attacking the very principle of universal Empire, no longer hesitated to say that a single monarch had never ruled over the world, moreover that there was absolutely no need for all men to obey a single prince and that in fact the Emperor, who claimed to possess everything, had virtually nothing. In these circumstances how can one do other than doubt that the terms 'universal Empire' and 'universal monarchy' carried any meaning in 1300?

Although these revolutionary declarations are justly considered important, since they mark the beginnings of the sovereign State, they should not make us forget what were still the convictions of the majority of the inhabitants of the West at the beginning of the fourteenth century: 'Imperator non est hodie super omnes reges et super omnes nationes, sed esse debet' (the Emperor does not have authority over all kings and all nations today, but he should do): this was the most widely held opinion. If in reality the power of the Emperor was weak, his claims to the government of the world remained justified in law. For although one large party of canonists had held the national State over the baptismal font, another pronounced that the Pope was the true Emperor and the Emperor his vicar. The warmest advocate of papal theocracy, Boniface VIII, was therefore consistent when he wrote in 1303 that no king escaped the authority of the Emperor. The old Pope was no out-of-date theorist swayed by sudden impulse. About this time Alexander of Roes, Engelbert of Admont, Pierre Dubois and Dante all still acknowledged that the peace of the world could only be safeguarded by the existence of a single, universal power. So it was not surprising when on 29 June 1312 (the day of his coronation at Rome) Henry VII sent an encyclical to the princes of Western Christendom in which he loudly proclaimed the universal power of the Empire: to which the king of England replied with a polite letter that did not challenge the imperial claims, while Philip the Fair set only the exception of France against them. The king of France was so far from despising the Empire at the beginning of the fourteenth century that in 1308 he urged the candidature of his brother Charles of Valois, and his son Charles IV sought the imperial crown for himself in 1324. Now civil law had given a solid basis to the Emperor's universal claims. The crime of *lèse-majesté* could only be committed against the Emperor; the laws of the Empire were valid everywhere, the creation of notaries public was an imperial prerogative and the legitimization of children born out of wedlock an imperial privilege, while an appeal could always be made from the king's court to the Emperor. And so States whose own sovereignty remained ill-assured did not consider imperial interventions impossible, even within their own borders. Perhaps the Empire was not of great importance in reality at the beginning of the fourteenth century, but the concept still loomed large in men's minds: they believed in it, desired and feared it still.

Should we say that towards the middle of the fourteenth century, after the final efforts of Henry VII and Lewis of Bavaria (1314–47), the Empire belonged to the past? That would be to underestimate a great many contemporary writings, claims and fears. In 1355 the humanist Niccolo dei Beccari encouraged Charles IV to restore the universal Empire, so that peace might reign. In the course of a disputation at Prague in 1385 a Pavian lawyer, Uberto de Lampugnano, claimed universal authority for the Empire. For Nicholas of Cusa in·the fifteenth century the Emperor, God's representative on earth, was still the ruler of the world. Were these no more than Utopian fantasies? Although Charles IV did not listen to Niccolo dei Beccari, Wenceslas affirmed in 1379 that God had granted him universal authority in the temporal order (*imperium universae rei publicae temporalis*) and in 1412 Sigismund asserted that God had called him to the government of the whole world (*ad totius orbis regimen*). No one made light of these claims. Yet in the course of the fourteenth century the Emperor ceased to be mentioned by name in the Mass in France and Spain, and when King Charles V of France (1364–80) received the Emperor Charles IV in Paris in 1377, he strained his ingenuity by underlining with almost two dozen details the Emperor's status as a friendly visiting prince rather than a sovereign. So, for example, Charles IV made his entry into Paris on an entirely black horse chosen for him because white was the symbol of sovereignty. In 1412 the Emperor Sigismund invited the rulers of the West to the Council of Constance, but the king of Aragon felt obliged to protest that he was not subject to the Empire. When in 1416 the same Sigismund was visiting Paris and invited to a session of the Parlement, he installed himself in the place reserved for the king without being asked and ennobled one of the supplicants on his own initiative, and 'many people were amazed', commented Jean Juvenal des Ursins 'that he was allowed to behave like this, in view of the fact that the Emperors once wished to have authority and sovereignty over the kingdom of France'. Nevertheless, in December 1419 the widow of John the Fearless, duke of Burgundy, sought the intervention of the Emperor who 'has received from God the administration of temporal justice in this world'.

Even in 1446, in his *De ortu et auctoritate imperii romani*, Aeneas Silvius Piccolomini appeared like a prophet of the old imperial faith: he counted upon the Emperor to reunite Christendom and lead a Crusade. Doubts have been cast upon his sincerity. Yet why should he not have been perfectly sincere? At Pavia in 1510 Jean Feu still had to argue many cases to demonstrate that the king of France was not subject to imperial authority; Francis I would have had no objection to being proclaimed Emperor in 1519 and Charles V, his successful rival, revived for himself the old medieval dream of universal monarchy, so natural in a Christian environment and so tenacious at a time when many still believed (especially in Germany) that this Empire would be the last and that on its survival depended that of the whole world.

It is somewhat premature to be burying the universal Empire in the thirteenth century. Two centuries later it was still alive, the hope of some, feared by others. However, when in 1452 Emperor Frederick III took up the orb, symbol of universal monarchy (*pomum, quod mundi imperium ostendit*), he was grasping only a shadow. If the universal Empire still existed *de jure*, no one disputed that since the beginning of the fourteenth century it had not existed *de facto*. By common consent therefore, there were already in 1300 States in the West free from all subordination to the Empire.

Did the Papacy not also threaten their sovereignty? Since the end of the tenth century rulers whose authority was insecure had sought the protection of the Holy See. About 990 Mesco I had 'given' Poland to the Pope and bound himself to the payment of an annual due. In 1059 Robert Guiscard did not simply bind himself to an annual payment for the whole of his States, including Sicily, but he also performed homage to the Pope. The prince of Aragon in 1068, the king of Portugal in 1144 and others – even King John of England in 1213 – gave their States to God and St Peter and were regranted them in return for the assurance of feudal dues and homage. A number of Western States were thus subjects or vassals of the Holy See in the thirteenth century.

But during the same period all the States of the West were threatened by the Papacy's theocratic assertions. Innocent IV gave utterance to claims prepared by Innocent III and repeated by Boniface VIII, that the Pope exercised universal monarchy (*regimen universale*) on Christ's behalf. Undoubtedly, neither Innocent III, Innocent IV nor Boniface VIII would have disputed the autonomy of temporal power. But the *plenitudo potestatis* which the Pope had at his disposal, the total and boundless sovereignty which he possessed in law on earth authorized him to intervene in the politics of Christian States. He could, for example, depose a king, release the subjects of a kingdom from obedience to their ruler and keep an eagle eye on the observance of laws. He had the power to do so, and did not neglect any opportunity in the thirteenth century. And when imperial authority collapsed in 1250, pontifical theocracy seemed more menacing than ever to the States of the West.

Nevertheless, the downfall of the Papacy followed hard upon that of the Empire. For, first and foremost, the destinies of these two hostile brothers, Empire and Papacy, were closely bound together; if one fell, the other had to fall also. At the beginning of the fourteenth century one of Philip the Fair's lawyers reasoned that, since France was not part of the Empire, she was no more subject to the authority of the Pope than she was to that of the Emperor. It was after this that to the vigorous opposition of the youthful States (expressed by the attempted deposition at Anagni of 1303, the assembly of Vincennes in 1329 and the Statute of *Praemunire* in 1353) were added the difficulties of the Avignon Papacy and the disaster of the Great Schism.

So in the fourteenth century the subject States and vassals of the Holy See, following the early attempt of Frederick II, vigorously rejected all notion of temporal dependence with regard to Rome. The formula (*Sedi Apostolice immediate subjecta*) which bound Poland to the Papacy was important in the thirteenth century; it still had a role to play in the first half of the fourteenth century; after that it lapsed completely. Of the former ties of allegiance, only the 'Sicilian' vassalage was remembered in the fifteenth century. And the Papacy's role was not so much a part of the internal political life of the kingdom of Naples, but simply a result of the diplomatic imbroglio of the Italian peninsula as a whole. As for the universal monarchy of the Pope, it was certainly defended by Agostino Trionfo and Alvaro Pelayo in the first half of the fourteenth century, and a few individuals here and there might even give their support to it at the end of the fifteenth century. However, undoubtedly its only concrete manifestation between the time of Philip the Fair and the dawn of the sixteenth century was Alexander VI's decision to divide the New World between Spain and Portugal in 1493, and it is reasonable to suggest that this was already arbitration within the jurisdiction of the law of nations rather than a sovereign decision by the Pope.

For the ebb of imperial and pontifical power left European diplomacy powerless. From then on, the West had no ultimate authority which might arbitrate its quarrels. It is not surprising that the decline of the Papacy and the Empire stimulated the formation of international courts and tribunals, nor that the Pope and Emperor themselves returned as arbitrators to the very places from which they had been driven as sovereigns.

The Empire in Italy

If Hungary, Poland, the Scandinavian states, England and France, Portugal, Castile and Aragon, and even the kingdom of Naples – all of them outside the limits of the Holy Roman Empire – were in effect sovereign kingdoms in the later Middle Ages, what was the position of the Emperor *within* the limits of the Empire? The Emperor was not a universal monarch; was he at least sovereign in the three kingdoms of Germany, Italy and Burgundy? The Empire was not universal; was it at least a sovereign State comparable with France or England?

In practice the Emperor was absent from the kingdom of Burgundy, whose different regions were dominated by French princes. The imperial vicariate granted in the second half of the fourteenth century to the eldest son of the king of France in Dauphiné was the only manifestation of sovereignty, with no practical outcome. The Emperor expended no more thought on the inhabitants of the kingdom of Burgundy than they did on him. Italy was an entirely different case.

At the beginning of the fourteenth century, and for a long while before that, the imperial question divided the inhabitants of the Italian peninsula into two violently opposed parties. The Guelphs were the enemies of the Emperor; the Ghibellines his faithful friends. From then on the gulf between the two points of view was not really so fundamental. For the Guelphs did not completely reject the institution of the Empire any more than the Ghibellines absolutely condemned communal liberties. In the course of the fourteenth century the Guelph and Ghibelline viewpoints drew imperceptibly closer. And soon everyone thought that the primary aim of their political activities should be to protect their autonomy against anyone else. Moreover, everyone admitted that the Emperor still had a role to play in the peninsula. It is not in fact open to doubt that the Emperor did intervene in Italian political life at the end of the Middle Ages.

It is on the importance of these interventions that historical judgement differs. According to some, like Jacob Burckhardt, the Emperor in Italy at the end of the Middle Ages was merely the main character in pitiful and meaningless charades. Others, on the contrary, such as Francesco Ercole, do not deny the importance of the Emperor's role, but place him in the context of foreign affairs: the Emperor was merely a trump card in the complex game played by what were in effect sovereign States. Finally, yet other historians give greater credit to appearances and believe that the sovereignty of Italy in the later Middle Ages was indeed still in the hands of the Emperor. There is some truth in each of these points of view, but it is important to differentiate time and place. Every country in Italy is subject either to the Pope or the Emperor, maintained John of Legnano in the fourteenth century. He forgot lagoon-bound Venice, which had always preserved its independence. But the kingdom of Naples was in effect a vassal of the Holy See, and the whole of the rest of the peninsula, from Savoy to the Papal States, had been part of the old kingdom of Italy. Within this kingdom, less as a result of the 'donation of Constantine' than because of a long series of specific, indisputable grants recognized by the Emperor, the Pope enjoyed complete sovereignty in the Papal States. But elsewhere the Emperor had not abandoned his sovereign claims in the least. These were founded in law, as much as on the imperial crown which the Emperor received at Rome, or on the iron crown with which Henry VII, Lewis of Bavaria, Charles IV and Sigismund took great care to have themselves crowned in the basilica of St Ambrose in Milan, in accordance with tradition.

The most impressive demonstration of imperial authority was undoubtedly the practice and teaching of Roman law, and no one disputed that the Emperor was still the source of the law. But he lacked the means to ensure more exact recognition of his sovereignty. There was no royal administration or capital in the imperial kingdom of Italy and only the most limited royal domain. The personal presence of the king was therefore of great importance. In 1282, for example, the citizens of Sienna and Florence had been granted exemption from the oath of loyalty unless the king himself or a company of at least 500 Germans came to Tuscany. In the last two centuries of the Middle Ages journeys to Italy by the kings of the Romans or by the Emperors were not so very rare. But on average there was only one approximately every ten years. Imperial continuity only finally depended on a single institution, the imperial vicariate.

This institution had been devised under the Hohenstaufen and was taken up and adapted by Rudolph of Habsburg. In 1281, after the vicariate of Charles of Anjou, Rudolph appointed his own vicar, who kept the peace, received oaths of loyalty, collected the king's revenue and had at his disposal powers comparable to those of an imperial bailiff in southwest Germany. Henry VII began to distribute local vicariates in northern Italy to men who had made themselves rulers of a city and were ready to pay a high price to legalize their power. Moreover, it was not always a question of straightforward legalization of *de facto* powers, for the Emperor's decision might still occasionally change established positions.

Under Charles IV it was Tuscan cities, such as Florence or Pisa, that obtained an imperial vicariate – not for a 'tyrant', but for themselves, after taking an oath of loyalty to the Emperor. Pisa was an old Ghibelline city. But how can one explain the Florentines who judged it right in 1355 to declare themselves *fideles Imperii* (loyal subjects of the Empire), recognize Charles IV as their lord and humbly request an imperial vicariate? One should be clear in the first place that, contrary to what has sometimes been said their attitude did not mark a divergence from the doctrine of Bartolus of Sassoferato. For, in the famous jurist's tag, *civitas sibi princeps* (the city its own prince), *princeps* has a very broad meaning: Bartolus's city is not yet an autonomous city, nor already a 'miniature Empire'. And the Florentine vicariate had the great advantage of legalizing the city's power over the territory which she had acquired. Later, in 1437, it was also by imperial vicariate that Venice legalized her control over the Terra Firma. It is impossible to dismiss this imperial legitimization as insignificant, since Florence paid 100,000 florins for it and promised besides an annual disbursement of 4,000 florins, while Venice agreed to pay 1,000 ducats a year.

The formula, vicariate of the Empire, was soon left behind. In 1395 Gian Galeazzo Visconti was made duke of Milan for 100,000 florins. In 1416 Amadeus VIII was made duke of Savoy. The lord of Mantua became count in 1432; the lord of Modena duke in 1452. Thus the Emperors made a hereditary class of imperial princes out of local lords. The Emperor ended by being no more in the eyes of the Italians than a machine that would legitimize and strengthen any acquired power whatsoever in return for payment. For the Emperor was always short of ready cash. And he increasingly ran up against what has been called Italian national feeling: Dante, loyal to the medieval ideal of universal monarchy, was not much troubled by the Emperor's nationality and longed for imperial peace in Italy; but his attitude became less and less common, and an increasing number of Italians thought of the Emperor as a foreigner because he was German.

Imperial sovereignty thus slowly evaporated in Italy. Henry VII still raised both many hopes and many fears. Charles IV still granted imperial vicariates whose importance there is no reason to doubt. But Bernabò Visconti of Milan (d. 1385) claimed to be 'Pope, Emperor and lord in all his lands'. Coluccio Salutati refused to entertain the notion that Florence was not sovereign. Sigismund still created a few great princes of the Empire. But Frederick III was not able to have himself crowned king of Italy at Milan in 1452; and when he returned to the peninsula in 1469, he spent a whole day in his chamber at Ferrara receiving payment for and endorsing the appointments of 80 *conti, cavalieri, dottori* (counts, knights, doctors of law) and notaries. This was the sorry end of imperial sovereignty in Italy. Although the Emperors Maximilian and Charles V were later to return, the Emperors were henceforth no longer sovereigns in the eyes of the Italians, but foreign princes like the king of France or the king of Aragon.

Thus within the kingdom of Italy – which one most certainly could not call a State – there arose and developed city-states on the one hand and principalities on the other. Their theoretical submission to the Empire was rather better accepted because, once imperial favours had been bought, imperial sovereignty did not involve any intervention by the Emperor in their internal affairs and did not prevent them in effect from playing at sovereignty. Moreover, the fortunes of imperial power in the kingdom of Italy cannot properly be understood unless they are seen in the context of imperial power in the kingdom of Germany.

The Empire in Germany

Traditionally, historians studying the Empire in the last two centuries of the Middle Ages have turned their attention to the imperial towns and the principalities. There, they say, the State is henceforth to be found. Some facts support this position. The Emperor was quite without material resources at this period: while the king of Bohemia had an annual income of 100,000 marks of silver and the duke of Bavaria 20,000 in the second half of the thirteenth century, the royal domain only brought in 7,000. What did remain was almost entirely squandered in the reign of Lewis of Bavaria. No money, so no army and no royal administration. Without these means, the Emperor had finally to renounce the claims which he had once maintained against the two rising forces – the rich merchant bourgeoisie of the towns and the princes.

Henry VII had reacted violently when the townsmen of Strasburg had referred to members of their council as lords. But Charles IV himself said 'You are lords' to the council of Lübeck. In the fourteenth century the Emperor willingly granted to the citizens the kingly rights which he still possessed in their towns. Moreover, once this sovereignty was proclaimed and recognized, it did not prevent the towns from declaring their attachment to the Empire. The citizens of Nuremberg, where the imperial regalia (*insignia que imperium dicuntur*) were kept, grown rich from the pilgrims and tourists who came to see this treasure, willingly declared themselves the most loyal citizens of the capital of the Empire (*capitis imperii fidelissimi burgenses*); and perhaps they had a genuine concern for the grandeur of the Empire. But very often the towns who spoke of the grandeur of the Empire reduced it in direct proportion to their own egoism and had – to use the expression of K. S. Bader – a purely 'negative concept of the Empire': they had no intention whatsoever of reanimating it and invoked it simply to combat the activities of excessively threatening princes.

For the future belonged to the territorial princes. In 1198 Premysl, ruler of Bohemia, gave himself the title of king; in 1212 he obtained vast concessions from Frederick II which assured Bohemia of very considerable autonomy; in 1216 the Emperor acknowledged Premysl's eldest son as his heir. After that the hereditary kingdom of Bohemia could have achieved rapid independence had the German ambitions of its kings not furnished them with a motive for staying in the Empire. The concessions made to Bohemia were exceptional. But the princes of the Church obtained their first privileges in 1220 (*Confederatio cum principibus ecclesiasticis*) and the secular princes in 1231 (*Statutum in favorem principum*). The Golden Bull of 1356 was the second important stage in the development of the principalities. This transferred to the prince-electors almost complete sovereign rights. The crime of *lèse-majesté*, which until then was only a crime against the Emperor, was henceforth also a crime against the prince-electors, and the privilege *de non appellando et non evocando*, which Bohemia alone had possessed until then, was extended to them all. The privilege *de non evocando* protected all the subjects of a prince from any summons before a foreign court; the privilege *de non appellando* forbade them all recourse to such a foreign court, so that any appeal outside the principality was impossible from that time onwards. What the princes obtained by the Golden Bull, Rudolph of Habsburg (d. 1365) attempted to obtain by fraud – for he, too, like Bernabò Visconti, wanted to be Emperor and Pope in his own dominions. The fraud was denounced by Petrarch and Charles IV refused to confirm it, but when the Habsburg Frederick III received the imperial crown in 1453 he confirmed these spurious Austrian privileges. Whether by deceit, grant of privilege or usurpation, other princes soon enjoyed the same rights. Thus royal prerogatives passed to insignificant rulers. It was the same with royal titles: only the Emperor was addressed as *serenissimus, durchlautigst* in 1300; in 1375 the prince-electors and, at the beginning of the sixteenth century, all the princes of the Empire acquired a right to them.

This rise of the principalities did not provoke any conflict between Emperor and princes, however. For although at one time the Emperor had dreamt of defending the Empire against the princes, with the support of the towns, he soon decided to abandon the towns and be no more than a territorial prince himself, putting what still remained of the Empire at the disposal of his lands and his ambitions abroad. Given these circumstances, how can one deny that even in Germany at the end of the Middle Ages the Empire was no more than an illusion and that the political reality of the State lay elsewhere?

Nevertheless, the attachment to the Empire remained. Certainly not in the West, in the Low Countries, where it was well and truly forgotten. Nor in the East, in Bohemia, whose Slav population remained within the Empire only by the wish of their king. But the Swiss Confederation remained attached to the Empire longer than has sometimes been maintained: in the fifteenth century they were still capable of distinguishing the Empire from the Habsburg who was at its head. During the war of 1436–44, in which the town of Zurich was at war with the canton of Schwyz, both parties appealed to the Empire. If it is well known that the citizens of Zurich supported the universal Church and the traditional Empire, the inhabitants of Schwyz were quite capable of protesting vigorously against the calumnies which alleged that they were enemies of the Empire.

Consciousness of the Empire survived elsewhere. More than that, it became stronger, but at the same time it became warped. For the notion of Empire was the means by which the Germans acquired self-awareness at this period. After the fall of the Hohenstaufen, German clerics, merchants and princes created the cradle of German national sentiment from the Empire that had been reduced to the kingdom of Germany; and by the same means they gave new life to the old kingdom. Alexander of Roes claimed the Empire for the Germans at the time when Rudolph of Habsburg's Chancery abandoned Latin for German. Fifty years later Lupold of Bebenberg wanted to make the king of Germany an 'Emperor in his own kingdom', like the king of France or of England, at almost exactly the time when at Rhens in 1338 the princes rejected all papal claims to any right of intervention in the election of the king. After 1356 the Golden Bull of Charles IV – meeting these wishes – spoke neither of the vicariate claimed by the Pope during any vacancy of the German throne, nor of any pontifical approval required after the election of the German king: the Empire withdrew into the kingdom of Germany and sought a German identity. In 1358 the merchants of the Hanseatic League replaced the expression *universi mercatores romani imperii* ('merchants of the universal Roman Empire') with that of 'German Hanse'. Under the Emperor Frederick III (1440–93) people had begun to indicate that the Holy Roman Empire was also German; it was only at this juncture that the complete formula appeared: *Sacrum Romanum Imperium Nationis Germanicae* ('the Holy Roman Empire of the German Nation'). Maximilian did not bother to have himself crowned at Rome. The German humanists mingled the Germany of Tacitus and Maximilian's Empire with an equal enthusiasm and in 1519, to the great delight of the Germans, Charles V of Habsburg rather than Francis I of France was elected Emperor, simply because he was German. Thus the Empire revived by becoming German. But neither Alexander of Roes nor Lupold of Bebenberg nor many other

Germans in years to come forgot the old idea of universal Empire, and thus that confusion was created which was ultimately responsible for the persistence of the German dream of universal hegemony. But to return to the Middle Ages: the Empire was not dead; transformed and adapted, it was deeply rooted in the hearts and minds of the German people.

Their conviction that imperial reform was difficult, but essential, stemmed from this fact. Charles IV is supposed to have said after 1350 to Cola di Rienzo that 'the [Holy] Roman Empire could not be reformed without a miracle from heaven.' But it was in the fifteenth century, in connection with the conciliar movement, that the Germans became really interested in the reform of the Empire. In 1433 Nicholas of Cusa produced his *De Concordantia catholica*. The treatise traditionally called the *Reformatio Sigismundi* (although written in German) appeared a few years later and in 1442 there was the first vain attempt at reform, the 'Reform of King Frederick'. The problem of imperial reform existed at two different levels in the fifteenth century. If the Empire was to be reformed it was necessary first to attempt to forbid all private war and to establish a general territorial peace within its boundaries. But that also involved the creation of an imperial army and a judicial system to enforce the peace; this in turn necessitated imperial taxes and fiscal administration – in short, an imperial government. In the fifteenth century the German desire for reform led in the reign of Maximilian to the establishment of a perpetual territorial peace (the *Ewiger Landfriede* of 1495), the setting up of an imperial court of justice (*Reichskammergericht*) at Frankfurt in the same year and even the formation of an imperial government (*Reichsregiment*) in 1500, with its seat at Nuremberg. But from the outset the activities and even the existence of these bodies was compromised: too many parts of the Empire escaped the jurisdiction of the law courts; it proved impossible to collect the imperial tax which had been envisaged, the *Gemeine Pfennig* (Common Penny) and, above all, the princes and the Emperor fought for control of these imperial institutions. Thus we also find in the kingdom of Germany one of the fundamental characteristics of the States of the West in the late Middle Ages: the opposition between the ruler and his country – between a prince and his *pays*.

It is impossible to deny some kind of existence to the Empire reduced to Germany. The Empire was perhaps not a State of the same kind as England or France, but it was a State just as the countries within the Empire (the kingdom of Bohemia, the Swiss Confederation, the principalities and the imperial towns) were States very different from imperial Germany and very unlike each other.

THE UNITY OF THE WEST

At the end of the Middle Ages the Empire, the old independent kingdoms, the new principalities and the city-states were different types of political structures. Moreover, between England and Poland, Scandinavia and the Iberian peninsula, historical and geographical conditions created such differing situations that all these States had quite different characteristics. Even if we suppose that such and such of these were the result of similar developments, they did not inevitably occur at the same time. In a comparative study of the States of the West in the fourteenth and fifteenth centuries the great obstacles are the disparate character of the States and the diversity of the West.

This evident diversity should nevertheless not conceal what all those States had in common. The German State was perhaps less different from England or France than might at first appear. For the latter were far from constituting a homogeneous political body: an English dukedom was an autonomous body; and surely we cannot deny the name of State to the *vicomté* of Béarn (sovereign at one point in the fourteenth century), or the Burgundian lands, sovereign for a long period in the fifteenth century, or the duchy of Brittany whose ruler claimed to be 'king in his country' (*roi en son pays*) at the end of the fourteenth century and styled himself duke 'by the grace of God' in 1417? In the same way, although German historians insist on the originality of the principality and Italian historians on that of the city-state, there are undoubtedly grounds to question whether, beyond their individual originality, they do not both have a number of funda-mental traits in common. Moreover all these States, of whatever type, shared the same intellectual and cultural ambience, reacted to the same demographic and economic difficulties, knew their neighbours' political problems and their solutions and drew inspiration from them. There is no question of playing down the disparate nature of the States of the West, but this book is concerned rather with indicating in what respects they were alike beyond that diversity, and what constituted the unity of the West in the fourteenth and fifteenth centuries.

The significance of the period

What then, did the fourteenth and fifteenth centuries stand for in the development of the West? What sense have historians been able to make of this period? The most general and widely encountered theme is that these centuries were part of a transitional period when the medieval State gradually gave way to the modern. Whether medieval or modern predominates in the period between 1300 and 1500 is an open question. But in reality the situation is too complex, the concepts of 'medieval' and 'modern' too fluid, for such a statement to be adequate. Some, French medievalists among them, believe that this period should be considered primarily as the end of the Middle Ages. Others, on the whole more numerous and with French legal writers prominent amongst them, believe, on the contrary, that the modern period really began about 1300. Besides, the States did not all develop at anything like the same rate. Historians find the awarding of prizes for modernity irresistible. The Norman State of Sicily most frequently carries off the first prize. But people have also been able to say that Florence was 'the first modern state in the world'. Frederick II's Sicily was 'already modern', as Charles V's Empire was 'still medieval'. The England of Edward I was 'already modern', that of Henry VII 'still medieval'. These contradictions are surely revealing. Do they not prove that historians are mistaken in denying all individuality to a period which is reduced, in their eyes, to prolonging the past or heralding the future? Is there not a case for putting this period, so often left in the wings, resolutely in the centre of the stage and making the fourteenth and fifteenth centuries a period as autonomous and individual in the development of the States of the West as the 'medieval' or the 'modern' periods? Some historians have found the solution: the 'medieval' and 'modern' States were opposed in futile combat; the 'Renaissance' State separated them.

Fortunately, historians' endeavours have not stopped at this terminological argument. More precise variations make these grand abstract themes more meaningful. From the tenth to the thirteenth century the political life of the West was dominated by feudalism: feudal relations – based on the personal bond of vassalage and the concrete tie of the fief – played a vital role. French historians have sometimes called the thirteenth century the period of the 'feudal monarchy' and German historians traditionally use the term *Lehenstaat* (from *Lehen* = fief). Everyone is agreed in saying that in the fourteenth century there was a singular decline in the importance of feudalism in the State. The State of that period was certainly no longer feudal. Nevertheless vassalage and fief still occupied an important place in the State which we must discuss in greater detail.

If some historians demonstrate the decay of feudalism in the fourteenth and fifteenth centuries, others clearly indicate the first steps of absolute monarchy at this time. Whether they already consider Francis I to be an 'absolute monarch', whether they place the flowering of absolutism at a later date or whether they even see it as an unfilfilled dream, many historians view the progress of absolutism as one of the characteristics of our period. Whatever the precise meaning they would give to the term,

B

those who have spoken of the progress of absolutism at the end of the Middle Ages have wanted to emphasize the remarkable advance in the power of the ruler.

The authority of this new type of prince was essentially based upon a bureaucracy whose importance is so striking that a historian such as F. Chabod makes this the distinguishing characteristic of the Renaissance State. The endeavours of the prince and his officers resulted in a central administration that became increasingly extensive. The external boundaries of the State had a purely jurisdictional importance and were scarcely more important than any feudal boundary. But the new State constructed increasingly solid borders for itself, to which it gave political, fiscal and above all military meaning: in the fourteenth century the bondary in effect became a frontier. And within these frontiers, little by little, the prince regained his old regalian rights, imposing his laws and his tax system with increasing effect, thanks to the growing number of his agents, controlled from the capital by an ever-expanding network of services. Thus, after the feudal State, the territorial State came into being as a result of the administrative action of the ruler. The monarchy of the Renaissance was not yet absolute, but it was already an administrative monarchy. Indeed, if a whole school of historical thought insists on the fundamental role of the prince and his servants in the new State and is not far from seeing the Renaissance State as an 'artistic creation', as Burckhardt put it, another view underlines the presence of those on whom this administration impinged, placing the governors opposite the governed and the prince opposite his country.

It is in this way, according to historians such as H. Hauser, that the stability of the new State is to be explained, above all by the birth of national feeling, which regrouped all the subjects of the prince in a real community. This assertion has been the subject of many reservations and refinements: what is meant, after all, by national sentiment? Should one not rather speak of national feelings, varying according to the country? Were all the States of the West bound together by national sentiment? And was this support really the vital ingredient? Whatever the case, it is very rare to find a historian who denies that the Renaissance State was, if not always, at least often, a national State.

But the community within it was not a monolithic structure. Nineteenth-century historians traditionally distinguished the Church, the nobility and the bourgeoisie. One of the historical themes most dear to French historians in the age of Louis-Philippe was that of the crown, supported by the bourgeoisie, overcoming the nobility and the Church. This theme, which has been the more or less conscious foundation of many works, today seems much less convincing, even in France, and even more so in other countries. For while the rise of the bourgeoisie is not apparent in all the States of the West at the end of the Middle Ages, the economic and political decline of the nobility is certainly nowhere evident. Even in France the king had to abandon his attempts to tax the nobility at the end of the Middle Ages. At present the relationship in the new State between the nobility and the bourgeoisie remains an unanswered question. To resolve it, we would have to ascertain precisely what is meant by 'nobility' and 'bourgeoisie' and animate these abstractions with individual examples.

However, the princes encountered stronger opposition that that of social classes: the local forces and influences which operated against him. A deep-seated 'regionalism' was one of the primary characteristics of the West in the fourteenth and fifteenth centuries. Villages, towns, castellanies, dioceses and counties all had a role that was sometimes powerful, always active. Within these boundaries groups formed whose outlines had long been indistinct – of clerks,nobles, merchants and sometimes even peasants. When the feudal ties of vassalage were becoming less effective it was with these forces and interest-groups that the prince had to communicate. The problem is to assess whether the initiative came from the prince or from the region itself. But it is a fact that, on the one hand, these bodies and groups tended to take shape opposite the prince in the 'estates' or 'orders' that were increasingly well defined and self-aware, and that, on the other hand, these classes gave their representatives powers to negotiate on their behalf and defend them. Historians who attach a primordial importance to the organization of society into estates speak of 'assemblies of estates'; the others simply call them representative assemblies. Without exception, such assemblies played an often vital part in the life of the States of the West from the fourteenth to the sixteenth centuries. Their role was so important that some historians have wondered whether, instead of speaking always of the progress of absolutism and princely power, it would not be better to delineate clearly an intermediate stage between feudal and absolute monarchy, whose essential feature would be the active presence of the regions (*pays*) beside the prince. The representative assembly characterized the State of this period as the Council characterized the Church.

In this debate French historians believe that the initiative remained with the prince. They always share the ruler's perspective and this has resulted in the definition of monarchy at this period (between the feudal monarchy and absolutism) as modified, limited or even controlled. By contrast German or German-speaking historians since O. Gierke (see pp. 221–3 below) have seen this period as one of dialogue between equals, with on the one side the prince, on the other the country organized into Estates (*Stände*), whose representatives grouped themselves into assemblies and had the power to conclude real agreements with him.

These were veritable treaties (dubbed *Herrschaftsverträge* by W. Näf) which henceforth regulated the life of the State. These historians either call this period that of dualism, or – following the pattern of *Feudalstaat* (feudal State) – they call it *Ständestaat*. Unfortunately, it is impossible for French historians to translate this as *Etat d'états* and in the past some of them proposed the term *Etat corporatif* ('corporate state') to remedy this, while today others seem to be settling rather for *Etat d'ordres* ('State composed of orders'), but there is no general consensus.

And so, as these theories are discussed, the principal traits of the Renaissance State begin to appear with the emergence of the national and the territorial State, a monarchy that was administrative, bureaucratic and centralized, with the development of modified, limited or controlled monarchy, and the dualist or corporate State.

The chronological limits of the period

The problem of perpetual change and of continuity must also be taken into account. On the one hand, whatever they have in common, there are enormous differences between 1300, 1400 and 1500. On the other, neither 1300 nor 1500 are convincing cut-off points. If the reigns of Edward I or Philip the Fair are turning-points in many respects, they are the inheritors of Henry III and of St Louis in every sphere of activity. Without them they would be inexplicable. As for the end of the fifteenth century, no one makes a break here in the political life of the West. Some encompass the three centuries of 1300 to 1600 with a single glance. Others will not countenance the smallest break between the beginning of the fourteenth and the mid-sixteenth centuries. They cannot bring themselves to separate the England of Henry VII from that of Henry VIII, the France of Francis I from that of Charles VII, the Germany of Charles V from that of Frederick III. Finally, others see essential changes occurring around 1500: according to G. R. Elton, for example, it was the 1530s, with the reforms of Thomas Cromwell, that really changed English political structures (see pp. 238–9 below). We should not be misled by round figures. We are forced by necessity to talk of the fourteenth and fifteenth centuries as an entity, but without conviction. We shall concern ourselves rather with identifying the originality of the political structures of the States of the West at a time which was no longer truly 'feudal', but not yet really 'modern', whose characteristics began to appear in the second half of the thirteenth century and persisted into the first half of the sixteenth.

Part I

Intellectual Attitudes

The reader may perhaps be surprised to approach the history of the States of the West at the end of the Middle Ages through a study of mentalities. Some historians refuse to relate political facts on the one hand to contemporary ideas and feelings on the other. One man maintains that the development of the monarchy in the fifteenth century is explained by the development of administrative and financial techniques, and not by futile speculation on the relationship between the king and the law. Another refuses to grant the great intellectual debates of the humanists any role in the political evolution of fourteenth- and fifteenth-century Italy. Of course the Middle Ages were not free from thinkers without wordly experience and had its share of administrators quite lacking in profound thought. But very often the theorists did play a role of prime importance in the life of the Church or the State. Moreover, we must 'realize the importance, in everyday life, of what we call abstract ideas' and which F. M. Powicke simply prefers to call 'man's capacity to think'.[1] These men had a sense of direction and purpose that was neither more nor less highly developed than in other periods. Ideas and facts cannot be separated.

Without denying this close relationship, some historians believe that 'the facts precede the theory', that political theory is never anything other than the rational expression of perceived experience. In these circumstances it would be putting the cart before the horse to set out the ideas before establishing the facts. It is true that other historians, like W. Ullmann, go so far as to say that 'facts are merely symptoms of underlying ideas and principles'.[2] We shall stop short of that and recognize the weight of economic, social and institutional reality in political life, the importance of simple power distribution. These realities influence contemporary and, above all, future theories. But at any one moment they can only act on and through minds, characterized by ideas, experiences and dreams that are often very old. To start the history of States with the study of mentalities is simply to recognize that politics are the work of men who do not submit passively to facts, but react to them according to the character and requirements of their own minds.

[1] 'Reflections on the Medieval State' (55).
[2] *Principles of Government and Politics* (393).

1

Information and Propaganda

The clergy had long realized the power of the arts and were skilled in instructing and persuading their flock with works whose themes they determined. Following their example, princes and towns soon learnt how to put art at the service of the State or of their own political ends. As early as 1200 the windows of Strasburg cathedral reminded the faithful of the imperial succession. In France the cathedrals of Paris, Chartres and Reims already offered the onlooker 'galleries of kings' in glass or stone, while the *Grande-Salle* of the Palais de la Cité (see figure 2), built at the beginning of the fourteenth century, was decorated with royal statues designed to kindle loyalty to the monarchy in countless visitors. In Venice at the same time art had to glorify the ruling power and praise the order and prosperity which it had created. Between 1337 and 1339 Ambrogio Lorenzetti painted his frescoes of Good and Bad Government in the communal palace at Sienna, translating Aristotelian teaching into pictures. In 1347 Cola di Rienzo had the sufferings and humiliation of Rome painted on the walls of the Capitol in order to incite the people. These examples will suffice. To set out ideas, strengthen feelings, rouse the passions – this is what was expected in the fourteenth and fifteenth centuries of an art that always exacted its price.

The decoration of palaces and cathedrals could only affect a minority. But at the end of the Middle Ages a taste for lavish spectacle also developed. Each country shaped these spectacles according to its own traditions. The humanists had no difficulty in discovering a classical origin for the Italian 'triumphs'. In contrast, old chivalric fantasies were staged in processions and banquets north of the Alps. But here and there, throughout Europe, these festivities developed in increasingly complex forms. By these means art was decorated to the point of exuberance, became animated, descended to the streets and affected an entire population. Some of these festivities were simply celebrations, but there were numerous occasions when they were organized by the ruling power, and had a political meaning; these greatly affected the life of the States.

The old ceremony of coronation which had made kings down the centuries had at first been conducted according to very simple procedures, recorded in very brief *ordines*. The ceremony was gradually embellished to such an extent that at the dawn of the fourteenth century it had reached full maturity. At almost the same time – about 1300 in France, 1307 in the Empire and 1308 in England – new *ordines* were drawn up which, without breaking with tradition, were at the same time fuller, clearer and more detailed than their predecessors. The importance of this new generation of *ordines* is considerable. Henceforth the liturgy of the coronation was essentially fixed. Nevertheless, innovations and revisions gradually modified the course and even the meaning of the ceremony. In England a new *ordo* was composed in the household of Nicholas Lytlington, abbot of Westminster, and followed for the coronation of Richard II in 1377. In France Charles V had the coronation ordinance revised by his clerks and again in 1484, on the accession of Charles VIII, a body of experts produced a new version of the ceremonial. Charles V wanted to make the royal coronation more like an episcopal consecration, while a century later the chosen aim was to restrict the significance of the coronation, to base royal legitimacy on heredity alone and to remove all traces of rights conferred by the ceremony at Reims. But the coronation gained in splendour what it lost in importance. The *ordines* of the fourteenth and fifteenth centuries were always longer and more detailed; the festivities more sumptuous and costly. The organizers always tended to neglect the religious ceremony, at which only a minority could be present, for the street spectacle, where a whole people could see the king. Our earliest description of the coronation-day procession of the king of England from the Tower of London to Westminster Hall dates from 1377. The considerable sums disbursed on this occasion would appear extravagant if one did not know the political importance of this procession from contemporary accounts.

In two centuries the funerary ceremonies of kings also became grandiose spectacles. But the symbolic importance increased precisely when that of the coronation waned. Since coronation no longer made the king, the funeral ordinance had to demonstrate that 'the king never dies'. Thus in France, at the beginning of the fourteenth century, the funeral was essentially a simple procession of mourners that led the body of the dead king from Paris to Saint-Denis. Soon the procession became increasingly large with the participation of ever-growing numbers of members of the Parlement (supreme court of appeals) and of the royal household. Then, following English custom, an effigy of the living king appeared beside the corpse at the obsequies of Charles VI in 1422. In the second half of the fifteenth century this effigy became the centre of the ceremony and gave it a new dimension: the king was not yet dead; and moreover his successor did not appear in the cortege, which was no longer a funeral procession, but a triumphal entry. It was only at Saint-Denis, when the body of the dead king had disappeared into its tomb, that the cry of 'The king is dead' was immediately followed by that of 'Long live the king'. For all its simplicity, however, the formula was slow to gain widespread acceptance. It was not until the death of Charles VIII in 1498 that they cried at Saint-Denis 'Mort est le Roy Charles, vive le Roy Louis' ('King Charles is dead: long live King Louis'); nor until 1509 and the funeral of Henry VII that you would have heard after the ceremony, 'The Noble Kynge Henry the Seaventh is deade', 'Long live the Noble Kynge Henry the Eighth.' It was only at the funeral of Louis XII in 1515 that the simple impersonal cry marked at the same time the continuity of regal dignity and the beginning of a new reign.

Coronations and funerals drew large crowds but in a strictly limited area. Nor were they so very frequent. Between one occasion and the next the people might well forget their message as royal officers sometimes forgot their ordering. Betweenwhiles popular sentiment was rekindled by the solemn entries which during the course of his travels the king made into his *bonnes villes*, the larger and more important towns in the kingdom. At the beginning of the fourteenth century princely entries, like coronations, were not the occasion for anything other than the most simple ceremonies. In the fourteenth and fifteenth centuries they became complex celebrations, grandiose and rich in meaning, with a ceremonial to which the modern world has been able to add only a few details. Indeed, at the beginning of the fourteenth century, when the king approached one of his towns his main concern was to find food and shelter. The most important moment of his exceedingly brief entry was when the citizens gave him the gifts which the right of lodgement (*gîte*) demanded, and without which neither he nor his entourage could possibly survive. But from the middle of the fourteenth century no one dreamt of having an entry without a long procession whose participants changed into a 'uniform' for the occasion. The tendency to transform the previously simple occasion into a noisy and colourful parade is apparent throughout the kingdom. Moreover, the reign of Charles VI was a decisive period for the history of the formal entry. For the first time in 1389, and from then on, the king rode along streets draped with hangings 'like temples' and underneath a canopy which was a copy of that which had appeared above the Holy Sacrament in the Corpus Christi procession a few years earlier. A royal entry thus became a semi-religious occasion, a veritable Corpus Regis, or glorification of the king. And at Paris in 1380 a royal entry first provided an opportunity for animated tableaux, at the same time that the first theatrical fraternities appeared at Nantes, Rouen and at Paris. For a long while these *histoires* and mystery plays remained few in number and were content to elaborate upon devotional themes, such as the life of Christ, or simply to entertain the king and the crowd. But from the reign of Louis XI (1461–83) the number of mystery plays along the royal route increased. The casual onlooker had them constantly before him, poets described them endlessly and, without abandoning the religious scenes, the organizers of the occasion sometimes chose for their drama themes designed to strengthen this royal 'religion', to exalt the person of the king and justify his policies. Initially a simple celebration, then a semi-religious ceremony, by the end of the fifteenth century a royal entry had become a grand spectacle in which the king's advisers adeptly developed all the themes of monarchical propaganda.

Nothing was better calculated to rouse the loyalty of the people than these great spectacles of coronations, funerals, entries and any other solemn ceremony where – as the chancellor said to the representatives of the Estates General at Tours in 1484 – his subjects had the opportunity of seeing the king in an appropriate context.

The king could not be everywhere and royal propaganda had plenty of other means at its disposal. In the household of the ruler, university scholars, churchmen and royal officers were all busy translating and compiling, and they assembled voluminous dossiers which – whether they were brilliant syntheses or undigested hunks – were an invaluable propaganda arsenal. We should not underestimate the intellectual abilities of nobles and citizens: these fat books can be traced in their libraries and they were well able to read and understand them. But the audience for such works was much wider than the number of extant manuscripts would at first suggest, for they had also influenced a whole group of people more or less conscious of their intermediary role. From them Chanceries could draw circular letters which were carried to the towns by the messengers of the prince and read by heralds at the crossroads on market days. Their themes inspired many sermons: in France, since the beginning of the fourteenth century, Philip the Fair and Philip VI of Valois were aware of the advantages of requiring their bishops to organize general processions, celebrate solemn masses and have prayers said, in the course of which sermons would be preached with themes specified by the king and designed to justify, for example, the war in Flanders or that against the English. Minstrels were doubtless much more difficult to inspire and control than preachers. They could even constitute a real danger for the ruling power. At the beginning of his reign Henry IV of England had to organize a campaign against the Welsh bards. But Henry IV was still an insecure usurper. In a stable State, if a minstrel wanted to live peacefully and go about the countryside, it was better for him if his poems and stories were not 'seditious or touching contentious issues'. He would more easily attract the benevolent attentions of the State's agents by composing or reciting short lyrics or interminable verse narratives that knew how to work up some of the themes dear to the regime.

Thus, until the end of the fifteenth century, minds were shaped by these spectacles and by what was said by heralds, preachers and minstrels. But about 1485 insubstantial pamphlets began to appear, printed at minimum expense on mediocre or even very poor quality paper, prompted by the regime, or controlled by it. The reign of the printed word and the journalist had begun. These writings reinforced and extended the effects of the spoken word and drama. For whether they were pamphlets which repeated the former, or broadsheets which recounted the latter, they could be sold at street corners several days later. The oldest of these *Neue Zeitungen*, as the Germans call them, appeared in 1486 and described the crowning of Maximilian. Of sixty-five extant French examples dating from the reign of Louis XII thirty-three gave news of the Italian Wars and the others reported the king's coronation, his entries, the obsequies of Queen Anne, the coronation and entries of Queen Marie and the funeral of the king.

With the advent of printing, communication and propaganda entered a new era and became more intense. However, before 1485 they had from time to time experienced varying levels of activity which are not explicable by the different means available, but reflect the tension of current events and the temperament of the rulers. The number and quality of political works provoked by the quarrel of Philip the Fair and Boniface VIII or that of John XXII and Lewis of Bavaria are too well known to need emphasis here. But take instead the case of Charles V. He was only dauphin and quite young when, in the crisis of 1357, he had platforms erected and, accompanied by a very small retinue, he addressed the crowd. Wise and eloquent, he had quickly learnt the political value of influencing men's minds. Once king, he collected a large number of books in his library. He commissioned translations of a number of major works that had an important influence on his own thought and action: Aristotle's *Politics* by Master Nicholas Oresme; St Augustine's *City of God* by Raoul de Presles; John of Salisbury's *Policraticus* by the Franciscan Denis Foulechat; the *De Regimine Principum* of Giles of Rome by the Carmelite Jean Golein. He had the long *Songe du Vergier* compiled (probably by a team of clerks) from works written in the previous century – a compendium that dealt with all contemporary political and social problems. To justify his war against the English he had dossiers of memoranda drawn up which earnt him the scornful epithet 'the Advocate' from his enemies, but succeeded in convincing his subjects – if, indeed, there was any need to do so. Finally, as his grandfather had ascended the throne in 1328 in questionable circumstances and his father had been defeated at Poitiers, in order to secure the legitimacy and raise the prestige of his house, he commissioned long verse narratives like *Florent et Octavien, Hugues Capet, Charles le Chauve,* and *Théséus de Cologne,* where the French might discover the characters to whom the king was pleased to link his dynasty: Hugues Capet and, above all, Dagobert and St Denis. Charles V knew all the secrets of controlling men's minds and he made most felicitous use of them.

Fifteenth-century Italian rulers were as convinced as Charles V of the importance of propaganda and they had the advantage of the humanists who, whether from conviction or vested interest, were exceptional propagandists. All the new forms of art and thought – painting, sculpture, poetry, history and philosophy – were put to the service of the princes and their States. Gian Galeazzo Visconti had already recognized and asserted the value of humanist propaganda. Lorenzo de Medici exploited it masterfully. After the bloody events of the Pazzi conspiracy of 1478, which had cost the life of his brother and shaken his own authority, Lorenzo organized a vast propaganda campaign, calling on the theologians, canon lawyers and the humanists of his household: it was in this way, for example, that Angelo Poliziano wrote a tendentious *Conjurationis Commentarium* in a classical form inspired by Sallust and Suetonius, where the radiant figure of the victim Juliano stands out against a background of hideous conspirators.[1] Afterwards, more sure of his power, Lorenzo the Magnificent was able to dedicate all his efforts to the praise of the Medicis and of Florence. Landino wrote a history of Florentine art in 1481 within the framework of the traditional civic eulogy. In 1488 Filippino Lippi made a tomb for Cosimo de Medici in Spoleto cathedral with an epitaph composed by Poliziano. And it was Poliziano again, in 1490, who composed the inscription of the monument set up in the church of Santa Maria del Fiore to the glory of Giotto. Thus Lorenzo himself sketched the first lines of the legend which the propaganda of his descendants was to consecrate in the next century: that of the golden age of Florence in the fifteenth century, under the Medicis.

At the end of the fifteenth century printing was added to all the traditional forms of propaganda. By this point the German Emperors had exhausted all their material resources. As a result of external circumstances and his own character, and so that he might pursue his foreign policy successfully and effect the reform of the Empire, to convince the Reichstag, the Reichstände and, beyond them, the whole of German public opinion, Maximilian became the instigator of a lively body of written propaganda. His Chancery was ordered to draw up numerous and

---

[1] Maïer, *Ange Politien* (303), pp. 358–71.

increasingly lengthy instructions that were corrected by the Emperor himself, printed in several hundred examples and sent to all the States of the Empire in the form of letters-patent. He also circulated pamphlets and memoranda on every possible issue, and even had a kind of 'white paper' published in 1509 to justify the war with Venice. These writings entered the German collective mind to such an extent that numerous popular songs are, surprisingly enough, simply the versification of an imperial instruction.

Thus the governments of the fourteenth and fifteenth centuries knew how to secure their rule and base their actions on many methods of propaganda. To be effective this propaganda still had to take account of the ideas and beliefs which were then dominant in people's minds.

2

Ideas and Beliefs

In the later Middle Ages a political doctrine was always the result of a theory created in another discipline. This was so much the case that one could say that the diversity of political theories is explicable purely in terms of the diversity of intellectual disciplines. Amongst those who ultimately affected the political arena, the 'apologists' constitute the best-known group, who, precisely because they wanted to write for a broader public, set out their ideas more clearly and made themselves better understood by their contemporaries and by historians. This is why a special place is always reserved for William of Ockham and Marsilius of Padua in the history of ideas. Their philosophical stance often explains their political position. And so, for example, the great realist–nominalist debate (where for so long the realists, convinced of the reality of general concepts, were set against the nominalists, for whom the individual alone existed) largely determined the poles of political thinking: whilst a realist readily sacrificed a part to the whole, the individual to the State, for a nominalist like William of Ockham the individual was all-important and the common good no more than the sum total of individual interests. The 'democratic' trends characteristic of the fourteenth and fifteenth centuries, which set the conciliar movement against the Pope and the Estates against the princes, coincided with an upsurge of nominalism. In this way the apologists diffused opinions which were often the expression of a philosophical response in political terms.

The theologians are less well known. Their works are difficult, scarcely ever read outside academic circles, and survive in fewer manuscripts. Nevertheless, the theologians vociferously demanded a position of prime importance for themselves and their discipline in the life of the States. Were governments not to exercise virtue and to avoid mortal sin in every sphere, making their actions conform to divine law? As the human and divine were inextricably intertwined, the boldest theologians claimed the exercise of power for themselves; others were content to have the ear of princes. This was not the chief role of the theologian, however. For even if he was happy to reflect in his study, address his pupils and write for learned men without leaving his university environment, his thought was all the freer: lacking a specific audience he did not have to concern himself with individual problems, and eventually the time came when his ideas did reach the ruler, his councillors and subjects, and became responsible for determining part of their political behaviour. The meditations of St Thomas Aquinas on the law had surely penetrated the general consciousness to this extent when, on the occasion of the entry of King Charles VII in Paris in 1437, the officers of the Châtelet (see figure 2) decided to represent 'la Loy divine, la Loy de nature et la Loy humaine' ('divine, natural and human law') on a scaffold-stage. The teachings of the followers of St Augustine – on the state of innocence which the human race had first known, the equality which then existed between men, the justification of the State in terms of original sin and, consequently, the equivocal bond between sin and power – all these teachings, once they had reached the masses, must have fostered revolutionary tendencies and threatened the structure of the States. God was everywhere in this period. How could theology possibly not have impinged on politics?

Historians have always underlined the importance of philosophy and theology in shaping political thought, but they have only slowly recognized the considerable role that law played in this sphere. However, libraries have always had many more manuscripts of Bartolus of Sassoferato than of Marsilius of Padua. It is well known that, after a long period of neglect, there was renewed interest in Roman law with the discovery of the Code of Justinian in the second half of the eleventh century. The Glossators, for the most part Italian, continued the study with enthusiasm throughout the twelfth century and their persistent effort resulted in the gloss composed by Francesco Accurso in the first half of the thirteenth century and which soon became standard. North of the Alps Roman law was welcomed in two quite different worlds. It penetrated the courts of justice and also affected notarial practice in southern France. It fed the thought and writings of the greatest French and English legal experts of the thirteenth century. The work of Bracton is justly considered vital in the development of English law; but it was from Roman law that he took many procedures and, more than that, even the substance of common law was affected by Roman law as a result of his work. In France, Roman law lay at the centre of the great legal tradition which developed at Toulouse and Orléans in the thirteenth century and then found its most complete expression in the works of Jacques de Révigny (d. 1296) and Pierre de

Belleperche (d. 1308). In the fourteenth century, by contrast, French and English lawyers were more conscious of their own past and more scornful of Roman law. In his *Grand Coutumier*, Jacques d'Ableiges clearly states that he will not write any more because the rest is imperial law. English lawyers, trained at the Inns of Court, were familiar only with English law. Out of favour north of the Alps, legal scholarship maintained its popularity at Bologna, Sienna, Pavia, Padua, Naples and especially at Perugia, where the so-called Post-Glossators taught and wrote, dominated above all by the genius of Bartolus of Sassoferato (1314–57). The Post-Glossators put a very high premium on law as a legal science, in the same way as theologians esteemed theology. For them it was both a source of wisdom (*sapientia*) when directed towards the study of things divine, a science (*scientia*) when turned upon the concerns of men, and a practical discipline (*ars*) as well. Undoubtedly few things affected the life of the States of the West in the late Middle Ages as much as did the law, and especially Roman law as reformulated by the Italian Post-Glossators of the fourteenth century, which then enjoyed renewed influence in Northern Europe. It is true that no formal exposition of a political doctrine is to be found in the legal writers. But whether they wrote a commentary on a book of the Codex, or whether they gave an opinion, they tackled certain themes and found particular solutions that could have immediate political application. Moreover, others looked to them to administer the State: 'hi enim sunt quibus respublica regenda committitur', Bartolus proudly maintained. More generally, every cog in the later medieval administrative machine – from the most prestigious to the lowliest position – was manned by great numbers of people who had read law at university, had some legal works in their libraries and attempted to put into practice the principles which they had read or heard. Many of the problems of the fifteenth century, in the towns or the countryside of the Empire, or in the dominions of Charles the Bold of Burgundy (1467–77), can be explained by the work of standardizing and centralizing administrators infused with Roman law, whose efforts were resisted by populations deeply attached to their ancient customs and liberties. More than any other discipline, law determined the political atmosphere at the end of the Middle Ages.

But it was not just civil law that exerted this influence. Indeed, one of the ideas most highly regarded in the later Middle Ages was the parallelism of civil and ecclesiastical societies, the notion that Church and State (*regnum* and *sacerdotium*) were built on the same principles. Indeed, the great problem of the medieval period was to establish the precise nature of the relationship between *regnum* and *sacerdotium*. Its ecclesiological expression appeared later and was less sustained: no section of Aquinas's *Summa* is devoted to the Church and none of the earliest treatises on this subject antedate the fourteenth century. Nevertheless, at the end of the Middle

Ages canon law applied itself to the organization of ecclesiastical society just as civil law attempted to organize secular society. Canon law followed a development fairly similar to that of civil law. About the middle of the twelfth century Gratian composed his *Decretals*. In them he achieved such a remarkably judicious synthesis of earlier texts that his work quickly received official sanction and became the standard basic text for all future canonical thought. At the beginning of the thirteenth century the labours of the 'Decretists' resulted in the elaboration of a standard gloss. After this the main concern of the canonists was to regroup and to establish the concordance of new papal decretals: this was the age of the 'Decretalists'. Their work is difficult to approach. For the greatest of them – and this is as true of Giovanni d'Andrea (1270–1348), the 'source and trumpet of canon law', as it is of Niccolò de' Tudeschis (called Panormitanus; 1386–1453), the 'lamp of law', a century later – left glosses that were remarkable but sparse: their labours never resulted in a comprehensive work with a body of doctrine. These difficult works are inseparable from their period, however. Like civil lawyers, they drew their inspiration from Roman law. Processes of thought and solutions that the theorists of secular society had often used to advantage are found applied to ecclesiastical society throughout the works of the glossators. For example, in the thirteenth century the canonists had cogitated at length on the relations between the bishop and his chapter; they asked themselves in what sense one could say that the bishop represented the chapter. Moreover they had examined the nature of the mendicant orders, and the means by which the assemblies of this new type of body were convened and made their decisions. Now the theories which they had gradually elaborated on the nature of representation and the role of the 'bodies' or 'universities' in the Church did not simply prompt the first steps towards the conciliar movement; they also fostered the development of representative and corporative theories in secular society. The defeat of the conciliar movement in the middle of the fifteenth century occurred shortly before the heyday of absolutist tendencies in civil society. The destinies of lay and ecclesiastical society were bound closely together in the Middle Ages. The words, the ideas and the theories of the canonists were echoed more or less consciously by the theorists and administrators of the secular States. So much was this the case that the historians who have made the greatest recent contribution to the study of medieval political thought have approached the subject not from philosophy or theology, nor even from Roman law, but from the study of canon law.

North of the Alps canon and civil law, theology and philosophy were the only ways to express political thought in the fourteenth century. But in Italy rhetoric, with law, had remained the fundamental discipline for centuries. The notaries public and legal clerks who were to be found in almost every Italian town or village learnt the *ars dictaminis* and the *ars notaria* in the course of their legal training. Now these men were professional rhetoricians who had studied the classical authors and philosophers in order to perfect their written style and their eloquence in court; this was the milieu in which humanism was born. It was at first a literary movement. To begin with, the Florentine humanists stayed in their ivory towers to lead a contemplative life. But, thanks to Coluccio Salutati in 1375 according to one theory, or Leonardo Bruni in 1402 according to another, they were thrown into the maelstrom of the active life in order to make an impassioned defence of Florentine liberty (see pp. 231–3 below). And so 'civic humanism' was born. It is true that many historians are sceptical about the political convictions trailed by these humanists: they opine that humanism was always traditional, rhetorical and politically neutral. But – this theory maintains – since they lived in Florence, humanists in this city cultivated a certain number of themes from the second half of the fourteenth century onwards (the eminence of the active life, the need to defend Florentine liberty and the grandeur of the Florentine past) to which the humanists at the Visconti court replied by drawing a portrait of the ideal prince and calling for Italian unity. Whatever the truth of the matter – political conviction, rhetorical game or political propaganda – these literary and historical themes characterize the atmosphere of the Trecento and the Quattrocento to such an extent that all attempts to explain Italian political life at this period without them seem doomed to failure. The ideas of the humanists soon spread across the Alps and were known from Aragon to Poland. To take only one example, the fifteenth-century French writer Thomas Basin had read Leonardo Bruni and was familiar with his ideas, for he followed Bruni's *Liber de Militia* in demanding a national army and refusing mercenaries. The diffusion of humanist thought was so widespread that it affected the shape of political thought throughout Europe at the end of the fifteenth century.

Historians have postulated a very crude relationship between political training and political attitudes. So it is assumed that, with a few negligible exceptions, all canon lawyers supported pontifical theocracy and all civil lawyers laboured to increase the ruler's power, while on the other hand philosophers, characterized from the fourteenth century onwards by nominalist and Aristotelian patterns of thought, all displayed 'democratic tendencies'. According to this theory the distinguishing features of late medieval political thought are easily explained: while in the thirteenth century canon and Roman law reigned supreme and justified the claims of Popes and kings, in the fourteenth century the law lost its vitality, intellectual primacy passed from theology to philosophy and text books were the work of apologists who provided councils and assemblies of

Estates with their theoretical justification. In this way the new political atmosphere is explained primarily in terms of a new hierarchy of academic disciplines.

However, it is too simplistic to maintain that a discipline always corresponds to the same political position. The canonists were not always enthusiastic supporters of papal power; a number of them respected temporal authority and adopted a dualist attitude to the problem of Church–State relations; even within the Church there were many who supported the community of the faithful against Pope or bishop. Similarly, amongst the Post-Glossators, some, like Lucas de Penna, enjoined absolute obedience on the people, while others, like Bartolus, were aware of the constraints that should operate on the power of the ruler. Thinkers trained in one and the same discipline could hold different political positions.

Still more important is the fact that almost all these thinkers had personal experience of contemporary political life. The apologists played their part in times of crisis, but the councils of Popes and princes were peopled from day to day by canon and civil lawyers and humanists. The theorists consequently prized above all else *experientia* ('experience') and *prudentia* ('prudence', defined as the capacity to act with wisdom in practical affairs). Perceptive observers of contemporary reality, aware of the decline of feudal institutions, the advance of centralized administrations, the financial difficulties of newly established States and many other trends – or even informed, like Pierre Dubois, about the customs of the Tartars – all these intellectuals of the same generation freely interpreted the conclusions of their sources in the light of common experiences and, although not always in the same way, at least in the same atmosphere.

SOURCES OF POLITICAL THOUGHT

Some historians are prepared to explain the entire evolution of political thought in the last two centuries of the Middle Ages solely in terms of Aristotelian influence. This was indeed very considerable. The work of Aquinas was permeated with Aristotelian concepts and Aquinas, dubbed 'most learned doctor' by his contemporaries and 'the universal doctor' in the fourteenth century, was henceforth one of the great authorities of the Christian West. Numerous individuals were also directly influenced by reading Aristotle's works, either in the original or in translation. Pierre Dubois invokes his authority dozens of times, referring to him simply as 'the Philosopher'. It was Marsilius of Padua's intention to ask for 'the doctrine of truth from the oracle of pagan wisdom, the divine Aristotle'.

Nicholas Oresme translated the *Politics* into French and wrote a commentary on them for Charles V. The Florentine humanist Leonardo Bruni made a new Latin translation in 1438. In the second half of the fifteenth century the University of Padua always followed the lessons of Aristotle. At Venice in 1498 Aldus Manutius published Aristotle in Greek for the first time. Seyssel, Machiavelli, Erasmus and Thomas More were all influenced by the divine philosopher. The great influence of Aristotle is not open to doubt.

It still has to be evaluated, however, and placed in context. Many readers of Aristotle sought political instruction but others, like Bruni, studied rhetoric through his works. The former were extremely selective in their use of his political writings: Aristotle distinguished six forms of government, but they were really only interested in one of them, monarchical government; he insisted on the economic role of the State, but no one before Thomas More took any notice of that. In short, Aristotle was a vital source, but only one of the sources of political thought in the fourteenth and fifteenth centuries, for he affected minds that remained deeply impregnated with the most traditional concepts. It is important not to lend too much weight to Aristotle here.

At the end of the Middle Ages the Bible remained the book most widely read, or more precisely, the Vulgate, the Latin translation made by St Jerome which Gregory the Great decided should be the official version of the Holy Scriptures in the Catholic Church. Now St Jerome thought and wrote like a fifth-century Roman. It is therefore not surprising that his work reflects contemporary institutions and that political terms like *imperium* or *potestas* are used with the meaning they then possessed. A little of the last years of the Roman Empire survives in the Vulgate. But classical thought was evidently known to the Middle Ages through many other channels. About the year 500 a Syrian who was a Christian disciple of the Neoplatonic philosopher Proclus passed himself off as Dionysius the Areopagite (who had converted St Paul) in order to gain a wider audience for his works. The success of his deception surpassed his dreams. Throughout the Middle Ages the works of the Pseudo-Dionysius were read with respect and through him Neoplatonic ideas were familiar, in particular the 'realist' theory or notion of hierarchy that characterized so much of medieval political thought. However, the impact of the Pseudo-Dionysius was minimal compared with the enormous and sustained influence of the Fathers of the Church, above all St Augustine (354–430). In his huge and complex oeuvre, where Plato, Cicero and many other thinkers are to be found, St Augustine was not essentially concerned with politics as such. Even in the *City of God* his aim is not to construct a political system. But he tackled and developed a certain number of themes, like that of the origin of temporal power or the role of the State, or the nature of law, which remained fundamental for the whole of the medieval period because St Augustine was read and pondered throughout the Middle Ages. Charlemagne read the *City of God*. The eleventh and twelfth centuries were especially influenced by Augustinian thought. The ever-increasing influence of Aristotle did not check that of Augustine, whom Thomas Aquinas cites thousands of times. In the fourteenth and fifteenth centuries every cultured person, from the greatest thinker to the humblest lawyer, repeated quotations from St Augustine, sometimes faithfully copied from his works, sometimes summarized by an intermediary and sometimes quoted from memory inexactly, but with evident familiarity. Through the Bible, the Pseudo-Dionysius, Augustine, Isidore of Seville and many others the whole of antiquity – pagan and Christian – continued to leave its mark on later medieval political thought.

Besides these classical traditions the historians of fifty years ago, especially the Germans, ascribed great importance to Germanic traditions. It was to these, for example, that the Middle Ages owed its ideas of contract and freedom. Barbarian mentalities undoubtedly continued into the Merovingian and Carolingian periods. But the more time passed the more Germanic memories faded, whereas antiquity was continually revitalized by books reread or rediscovered and by the original works which it inspired – to such an extent that at the end of the Middle Ages notions of contract and liberty owed more to the Decretists and the Glossators than to old barbarian traditions, whose influence was minimal hereafter.

On a general level it is important not to overemphasize the Greeks, Romans and barbarians and neglect all that the fourteenth and fifteenth centuries drew from works written in the immediately preceding periods. One thinks immediately of the legal writers and Aquinas, less readily of an author such as John of Salisbury. However, there are numerous manuscripts of the *Policraticus* throughout the libraries of Europe; Dante had read it; the Neapolitan jurist Lucas de Penna was greatly influenced by it; Denis Foulechat translated it for Charles V and Jean Molinet quoted it. The *Policraticus* was the source of some of the great political themes of the fourteenth and fifteenth centuries, such as the notion of the king as the image of God (*Rex imago Dei*) and the apology for tyrannicide.

Mention must also be made of the rediscovery of Cicero, whose letters were found in the mid-fourteenth century, and that of Plato, whose works were available in Greek in the fifteenth century and whose *Republic* was cited by the chancellor of France to the Estates General in 1484. But what is the point of getting lost in the tangled maze of these influences? It is clear that too much importance should not be attached to Aristotle. And we have proof that when Marsilius of Padua said that nature always creates new forms which render new laws necessary, he was not – as was long believed – following Aristotle, but Justinian and the legal writers influenced by him.

So we shall not attempt the impossible, an exhaustive review of all the sources of later medieval political thought. It is more fruitful to ask ourselves how the more important of them affected the political thought of the fourteenth and fifteenth centuries. It has often been thought that a great work, like those of Augustine or Aristotle, could have been responsible for a specific doctrine and political stance. According to H.-X. Arquillière, the political theorists of the ninth century had undoubtedly discovered the principal characteristic of Augustinism, which was to absorb the natural into the supernatural order. From this they had drawn the inevitable justification of pontifical theocracy; the Augustinian theory of politics and pontifical theocracy supposedly triumphed together and then receded under the pressure of Aristotelian thought. In reality things were not so simple. God said in the Bible, 'By me kings reign' ('Per me reges regnant') and thereby justified the divine right of kings; but in Exodus one reads 'Moses arose from the water' ('Assumptus est Moyses de aqua') which, glossed in the Institutes of Justinian 'Eligitur rite magistratus de populo' ('A magistrate is properly chosen from amongst the people'), justifies popular sovereignty. The Emperor's supporters were just as Augustinian in the twelfth century as those of the Pope. The political theorists James of Viterbo, Engelbert of Admont and Marsilius of Padua all invoke the authority of Aristotle, but James (1301) defended pontifical theocracy, Engelbert (1310) supported the Empire and Marsilius demanded total subordination of the spiritual to the temporal realm. As for Aquinas, he maintained such an unstable equilibrium that the English made him spokesman for the royalists in the sixteenth century, the first of the Whigs in the nineteenth. Everyone was more or less Augustinian in the twelfth century, Aristotelian in the fourteenth. These great systems of thought were at the same time too rich and too subtle ever to have justified one single political position. In the fourteenth and fifteenth centuries on the other hand, they were able to impose upon diverse times and national traditions a common atmosphere and a common stock of words, themes and images to which every specific political attitude had to pay attention or adapt itself. The political mentality of a period is less well defined by powerful and original systems that were able to flourish with it, than by the commonplace, even banal, expression of its fundamental assumptions.

FUNDAMENTAL ASSUMPTIONS

Everyone was agreed that the fundamental task of the State was to ensure peace. The only means of ensuring peace was to establish justice, 'Remota itaque justitia, quid sunt regna nisi magna latrocinia?' ('If justice is not present, what are kingdoms but robbery writ large?'): thus Augustine. He was most certainly not contradicted by Aristotle, for whom 'the administration of justice [was] the very structure of the political community'. In the later Middle Ages this ancient and unceasing concern was still shared by everyone in the West. For them justice remained the dynamic and the purpose of the State. Everyone saw justice in a hundred guises from the streets to the palace. They were all familiar with the Augustinian tag and repeated it more or less accurately. And they were all convinced, like an advocate at the Paris Parlement, that 'no power endures without justice'.

Justice was an abstract notion that the Middle Ages defined with facility by adopting the famous phrase – influenced by Aristotle – of the Roman jurisconsult Ulpian: 'Justitia est constans et perpetua voluntas jus suum cuique tribuendi' ('Justice is the constant and ceaseless will to render to each his due'). But the intervention of the law was absolutely necessary to impose the simple and abstract notion of justice on the complex reality of human affairs. It is not therefore surprising that speculation upon the law is central to all medieval political thought. This or that theorist was undoubtedly able to embroider variants and subtleties around the law. But opinion in general very broadly distinguished three laws: divine or eternal law; natural law; human or positive law. Eternal law underpins the whole of the universe, animate and inanimate, the sum total of beings and things from the seraphim to a grain of sand; it would, as humorously explained in Oxford, be contrary to universal law to expect a cow to give whisky rather than milk. Natural law governs the interrelationships of all human beings; it is the entire body of all the principles dictated by reason to the human conscience; first principles such as, 'Do not do to others what you would not wish them to do to you' or, 'Do to others what you would wish them to do to you' and second principles deduced from these. Finally, positive law is the entire body of laws or customs which specifically govern the life of a people. Whereas eternal and natural laws are immutable, positive law, on the other hand, varies with time and place, and is even perfectible: it is possible to make alterations to correct its defects and to make it correspond more exactly to the exigencies of natural law.

These fundamental distinctions imposed precise limits upon a government that wished to be just. It had to respect the rules of natural law; as for positive law, it was meant to complete it; the State could modify it with circumspection provided that, first, it respected the natural law and also that it was motivated by concern for the common good. For the common good (*bonum commune*), the common interest (*utilitas communis, utilitas publica*) the public good (*bonum publicum*) and the public weal (*res publica*) were, with law and justice, the key-words of medieval political thought. 'The first duty of a ruler', says Aquinas, 'is to govern his subjects according to the rules of law and justice with a view to the common good of the whole community.'

But the notion of the common good, constantly invoked, was ambiguous. For nominalists like William of Ockham, the common good was no more than the sum total of what was good for each individual. For the realists, however, the totality had an existence in its own right, the collective whole was more than the sum of individual interests and, if these interests conflicted, the individual right should bow to the common good. The nature of the commonweal thus varied according to the relationship postulated between the individual and the State. This relationship itself was determined by the way in which the Middle Ages apprehended the origin and nature of temporal power.

According to Aristotle man was 'by nature a political animal', that is to say that the city-state (*polis*) was 'by nature antecedent . . . to each of us taken as individuals'. Aristotelian theory justified the complete submission of the individual to a State without which he would have been unable to exist. Enlightened by the Stoics and the Old Testament, the Church Fathers refused to accept this scheme of things. Before the Fall, said Augustine, man was good and the State redundant. Man was by nature a social animal in the sense that he was unable to live alone, but not a political animal; man himself antedated civil power, which was justified only by sin. The State was like a hospital; if mankind were perfect, there would not be a perfect hospital – there would be no hospital at all. It was unthinkable that man should be crushed by a State that came into being after he himself. This traditional Christian concept was not entirely abandoned with the return of Aristotle in the thirteenth century. It is true that, for Aquinas, man was certainly 'naturaliter animal politicum et sociale' ('by nature a political and social animal') and for Buridan 'animal civile a natura' ('by nature a social animal'). The natural state weighed heavily on the individual. But the individual continued to be protected from it by the Augustinism of some, the nominalism of others and by universal Christian precepts.

Moreover the myths of the state of innocence and of the Fall characterized other developments of the political atmosphere at the end of the Middle Ages. Before the Fall men were not merely good; 'all men were equal and they possessed nothing in their own right.' What Jean de

Meung said all clerics said or knew; the humblest Christian was not unaware of it. Fourteenth- and fifteenth-century revolutionaries often intended to re-establish the equality between men and the holding of goods in common that had disappeared with the advent of sin. 'They believe that everything belongs to all men, whence they conclude that theft is permissible', said the bishop of Strasburg of some rebels in 1317. 'When Adam delved and Eve span, who was then a gentleman' demanded the English in revolt under Richard II. 'They claim equality between men' it was said of 'brigands' of Forez in 1422. In this sense it is true that the notion of equality is at the very foundation of medieval thought.

But these robbers and rebels made the mistake of expecting a return to the state of innocence on this earth; it was because of this that they earnt the condemnation of Church and State. True Christians knew that equality and the community of possessions were irredeemably lost upon this earth in lay society. Then and always men were to be different and unequal; some were well endowed, others not; some were wise, but 'the number of idiots is infinite.' Rebels aside, the general belief was that inequality was inevitable in a political society.

More than that, it was necessary, for society could not survive unless everyone played a different role within it, for which he had been differently endowed, and so diversity and inequality were organized into hierarchy and order. 'Order', said Augustine, 'is the arrangement of equal and unequal beings, appointing to each the place fitting for him.' 'The diversity of matter', said Aquinas, 'ordains that all things cannot be equal, but that there should be order and gradation amongst them.' In the later Middle Ages all these traditions – Platonic, Aristotelian or Augustinian – combined to impress upon men's minds the idea that they were different and unequal and that they should respect a certain hierarchy so that the order indispensable to society might be secured. In this sense the idea of inequality was at the very root of medieval political thought.

To express these abstract notions of inequality, order and hierarchy better, the Middle Ages had inherited from antiquity an image which they took great pains to render more precise and embellish and which, floating more or less consciously in everyone's mind, was an essential link in the chain of fourteenth- and fifteenth-century commonplaces: this was the organic image of society. Society as a whole was first conceived of as a human body, Christendom likewise. These comparisons had always been used. But the image which soon became predominant with the rise of nation States was that of the State as a body. John of Salisbury put it like this: the priests are the soul of the body, the ruler its head, the judges its eyes, mouth and tongue, the financiers its stomach and intestines, the peasants and artisans its feet. And three centuries later Nicholas of Cusa compared legislation to the digestion: the Privy Council was said to chew, like teeth; the Great Council to digest, like the stomach; the judges to administer the law for each member, just as the liver ensured health for the body. Not everyone carried the comparison to such extremes of precision. But the innumerable texts that refer to the ruler as the head and compare peasants with the feet are adequate proof that everyone thought of the State as a body. Now this commonplace image is redolent with precise political interpretations. Not only did it clarify the need for inequality and hierarchy, but further reinforced the conviction that the State was more than the sum of its members, upheld the mystical notion of unity and justified monarchy without further appeal to reason, for although a ruler might live without a hand or a foot, no one had ever survived without a head.

This, then, is one of the images which undoubtedly had a much greater effect upon men and their behaviour than abstract ideas. The metaphors themselves, however, were less influential than the myths and beliefs to which everyone avidly turned for guidance as to their own conduct and for revelations about the future.

PROPHETIC WRITINGS

There could surely have been no one at this period who did not believe in prophecy. In the reign of Louis XI the unassuming peasants of the Rouergue were convinced that the king of France would conquer the world, in accordance with Sibylline prophecy. When the usurping Henry IV of Lancaster entered London in 1399, the people cried, 'Now the prophecy of Merlin has come to pass.' At the beginning of the fifteenth century the Welsh rebel prince Owen Glendower believed himself personally called to fulfil certain prophecies. Seventy-five years later Edward IV consulted prophetic writings when he found himself in difficulties. The clergy could not criticize him: no one doubted that God himself was responsible for Balaam's ass, the Sibyl, Merlin and many more; everyone was busy interpreting their prophecies, whether it was the Dominican Vincent de Beauvais in the thirteenth century, the Spiritual Franciscans or the Venetian Camaldolesi in the fifteenth.

So it was not surprising that each period of internal or external disturbance spawned numerous prophecies. In England prophecies abounded during the troubled reign of Edward II; during the wars with the French in Edward III's reign; around 1400, when Richard II was deposed and war raged on the Scottish border; and finally during the Wars of the Roses. In France prophecies appeared at the darkest moments of the Hundred Years Wars, then later when Charles VIII swept a restored France into the Italian Wars. It was the same elsewhere.

Poor shepherds and illiterate artisans could prophecy. But so could politicians who were far more astute, such as Filippo Buonaccorsi, who had prophecies of his own composition distributed on loose sheets in the market-place when he conspired against the Pope in 1468. However, almost all surviving written prophecies are the work of specialists, consummate experts in the prophetic tradition and its literature. In 1445 a certain Jean Du Bois presented a collection of prophecies to Charles VII that had been drawn from the great prophetic writings familiar at that period: the Sibyl, the Benedictine abbess St Hildegarde (1098–1179), Joachim de Fiore, inspiration of the Spiritual Franciscans (1132–1202), and prophetic writers of the fourteenth century who are less well known today than they were then, like the French Jean de Bassigny, the English John of Bridlington or the Calabrian Telesphore de Cosenza, besides minor prophets like Marie Robine whose memory is linked to the great enterprise of Joan of Arc.

Everything was grist to the mill of prophecy for minds which, as Philippe de Commynes put it in the fifteenth century, 'tous se fondoient en prophetie' (thought entirely in prophetic terms): a white pigeon indicated the presence of the Holy Spirit and announced the Peace of Picquigny in 1475; a stone falling from the sky in 1503 heralded the Crusade of Maximilan's dreams. But these were occasional prophecies, not worth the attention of experts who had more rigorous techniques and more convincing authorities. It was – not surprisingly – in Holy Scripture that they sought to penetrate the secrets of the future: the Books of the Prophets and the Book of Revelations offered them food for thought, and so did the Psalms. Jean Du Bois, with some justification, saw the prefiguration of the events of 1442 in the nineteenth verse of Psalm 82, the 1442nd verse of the psalter as a whole, and using the same method he announced the history of the years to come. And yet the Scriptures as a whole were invoked less than the two great authorities of the late Middle Ages, the Sibyl and Merlin.

Since classical times a mixture of Greek, Roman, Jewish and Christian traditions had created the figure of the Sibyl, whose supposed utterances and writings prophesied the future. During the early Middle Ages the West hardly remembered the Sibyl. But the East had faithfully preserved her memory and retransmitted the tradition to the West in the eleventh century, after which Joachim de Fiore made the Sibyl the greatest prophetic figure in the West for several centuries, invoked even in the *Dies irae*:

> Dies irae, dies illa
> Solvet saeculum in favilla
> Teste David cum Sibylla

– the world will turn to dust, as David and the Sibyl foretold. Some of the most important themes of political life at the end of the Middle Ages were bound up with this cycle of Sibylline prophecies. Firstly, the old Christian theme of Antichrist: there is so much talk of Antichrist and he is described in such exact terms, said Matthew of Janow during the Great Schism, that even children would recognize him and not be surprised. Then there was also the old Roman theme of the universal Empire finally establishing a world-wide peace. There was perhaps no one in the later Middle Ages who did not anticipate the imminent reign of the last Emperor, shortly preceding the coming of Antichrist, as prophesied by the Sibyl. Now only two possible names could be envisaged for this monarch with such a prestigious future. The legend of Charlemagne dictated that of Charles: the last emperor would be called Charles, who would go ultimately to Jerusalem, and lay down his crown there. However, the memory of Frederick II, with whom a number of myths had become associated (among them Prester John, the Old Man of the Mountain and the Crusade), supported the expectation of a third Frederick, who would be the last Emperor and would not lay down sceptre, crown and shield on Golgotha but near the dry tree.

Did Geoffrey of Monmouth invent the character of Merlin in the first half of the twelfth century? Or did he rework old Welsh themes? It is of little consequence here, for it is clear that with the *Libellus Merlini* and the *Vita Merlini* Geoffrey was at the bottom of Merlin's overwhelming international success, commented upon by Alain de Lille before 1179 and by Joachim de Fiore in 1196. After that, although he was scarcely known in Germany, Merlin's authority was enormous in England, France and in Italy and it was around Merlin that the second great prophetic cycle of the later Middle Ages revolved.

Regardless of whether subsequent events appeared to have confirmed a prophecy, it was taken up by generation after generation, adapted, interpolated, altered, commented upon and survived every disappointment. One such prediction was first applied to Henry II of England, then taken up two centuries later and adapted to Henry IV's advantage. The Latin prophecies attributed to Merlin were drawn up by someone at the court of Frederick II; translated and adapted, they appeared in French in 1276, in Italian in 1379; edited and translated once again they were published in Italian at Venice in 1480, in French at Paris in 1498 and in Castilian at Burgos. At the end of the fifteenth century *The Prophecies of Merlin* were an anarchic collection of prophecies of differing ages. From the thirteenth to the sixteenth century all the margraves of Thuringia were called Frederick in the perennially renewed expectation of the third Frederick. The accession of Frederick III aroused great hopes; one chronicler reports that 'most of the people remember what the Sibyl said about a future Frederick.' The hope of seeing a Charles conquer Italy, cross the seas and reign at Jerusalem sustained the adventures of Charles of Anjou in the thirteenth century and it was successively adapted to Charles VI, Charles VII and even, paradoxically, Louis XI, before justifying the expedition of Charles VIII in French eyes. It was no mere coincidence that John of Luxemburg's son eventually preferred the name of Charles to his baptismal name, Wenceslas, nor that, as the Emperor Charles IV, all the hopes of his adversaries were centred on a Frederick. Doubtless here and there there may have been a few brave individuals prepared to ignore or even ridicule them; but that did not prevent the prophecies of the Sibyl or of Merlin, the expected coming of the last Emperor or of the Antichrist, the myths of Charles and Frederick, and many similar hopes from playing their part in the political life of the fourteenth and fifteenth centuries. At the end of the fifteenth century Savonarola still based his assertions upon predictions, Maximilian toyed with them and innumerable books of prophecies were printed at the beginning of the sixteenth century.

The attraction of prophecy thus continued unabated. But the authority of Merlin and the Sibyl diminished, whilst astrologically based forecasts drew more attention. The West had been initiated into astrology in the second half of the thirteenth century and its increasing popularity in the course of the fourteenth and fifteenth centuries was bound up with the development of the spirit of scientific enquiry. Astrology in fact attempted to explain a world hitherto subject to random chance. It started from the principle that there is a correspondence between heaven and earth. This resulted in three main consequences: firstly, that an individual's future can be deduced from the position of the stars at the time of his birth; secondly, that the destinies of a town or nation are similarly inscribed in the heavens, and finally that the movement of heavenly bodies results in moments of great astral conjunction which determine important events upon earth that can also be predicted by astrology. To be sure, men like Nicholas Oresme, Gerson or Pico della Mirandola were engaged in combatting astrology, which reduced free will to nothing. But a *judicium astrologicum*, an astrological judgement which treats one astral conjunction and its consequences 'is, in many respects, the supreme act of medieval thought, insofar as astrology represented the summit of lay reflection at this period and the synthesis of philosophy at the stage when it ceased to be subordinate to theology'.[1] Nevertheless, Pierre d'Ailly, a good Christian, defended astrology, and a bishop, Paul of Middelburg, was a masterly exponent. Astrology very soon introduced a new note into politics: as early as the beginning of the fourteenth century Pierre Dubois

[1] Abel and Martens, 'Le rôle de Jean de Vesale' (286), p. 47.

had used the stars to explain both French hegemony and the pre-eminence of Paris in France. Astrology provided a scientific justification for national sentiment and in the fifteenth century astrologers and astrological pronouncements occupied an increasingly important place in princely propaganda. Charles the Bold, duke of Burgundy, dabbled constantly with it: this conjuncture of the stars had heralded the War of the Public Weal (1465); this other should have a deadly influence upon Louis XI. In 1474 his confidence in the popular astrologer of Geneva cost him dearly.

Thus ideas and beliefs, fundamental assumptions and banal commonplaces, myth and prophecy all shaped modes of political thought and every ruler had to take account of them. Against this general background two figures now stand out: the prince on the one hand and the country he ruled on the other.

3

State and Nation

In 1369 Philip the Bold, duke of Burgundy, married the daughter and heiress of Louis de Male. This marriage soon enabled him to join the county of Flanders to his duchy. The 'Burgundian State' had taken its first step. In 1370 Casimir the Great, king of Poland, died. His kingdom reverted to his nephew Lewis the Great, already king of Hungary. When Lewis the Great died in 1382, Poland reverted to his daughter Edwige who had married Ladislas Jagellon, duke of Lithuania: the Polno-Lithuanian State was born. In 1397 a century of laborious marriage alliances and unexpected deaths resulted in the formation of a union of the three Scandinavian kingdoms. Three-quarters of a century later, the marriage of Ferdinand and Isabella in 1469 prepared the way for the union of Castile and Aragon. In 1477 that of Maximilian of Austria and Mary of Burgundy announced the rise of Habsburg fortunes. The State of Charles V was only the most spectacular of all these matrimonial edifices. Marriage alliances and chance decease made the Middle Ages, more than any other, the period of united kingdoms.

In reality, even at this date, marriages and lines of succession were unable to create or sustain any State. Indigenous opinion had to be reckoned with. In 1328 Edward III, grandchild of Philip the Fair, had plenty of legal arguments for his case which would have enabled him to succeed Charles IV on the throne of France. But his rights ran up against the French feeling that, as king of England, he was a stranger in France and could not reign there. In England and France the sense of national identity was more precocious and more exacting; it made any union under one king impossible from the beginning of the fourteenth century onwards. Even where the formation of new kingdoms was possible, they were merely ephemeral because they were held together only by the fortuitous circumstance of a marriage or a life. Only the person of Lewis the Great bound Hungary and Poland together: on his death they each returned to their previous course. On the other hand, if the Polno-Lithuanian union proved enduring, it was because the marriage of Edwige and Ladislas, far from being a mere game of princes, had been desired by the most powerful class of the country, the nobility; the union was slowly accepted by everybody, and still existed, in a closer form, in the eighteenth century.

Multiple State or simple kingdom, the late medieval State was still more stable when its population was conscious of a common identity which they wished to preserve. A State of the West was no longer simply the result of chance or conquest. It drew its strength from the cohesion of the people who inhabited it. In order to flourish and endure a State had to be grounded in a nation. The crucial question is to determine the extent to which the nations of the West had developed at the end of the Middle Ages and what their relationships were with the States.

THE NAMES OF PEOPLE AND COUNTRIES

Undoubtedly, the first sign by which a community indicates that it has become conscious of its own identity is by giving itself a name and giving one also to the country which it inhabits. Antiquity left a considerable legacy of peoples and place-names to the centuries that followed. Under the Romans, for example, the Rhine separated the *Galli* from the *Germani*, *Gallia* from *Germania*. At the end of the thirteenth century these old scholarly words still persisted, but they only survived because of the erudition of a few clerics; they were rarely used and princes and peoples would not have recognized them. Since the beginning of the Middle Ages, by contrast, new names had appeared, originating in the peoples themselves. The name of Frank, *Francus,* appeared from the fourth century onwards. *Francia* was slightly later. The adjective *Theodiscus* appeared in the eighth century to describe a language. However, the word had no future. It was supplanted by the adjective *Teutonicus* which initially, in the ninth century, qualified the language and was later – in the tenth century – transferred to the people who spoke it. The name of *Teutonici,* the Teutons, was used in an absolute sense from the middle of the eleventh century onwards at the latest. Finally *Teutonia* appeared in the middle of the twelfth century. About the year 1000 the words *Polenia, Polania* or *Polonia* and the word *Poloni,* describing the kingdom founded shortly before by Mesco I and its inhabitants, had developed from *pole* meaning 'field'. From before 1100 the words *Catalan* and *Cataliung* appeared in the native language. In 1114 the Italians spoke of *Catalani* for the first time. And in the twelfth century *Catalonia* became the name generally used to indicate the inhabitants of the half-Pyrenean, half-Mediterranean State ruled by the count of Barcelona.

Polonia and *Catalonia* came into being to describe existing States. *Francia*, on the other hand, antedates by far the kingdom it eventually described. The adaptation of name to object was the result of a lengthy evolutionary process. Thus in 1100, at the time of the *Chanson de Roland* and the First Crusade, there was on the one hand a kingdom hardly ever called anything other than *regnum* and on the other the word *Francia*, which had only two possible meanings: for the learned it might refer to the former Empire of Charlemagne, or rather the countries of that Empire situated to the north and west of the Alps; for the people, it was a small and, moreover, somewhat indeterminant region in the north of the kingdom. In the course of the twelfth century the kingdom acquired powers and personality. It had to be named more frequently. People spoke of *tota Francia* to avoid ambiguity. But at the end of the twelfth century, *Francia* was sometimes used, in a few unquestionable cases, to refer to the whole kingdom. On 24 June 1204 Rouen finally fell to the forces of Philip Augustus. It was also in June 1204 that the king officially styled himself *rex Franciae* for the first time; it was in June 1205 that the expression *Regnum Francie* – henceforth common parlance – was used. France was now aware of her identity. Henceforth she had a name, in the same way moreover as most of the States of the West from the end of the thirteenth century. Admittedly the existence of a proper name is only proof of very rudimentary national consciousness. It is at least an indication that, from the end of the thirteenth century almost all the States of the West were no longer simply artificial constructions and could at least reckon on an elementary collective consciousness. And the fact that neither the States nor the subjects of the duke of Burgundy had a common name was more of a threat to Charles the Bold than the policies of Louis XI.

The popular words *Francia*, *Teutonia* or *Alemania*, *Polonia* and so on were used almost exclusively throughout the fourteenth century. They prove the existence of nations. They also supported their national pride. The French, for example, were proud of being *Franci*, that is *libri* ('free men'). Their name proclaimed that their freedom was vital to them: 'Considering', said an ordinance of Louis X in 1315, 'that this kingdom is called the kingdom of France and desiring that all things should be in keeping with the name . . .' Then the Renaissance brought about the revival of the old classical names that had long been almost forgotten. In France, as early as the reign of Charles VI, Jean de Montreuil virtually always speaks of *Gallia* in his *De gestis et factis memorabilibus Francorum*. On the other side of the Rhine it was in 1438, at the Reichstag of Nuremberg, that people spoke for the first time of the *natio germanica*. Since the middle of the fifteenth century the adjective *germanicus* and the names *Germani* and

Germania had been in general use. The Hanse soon described itself as 'of the German nation'; likewise the Holy Roman Empire in 1471. Finally, a little before 1500, people spoke of *Sarmatia europaea* to designate the Polno-Lithuanian State born a century earlier. *Sarmatia* scarcely survives. But *Gallia* and *Germania* took root and prospered. The contemporaries of Louis XII and Maximilian returned to the classical terms, speaking of a *Gallia* and a *Germania*. But in classical times the Rhine was the boundary between Gaul and *Germania*. What is the position today? The position is no different now, say the French. France is the heir of classical Gaul: she should regain her true borders, which were established by nature and the ancients, and her territory should once more extend as far as the Rhine. The names of Western people and countries in the later Middle Ages are not so unimportant after all. Not only does their mere existence indicate the crystallization of a collective consciousness, an elementary sense of national identity without which no State can long survive, but their very nature at the same time translates, sustains or determines certain fundamental myths about the nation and the State that bears them.

But to return to *Gallia* and *Germania*. The German attitude is quite different; for them the *Germania* referred to in 1500 no longer had the same boundaries as classical *Germania*; for, they say, the German language is spoken well to the West of the Rhine; if rivers divided nations in classical times, in our day it is language that distinguishes them.

NATION AND LANGUAGE

Throughout the Middle Ages the definition of a nation given by Cicero and recast by Isidore of Seville was accepted. A nation was defined by its birth – as, indeed the etymology of the word demands; it is a group of men of common origin, bound together by ties of blood. In the Middle Ages it simply meant race.

How can one in fact determine whether or not men share a common origin? What do the people of the same nation in fact have in common? The legate Tadwin, said John of Salisbury, was of the Teutonic nation: he differed from the French in his manners and language. Three centuries later Jacob Wimpheling explained that the Germans differed from the French in the colour of their hair, their physiognomy, their language, character and customs. His contemporary Claude de Seyssel maintained that reasonable men would prefer to be governed by people of their own nation 'who knew their manners, laws and customs and shared the same language and way of life'. Throughout the Middle Ages a nation was characterized by language, physique and customs. But analysis of manners and appearance leads to misunderstandings and endless debate. Ultimately, the only definitive 'national' characteristic that applies to everyone, learned and ignorant, is language. A nation in the Middle Ages was primarily a language.

Now in thirteenth-century Christendom there were many languages as yet untamed by any cultural or political institution. Clerics had their Latin. The others, more numerous, experienced the linguistic confusion of this modern Tower of Babel acutely. There were not simply the three large groups of Romance, Germanic and Slavonic languages, distinct from, scornful of and sometimes positively hostile towards each other since the ninth century. Even within each of these groups there were not simply the broad divisions to which we are accustomed. In 1323 Pope John XXII, a native of Cahors, had a letter which he had just received from the king of France translated into Latin. In 1439 the archbishop of Salzburg found a letter sent to him from the Rhineland very difficult to understand. What is more, within a single language, such as the *langue d'oïl* (the language of northern France, precursor of modern French) there were still considerable differences between the dialects of the Ile-de-France, Normandy, Picardy and Burgundy. Roger Bacon tells us that in his day 'a Picardism was an abomination to some-one from Burgundy and likewise for an inhabitant of the Ile-de-France.' Each claimed to speak the oldest and the most beautiful language in the world: for Parisians, true French was spoken at Paris; the inhabitants of the Murcian region boasted that they spoke the 'plus bell catalanasc del mon' ('the most beautiful Catalan in the world'). German scholars of the Renaissance thought that Adam spoke German. In short, thirteenth-century Christendom throbbed with languages and dialects; between one and the rest there was incomprehension, scorn, hostility, indeed hatred. But linguistic boundaries had no relation to political frontiers. At the beginning of the thirteenth century no one would have thought that a State should correspond to a 'nation'.

Now we must look at the way in which the intellectuals debated the nature of the ideal community. The Augustinians thought that there was no relationship between the political and the racial communities, *populus* and *natio*. But there were few Augustinians. And all those who were tainted to a greater or lesser extent by Aristotelianism did link the two communities. According to the Averroïsts the *populus* was merely the political form that the *natio* had necessarily to take. According to Thomist theory the State was simply the inevitable consequence of a race; however, there was no perfect political community without a racial foundation, no real *populus* without *natio*. Thus most theorists established a close connection between State and race, that is State and 'nation' in the medieval sense, which meant above all between State and language.

Towards the end of the thirteenth century rulers began to emphasize the fact that their subjects constituted a 'nation' and to make language one of the props of their States. In 1274 the monk of Saint-Denis who translated the *Grandes Chroniques* of the kingdom from Latin into French spoke of France as a nation for the first time. In 1295 Edward I called upon his subjects to defend the English language against the king of France. Some years later Denis the Cultivator, king of Portugal, insisted that Portuguese should be used as the kingdom's official language.

Certainly the concept of nation retained an inexact significance for a long while afterwards. It could refer to different entities. Froissart spoke of the nation of London, the Bourgeois de Paris (author of a journal recording events there between 1420 and 1449) of the nation of Paris, Chastellain of the nations of the kingdom of Charles VII. The important thing is that beyond the towns and regions the French conceived of France as a nation and made the French language one of the characteristics of that nation, one of the elements of the State's grandeur and solidity.

At the end of the Middle Ages not all the States of the West were as fortunate as France in realizing the correspondences between State, nation and language; even in France the correspondence was not perfect; it existed more in theory than in fact. But everyone admitted that this coincidence was the ideal to be attained. With more or less success the later medieval States of the West were concerned to distinguish themselves from each other by their language, and each to rely on one language and the conviction of their inhabitants that they constituted a 'nation'. These States were undoubtedly 'nation' States.

NATION AND COUNTRY

The Middle Ages took up and tirelessly repeated all the themes woven by antiquity around the idea of *patria*, one's native land. (In French this must be translated as *pays*, country or region, since the word *patrie* – which has no English equivalent – was a sixteenth-century development.) Jurists, theologians and indeed all writers extolled *amor patriae* ('love of one's country') and condemned the *patriae proditor* ('traitor to one's country'). On the model of Cicero and Horace they encouraged each man to die for his country (*pro patria mori*) and in the manner of Cato exhorted them to fight for it (*pugna pro patria*). Patriotism will not be discussed since the word only dates from the eighteenth century. Let us say simply that throughout the medieval period everyone was constantly exhorted to love his country, to fight and, if necessary, die for it. From the ninth to the sixteenth century love of his country was rooted in every man's heart.

Which country? The *Digest*, heir to a long tradition, recognized two senses of the word *patria*. Each of the citizens of the Roman Empire had a *patria propria* ('native land') and a *communis patria*, which was Rome. With the disappearance of the Empire and the triumph of Catholicism, *patria* was engulfed in vagueness. Here it meant merely 'our region'; there it referred, more accurately, to the birthplace. Generally, the name *patria* was reserved for wherever a man first felt he belonged. Paradise was the Christian's country in the high Middle Ages; the Empire was Gerbert's;[1] that of the archbishop of Reims in 1297 was this earth. These were men with distant and lofty horizons. But the monastery was more usually a monk's 'country', the village a peasant's, and a townsman's his town.

But then the new States became more forceful. Men became ever more aware of them, accustomed to considering as their country these political entities which increasingly formed the real parameters of their existence. As early as the twelfth century Geoffrey of Monmouth explained that by *patria* he meant the monarchy of the whole island, *totius insulae monarchia*. In the second half of the thirteenth century the inhabitants of Liège consciously formed a political unit when they developed common institutions: at the same time they began to speak of the country of Liège. As for France, it would appear that the lawyers trained at Orléans in the reign of St Louis (1226–70) first thought of the kingdom as their country. Not without some qualifications. About 1250 Jean de Blanot spoke of the *tota patria*. Jacques de Révigny, about 1270, adapted the conclusions of the *Digest* and spoke of *communis patria*. But people quickly became accustomed to seeing France as their country. Guillaume de Nogaret cleared himself of the accusations made against him by explaining that he had wanted to defend his king 'and also his country, that is the kingdom of France' ('nec non et patriam suam regni Franciae') after the assault on Pope Boniface VIII at Anagni (1303). And soon the French, like Charles of Orléans, were simply to speak of the *país de France*.

Since at the end of the Middle Ages men now considered their State to be their country, all the affective and emotional power attached to the name and concept of the country henceforth upheld the State. The later medieval State did not draw its power simply from its people's hazy notion of being a 'nation'. It relied also on love of one's country – a much more highly developed sentiment – and on the conviction that the country for which each man should henceforth live and die was this State.

[1] Founder of the cathedral school of Reims; d. 1003.

NATION AND RELIGION

The fact that everyone believed in one and the same God might have checked the development of national sentiment. But a collision between patriotism and the Christian faith was avoided, for governments were very soon able to persuade their people that to fight for one's country was to defend God. The propaganda of Philip the Fair made the struggle for justice, the Church and the public good, for the king and the kingdom one and the same fight. Joan of Arc did not doubt that 'all those who fight against the said holy kingdom of France fight against Jesus the King.'

Moreover, for greater clarity, the incipient States invoked God less frequently than his saints. The sense of national identity was translated, strengthened, and given a more exact expression by the choice of a patron saint. Far from smothering the nations, religious sentiment had to adapt itself to them. Europe created Paradise in her own image. But if the union of a nation and a saint was realized everywhere in different places, it was done at different periods and in different ways. The historic role of the saint, the spontaneous reaction of the common people, the deliberate policies of rulers, as well as the random patterning of events, all explain the great variations between one country and another.

Take Bohemia. The young Duke Wenceslas only reigned a few years. Scarcely had he adopted the Latin rite and acknowledged imperial suzerainty than he was assassinated by his brother on 28 September 929. The priests who surrounded him at once spoke loudly of martyrdom. The people did not forget their duke and remained beneath his protection. Already on 4 March 932 the repentant brother-assassin had Wenceslas solemnly buried in the cathedral of St Guy at Prague. From the tenth century the cult of St Wenceslas grew. In the eleventh century 28 September became the Czech 'national' day. St Wenceslas was now associated with all Bohemia's triumphs and misfortunes. In 1278, after the death of Premysl II, when Czechs had everything to fear, one of them composed the chorale of St Wenceslas ('Good King Wenceslas'), which has been sung continuously ever since and will be for a long while to come. Later Charles IV was able to increase the evidence for veneration of Wenceslas's miraculous powers. Jan Hus often invoked him:Wenceslas had been Bohemia's patron saint for a long while already and the cult of their former duke strengthened the Czech community.

Saints Denis, Martin and Rémi had played a vital role in the introduction of Christianity to Gaul. But Denis had been the first bishop of Paris; he had been martyred near Paris; he was buried near Paris, at the centre of the Capetian domain. When France began to regroup around the

Capetian rulers, the people's enthusiasm coincided with the wishes of the ruler: St Denis, patron saint of the dynasty, relegated Martin and Rémi to second place and quite naturally became the kingdom's principal protector. It was Louis VI, who, in 1120, solemnly acknowledged St Denis as patron and protector of the monarchy. It was he again who in 1124 first raised the *oriflamme* of St Denis, the sacred red banner of the kings of France, at the head of his army. It was in his reign that the *chansons de geste* (vernacular epic poems) began to give St Denis a preponderant role. In the thirteenth century no one could doubt that St Denis was the protector of France. Any and every occasion served the monks of the great Parisian abbey of Saint-Denis to present traditions associated with the saint in an increasingly nationalistic light. Admittedly the cult of St Denis suffered a mild eclipse in the fifteenth century: in the Hundred Years War St Denis had been unable to protect Paris, his own city, against the English, whilst St Michael, on the other hand, had never faltered in his defence of Mont-Saint-Michel; it was not remotely St Denis, but St Michael, who had sustained Joan of Arc; later, Louis XI was to found the Order of St Michael and was not even buried at Saint-Denis. But that was only a temporary lapse and under Louis XII, as it had been under Charles V or, earlier, under Louis VI, it was from Saint-Denis that a French king in difficulties sought security, from St Denis that France in distress expected deliverance. It seems that the English – whose national sentiment was so precocious – relied less on heavenly intervention. They did not find a great popular saint in their distant or more recent history. It was to St George – whom nothing had marked out for this role – that the kingdom was entrusted. It was only in 1222 that the Council of Oxford decreed that St George's day should be celebrated as a national feast day, and it was not until the reign of Edward III that St George became the kingdom's official patron.

Let us return to the Continent. Poland's first capital, Gniezno, especially honoured the saint and martyr Wojciech. But in 1079 king Boleslas Sczcodry assassinated or had assassinated Stanislas, bishop of Cracow. The martyr of Cracow was canonized in 1253. And when the Polish kingdom was reconstructed around Cracow in the fourteenth century, it was Stanislas who became Poland's protector. And similarly Philip the Good of Burgundy placed his young State under the protection of St Andrew in the fifteenth century.

There is no need to multiply examples: Ambrose at Milan, Mark at Venice, Stephen in Hungary, Olaf in Norway, Andrew in Scotland. In the later Middle Ages, sooner or later, each and every people and State set out on different paths under the protection of a different saint. But no State or people believed they could manage without the aid of a patron saint. In the mind of a contemporary of Philip the Fair or Edward I, of Ferdinand or of Isabella, a true political community should be at the same time a religious community. The Jews thus posed a problem not only at a religious level, but also on a political plane. There are many other causes of the expulsion of the Jews from England in 1290, from France in 1306, from Spain in 1492, but one of the essential reasons was the conviction that religious unity was a necessary constituent of political unity. Since later medieval States drew their strength from the protection of a saint, the growth of nation States and the persecution of the Jews went hand in hand.

NATION AND HISTORY

From the day a nation developed self-awareness it wished to justify the present by its past or to use the past to justify the present. Nothing gave it such proof of its existence as its history. In one sense it is historians who make nations. There is no nation without a national history. The first of these histories appeared in the twelfth century. About 1135 Geoffrey of Monmouth wrote his *Historia regum Britanniae*. In the second half of the twelfth century Saxo Grammaticus wrote the first Danish national history, at the instigation of Archbishop Absalon. Between 1185 and 1204 the monks of Saint-Denis compiled a *Historia regum Francorum* from thousands of scanty fragments. In the second half of the thirteenth century a more complex version was compiled under Matthew of Vendôme, abbot of Saint-Denis. The monk Primat accordingly made a French translation in 1274. In the fifteenth century the *Grandes Chroniques de France* had almost the authority of a Bible for the French.

The most pressing role of these national histories was to uphold or sustain the pride of an entire people by calling to mind their unfailingly glorious origins. On 1 August 1291 the three Swiss cantons of Schwyz, Uri and Unterwalden concluded a treaty against the Habsburgs in which they promised each other mutual support in perpetuity: the Confederation acquired a body. In about 1470 the *White Book* of Sarnen was compiled, in which the origins of the Confederation were related and where William Tell made his first appearance: now the Confederation had a soul; henceforth her future was secure. In fact William Tell was an exception in Western Europe in the later Middle Ages. For nations in general sought far more distant origins. Not without reason the Spaniards went back to the Goths and the Hungarians to the Scythians. But almost all the European nations endeavoured to connect themselves with the two great shadowy visions of Rome and Troy.

Take Rome in the mid-fourteenth century. A surprising character was of prime importance. Politician and mystic, half Brutus and half Shakespearian fool, Cola di Rienzo was also a historian and a talented epigraphist. The man who styled himself 'Tribunus Augustus, liberator Urbis, zelator Italiae, amator Orbis' ('Imperial tribune, liberator of the City, zealot of Italy, friend of the world') in 1347 had no problem in finding cause for pride for his fellow-citizens in the history of Rome. But it was not only the Romans who were sustained by the pride of being Roman. The Florentines were glad to read in Villani's chronicle that Florence was founded by Fiorino, king of Rome, that their city was a little Rome and built like Rome. Henry V's subjects were proud to say that the Tower of London had been built by Julius Caesar. If educated Frenchmen talked of prefectures rather than *bailliages* at the end of the Middle Ages. of quaestors rather than *receveurs* ('receivers'), senators rather than counsellors of the Parlement, it was not simply a case of gratuitous pedantry: they knew from the *Grandes Chroniques* that Clovis was a new Constantine, they were convinced from the thirteenth century that Paris was a new Rome: *Les Faits des Romains* (a history of the Romans written in Flanders in 1213–14) was perhaps such a success, so often read and frequently translated right up to the Renaissance, because its readers simply had a taste for : history and also perhaps because they wished to be better informed about their origins.

In fact pride in things Roman often remained a subject for clerics and the concern of the scholar. It is difficult to believe that some scholarly problems troubled the sleep of the masses. In Florence, for example, King Fiorino was forgotten at the beginning of the fifteenth century. Florentine historians believed that the city had been founded by Caesar, because like all medieval peoples, it was imperial Rome that they admired. But at the same time the Republic was at war with the tyranny of the Visconti. She believed herself to be defending Italian liberty against it. Florentine historiography accordingly revised its attitudes. Caesar was a tyrant, Brutus a hero; it was the Republic, not the Empire, which was the high point of Roman history; it was Sylla who had founded Florence. It is difficult to believe that these impassioned speculations, engendered in the seclusion of the study, were able to survive long in the bright light of public debate.

But that is not our primary concern here. In the West the Emperor claimed to be the heir of Rome. A State that insisted too much on its Roman origins could give rise to imperial claims. To invoke the spirit of Rome, the Roman senate and Roman law was all very well so long as it was understood that the king was emperor in his own kingdom, disastrous if the current Holy Roman Emperor had the power to claim his inheritance. Whence the hesitations and reticence of the kings of France for things Roman. For the young nations of the West in the later Middle

Ages, Rome was an ambiguous notion. Roman origins were both glorious and compromising. To claim descent from Æneas was not without danger. But Æneas himself was a Trojan. A nation that was able to claim Trojan origin would not yield an inch to another nation, however glorious, on this issue.

In the seventh century the chronicle attributed to Fredegar first spoke of the Trojan origin of the Franks. In the eight century the *Historia Britonum* mentions the Trojan origin of the Britons for the first time. Little by little this theme was extended and elaborated amongst the Franks and the Britons. But it was only in the twelfth century that it reached its full development, in the *Historia regum Britanniae* of Geoffrey of Monmouth and the chronicles of Saint-Denis. And it was only at the end of the thirteenth century that Alexander of Roes spoke of the Trojans in Germania. From then until the end of the Middle Ages, still distorting or embroidering them, everyone recounted the story of the Trojan migrations.

Take Brutus. Having left Troy, he travelled to Greece where he fought and defeated the Greeks. After Mediterranean voyages strangely reminiscent of those of Æneas he stayed in Gaul, then arrived at the Isle of Albion which fate had assigned him. He triumphed over the giants who lived there and finally founded *Troja Nova*, later to take the name of London. From Troy to Paris the story inevitably had several variations. We shall summarize the most popular version. Troy was destroyed in 1383 BC. While Æneas went to found Rome, the other Trojan princes were scattered throughout the European continent. Francion founded the town of Sicambria, in the Palus Maeotis (now the Sea of Azof). Later, in 905 BC, inhabitants of Sicambria founded Lutetia. Later, in AD 196, the duke of Sicambria, Marcomir, named Gaul France in honour of Francion, and Lutetia Paris after the abductor of Helen. In Germania it was Priam himself who founded Klein-Troja (Xanten) and several other towns. The Trojans who came with him mixed with the Germans. The latter, descendants of Priam, were thus brothers of the Romans. And the Romans were so ready to acknowledge this that they gave them the name of *Germani*.

The young European nations took pride in their Trojan origins, which no one contested, and their rulers found it a source of powerful arguments. In 1282 John Peckham, archbishop of Canterbury, wrote a long letter to prove to the French that there was no argument to be drawn from the life of Brutus against the English. Some years later Edward I attempted to justify his claims to Scotland in the eyes of Boniface VIII with the life of Brutus. During the Hundred Years War the English and the French also fought over Brutus: in the *Débat des Hérauts de France et d'Angleterre* the English maintained that the wars of Brutus in Gaul justified the enterprises of their fellow-countrymen; to which the French replied that the

Britons, not the English, were descendants of Brutus. In his *Libellus de cesarea monarchia* (1460), Peter of Andlau used their Trojan origin to prove that the Germans were the equal of the Romans and superior to the French. When Louis XII left for Italy in 1499 he took his motto from the *Æneid: ultus avos Troiae* (avenging his Trojan ancestors). At the end of the fifteenth century pride in Trojan origins continued to uplift peoples to such an extent that Ferdinand and Isabella thought they should encourage the emergence of a newcomer, the Trojan Hispanus.

Without always going back as far as their founders – Æneas, Brutus or Francion – the people of all nations loved to discover exceptional individuals in their more recent history whose virtues and glory protected and reinforced their collective identity. Amongst these national heroes, none played a more significant role on the Continent than Charlemagne. From the ninth century, amongst the Saxons and the Bavarians, in the cathedrals and cloisters of the German kingdom, the memory of Charlemagne was vivid and fecund. The traditions it inspired were diverse and sometimes contradictory. At some times and in some places they were more active than others. Imperial initiative was responsible for the tradition's greatest moments, above all Otto III's discovery of Charlemagne's tomb at Aachen at Pentecost in the year 1000 and then his canonization on 29 December 1165 in the presence of Frederick Barbarossa. Charlemagne's influence upon Barbarossa's empire was great. But the vicissitudes of imperial policy caused the image of the great Emperor to fade in thirteenth-century Germany. By contrast, in France, Charlemagne was an epic character from the end of the eleventh century. A hundred years later politics made allies of the Carolingian emperor and the Capetian king whose combined shadows soon covered the entire kingdom. Through his mother Adela of Champagne and his wife Isabella of Hainault Philip Augustus claimed descent from the lineage of Charlemagne. The Capetian had nothing to fear from the memory of the Emperor – on the contrary. From the late twelfth century the *oriflamme* of Saint-Denis was assimilated to the standard of Charlemagne. When Philip Augustus exhorted his soldiers on the eve of the battle of Bouvines, Guillaume le Breton has him address them in these terms: 'Magnanimous descendants of the Trojans, distinguished race of Franks, heirs of the powerful Charles, of Roland and the valiant Oliver.' Francion and Charlemagne combined to ensure the Capetian triumph.

When our modern nations emerged towards the end of the thirteenth century, and when French and German began to align themselves more clearly in mutual opposition, the Emperor of the Franks, claimed by both peoples, became a cause of friction. Everyone recognized that Charlemagne had then governed both the territories of the Empire and the kingdom of France: it was doubtless Adenet le Roi, minstrel at the court of

Brabant, who about 1275 had envisaged Charlemagne's coat-of-arms with the fleurs-de-lis of France on one side and the black eagles of the Empire on the other; everybody, French and German, ascribed these arms to Charlemagne until the Renaissance. But what, then, was the origin of Charlemagne himself? Did he leave Germany to conquer France, or leave France to conquer Germany? Was the Emperor of the Franks French or German? People still continue to ask this ridiculous question.

For the subjects of Capetian and Valois France, who had always held him in honour, Charlemagne was firstly king of France; he was born at Aix-la-Chapelle well to the west of the Rhine and was buried there; he had conquered Germany and even England; he was clearly destined to be the powerful protector of the kingdom whose greatness he had established. In 1369 Charles V granted the same privileges enjoyed by his subjects to the citzens of Aix-la-Chapelle, where 'the body of the holy Charlemagne, once ruler of the kingdom of France', lay. In 1469 Louis XI declared the feast of 'Monseigneur saint Charlemagne, once our predecessor, king of France' an obligatory public holiday to be celebrated throughout the kingdom. Since the middle of the fifteenth century the Parlement had had an altarpiece placed in the Grand Chambre, showing Christ on the Cross with St Denis and Charlemagne on his left, with a background of Paris and the Seine. In the Empire the memory of Charlemagne faded somewhat in the thirteenth century. Then Lewis of Bavaria and his propagandists invoked the great figure once more. Charles IV, whose baptismal name was Wenceslas, particularly venerated him. Soon German national sentiment grew stronger in the shadow of an ever more popular Charlemagne: a Charlemagne born at Ingelheim, on the right bank of the Rhine, of Germanic as well as Frankish extraction, speaking German, whose actions demonstrated that his principal interests lay in Germany. In 1519 Francis I of France and Charles of Habsburg both believed they had a claim to the succession of Charlemagne. The Habsburg Charles finally won the imperial crown, thanks not only to the financial resources of the Fugger, but also perhaps because of a feeling that because Charlemagne was German the Emperor ought to be German too, and because his own name was Charles.

Was there really a sixth-century Briton general who successfully opposed the Saxons? Was that the origin of King Arthur? How did Arthur become a popular Welsh hero? Was Geoffrey of Monmouth content to make a written record of an existing tradition in his *Historia regum Britanniae* or did he largely invent it? We shall never know. Moreover it has little relevance to our concerns. For us the important thing is that, after the astounding success of Geoffrey's work towards the end of the twelfth century. Arthur became a historical character whose stature rivalled that of Charlemagne: he remained the Welsh national hero and became one of the great models of the chivalric world. Association with the hero was now so advantageous that the kings of England – aided by the monks of Glastonbury – endeavoured to share it. In 1191 the bodies of Arthur and his second wife, Queen Guinevere, were found in the barely cooled ashes of the monastery. In the reign of Edward I Arthur attained his full political power: in 1278 the remains of Arthur and Guinevere were transferred to a new tomb before the high altar at Glastonbury; in 1283 Edward I seized the crown of Arthur from the Welsh and had it placed in Westminster Abbey; many times in the course of his reign he held solemn Round Tables, at Kenilworth, in Wales and in Scotland. Afterwards, admittedly, the English lived in a less specifically Arthurian atmosphere. But at the end of the fifteenth century Henry VII still took care to ensure that his first son was born at the palace of Winchester where the Round Table was preserved; and he called him Arthur.

Brutus or Francion, Arthur or Charlemagne, and others besides them, watched over the young nations of Europe for centuries. But then came the Renaissance, when historians confronted all those familiar heroes with the evidence of the classical world. They came to doubt and then to deny them. The Italians who were the inheritors of Rome had no inhibitions in this respect. The first was Æneas Silvius Piccolomini who in 1443 denied the Trojan origin of the Franks and the existence of Brutus. To the north of the Alps the painful truth was slowly acknowledged. In France, Robert Gaguin in 1497 and Paul Emile in 1500 no longer believed in the Trojan origin of the Franks; in Germany Beatus Rhenanus rejected the Trojan origin of the Germans in 1531; and in his *Anglicae Historiae* (1534–55) Polydor Virgil cast doubts on almost all aspects of Brutus and Arthur. Some time had to pass before the frustrated peoples were convinced. Moreover these historical advances did not stifle what were by then vigorous national feelings. The historians of the Renaissance were ardent patriots themselves. The *Germania* of Tacitus was here for the Germans what Caesar's *Gallic Wars* were for the French: both books enabled the writing of new national histories with fresh foundations. From this point of view the late Middle Ages have a curious aspect. It was the time when the new nations of Europe became conscious of their own identities, bolstered by the themes and historical characters that in the sixteenth century were soon to lose all credibility.

NATIVE AND FOREIGN

In sum, after a slow process of adaptation and evolution, people, country and State were tied together by particular bonds. At some point they became aware of this understanding that had gradually been established.

Paradoxically, they believed in a harmony desired by nature herself at the end of a period of secular evolution. The word natural, *naturalis*, was used in a feudal context in the eleventh and twelfth centuries. The tie which bound the vassal and his lord was deemed natural if it was hereditary and legitimate. In the thirteenth century the word began to be employed to characterize the complex but distinct relationships that bound together the ruler, the people and their country. The strength of the majority of later medieval European States was that they appeared natural to their inhabitants.

Gerald of Wales died in 1220: he spoke of the Welsh and of the country of which they were the 'natural inhabitants'. The author of *Siete Partidas*, written about 1265 in the reign of Alfonso X of Castile, defined *desnaturar*. '*Desnaturar*', he wrote, 'means in Spanish to break the natural tie which binds a man to his lord and to the country in which he lives.' In France at the same time the mendicant theorists at the University of Paris defined the *fraternitas naturalis* which bound together the inhabitants of a kingdom and prevented them, for example, from entering into any allegiance beyond their frontiers.

Moreover, people were not unaware of the concept of foreignness before the thirteenth century. They spoke of *extranei*, of *albani*, and of those who came from elsewhere (*de foris venientes*). But 'elsewhere' might mean from another lordship, jurisdiction, castellany or town. Then, gradually and in direct relation to the State's own stability and the realization of its inhabitants that they constituted an increasingly secure political community, the foreigner was relegated to parts further afield. At the end of the thirteenth century or the beginning of the fourteenth the French distinguished clearly between 'people ... born outside the kingdom' and 'those born in the kingdom', the natural inhabitants or subjects of the kingdom from the strangers or casual visitors.

With the appearance of these words and the national consciousness which they betrayed, one can say that the edifice of the nation was essentially complete. 'National sentiment' could still develop, become specific and stronger but it was well and truly there. Take the case of France. In 1328 Edward III was unable to become king of France, not only for goodness knows what complex legal reasons, but simply because he was English: 'Philip de Valois', admits an English chronicle, 'was crowned because he had been born in the kingdom.' In the fifteenth century the French were unable to accept English government, which was 'unfitting' for the nature of the country. Should we believe that Thomas Basin's constant use of the word 'natural' in his description of the Normans' surge towards France about 1450, was merely coincidental?

Since they perceived the way in which they might break the gross servitude of fear and violence, as if joyously pushed by a natural movement, they endeavoured not only to welcome but also to call upon and invoke their natural kingdom, the oldest on earth, namely the kingdom of France, and they hastened towards it as towards the seat of their natural tranquillity.

This admirable phrase perfectly expresses French national feeling at the end of the Hundred Years War. But when Thomas Basin was writing, the kingdom of France had already been a natural kingdom for two centuries in the eyes of the French.

National consciousness did not limit itself to distinguishing the 'natural' from the foreign. It exalted the former as much as it denigrated the latter. For centuries clerics had enumerated national virtues and vices. But their routine and traditional lists – where the envy of the Jews went perennially alongside the perfidy of the Persians, the wisdom of the Greeks, the Gauls' love of food, the pride of the Franks, the anger of the Bretons, the cruelty of the Huns or the treachery of the Poitevins – owed more to the authors' scholarship than to their powers of observation. Gradually, however, the lists of nations became appropriate to the period. The combination of vices described and virtues assigned, the result of habit and prejudiced observation, resulted in two portraits of each of the new States of Europe, one black and one white. For centuries English, French and Italians had described the Germans in terms of their fury (*furor*), rage (*rabies*), anger (*ira*) and pride (*superbia*) when Jacob Wimpheling undertook to demonstrate their bravery (*fortitudo*), nobility (*nobilitas*) and generosity (*liberalitas*) in 1505. This elementary national psychology, which gave nations a sense of identity, a yardstick for comparison and the wherewithal for self-glorification, was another means by which national consciousness grew stronger and developed self-expression.

CONCLUSION

It goes without saying that the nature and depth of feeling that bound an individual to his country in the fourteenth and fifteenth centuries varied in the different States of the West, as well as in different social classes and from one person to another. It also goes without saying that this 'national' sentiment was very different from our modern national sentiments. It was the product of a common name, ruler, interests and language, awareness of a common origin, pride in a common history and religion. From this period onwards, however, a State was the more stable and lasting when its inhabitants had some consciousness – more or less complex or elaborate – of constituting a nation.

4

The Image of the Prince

THE NECESSITY OF MONARCHY

When exactly did the passion for freedom erupt amongst the Florentine humanists? Was the republic a deep political conviction for them or merely a rhetorical theme? It has always been maintained that at the beginning of the fifteenth century many Florentines were consumed with the pure fire of republicanism and that their writers and artists proudly linked Florentine liberty to the Roman republic. A fresh crisis, in 1436, reinforced the Florentines' republican convictions. And in this milieu in the fifteenth century, whether it was the result of Florentine influence, communal traditions reawakened, or the reading of Latin authors at first hand, republican sentiments were manifest in all the large Italian towns. In 1436 Giannozzo Manetti wrote a *Laudatio Ianuensium* to the glory of the Genoese; in Milan the 'Ambrosian Republic' was declared on the death of Filippo Maria Visconti (1447); at Rome Stefano Porcari preached the restoration of the republic and hatched a conspiracy in 1453. But the *Laudatio Ianuensium* had no imitators; Francesco Sforza put an end to the Ambrosian Republic in 1450; Stefano Porcari's plot was soon discovered and punished; and even at Florence the rise of the Medicis soon caused the republican ideal to languish. Nevertheless, republican convictions did exist in fifteenth-century Italy. They were episodic and sporadic and doubtless only affected a few people. The 'tyrant', not the republic, was the reality.

Now if republics were rare in Italy, they were virtually non-existent elsewhere. Political theorists, observing contemporary reality, confined themselves almost entirely to monarchies. Italian jurists themselves recognized that, if a republic was strictly possible within the framework of a town like Florence or Venice, it was not in any circumstances possible to envisage anything other than a monarchy in a larger State. And everything pushed the theorists towards a justification of monarchy alone. There was the scholastic argument of economy, used by Dante in his *De monarchia*: 'What can be done by one man is better done by one man than by several.' There was the classic organic image of the State: the State is a body; it has only one head; it needs only one leader. And there was the microcosmic view of the State: the World is ruled by one God alone; the State can only be ruled by one prince alone. Monarchy was not simply the best possible form of government; it was almost the only conceivable form. With the exception of Italy, the word *respublica* was often used but only to mean the public weal, the State. When they were speaking of the body politic in general, the theorists, still lacking the word State, *status*, often simply used *regnum*, besides *respublica*.

THE LEGITIMACY OF THE RULER

So that the monarch could play the role expected of him in this necessarily monarchic State, he had to possess a number of qualities, of which legitimacy was the first. Here our modern minds would tend to place heredity and election in distinct opposition, and think that a ruler's legitimacy should be defined in terms of one or the other. In fact for centuries the two procedures were more complementary than mutually exclusive. For the laws of hereditary succession were inexact and ties of blood designated not one person, but all the members of the same family to the crown. Moreover an election decided between them without re- course to our modern arithmetical methods – bargaining and power struggles within an ill-defined electoral college finally resulted in the unanimous acclamation of the future king. Then in the twelfth and thirteenth centuries succession practices and the rules governing elections became more exact. There began to be a polarity between heredity and election. But no force swept all the monarchies of the West *en bloc* towards one method or the other. For a long while secular princes made use of one or the other as circumstances dictated. As for the Church, where elections were increasingly numerous and better organized, both at Rome, in the dioceses and amongst the religious orders, in some cases her example and influence favoured the election of the monarch; in others, such as thir- teenth-century Norway, the clerics judged it preferable to support the hereditary principle in order to strengthen royal power.

Nevertheless the divorce between heredity and election led to totally different results in different places, depending on circumstance. In England the bishops or barons might speak of choosing a king during the disturbances of the first half of the thirteenth century, yet shortly afterwards the succession of the eldest son of the deceased king was so generally admitted and even the idea of an election so firmly rejected that the writer of the *Ordo* (Coronation Order) of 1308 was careful to substitute the phrase 'in regem consecramus' for the formula 'in regem eligimus'. Moreover, no one disputed the fact that the ordinary practices of inheritance applied to the crown and that in the absence of sons, the eldest daughter of the deceased king could certainly assume office. In the kingdom of Germany, on the other hand, after the death of Frederick II of Hohenstaufen (1250), the principle of election triumphed: the king was to be chosen by an electoral body reduced to seven members where a definite numerical majority was henceforth to decide the matter. In France at the same time the oldest son had in fact long succeeded his father, but the principles were still ill-established when, at the beginning of the fourteenth century, the sons of Philip the Fair had no male heir and their daughters – with incontestable rights – were deprived of the crown as a result of assemblies called together by claimants only too happy to screen their force of arms behind a moribund elective principle. Afterwards the Valois worked hard to ensure that these doubtful assemblies were forgotten and to base their legitimacy upon the hereditary principle. It was then that the principle of succession by the oldest son (or in default of sons, by the nearest male heir) triumphed conclusively in France. In Poland, on the other hand, the chance of royal descent and the progressive organization of assemblies gradually reinforced the elective at the expense of the hereditary principle. So not all the monarchies of the West were hereditary at the end of the Middle Ages. But the strong monarchies were undoubtedly those where hereditary right unequivocally revealed their natural lord (*dominus naturalis*) to his subjects.

To begin with, heredity and election appointed the future king but only the coronation ceremony made him king in reality. This was so much the case that in the first half of the thirteenth century the kings of England, France and Germany only assumed their title after coronation and counted their regnal years from that day. In places where election disappeared and hereditary right was affirmed, the coronation gradually lost its constitutive force. When Louis IX died at Tunis in 1270, his son Philip was proclaimed king on the spot and counted the years of his reign from the actual assumption of power and not from his coronation, when only took place in 1271. Several months later, in 1272, Edward I was proclaimed king four days after the death of his father and was not crowned until 1274. From then on the coronation had no power in England to make a king: in 1307, Edward II, *ja roi d'Angleterre par descente de heritage* ('already king of England by inheritance and descent'), began his reign the very day after his father's death and for 200 years his successors did the same; in the middle of the sixteenth century this day's interregnum disappeared in its turn. In France things were ill-defined for a long while. Whenever possible official circles put their weight behind heredity and affected to attach less and less importance to the coronation. But the uncertainties of the first half of the fourteenth century and the misfortunes of the period after the death of Charles VI (1422) explain the persistent attachment of French public opinion to the coronation. For Joan of Arc Charles VII remained dauphin until the expedition to Reims, where he was crowned. It was only at the obsequies of Charles VIII in 1498 that ceremonial, with the cry 'Mort est le Roy Charles, vive le Roy Louis' (King Charles is dead, long live King Louis) clearly succeeded in suppressing any interregnum and denying all constitutive value to the coronation. In the later Middle Ages it was no longer the coronation, rarely an election, but almost always clearly defined hereditary right that now made a legitimate king.

THE IDEAL RULER

Birth was necessary to make the prince legitimate; it did not suffice to make him a good prince; personal merit was an additional necessity. The ideal prince is a timeless necessity and the virtues expected of him are documented in an abundant and continuous literature throughout the Middle Ages. Not only were the *Ordines* drawn up for the coronation careful to point out very specifically in their formulas the qualities expected of a new king, but also works of fiction, such as the *chansons de geste*, set the scene for accomplished kings; historians or annalists placed under the eyes of the reigning king the model of his predecessor, robed in every virtue – like the Charlemagne presented by Einhard, the Louis VI of Suger, Joinville's St Louis or the Charles V of Christine de Pisan; lastly, numerous theorists set out in a *Mirror of Princes* what they thought the perfect king should be. It was undoubtedly in the *City of God* (V, 24) that the Middle Ages found its first portrait of the ideal prince. The *Formula vitae honestis* of Martin of Braga in the sixth century, or the *De institutione regia* of Jonas d'Orléans in the ninth are sufficient proof that the genre never disappeared. It received a fresh impetus in the twelfth century from John of Salisbury's *Policraticus* and undoubtedly reached perfection in the second half of the fourteenth century with the *De regimine principum* of Giles of Rome. It was moreover this work, frequently read and translated, that was the inspiration of writers for two centuries until the copious flowering of *Mirrors* in fifteenth-century France, Burgundy and Italy bore fruit in three major contemporary and very different works – Machiavelli's *The Prince* (1513), Erasmus's *Institutio principis christiani* (1516) and the *Instruction d'un prince* of Guillaume Budé (between 1516 and 1519).

Several brilliant exceptions aside, it cannot be said that this plentiful literature has often held the historian's interest. It appears that they have been discouraged from the outset by works thought to be stereotyped and conventional, with no visible relation to concrete political life. It is true that the predictable and the abstract frequently triumph in the *Mirrors*. But it is important not to underestimate the influence of these *Mirrors* on political activity. They give a portrait of the prince to which the people were deeply attached and to which their propaganda, if not the princes, had to conform. In a period when the scientific mind had begun to impose the use of a number for rulers with the same first name, but had not yet seen such usage triumph, the traditional use of a surname remained; now these qualifying epithets – the Fair, the Good, the Wise, the Brave – were not ascribed by chance; by emphasizing a particular quality in the ruler that conformed to the received ideal, they wanted to convey to the prince himself or his successors the support of his people. Besides, the ideal prince of 1500 was not what he had been in 1400; the evolution had been slow and imperceptible; nevertheless it did take place and forces one to distinguish between different periods. What is more, at the same period different milieux dreamt of different rulers. It is thus far from pointless to assess what is new in the image of the ideal prince constructed in the West in the later Middle Ages.

Tradition demanded first that the prince should practice the personal virtues expected by the Church from every Christian, regardless of rank. Thus for St Augustine and thus, eleven centuries later, for Erasmus. The ruler was first a Christian and then a prince and should 'practice perfection'. Only these personal virtues, moreover, would enable the ruler to attain sanctity. For although there were kings who were saints in the Middle Ages, they never owed their sanctity to the perfect exercise of their royal role. When Henry VII attempted to obtain the canonization of Henry VI from the Pope at the end of the fifteenth century he put forward the holiness of his life, his habits, his fasts, vigils, prayers, his charity and his miracles. Admittedly he could hardly have made much of the success of his ancestor's reign. But the same lines of argument won St Louis his halo. The personal virtues were therefore indispensable, and all the more since 'the prince cannot prevent every eye from resting upon him' (as Christine de Pisan expressed it)[1] and since it was impossible to differentiate in him between the public and the private man. His personal virtues might therefore in one sense be considered as necessary for the right performance of his 'office' or royal 'ministry', which, however, demanded plenty of other virtues as well. The good prince was in effect known by establishing the rule of peace. He achieved this by the practice of justice.

[1] *Le Chemin de long estude*, ed. R. Puschel (Berlin/Paris, 1881), v. 6129–31.

'The king earns his title by ruling justly' ('Rex a recte regendo vocatur'),
Isidore of Seville had already said in his *Etymologies*. Again, 'For it is the
function of the crown to dispense justice, administer the law and keep the
peace' ('Est enim corona facere justitiam et judicium et tenere pacem'),
said Bracton. And the theme of the just king was as central to the fifteenth
as to the thirteenth century. However, to establish peace and justice the
prince could not merely 'spend much time in long prayer' ('moult vaguer
en longue oroison');[2] he has also to exercise the three qualities which were
those of God himself: *potentia, sapientia* and *bonitas* (power, wisdom and
goodness). By his might, his strength or his power the king imposed
justice on everyone. But since great injustice was also caused by the law's
supremacy, the king, by his goodness, charity, clemency and mercy had to
temper justice with regard for the weaknesses of men and their misfortunes for, as the anonymous author of the fourteenth-century *Avis aux
roys* wrote, 'it is impossible to hold sway over everything with an unbend-
ing iron rod . . . but sometimes you will have to use one of lead which can
accommodate itself to that which is being ruled.'[3] But power and goodness were essentially only accessories to that supreme royal virtue, wisdom: 'By me kings reign and princes decree justice', says Wisdom in the
Book of Proverbs (8, 15) and it was repeated throughout the Middle Ages.
At least, to be precise, the first centuries of the Middle Ages, for the
Carolingian period and even the eleventh century continued to conceive
wisdom as that of Solomon in the Book of Proverbs: according to them it
was simply virtue. But when, in the twelfth century, there was a real
cultural revival, the ruler had to add knowledge to virtue, in order to be
wise. 'A prince without learning is like a crowned ass' ('Rex illiteratus
quasi asinus coronatus'); the phrase first appeared in the twelfth century
and was repeated in all the *Mirrors of Princes* before being adopted by the
humanists of the Renaissance. To earn the epithet 'the Wise', Alfonso X of
Castile (1252–84) had to read widely and remember much of it; in another
period he might have been called Alfonso the Scholar. But soon wisdom
became even more difficult to attain. Smaragdus had already defined
prudence (*prudentia*) as the quality enabling the practice of wisdom. The
men of government, the administrators, whose political power gradually
increased in the second half of the thirteenth century, emphasized the
importance of this practical wisdom that looked to the future, so that it
became a political virtue of prime importance. The quality of prudence
enabled the prince to focus his action upon a clearly defined aim, just as
an archer cannot aim his arrow properly unless he can see the target.
Charles V was wise because he was virtuous and well informed, and also

[2] C. de Pisan, *Le Livre de corps de policie*, ed. R.H. Lucas (Geneva, 1967), p. 15.
[3] D.M. Bell, *L'idéal éthique de la royauté en France* (Geneva/Paris, 1962), p. 73.

because he was able to make good use of 'prudence'. Wisdom was thus not defined in the same way in the fourteenth century as it had been in the fifth. This did not prevent good fortune and happiness from being promised in the fourteenth century, as they had been in the fifth, only to those rulers of States who were capable of placing their strength, wisdom and goodness at the service of justice and peace.

That was how the clerics saw it. The knights dreamt of quite a different prince, whom they saw as handsome, good, brave, worthy, valorous, faithful, protecting his vassals and his people by the chivalric virtues cultivated to perfection. As opposed to only Charles V 'the Wise', the epithets of numerous kings of France like Philip III the Brave, Philip IV the Fair, John II the Good, or of numerous dukes of Burgundy like Philip the Bold, John the Fearless, Philip the Good, Charles the Bold· (thus before his misfortunes turned him into Charles the Rash) and Philip the Fair, are adequate proof that in the fourteenth and fifteenth centuries the peoples of the West undoubtedly looked for their ideal prince more frequently in chivalric romances than in the *Mirrors* of clerics.

To which one must add that, if some of these *Mirrors* continued to reflect the traditional image, in others, more sensitive to new trends, the portrait of the prince was altered out of all recognition. Beside the just and good king who judged according to the law, but did not make judgement on the law, the lawyers who invaded government departments in the second half of the thirteenth century imposed throughout the West, from Italy to Scandinavia, the cold and abstract ideal of the legislating ruler, of *rex lex animata*, the king as instigator of the law, who was able to suppress evil customs and make new arrangements to adapt the eternal law to the conditions of everyday life. Moreover the encroaching zeal of the bureaucrats aimed to extend this principle to all areas of State action. Erasmus's ideal prince is not content to sit in the law court and prepare the laws; he is feverishly busy building bridges, draining unhealthy marshlands, regularizing the courses of rivers, uprooting unprofitable vineyards. For him the common good is not simply peace, it is also prosperity. Was this the influence of Cicero, then? Was it the result of the events of 1356–8 when the Dauphin Charles had frequently to make payments from his own resources and calm the threatening crowds in his own words? Was it a realization of the enhanced significance of assemblies in the political life of the fourteenth and fifteenth centuries? It is always said that after Charles V the prince had to ensure that he was eloquent. Opinions changed to such an extent that, in the portrait of the later medieval ruler, justice follows wisdom and wisdom is composed less of knowledge than of prudence, less of prudence than political acumen; the prince was becoming increasingly an administrator, technician and expert.

The old problem of the ends and the means then began to take a new turn. Like all theorists down the centuries before him, Nicholas Oresme still wrote that, 'according to the doctrine and philosophy of St Paul, no one may do evil in order to achieve good.'[4] But Charles V maintained that 'things are made good or evil by circumstances, for something may be presented in such a way that it seems good or in such a way that it appears evil.' Undoubtedly one should not overemphasize the significance of this sentence. The wise king explained it himself: 'It is good sense to dissemble when necessary in the face of the anger of wicked men, but to dissemble and conceal one's true intentions with a view to harming someone, that is wrong.'[5] By this first concession of the moral to the politic the ruler had nevertheless embarked on a slippery slope. Moreover, in the thirteenth century the ruler had to surround himself with wise counsellors. A century later these counsellors had to be able as well as wise, competent as well as virtuous. But what was to be done if there were insufficient virtuous and competent individuals? Ghillebert de Lannoy was bold enough to say that in affairs of state the prince might then make use of skilled men lacking in virtue; he advised merely that they should not be given roles of the first importance.

In this way the Augustinian definition of the happy prince was gradually obliterated and increasingly the fortunate prince was considered the one who was most successful in his endeavours in this world. Soon the need for temporal success excused all behaviour. Indeed, certain Arabo-Oriental works (such as the *Secreta secretorum*, which, translated into Latin in the thirteenth century, experienced an astounding success from that time onward) contributed to the West's gradual acclimatization to the idea of an amoral prince. Soon the *Mirrors* were advising rulers that, if they could not be positively virtuous, at least to save appearances: 'if you cannot live chastely', John of Viterbo advised his ruler in the fifteenth century, 'you must at least act prudently' ('Si caste non vivere potes, caute tamen agas'). Macchiavelli did not therefore surprise everyone in the least by turning dissimulation into a general principle: 'It is not essential for a prince to have all the good qualities [listed above]; but it is important that he should appear to possess them.' Thus in the fifteenth century the prince had always to seem virtuous, just and wise, but an increasing number of individuals knew that henceforth to succeed he needed above all to give evidence of *savoir-faire*, ability, subtlety and cunning. Cunning (*cautele*) had often, but not invariably, been used in a pejorative sense since its appearance in the thirteenth century; subtlety (*subtilité*) still lacked derogatory overtones in 1500. But to subtlety and cunning were added so

---

[4] See Shahar, *Morale et politique en France* (382), p. 216.

[5] C. de Pisan, *Le Livre des faits et bonnes moeurs du sage roy Charles V*, ed. S. Solente, II (Paris, 1940), pp. 74–5.

much deceit and violence that in the sixteenth century *subtil* and *cauteleux* were always pejorative epithets.

THE CEREMONIAL PRINCE

Neither the virtues nor their appearance sufficed. Wise, devious or chivalric according to their means and temperament, the rulers of the later Middle Ages shared a concern to communicate to everyone their power and to present their majesty against a fitting backdrop.

To achieve this they first made use of the 'insignia of power' to which P. E. Schramm has convincingly drawn the historian's attention. The insignia of power had different connotations from one kingdom to another. Take the kingdom of Germany. No one entertained further doubts as to the legitimacy of Conrad II in 1024, after the widow of Henry II had bestowed on him the insignia which her husband had entrusted to her, amongst them the crown which Charlemagne was said to have worn and the spear that he had received from an angel. At the beginning of the fourteenth century, in the dispute between Frederick the Fair, duke of Austria and Lewis of Bavaria, the former held the advantage for a long while as possessor of these insignia; Lewis only became master of the situation when, after his victory at Mühldorf, he was able to lay hands on these precious objects and display them to all beholders at Munich in 1324. Consider too the example of Hungary. Charles-Robert of Anjou had already been crowned twice, the first time during an improvised ceremony in 1301, and then again more formally in 1309. His power did not remain uncontested, however, until 1310, when he was crowned with the crown universally believed to have been St Stephen's. In 1403 Sigismund was acknowledged king because he had possession of the same crown. In 1440, in order to promote the affairs of her son and to discredit his opponent Ladislas Jagellon, Queen Elisabeth, widow of Albert II, started a rumour that the crown given to the former was not authentic. And when Mathias Corvinus was elected king in 1458, that humanist prince thought at first that he would be able to do without the precious relic. But, his historian tells us, the 'superstition', 'idiocy' and 'ignorance' of the Hungarians was such that in 1463, in order to establish his legitimacy definitively, he had at all costs to recover St Stephen's crown and assume it with great pomp. Amongst the insignia of power, therefore, there were irreplaceable objects which the prince had to possess and exhibit to assert his rule.

There were others that had no intrinsic importance and were mere symbols: at the battle of Aljubarrota in 1385 the Portuguese seized the banner of Castile; they still owned it in the fifteenth century, but the

Castilians were not in the least affected by it; royal dignity was not bound for them to that banner, which was merely a symbol and could be replaced. Rulers could have many such emblems when their finances were good, sell or pledge them in time of crisis. At the end of his reign Henry III had four crowns; Edward I had four others made in 1277. Charles V had dozens of crowns. Conversely, Edward III did not hesitate to mortgage his great crown in Flanders for 25,000 florins. In 1399 the crown of Aragon was broken into pieces and in the hands of creditors; likewise that of France in 1413. Finally, in 1496 Isabella of Castile pledged her golden crown. Admittedly the crown had virtually no importance in Castile, where the kings crowned themselves after 1332 and did not even bother to do that after the end of the fourteenth century. Generally speaking, Castile was the country of the West that displayed least interest in these signs of power.

Nevertheless, it was indeed in Castile in 1465 that the nobles in revolt against Enrique IV, having set an effigy adorned with the royal insignia upon a scaffold, solemnly stripped it of its crown, sword and sceptre. Even if they were only a motley collection of objects, mere symbols without a past, these insignia of power still retained sufficient importance at the end of the Middle Ages to play a political role. Rulers entrusted them in some cases to a respected monastery, as the kings of France to Saint-Denis, in others to a church, as Charles IV to St Guy of Prague, or even to a town, as the Emperor Sigismund to Nuremberg. Conquerors seized them, destroyed them or engineered their disappearance: after 1270, in the disturbances which followed the death of Béla IV, Ottokar II of Bohemia laid hold of the Hungarian royal insignia; after defeating the Welsh in 1285 Edward I returned to London with the crown of Arthur which was never heard of again. After his victory over the Scots in 1296 the same king seized the crown of John Balliol, had the throne of Scotland, made of Scone stone, destroyed and brought the seat to London, which he incorporated in the superb wooden throne he had made for himself in 1300.

The power of a ruler was thus in some sense bound to the very existence of such insignia. In everyone's eyes the richer these objects, the greater his power. Above all the shape of the former clearly specified the nature of the latter. Around some princes, more frequently with the approach of the modern period, artists were undoubtedly able to create complex forms with a difficult symbolism. On a triumphal arch raised to the glory of Maximilian (1515), Albrecht Dürer represented a sceptre surrounded with a serpent whose body was transfixed by an arrow: one had to infer that the Emperor governed the world in law but not in practice; similarly the falcon on the imperial globe symbolized brilliant victory; the basilisk with a bird's head inside the crown signified immortal glory. But this obscure symbolism was only a meaningless game. Medieval symbolism owed its power to a simplicity and clarity that were the more comprehensible the closer they stayed to the traditional forms inherited from Byzantium or the Carolingians. It is thus possible to follow the varied fortunes of the *kamelaukion*, carried by the Byzantine Emperor in the ninth century, in many of the crowns of the West, from the imperial crown to the Doge's cap.

Amongst the insignia of power it was undoubtedly the crown which was richest in traditional meaning, and it was through the crown that rulers best expressed their claims. After two centuries of hesitation, in the tenth and eleventh centuries, the 'closed' crown, symbol of sovereignty, became the Emperor's exclusive privilege from the twelfth century onwards. This closed crown might, as in the crown of Otto I, consist of a circle at the base surmounted by a single longitudinal arch, in such a way that the two points of the imperial mitre sloped at a gentle angle; or the same circle might be topped with two arches intersecting at right angles. On the reliquary of the arm of Charlemagne, executed between 1166 and 1173 on the instructions of Frederick Barbarossa, Louis the Pious and Otto III wear crowns with one arch, whilst Conrad III and Barbarossa have crowns with a dual arch. But in both cases it is undoubtedly a crown, which Barbarossa's contemporaries could distinguish perfectly from a simple circlet, which was sufficient to designate the power of any king whatever. Although kings might later expand their circlet or decorate it with fleurons like the king of France, the fundamental distinction between the closed imperial crown and royal circlets or diadems remained. A miniature in the *Grandes Chroniques de France* represents the meeting in 1377 of Charles V of France on the one hand and the Emperor Charles IV and his son Wenceslas on the other: only the Emperor has a closed crown. But the simple crown with fleurons of the king of France placed him far above his greatest vassals, such as the dukes of Burgundy or of Brittany, who only had the right to wear a very simple, unornamented circlet, called a *chapeau* or *chaperon* by their contemporaries.

This three-tiered hierarchy was essentially that of the fourteenth and fifteenth centuries. But, whether from justified pretensions or mere vanity, this order was soon disturbed by the initiatives of an increasing number of princes. In 1448 an ordinance of Charles VII permitted Philip the Good, duke of Burgundy, to adopt the insignia of a gold circle decorated with cabochons and, some years later, Charles the Bold of Burgundy had a 'most triumphant' *chapeau* made for himself, of unheard-of richness, where the gold band, ornamented with sapphires and large rubies, was extended downwards with a broad rim and surmounted by a tall hat of yellow velvet embroidered with pearls and topped by a long, pointed ruby fastened to a golden ornament; finally at the front of the *chapeau* were two real feathers decorated with gold and pearls. Even this debauched product of the imagination and love of vulgar display of the 'Grand Duke' of the West did not result in any confusion. But almost at the same time Francis II of Brittany had the audacity to wear a crown *with* fleurons. When in 1463 Louis XI complained loudly that 'a crown has been placed on the coat of arms of the Duke instead of a ducal coronet' it was certainly because for himself, for the duke and for their subjects this act of daring was not a gratuitous fantasy but, on the contrary, the outcome of a theory that claimed royal rights for dukes.

In the same way it was the claim of kings to be sovereigns or emperors in their own kingdoms that drove them, one after another, to adopt the closed imperial crown. This *imitatio imperii* was first manifest in the Eastern kingdoms (Bohemia, Poland, Hungary) most threatened by the Empire and most anxious to affirm their *libertas*. By contrast, although the sovereignty of England and France had not been contested since the thirteenth century, or perhaps precisely because it was no longer threatened, the closed crown was introduced at a much later date in these countries. It was not until the beginning of the sixteenth century that it appeared in England and 1533 before Henry VIII definitely adopted 'the imperial crown of this realm', to affirm his sovereignty not so much in the face of the Emperor as of the Pope. In France there may have been a 'great imperial crown' in the treasury at Saint-Denis in 1340, but the kings were proud of their fleurs-de-lis and remained faithful to their traditional crown until the end of the reign of Francis I. The closed crown did not establish itself permanently as a symbol of absolute monarchy until the second half of the sixteenth century.

Slow to assume an imperial crown, the kings of France always scorned that other symbol of sovereignty, the orb surmounted by a cross, which the Emperor held in his hand from 1014 and the king of Sicily adopted in the twelfth century, the king of Aragon in 1204, the kings of Hungary and Bohemia and the kings of the Scandinavian countries in the thirteenth century, the kings of Poland and England in the fourteenth century. In contrast later medieval French kings attached greater importance to their sceptre, their *main de justice* and their sword of State. The kings of the Old Testament already carried a long *baculus* and a short *virga*. Likewise, copying them, did Charles the Bald. While one of the two rods disappeared in almost all the kingdoms of the West, they both survived in France. After several metamorphoses their form crystallized towards the end of the thirteenth century. Henceforth the king carried a long sceptre, symbol of royalty, in his right hand, and in his left the famous short rod topped by an ivory hand, the symbol of justice that had appeared under St Louis and was familiar under the name of *main de justice*. The Constable of France carried a sword in front of the king, supposedly *Joyeuse*, the sword of Charlemagne, which had long symbolized the king's justice until the invention of the *main de justice* gave it a war-like dimension, causing it to pass into the hands of the Constable.

By these crowns, orbs, sceptres and swords, as also by a throne, robes, a standard and many other tokens, both traditional and original, and of varying shape, meaning and importance, each Western ruler gradually built up a setting for himself which was intended to glorify his person and define his function. Consider the Emperor, with his closed crown and his mitre, his orb and sword, his celestial cloak, his belt of little bells modelled on that of a great prelate, whose every attribute proclaimed his sovereignty and his religious pretensions. Take the king of France, whose *oriflamme*, crown with fleurons, sceptre with fleur-de-lis, *main de justice*, semi-priestly vestments and (from the reign of Charles VI) canopy, effectively communicated that the personage was sacred and his position amongst the rulers of the West unique. Finally, think of the Doge of Venice, whose entire appearance – crown, golden robe, red shoes, golden canopy, standard and trumpets of silver – was designed to convey the image, not of the Duke's sovereignty, but that of his city.

Soon these solemn occasional spectacles were not enough. The people expected to see their ruler in princely garb every day. Towards the end of the Middle Ages this expectation constituted a new demand. In the majority of the States of the West in the thirteenth century the prince was still best assured of his subjects' loyalty if he remained faithful to a simple life and modest life-style in the midst of his itinerant court. But, under pressure from both Byzantine and Muslim examples – probably first in Sicily – this patriarchal ideal receded and the conviction gradually became widespread that luxury and magnificence were necessary constituents of a ruler's daily setting. From then on, and with greater ease as his moves became increasingly rare, an enormous and disparate world developed around each prince, charged with providing for his necessities and glorifying his majesty: the Household.

At first only the composition of these new-style Households are known to us. We know that the Household of the king of France, organized at an early date with its six departments, served as a model from the second half of the thirteenth century for many princes of the West, such as the king of Naples or duke of Burgundy. From the beginning of the fourteenth century we have some idea of the groups that gravitated around the ruler: perhaps 300 or 400 individuals at Avignon around Pope Clement V; some 400 around Charles IV the Fair in 1322; more than 200 around the king of Aragon in 1344; 150 persons around the modest King James II of Majorca in 1337, and these figures only grew larger: the Household of Charles VI comprised 700 to 800 persons; that of Henry VI of England, in 1454, 424 individuals, to whom must be added the 120 members of the queen's Household and thirty-eight of that of the prince of Wales. Undoubtedly the titular employees of the Household were never in attendance upon the ruler at the same time; no building could have held them all. Nevertheless, taking account of visitors and their retinues, several hundred individuals permanently surrounded a great ruler and considerable sums were swallowed up by the Household. In normal circumstances in the reign of Charles VI the court annually expended between 100,000 and 110,000 francs. It passed this figure by a wide margin in a period of celebration or travel. This was far beyond the sums expended by other Western rulers. That did not prevent Edward III from reckoning in about 1330, in the middle of his worst financial difficulties, that he had to spend about 10,000 pounds a year on his Household, and Edward IV (1461–83) did not envisage expenditure of less than 13,000 pounds although, however, he was never able to adhere to this figure. Nevertheless, 10,000 and 13,000 pounds were very considerable sums of money. The magnificence thought necessary for princes was a cause of constant financial concern to them.

The most foolish did not worry about it at all. The wisest attempted to adapt their splendour to their means and to control their expenditure. 'Vix sine mensura durabit regia curia' ('Without moderation, the royal court could hardly survive'), said James II of Majorca in 1337; and in the Black Book of the Household of Edward IV there are two miniatures: one portrays the *Domus Regie Magnificiencie*, the other the *Domus Regie Providencie* which, by wise administration, makes the magnificence possible. Initially and for a long while to come the main object of Household ordinances was to draw up a list of its officers and lay down their wages. This is true of the first French ordinance of the Household (1261), of the English ordinances of 1445 and 1478, and even of the ordinance made in 1499 by the Grand-Master of the Teutonic Order, which is one of the earliest Household ordinances recorded in Germany.

To these calculable concerns was soon added the notion that there should be a permanent, highly organized display at the palace, where everyone should receive the honours due to his estate. This concern for the setting and this sense of the necessity of hierarchy produced a second category of household ordinances regulating ceremonial as well as expenditure and where etiquette might be said to have taken its first steps. An ordinance of the Dauphin Humbert II of Vienne in 1336 fixed the composition of menus, the order to follow at meals, the price of fabric and furs allowed to each individual for court dress, according to his rank and the season of the year: it was undoubtedly the first of its kind in the West. James II of Majorca tackled the same problems in 1337 in his *Lois palatines*. And in 1344 Pedro IV of Aragon did little more than translate James II's *Lois* into Catalan, further emphasizing the heavy dignity of their ceremonial. In doing so he earned the epithet 'the Ceremonious' and his *Ordenacions* were the inspiration of many European courts, and especially of Burgundy. This last glittered in its turn with incomparable brilliance in the fifteenth century and served in part as a model in the Northern courts (the English in 1493 and the Prussian at the beginning of the sixteenth century) who were the last to establish ceremonial in their written ordinances.

A court had thus become a sumptuous setting where a prince and his entourage henceforth played a role determined by ceremonial down to the smallest detail. In this grandiose spectacle some rulers with an exaggerated sense of their own glory could seek personal triumph. The ideal prince knew that this setting 'doit honnourer l'estat de sa dignité, non l'estat de sa personne' ('should be to the honour of his position, not his person').[6] Far from exalting his personal pride, the insignia and ·quasi-liturgical ceremonial reminded the ruler of the limits of his power.

[6] *Les Demandes faites par le roi Charles VI, touchant son état et le gouvernement de sa personne, avec les réponses de Pierre Salmon, son secrétaire et familier*, ed. G.-A. Crapelet (Paris, 1823), p. 27.

5

King and Tyrant

The law

The resurgence of Roman law in the twelfth century validated some principles which permitted certain theorists to claim unlimited power for the ruler. Starting from the proposition drawn from the Code 'Quum omnia principis esse intelligantur' ('Since everything belongs to the prince'), the legal writer Martinus (*fl. c.*1150) attributed to the Emperor the effective ownership of all goods and the power to arrange all rights in individual cases according to his pleasure. Afterwards, when kings were affirming their sovereignty they sometimes revendicated this universal ownership in their kingdom. But the two Roman tags most frequently quoted were: 'Princeps legibus solutus est' ('The prince is not bound by laws') and 'Quod principi placuit legis habet vigorem' ('What the prince decides has the force of law'). From the time of John of Salisbury, the flatterers of the powerful concluded from this that the prince was above the law and that all his decisions, whatever they were, had the force of law.

In fact the author of the *Policraticus* was already indignant at such propositions and those who supported them remained very rare throughout the Middle Ages. For almost all medieval theorists aimed at limiting the power of the ruler. After the end of the twelfth century there was no support for Martinus's error. Certainly it was admitted that the king was *dominus* in his kingdom and had *dominium* there, but, it was said 'non quoad proprietatem sed quoad protectionem', his *dominium* gave him a right of protection not one of ownership and certainly did not give him the right to dispose of his subjects' goods and, therefore, to tax them. As for 'legibus solutus' and 'quod principi placuit' there was almost unanimous agreement that one should understand by this that the king was compelled to obey the law, not because of some external judicial sanction but simply because of his goodwill and innate sense of justice. The first president of the Parlement of Paris (supreme court of appeals in the kingdom of France) did no more than follow an age-old tradition when he declared in 1527: 'We know well that you are above the law and that laws and ordinances cannot constrain you . . . but it is common belief that you should not exercise unlimited power (nor should you wish to do so), but only that which is good and equitable.'

The king was therefore beneath the law, or rather beneath the laws, and he should respect them all, natural as well as divine law, and also the actual laws of his kingdom, where the customs and privileges of his people were recorded. In principle this positive law was immutable, but in the later Middle Ages everyone agreed that the king might make additions to it, provided that they conformed to natural law and enhanced the common good. Furthermore, the king could modify the provisions of the positive law if they were not in harmony with natural law, so that natural law might triumph and the common weal prosper. In certain cases some writers, such as Lucas de Penna, were even of the opinion that the king could legislate against the natural law, provided that he was motivated solely by concern for the common good. That is to say that the power of the king, already limited by the law, was also checked by the community.

The community

Although no one disputed that the king held his power from God, the manner in which he had received it still had to be explained. It was in this area that democratic trends became apparent, which historians of the beginning of this century believed to have stemmed from an ancient Germanic source but which were in fact also based on certain principles of Roman law. Virtually everyone believed in the divine origin of the ruler's power, in the sense that God inspired the people and that, when they chose a king, the people were the instrument of God: his political authority was mediately derived from God, immediately from the community. God, said the theologians, had entrusted his authority to the people so that they might confer it on a ruler, and the legal writers specified that this transfer of sovereignty, this *translatio imperii*, was effected by the people in the famous *Lex regia*, which was the inevitable starting point for every theorist since the twelfth century.[1] Now the crux of the question is whether this transfer in the *Lex regia* was provisional or final.

[1] The text is to be found in the *Digest*, I,I,4 and the *Institutes*, I,2,6: 'Quod principi placuit legis habet vigorem: utpote cum lege regia, quae de imperio ejus lata est, populus ei et in eum omne suum imperium et potestatem conferat.'

If, as the Ghibellines thought, it was final, sovereignty was then trans-
mitted from prince to prince, from dynasty to dynasty; popular authority,
recognized in theory, remained without any practical outcome. If it was
only provisional, real sovereignty remained with the people, who were to
take the initiative when the throne was vacant or the monarch powerless.
These consequences, constantly called to mind in countries where the king
was elected, were sufficiently to the forefront of minds elsewhere that they
were developed on a broad scale before the Estates General of Tours in
1484.

The role of the people did not stop there. Even if the sceptre was held in
a firm grasp, the people were still entitled to give the ruler their advice.
Admittedly, a few isolated writers already showed the most complete
scorn for the people and refused them all power in the State, even the right
to advise: 'Vanae voces populi non sunt audiendae' ('You should not
listen to the people and their foolish ideas'), said Lucas de Penna. Such an
assertion scarcely produced an echo in the Middle Ages, when almost
everyone declared that the ruler would derive the very greatest advantage
from the counsel of his people, if he listened to it. 'For', as Nicholas
Oresme explained in his commentary on Aristotle, 'although the common
people have no idea how to maintain order or establish laws, they are well
able to see inadequacies and to take note of any opportunities for
improvement and advise the legislators accordingly, so that they do not
make mistakes, and for this reason the people should be given a voice.'

The crown

The king did not only find the law and the people confronting him. You
will remember that the crown was the most important of the emblems of
power. It was natural that a word describing a material object of great
symbolic value soon acquired an abstract sense. The abstraction of the
crown first appeared in England: from the first half of the twelfth century
kings there spoke of Crown Pleas (cases, such as capital offences, reserved
to the crown). In France it was Suger who first used the word crown with
an abstract meaning in the middle of the twelfth century. This sense was
also found in Bohemia in 1158 and in Hungary in 1197. However,
although the concept of the crown henceforth had an important place in
English and Hungarian political thought, it was not found again in
Bohemia after 1169, and hardly at all in France, where the nobleman and
legal writer Philippe de Beaumanoir, for example, only makes one brief
allusion to the concept in the whole of his work. It was not until the
fourteenth century that the notion of the crown was common parlance in
the West. In France Philip VI sheltered his insecure legitimacy under the
crown. This same crown was often invoked after the French defeats at

D

Poitiers and Agincourt; Louis XI frequently referred to it. In Bohemia the concept of the crown reappeared in the first half of the fourteenth century. Charles IV made systematic use of it. It was finally in 1353, in the reign of Casimir IV, that mention was first made of the Polish crown, which was destined to play such an important part in Polish life until the late eighteenth century.

Although all the chanceries of the West finally welcomed this new abstraction, it carried more or less weight in different countries and its importance varied according to the political atmosphere in each kingdom. When a king of France spoke of the crown, he had his patrimony and domain to the forefront of his mind. 'The domain of the crown', 'the revenues of the crown' were expressions constantly repeated from the fourteenth century onwards. But the crown rarely had this patrimonial sense in England; never in central Europe. The king of France also used 'crown' to signify dynastic continuity, the chain of kings in which his person was merely a link. From the line of royal succession, the French chancery rapidly passed to the abstract notion of royalty, and in any case, whatever its precise route, it was in the sense of royalty that *corona* (crown) was generally used when it first appeared. Royalty was the king's power, his rights and, very soon, the territory over which he exercised this kingly power. In the countries where royal power remained strong, in France, in the England of Edward I or the Bohemia of Charles IV, the crown remained closely bound to the person of the king, who exploited and invoked it to protect himself; whilst it went beyond the king and limited his initiatives, the crown in these cases remained truly the king's crown. But, wherever royal authority was weak, the crown became detached from the person of the king and became the crown of the kingdom, symbol of the kingdom, which was entrusted to the people as well as the king and for which they were also responsible. In England the subjects of Edward II and Richard II endeavoured to maintain the state of the crown, if need be, against the king. In Bohemia, while Charles IV spoke of *rex et corona*, thus binding the king to the crown, the habitual expression after his reign was *regnum et corona*, relating the crown to the community of the realm. The Hungarians and the Poles had never said anything other than *corona regis*, *corona regia* until (in 1385 in Poland and 1401 in Hungary) the notion of *corona regni* appeared, which was used by the community of the realm further to limit royal power.

THE PUNISHMENT OF A TYRANT

Thus in the later Middle Ages the law, the crown and the community of the realm set certain limits on the ruler's power which the prince himself promised not to break by the oath before his coronation. But what happened if he did break them?

The iniquitous king was then branded with the name of tyrant. In the Middle Ages as in antiquity the tyrant was first the usurper who had seized power by illegitimate means. But this 'acquisitive' tyranny posed fewer problems to the theorists than 'regitive' tyranny, by which a wicked ruler abused his legitimate power. What could actually be done against this tyrant?

Everyone naturally demanded that he should be punished, and to achieve this many vigorously underlined the subject's right of resistance. In some writers this *jus resistendi* might even go so far as the assassination of the tyrant. In the Old Testament many tyrants suffered a violent death; Aristotle had recorded the frequency of this end amongst tyrants; in his *De Officiis* Cicero had judged it legal and just; Seneca had declared that nothing was more pleasing to the gods than the sacrifice of a wicked king. For a long while, the Commandment 'Thou shalt not kill' had deterred Christian thinkers from advocating tyrannicide, but in the twelfth century John of Salisbury was bold enough to make a fresh case for it, basing his arguments on the Bible and on Cicero. For a long time his was an isolated voice, until the fourteenth century when others started to echo him – whether because of the influence of the *Policraticus* itself and its translations or the direct influence of Cicero and Seneca. 'There is no sacrifice more acceptable than the blood of tyrants', said Bocaccio; 'No sacrifice is more pleasing to God than the death of a tyrant', said Gerson, chancellor of the University of Paris, in his sermon 'Vivat rex' (1405). Many tyrants did indeed die a violent death in fifteenth-century Italy; and the pro-Burgundian secretary Jean Petit justified the murder of Louis, duke of Orléans, in 1407 as tyrannicide. But it was precisely this assassination and Petit's apology that made Gerson aware of the dangers of high-flown classical formulas: generally speaking the fifteenth century was less enthusiastic in its recommendations to the people to counter force with force, 'vim vi repellere'. And many followed Thomas Aquinas in maintaining that, if tyranny was wicked, tyrannicide risked being an even worse remedy for the evil.

So the tyrant was not to be killed. But throughout the later Middle Ages writers as different as William of Ockham, Marsilius of Padua, Jean Buridan, Jean Gerson, Zabarella or Jacobus Alemannus followed Aquinas in condoning and recommending the deposition of an incompetent and tyrannical ruler. Who was able to depose him? Before each State became enclosed within its own sovereignty this might be the Pope or Emperor. Now all those who countenanced the deposition of a wicked ruler thought that he could only be deposed by the people, who had instituted him or at least had once delegated his powers: *Vox populi, vox Dei* ('the voice of the people is the voice of God'). The difficulty then was to know who were the people and who represented them. In countries where the king was elected his electors were of course fit to depose him; in Germany the prince-electors pronounced the deposition of Adolf of Nassau in 1298 and of Wenceslas in 1400. Where a regularly convened assembly represented the people it might take the initiative; and the English Parliament played an important role in the abdication of Edward II in 1327 and of Richard II in 1399. But the problem was precisely that the majority of the States of the West had no electoral body in the later Middle Ages, since the king was never, as it were, elected by a regular numerical procedure; elsewhere the representative assembly was never sufficiently powerful to enforce the deposition of a ruler which it had never elected. In England Edward II and Richard II were forced to abdicate, but, strictly speaking, they had not been deposed. Theory countenanced the principle of deposition of a tyrant. But, with few exceptions, the nature of the institutions involved prevented this from becoming a regular political event. Medieval monarchy was limited by theory but not controlled by institutions. Even if a people was absolutely determined to depose its ruler, there were, with very few exceptions, no legal paths to this end.

THE UNTHINKABLE SACRILEGE

However, more than these legal means, it was determination to punish their wicked ruler which the people lacked. Admittedly the responsible citizen was beginning to emerge from beneath the passive subject at the end of the Middle Ages; the necessity of collaboration between the ruler and his country was viewed in an increasingly favourable light and the idea of a contract binding ruler and country as equal parties became increasingly widespread. The fourteenth and fifteenth centuries were indeed the period of dualism. This did not prevent the dialogue from being a thoroughly unequal one between the people, who were just developing some kind of self-awareness, and the prince, who was supported by the age-old conviction that he was, in M. Bloch's words, 'something very different from a high-ranking official'.

Since the twelfth century, lawyers had gradually begun to construct the notion of community, society and 'university', which constituted a verit-able collective personage, a *persona ficta*, whose head was its representative in the sense that it was he who held all its powers. In this perspective, to say that the king represented the kingdom was simply to say that he acted *qua* mouthpiece and *qua* representative of this moral personage that was the community of the country. The relation of king to kingdom was on a legal and a rational plane. This scholarly explanation was new. It had not convinced everyone, far from it. For many, the king represented the kingdom in the sense that he personified the kingdom in himself alone, that he *was* in reality the kingdom. They were familiar with the ancient and universal theme of folklore (repeated in the Arthurian legend) which identified the king so completely with his kingdom that, once the king was wounded in his private parts, the kingdom was afflicted with sterility. Who would dare maintain that this old magic source had lost its power when the theorists of the fifteenth century demonstrated that the king *was* the kingdom and Louis XI said 'I am France'? Such ideas and beliefs in any case put the king beyond the reach of his subjects.

The kings drew their strength above all from the Christian faith of their subjects. For a long while this had not automatically been the case: in the thirteenth century the king was still not anointed in Scotland, and in Poland monarchical power retained a secular character. But soon afterwards kings throughout the West derived great advantage from religion. They did so in varying degrees, however, depending on the country and its temperament. In one land the king was simply king by the grace of God. But in others the king was the vicar of God, or even the image of God, shown occasionally to the people under a canopy, like the Holy Sacrament. Finally, some kings possessed a miraculous power and we know that sick people – clerics, nobles and peasants – came every year in their hundreds from all parts of the country and from abroad to have their scrofula touched by the king of England or the king of France, be he Edward II or Philip the Fair. It would be ridiculous to set out the relationship between king and country in purely institutional terms, for at the end of the Middle Ages the king was supported by a very real faith.

With such a prestigious personage the people could only appeal to his conscience or to God. The education of a future king therefore became of prime importance, since the only practical obstacle to tyranny was the horror of tyranny inculcated in the ruler himself. The *Mirrors of princes*, far from being the pointless chatter of moralists, were a political necessity throughout the Middle Ages. Would the adult king make the wrong decisions? His subjects thought that he would if he was surrounded by evil counsellors and they were universally detested – witness the attitude of the Bourgeois of Paris in the reign of Charles VI in speaking of 'the bad counsel that then surrounded the good king'. Wicked counsellors should be driven away from the king and the king himself warned about them, for, as Jean Juvenal des Ursins said in 1440, 'My countrymen think that if the king has been warned he can foresee the danger.' But what if he did not foresee it? Clerics might write treatises on the rightness of resistance; vassals might believe them. As time passed, an increasing number of scholars reverted to the traditional convictions which the loyal people, deep down, had never abandoned. One cannot offer resistance to one's natural lord, they said in Poland. The king must be obeyed, was the word in the England of Henry VIII. And in France, although Thomas Basin still attempted to justify the War of the Public Weal, Gerson in 1405, Jean de Terre Vermeil in 1420, Jean Juvenal in the middle of the century and many less favoured clerics at the end of the fifteenth century all declared that the matter should be left in God's hands, that kings and tyrants should be obeyed and that to rebel against them would be to commit the crime of *lèse-majesté*, if not sacrilege itself. The loyalty of his subjects to the person of the king was so deep that popular revolts, like that of the Jacquerie in France or the Peasants' Revolt in England soon came to nothing. Only God finally imposed a real limit on royal power and, in the last analysis, that was less a constraint than a source of support for the king.

Undoubtedly not all the rulers of the West had a position as assured as that of the king of France; undoubtedly the king of France himself came up against many difficulties; there was undoubtedly dialogue, sometimes brutal, between the ruler and his subjects. But a whole world of beliefs and convictions operated in favour of the prince. As the author of the *Rosier des Guerres* said of the Praguerie:

> It has always been the case in France that the sovereign lord has finally proved master and lord of those who are placed under him. And those who have remained set in their obstinacy have come to a bad end . . . over which many people rejoice, who mended their ways and made peace with him whom God has ordained to rule over them, just as in the proverb which says a lord of straw can overcome a subject of steel.

In the vigorous dialogue between the ruler and his subjects which was characteristic of the political life of the later Middle Ages, the prince had the convictions of his subjects behind him and there were no others.

Part II

The Power of the State

Although it is important not to underestimate the importance of mentalities in the life of the States, it is also vital to take account of concrete facts. The power of the State rested on its people's loyalty. It depended also on the resources available to it and the structures which it was able to forge in order to attain its ends.

6

The Resources of the State

Later medieval public opinion believed it was a fundamental necessity that the prince should 'live off his own' from the resources of his domain, that is, resources so ancient and traditional that no one dreamt of contesting his right to them. These traditional resources were the inheritance of vicissitudes down the centuries and constituted a rag-bag of all sorts of rights from which the prince was happy to benefit without troubling himself about their origin. The modern historian can certainly attempt to distinguish between property rights, seigneurial, feudal and regalian rights. The medieval ruler was content to total in all its disarray the income he received from his lands, his mills, his forests, his fishponds, from the tax his peasants paid him, the reliefs and aids granted by his vassals, the rights of toll which affected goods in circulation, the taxes on sales (*tonlieu*) which affected merchandise, above all grain and wine, sold in a shop or at market, the fines imposed by his tribunals, the coin manufactured in his mints and the income from mines on his lands.

Although there was little variation in the nature of traditional resources between one State and the next, this was not the case with the relative place each type occupied in the total revenue of different rulers. Combined political and economic realities explain why, for example, the king of England took more money from his vassals than any of his neighbours, while the king of France received more from his courts of justice and his forests, and the Elector Palatine relied primarily on the tolls by which he profited from shipping on the Rhine.

It is virtually impossible to evaluate the income which a ruler might receive from his domain. In the first place because the financial records which might have made this possible have generally been lost through mishap or carelessness, for these documents, which soon became obsolete and redundant, were also quickly jettisoned and abandoned. But even if they had all come down to us the investigation would not be very much easier. For no document shows the total revenue and expenditure of the State. Each receiver made a certain number of payments from his returns and the ruler was only interested in the surpluses at his disposal. So a medieval ruler knew the total of neither his income nor his outgoings. The historian, coming long after him, is frequently incapable of seeing the situation any more clearly.

All that we can say is that at the end of the Middle Ages the power of the ruler was still closely related (to a greater extent than has often been thought) to the importance of his domain. But this domain was constantly threatened with alienations and maladministration. When the ageing duchess of Brabant had to sell her estates to the duke of Burgundy at the end of the fourteenth century, the new owner found ruined castles on his lands, damaged forests, fishponds without fish, mills in disrepair and the legal system abandoned. A dilapidated domain was the hallmark of a weak ruler. The first concern of the ruler who wished to be powerful was to restore his domain by sending commissioners with a reforming brief to revoke alienations which should not have taken place, drive out incompetent or dishonest officials and recover all his rights. Even at the end of the Middle Ages the increase of his domain revenues was one of the means by which Henry VII aimed to restore royal power in England after the Wars of the Roses.

A powerful ruler needed firstly a prosperous domain. But the financial burdens of the new States were such that in any case the resources traditionally acknowledged as his in the thirteenth century were henceforth insufficient for any ruler. From the second half of the thirteenth century the States of the West all participated in a feverish search for fresh sources of income.

THE COINAGE

The right of striking coin was one of the royal rights which a good number of lords beside the king still enjoyed in the thirteenth century, as a result of more or less ancient concessions or usurpations. In the duchy of Burgundy alone the mint at Dijon was in ducal hands, those of Auxerre, Châlon, and Mâcon belonged to their counts, that of Autun to the cathedral church, that of Cluny to the abbey there, that of Tournus to the abbey of Saint-Philibert. All these mints produced coins of different values that no longer had any visible relation to their common Carolingian ancestor. Monetary exchange was then so limited that this numismatic anarchy inconvenienced no one initially. Then, with the resurgence of the State and of commercial activity, this situation soon appeared as intolerable to rulers and merchants alike, with the result that, whether as a measure of political authority or because of the free play of market forces, one after another the seigneurial mints closed or changed in character. There were four private mints in England from the beginning of the fourteenth century, but they received their coins from the king, and in effect manufactured royal money; only the profits of striking the coin escaped the State. After twenty years of provisional and contradictory measures in France the ordinance of 1315 finally authorized thirty-two seigneurial mints to continue to strike coins whose nature and value were fixed by the king. There were still good times ahead for some private mints. But the economic situation was definitely unfavourable towards them. One after another the seigneurial mints closed: Melgueil in 1316, Le Puy in 1318, Rodez in 1378. Slowly seigneurial coinage disappeared from circulation until at the end of the fourteenth century royal coins reigned supreme in France. In Castile, on the other hand, the king simply closed the private mints which were still producing coins of their own choice at the end of the fifteenth century. Sooner or later coinage became what it had been in the Carolingian period: the exclusive concern of the State.

Once masters of their coinage, what did the rulers do with it? The cost price of metal coin depended on three factors in the Middle Ages: the purchase price of the metal, the cost of manufacture of coins (or *brassage*) and the profit which the lord intended to make from the striking of coin, a principle which no one contested and which was called *seigneuriage* in France, 'seignoriage' in England. Charles V's mints paid 60 *livres* for a gold *marc* to the money-changers. The *brassage*, that is the manufacture of the sixty-three coins of a *franc* made from it, came to 30 *sous*. (The *franc* was worth one *livre* or 20 *sous*.) The *seigneuriage*, or profit, was thus 30 *sous*. Let us enter the realm of conjecture. The king could have manipulated the statutory composition of the coinage by adding worthless copper and manufacturing with this metal alloy the same number of coins of the same weight and having the same official value. He could have clipped the coins to his advantage by striking a larger number of coins from the same *marc* of pure gold. He could simply have changed the value of the sixty-three coins struck from the pure gold *marc* and decided that their official value was no longer 20 *sous* but, for example, 22 *sous* 6 *deniers*. In all three cases the result would have been similar: he would have altered the base of the coinage and in this way effected a change in value; more specifically, he would, in the example chosen, have weakened the coinage and effected a devaluation.

However, between 1300 and 1500 there were numerous rulers who made repeated monetary mutations, above all repeated devaluations,

resulting in a general and spectacular weakening of the European coin-
ages. Take France, for example: St Louis had created a monetary system
that endured many years; then, from 1295 to 1306, Philip the Fair effected
a series of adjustments, after which *bonne monnaie* – weaker however than
that of St Louis – was restored and survived more or less until a new
period of uncontrolled debasements of the coinage in 1337–43. France
thus experienced periods of monetary stability, of which the reign of
Charles V is the most famous, followed by stormy periods of fluctuating
rates (1295–1306, 1337–43, 1351–61, 1413–22), as a result of which the
royal coinage was considerably weaker at the end of the fifteenth century
than two centuries earlier. England did not experience these great monetary upheavals, but whereas the noble (a pure gold coin created in 1344)
was initially struck at the rate of forty-two coins to the pound sterling,
each noble being worth 6s. 8d., at the end of the fifteenth century, after a
number of isolated changes in the base rate, it was struck at the rate of
fifty coins to the pound sterling and each of these coins now had a nominal
value of 8s. 4d.

To account for these changes historians adopt two types of explanation.
According to some, their causes were purely economic: it was essentially
variations in the price of precious metal that forced a ruler to alter the
value of his money. Without denying the effect of economic causes, other
historians have, on the contrary, believed that the real cause of these
monetary mutations is to be found in the financial needs of the ruler.

It is important first to underline the fact that, whatever has been said to
the opposite effect, medieval monetary adjustments were not effected by
ignorant governments bent double under the weight of blind necessity.
Medieval monetary thought did exist and the rulers were guided by it.
Since the thirteenth century canon and civil lawyers had constructed a
monetary theory; the experts (the money-changers) had understood the
effects of monetary mutations and had written books of advice which the
rulers could read well before Nicholas Oresme, the inheritor of age-old
theory and experience, wrote his admirable *De Moneta* (1355–60), which
was to inspire the monetary policy of Charles V and of many other rulers
at the end of the fourteenth century.

That said, many of the changes in the value of the coinage were
undoubtedly forced on governments by economic necessity. Three sorts of
coin were in circulation: small 'black' (copper) coins needed for day-to-
day life, whose intrinsic value was virtually non-existent; silver coins, such
as the *gros* or the *sous*, necessary for more important transactions; and gold
coins, whose invention had been necessitated by the exigencies of international commerce and from the middle of the thirteenth century fell into
two main categories – the florin of Florence or Venetian ducat (which had
the same value) and the French *écu*. Monetary changes had at first been

necessitated by the continued rise in the price of precious metals. Mines were actively worked in Europe, however: gold mines in Hungary and Transylvania; silver mines in Bohemia, which achieved maximum production in the fourteenth century, but where technical problems and political disturbances resulted in reduced extraction at the beginning of the fifteenth century; the Serbian mines, which took the lead in the first half of the fifteenth century; the mines of central Europe (southern Germany and the metal-bearing mountains of Bohemia) where, once peace was restored, technical progress enabled miners to prospect for silver hundreds of metres below ground from the mid-fifteenth century onwards. But even this quantity of production could not meet the increased needs of international commerce, nor indeed compensate for the interest (*frai*), that is the inevitable usury of money in circulation. However, if this mining expansion explains the prosperity and international importance of Bohemia in the fourteenth century and of Serbia in the first half of the fifteenth century, it did not prevent any country of the West with an external trade deficit from having a shortage of precious metal and having to weaken its coinage, causing a fall in neighbouring and interdependent currencies. Besides, although the State could certainly stipulate a legal relationship between gold and silver, the commercial price of the two metals was constantly changing and eventually the legal rate had to be adjusted to the commercial rate, either by changing the value of gold or of silver coin. The fact that money was made not just from one but from two metals, whose price was subject to constant market fluctuations, explains a fair number of economically inevitable adjustments.

But economic grounds cannot explain all such medieval variations. People were still sympathetic to the old theory that the coinage was the ruler's affair, whose value he could establish arbitrarily in his best interests. Nicholas Oresme himself, who demonstrated that the coinage was not the affair of the prince but of the whole community and could only be adjusted prudently and in exceptional circumstances, admitted that in absolute necessity a State could decide to alter the rate to make a profit and increase the *seigneuriage*. This, he explains, is a mild tax felt less acutely than direct taxation and proportionate to the individual's lot since 'who has most pays most' and no one, be he noble or cleric, can escape it. To supply rulers with the money they needed, it was as if the peoples could now choose between direct taxes and changes in the value of the coinage. In order to resolve the financial problems caused by the resumption of war, Philip the Fair tried to establish direct taxation in 1294; he was unsuccessful; six months later his dramatic devaluations began. In 1303 the French king announced a return to 'sound coin', but in exchange the French had to grant him heavy subsidies. If Charles V was able to maintain a stable money supply, it was also because he had been able to impose direct and indirect taxes, which were infinitely more hated than 'sound coin' had been esteemed. The repeated devaluations to which the German princes had recourse throughout the fourteenth century were seldom anything other than a form of capital taxation. For if a prince lowered the value of his coinage, he could pay a higher price for precious metals than his neighbours; gold and silver flowed copiously into his mints and the striking of coin left the ruler with a considerable profit. When the currency was stable, *seigneuriage* brought the king of France virtually nothing, but it provided him with 65 per cent of his Treasury receipts in 1298, 50 per cent in 1299, 70 per cent in 1349, 80 per cent in 1417. But at the same time the revenues of his subjects were reduced, and the economic life of the country severely disturbed.

In the fourteenth century the problem was no longer whether the ruler should obtain new resources from his subjects, but what form they should take. The subjects themselves were still not reconciled to the payment of the necessary direct or indirect taxes, so that for a while devaluations were the only course open to the hard-pressed States. In later medieval France especially, avalanches of politically inevitable and fiscally motivated changes to the coinage were added to those caused by economic necessity, because this was the only weapon available to powerless governments. These quasi-fiscal devaluations, whose disadvantages were universally apparent, became less common once the State was able to levy new taxes from the country: these were just as profitable and entailed less risk.

INDIRECT TAXATION: CUSTOMS DUES

Amongst these new taxes, those which the States could operate effectively and with the greatest speed were naturally indirect taxes. After 1274 Genoa decided to impose a levy of 2 *deniers* in the *livre* (2/240) on imports and exports, called the *comerchium*. In 1275 Edward I decreed that a sack of wool or 300 fleeces leaving the country would pay half a mark and 200 tanned hides a mark: this first customs rate was distinguished from subsequent tariffs by the name of *Magna et Antiqua Costuma* ('Great and Ancient Custom'). Finally in 1277 Philip the Bold quite simply forbade the export of wool and a large number of other commodities from France. These three measures were contemporaneous, they differed from the long-established feudal rights on the movement of goods, and they all marked the first appearance of the young States at their borders. They are comparable but not in the least similar.

The small republic of Genoa had only a large port and a few kilometres of coast to watch over: it was easy for it to organize a complex, effective and profitable customs system in a short space of time. The *comerchium* established in 1274 continued to affect all imports and exports (with some exceptions), but from 1340 it was levied at the rate of 6 *deniers* in the *livre*, or 2.5 per cent. In addition, taxes called *drictus* could affect a geographically defined sector of external trade; thus at the end of the fourteenth century a 1 per cent toll operated on all goods from Provence and Languedoc. Certain products that were exempt from the *comerchium* and the *drictus*, such as cereals, paid specific dues. Finally, *Ambasciate* were sometimes added to all these taxes: as the name suggests these were temporary fiscal measures designed to meet the costs of particularly important embassies. The *Ambasciata Francie* fell into this category in 1340, the *Ambasciata Anglie* from 1374 to 1377, the *Ambasciata Alexandrie* in 1386. The sum total of customs dues provided Genoa with important resources without which the life of the State would often have been paralysed.

As for the history of England, it would be incomprehensible without the taxes levied on wool and hides after 1275. For English wool was indispensable to the European textile industry, and the king of England would allow himself to derive abundant profits with the sole disadvantage of putting up the price of continental cloth. Without wool Edward III could never have undertaken his French wars.

However, these customs dues were extremely difficult to collect. Although the levy of the Great and Ancient Custom caused no problems in the first half of the fourteenth century, this was not the case with the *maltote* (1303) with which Edward I and then Edward III attempted to increase the revenue afforded by the Great Custom. Edward I and his successors very quickly learnt that agreement of their subjects was vital. But which subjects? At first negotiations were conducted with the merchants, who agreed to the payments demanded the more willingly as they could obtain substantial advantages in exchange, and could use the tax as an argument for selling the wool at a higher price on the Continent and buying it more cheaply in England. The English quickly learnt that taxes on wool were not simply the business of merchants, but concerned them all. And they did not rest until the king promised that no new tax would be levied on wool or hides without the consent of Parliament. Edward III agreed to this request in 1362.

Once decided upon and accepted, the very collection of the tax posed further problems. For the English coast extended for hundreds of kilometres and wool could leave from dozens of ports. Gradually formulating a viable and profitable system of collection was no mean undertaking. The government first tried direct collection by royal officers. The yield was so small that a system of tax-farming was finally adopted in 1343. Farmers of taxes could undoubtedly have been established in each wool port. But many complex pressures, economic rather than fiscal, forced the government to limit the export of wool to a limited number of ports where the dues could be more easily collected. The problem then was the choice of these privileged 'staples'. After many variations it was decided in 1363 that all English wool exported to the Continent, with the exception of that exported to Italy by Italian merchants, should pass only through the town of Calais which Edward III had won shortly before (1347). This solution, which best reconciled conflicting interests, proved permanent. But there was inevitable friction between the farmers of the tax and the merchants who had to pay it. The organizational edifice was finally completed in 1399 by the creation of the Company of the Staple at Calais, grouping together between 300 and 400 'staplers' who – with the exception of the trade to Italy – had been granted the monopoly of the export of English wool and who undertook in exchange to organize the levy of the tax at Calais themselves. Farm, staple, monopoly: thus in the course of the fourteenth century a system was slowly constructed that was more stable and less subject to dispute. In the following century, as the English textile industry developed, exports of raw wool fell constantly and, as a result, the profit that the State could expect from it also declined. At the end of the Middle Ages taxes on the export of wool or hides were no longer so important. Nevertheless, for a 150 years they provided England with incomparable resources and left an enduring mark on her institutions. Without wool and the wool taxes, modern England would be incomprehensible, and contemporary Englishmen were sufficiently aware of its importance for the chancellor to sit in Parliament on a woolsack.

In contrast to both the republic of Genoa and the king of England, the king of France was acting on an economic rather than a fiscal plane when – with only temporary success – he forbade a number of exports in 1277 and repeated and even extended the ban in 1305. By preventing certain commodities from leaving the country he hoped at least to check the rise of prices in France. As a secondary consideration he soon realized that he could profit from the issue of individual export licences. He was thus increasingly aware of the fiscal aspect of the situation. Subjected to conflicting pressures he hesitated for a while, at the mercy of events, between unlimited foreign trade, a total ban on exports, concessions at a price for individual licences within a general policy of prohibition and finally the free export of all goods in return for a tax *ad valorem* (proportionate to their value). Then, in 1324, he established a dual customs system that proved more durable: certain commodities were regularly exported on payment of a tax proportionate to their value, called the *droit de rêve*; other commodities, such as those subject to Papal legislation forbidding their possession by infidels (arms, horses, etc.) or those needed by national industry (wool, flax, hemp) remained subject to a system of specific licence and paid a so-called toll of *haut-passage* once their export had been authorized. Finally all these complex measures were simplified in 1360 in order to secure the ransom of King John. A lasting customs system called the *imposition foraine* was established which, however – always faithful to previous perspectives – continued to tax exports alone. It was only in the sixteenth century that imports were also subject to customs dues.

Moreover the collection of customs duties in France, along the entire length of her interminable land border, was an infinitely more difficult undertaking than in England. Since, in addition, France did not have commodities for export on which her neighbours were so totally dependent that they would accept any price whatever, the *imposition foraine* never comprised more than a small proportion of the revenue of the kings of France. By contrast, it was in France that the greatest proportion of duties were levied with increasing severity on products for mass consumption, especially salt.

INDIRECT TAXATION: THE SALT TAX

First and foremost, salt is a biological necessity; moreover salt alone made possible the preservation of meat and fish, which made the next day a little less worrying for the inhabitants of the West. Salt was thus irreplaceable. However it is also one of those rare products which one cannot expect to find on one's doorstep. 'On a farm', runs an old Provençal proverb 'there should be everything, except iron and salt.' Although salt was not to be found everywhere, it was never far away, however, and in copious supply – whether in salt marshes, peat impregnated with sea salt, salt springs or as crystals hewn from the ground by the developing mining industry. The only problem was that its transport was costly and difficult and that before it could be made available for consumption it had to be stored to dry out for three or four years. The salt trade thus required considerable capital and was consequently vulnerable to capitalist speculation, which was already beginning to turn a common but irreplaceable product into an expensive commodity. At this point the State intervened.

It was in the twelfth century that the resurgence of Roman law encouraged the princes and towns of southern France to assert the right of the State to salt. This tendency never led to the possession of salt-marshes by the State. It sometimes led to a State monopoly of salt production and its sale; thus in 1184 Venice established her monopoly over the production and sale of the salt of Chioggia, and, following her example, Sienna did the same for the salt-marshes of Grossetto, and Rome for those of Ostia.

But this monopoly did not appear at such an early date and remained less common than a monopoly of the distribution of salt. From the middle of the twelfth century the count of Toulouse, the viscount of Carcassonne and the lords of Montpellier, Tarascon and Arles had a monopoly of the sale of salt in their lands. In the second half of the twelfth century and during the thirteenth, the monopoly of the sale of salt became one of the cornerstones of the finances of the Italian communes. But in order that the declared monopoly should be effective it was necessary for the State to control the movement of salt, and the establishment of mandatory granaries was therefore a logical necessity. Thus a unique institution developed in Southern Europe where the State did not draw her resources from a straightforward tax but from a monopoly that in fact created new structures. Progress continued: in 1259 Charles of Anjou perfected the institution that was soon given the name of *gabelle*; and established it throughout his vast State; by the ordinance of Burgos in 1338 Alfonso XI of Castile put the finishing touch to the efforts of his predecessors, giving the royal monopoly of salt a legal basis, and organizing it on foundations which were to survive until the death of Philip II.

A few months later the *gabelle du sel* (salt tax) appeared in France. All too often it has been asserted that this was at first a royal monopoly directed against unscrupulous merchants, to serve the interests of the kingdom as a whole. It is clear that it was never anything other than a fiscal expedient, not even invented by the hard-pressed counsellors of Philip VI, but simply borrowed by them from the long-established practices of the South.

The salt tax, which remained an uncertain phenomenon in the reigns of Philip VI, John the Good and Charles V, was suppressed in 1380, shortly after the death of the last, and was re-established on a firm footing in January 1383. It did not affect the whole kingdom equally. The combination of existing rights and political circumstance had different effects in different regions. At first some provinces such as Brittany, completely escaped the royal tax on salt. In others, such as Poitou, Aunis and Saintonge, salt was taxed at the rate of five *sous* in the *livre*, or 25 per cent, but was never subject to a monopoly. In Languedoc there were granaries – the legacy of previous centuries of experience – sited near the centres of production and through which all salt had to pass, but after which its movement and sale were unrestricted. Finally, to the north of the Loire, in a certain number of towns, granaries were established near the consumers where rich importers had to store the damp salt, pay their taxes and where all retailers had to purchase dry salt. To this first monopoly, that of supplying the granaries was often added; this was a new source of considerable profit to the king or those of his *bonnes villes* to whom his rights were relinquished.

It was thus that an irreplaceable necessity – but one that was not in short supply – ended by becoming an expensive item whose purchase was a heavy burden on the individual budget, as a result of State and capitalist intervention. As the most vigorous protests did not result in the disappearance of these scandalous innovations, producers, shopkeepers, consumers and even officials tried to turn them to their own advantage by innumerable fraudulent practices. The State was desperate rather than effective in its struggle against them. It soon decided that the most effective way to check fraud was undoubtedly to force every consumer to buy the amount of salt that roughly corresponded to his needs, so that any additional fraudulent purchases would be redundant. But this *sel de devoir* (obligatory salt), mentioned in certain Italian towns from the mid-fourteenth century and ordained by the king of France in 1370 at the latest, never succeeded in eliminating fraudulent practices.

So no State ever reaped the profits it had anticipated from the salt tax. Nevertheless, in Castile, Provence, the Papal States, Florence and Genoa, as well as in France, salt was one of the State's most important sources of revenue in the later Middle Ages. In 1502 Louis XII rightly believed that the *gabelle* was 'the easiest, simplest and most straightforward subsidy that could ever have been levied'. It is not an exaggeration to say that if England was partly built on wool, other late medieval European States, especially France, were partially founded upon salt.

DIRECT TAXATION

In the thirteenth century the impecunious prince could have recourse to many measures. He could impose a *taille* (land tax); demand an *aide* (subsidy) from his vassals, making great play of precedent and feudal custom; announce his departure on a Crusade and thus obtain Papal consent for the levy of a tithe or a tenth from the clergy; negotiate the grant of subsidies from the towns in return for concessions of a more or less illusory nature. As these partial solutions were all inadequate, rulers soon attempted to obtain more by demanding that all their subjects should consent to support them financially. Thus – earlier in some places than others – modern direct taxation was born and was familiar in one guise or another to all the States of the West by the end of the fifteenth century. Some historians have seen this tax merely as an extension of seigneurial revenues (*tailles*); they have underlined its origins in the lord's domain. Others have considered it a descendant of the feudal aid (aids were certain subsidies paid by vassals to their lord) and emphasized its feudal origin. In reality, although it may have benefited from earlier experience, modern direct taxation, theoretically granted and paid by everyone, is essentially different and specific. Just as seigneurial taxes and feudal aids characterized the feudal period, so direct taxation is indissolubly linked to the modern State. Moreover, in their desire to impose direct taxation, governments came up against considerable political and administrative difficulties.

The first obstacle was the ubiquitous necessity of popular consent. This occasioned vital developments in all States and played an especially important role in the history of representative institutions. But once the tax had been granted governments encountered even greater political and administrative obstacles at the time of imposition. When, under Philip the Fair, the French monarchy made its first attempts at direct taxation, it tried out all possible solutions over a period of some years: tax on capital, revenue or simply on hearths. All these methods produced equally deceptive results, for the government lacked the means to estimate individual capital or income or even simply to calculate the number of hearths in the kingdom. Moreover, this complete impotence resulted also – it was still the very beginning of the fourteenth century – from the immense size of the country, for at this period smaller political units were still a long way off.

For a long while before, the towns had assessed their taxes by hearths: nothing was easier, on a relatively small scale, than to count the number of hearths, that is the dwellings or heads of household and demand the payment of the same sum from each household. This system was simple but profoundly unjust and was quickly abandoned for another which made more allowance for individual means. To the best of our knowledge the *estime* appeared at Pisa in 1162, Sienna between 1168 and 1175, Lucca in 1182 and Florence in 1202. In this new system the *libra,* or direct tax, was no longer levied uniformly from each household but in proportion to the figure recorded, after an enquiry, in the register of estimates. This figure did not indicate the precise total of capital or revenue of the taxpayer. It was merely a number, to some extent abstract, higher or lower depending on an individual's means, and in proportion to which the total sum levied was divided amongst all the inhabitants. The determining of this simple number (periodically revised to take account of changes in fortune and of the parties in power) involved the exercise of considerable individual discretion. A further step forward occurred when the town undertook to compile a general and precise inventory of the property and chattels of each family. This was done in Toulouse in 1263. These Toulousain registers were called *estimes,* but they differed greatly from the Italian *estimes.* From the thirteenth century onwards the compilation of such inventories posed no insurmountable administrative problems within the limited context of a town. On a political level the practice encountered opposition from the rich, for whom the triumph of fiscal justice was not a primary concern. As the rich were also the holders of power, the example of Toulouse was slow to be followed. There were *estimes* at Albi only in 1343 and at Lyon (where they were called *nommées*) in 1388. As for the Italian city-states, they only resigned themselves to the practice in the fifteenth century: an inventory like the *estime* of Toulouse and called a *cadastre* was only drawn up in Florence in 1427; following this example a *cadastre* was compiled at Pisa in 1428. The Toulousain formula had hardly been adopted in Italy when it was abandoned in Toulouse, where the last registers of *estimes* date from 1459, and where, from 1478 onwards, the goods of the inhabitants were not recorded under one proprietor after another but listed in topographical order. This new kind of document was called a *cadastre* in France. Generally speaking, in the Italian city-states and the towns of France the tax on households was quickly replaced by a levy more or less proportional to the value of property and movable goods, with an emphasis on the former which was more easily assessed.

On the other hand in England, from the beginning of the fourteenth century onwards, everyone was resigned to paying a tax proportional to their personal fortune, which was generally called the 'pourcentage'. Although there had been a few isolated attempts to establish such a tax in the twelfth and thirteenth centuries, this acquiescence was largely due to the determination of Edward I. The 'pourcentage' was granted by Parliament and varied on each occasion. One time it would be a fifteenth, another a ninth, for everybody. A distinction was soon made between urban and rural wealth, the latter being taxed at a lower rate than the former. Thus, from 1332 Parliament regularly granted, at the king's request, a fifteenth and a tenth, that is a tax of a fifteenth on the movable goods of rural inhabitants and a tenth on the possessions of those who lived in towns. A vast inquiry into the eminently variable wealth of each individual had to be undertaken every time. The course of such an inquiry could never have been smooth.

As for the French administration, it was even less well equipped at this period and had to rely on the hope of counting hearths. It was in 1328 that a schedule of all the hearths of the kingdom was first drawn up – with countless inaccuracies and uncertainties – which henceforth enabled the *fouage* (hearth tax) to be assessed more accurately. In 1380 the *fouages* were abolished by Charles V on his deathbed. But a few years later the French had to resign themselves to the payment of a new direct tax, the *taille*, which was initially very similar to the old *fouage*. The nature of the *taille* soon changed; there came gradually to be a considerable difference between the north and the south. In the north the hearth always remained the basis for tax-assessment, with their actual number revised by periodic enquiry. Here the *taille* was a personal tax, born by individual heads of household. In the south, by contrast, the assessment of the *taille* by hearth ceased at the beginning of the fifteenth century. At first chattels and landed property were taken into account until, in about 1480, real estate was retained as the sole criterion because it was more accessible. Here, the *taille*, levied on land, was a property tax.

Whatever its basis, the tax might still be collected by quota or by distribution. In England the king demanded a certain proportion of the value of their chattels in tax from all his subjects, letting the sum total of the tax depend finally on individual variables. Here the tax was levied on a quota basis. In France the king initially tried the same approach. He very soon abandoned it and afterwards preferred to establish at the outset the sum which he wished to have at his disposal, then divide this sum. Thus in the second half of the fifteenth century the total required was divided between the *généralités*, then between the towns and the surrounding countryside of each *élection*, then between the inhabitants of each town and each village.[1] At every level the total to be paid was theoretically divided according to a single, known criterion, the number of hearths or the importance of landholdings. At every level, in practice, everything depended on the influence of the negotiators; at every stage there was nothing but barter and haggling, from which the clever and the powerful emerged at a lower rate of tax. The distributional system was therefore much less just. But as each community was completely responsible for the sum it had granted, the government laid hands on the money it needed more quickly and certainly. And so, although the young States of the later medieval West could sometimes dream of quota-based taxation, in the end they resigned themselves without too much difficulty to taxation on a distributional system which they knew to be less just, but which required more elementary and effective administrative methods. They had reluctantly to abandon other practices as well, which, without jeopardizing the principle of direct taxation, year by year reduced its yield. Initially they were powerless against fraud: an inn-keeper at Bristol in 1313 had movable goods worth 200 pounds sterling, but his tax was only calculated on 10 pounds sterling; in a town in the *bailliage* of Caen in 1484 ten couples and seventy individuals huddled together in a single house and were reckoned a single hearth. More serious still were the official exemptions which this or that section of the population obtained. At Florence the town succeeded in extricating itself from the payment of tax, whose entire weight fell upon the surrounding countryside. In England the clergy went untaxed. The very poor were given a similar dispensation. But just as the tax-payers' declarations were shamelessly false, so the numbers of the

---

[1] *Généralités* were regional sub-divisions stipulated by the French royal treasury; *élections* were fiscal units under a royal official entitled the *élu*.

'poor' grew every year: in Worcestershire in 1275, when the collection of taxes under the value of 15 s. had been waived, 7,373 individuals were affected; in 1327, when the minimum taxable sum was 10 s., this number had fallen to 4,642. Finally, in France not only were the clergy and the poor exempt, but soon the nobles as well and even the towns, with the result that the tax became an intolerable burden on the defenceless rural areas.

Let us confine ourselves now to this problem of the basis of the tax, leaving aside for the time being that of its collection. We have to conclude that although the principle of direct taxation was acknowledged in all the States of the West at the end of the Middle Ages, its distribution encountered such great political and administrative difficulties that returns generally remained extremely meagre, even when they did not actually fall. In England in 1290 a fifteenth brought in 116,346 pounds sterling; in 1334, thanks to fraud and exemption, a fifteenth and a tenth yielded a return of only 38,245 pounds sterling. The king was then only too happy to declare that henceforth in any case a tenth and a fifteenth could not be permitted to yield less than this sum. The young States of the West were unable to reap the harvest from direct taxation of which they had once dreamt. The history of direct taxation in the later medieval period is one of birth and growth in which hope was soon replaced by resignation.

PUBLIC CREDIT

The State was nevertheless frequently able to obtain subsidies in the form of loans from groups who escaped direct taxation. Historians, exaggerating the negative character of loans, have seen them as the last resort of improvident princes reduced to desperation. Numerous facts seem to support this view: in 1404 Philip the Bold, the powerful duke of Burgundy, could not have been given a fitting funeral without a loan from Dino Rapondi; in 1473 the Emperor Frederick III was unable to leave Augsburg, where his creditors had foreclosed on his horses; in 1518 Jacob Fugger had to make a loan to the Emperor Maximilian who otherwise 'would have had nothing to eat'. These occurrences were too commonplace to deceive contemporaries; these princes in supposedly desperate straits were not all incompetent rulers, far from it; it was the very structure of the State, whose resources were still too small for its new needs, that had first made a system of public credit inevitable in the late Middle Ages. Moreover this public credit was quite normal, for it was standard practice for a reasonably far-sighted and strong ruler to draw on new resources in order to anticipate receipts that were slow to enter his Treasury and cover his essential expenses as necessary. Moreover tax-farming and assignment were traditional methods. Now tax-farming paid in advance by the farmer, and assignment by which a creditor only received the promise of settlement on an anticipated receipt, instead of a cash payment, were the first forms of credit and prepared the way for others. Inevitable and normal, public credit was finally sometimes also the solution consciously desired in the fourteenth and fifteenth centuries by ruling classes who refused every form of direct taxation and preferred to lend the State such sums as it urgently needed. The creditors drew interest and recovered their capital once the crisis had passed. A highly profitable means of supporting the State.

In 1425 the duke of Brabant needed money. So he pledged jewels to merchants in Malines. At the same time he sold the income from his domain revenue and raised loans on the Bruges money market. There were many forms of public credit and each government could utilize them all. But they had to be adapted to a political and economic context that differed from State to State and permitted or dictated one formula rather than another.

With few exceptions, rulers to the north of the Alps made use only of short-term loans, repayable after a few months or after one or two years at the most, on which canon law forbade all interest. This ban had never prevented creditors from making substantial profits, by more or less convoluted routes, normally amounting (as far as we can estimate) to between 20 and 25 per cent of the capital involved.

In a country like Germany, with archaic economic structures, later medieval rulers were still forced to borrow either from the great landhold-ing lords with a vested interest in land, to whom they had to pledge the most profitable parts of their domain, or from the Jews, to whom they temporarily relinquished their jewels and crowns.

The States with an Atlantic sea-board experienced a similar situation at first. For them everything changed with the establishment of Italian merchant bankers at Paris, London and Bruges in the second half of the thirteenth century. From about 1290 and for the next fifty years these businessmen were informed advisors and creditors, all the more useful because although they had enormous resources at their disposal, they demanded pledges of neither land nor jewels but were prepared to accept promises of repayment on the future returns of direct or indirect taxation. Thus the Florentines Musciatto and Albizi Franzesi ('Biche' and 'Mouche') aided Philip the Fair from 1297 until their death in 1307. But it was in England that the collaboration of the State with Italian financiers went furthest. Edward I relied initially on the Riccardi, who farmed the customs dues for a long while. He abandoned them in 1294. Until 1311 it was the apogee of the Frescobaldi. Then in 1312 came the Bardi – twenty-five years later it was only their loans that enabled Edward III to embark on war with France. Loans to the ruling power brought the Italians enormous advantages but were not without risk. The time came in 1346 when the Bardi, drained by the demands of Edward III, went bankrupt and ruined other Florentine families in their fall. This disaster made the Italians more careful. Henceforth, as a general rule, they avoided loans to princes. After this date only the dukes of Burgundy continued to deal with financiers from south of the Alps. But although Dino Rapondi, who served Philip the Bold and John the Fearless, was highly satisfied with the arrangement, Tommaso Portinari, the agent of the Medici bank at Bruges who backed Charles the Bold, fell with the duke.

After the collapse of the Bardi the kings of England never found such reliable money-lenders. They continually experienced weakening financial crises. On the other hand, the kings of France, who had never relied on Italian resources to the same extent, were gradually able to find new creditors. They appealed to the clergy, the towns and (especially after the reign of Louis XI) to their officials. These multiple loans enabled the kings of France to have considerable sums at their disposal in a short space of time. However, these loans were frequently forced and granted without interest. What is more, these numerous small loans did not tie the king's hands on a political level. Jacques Coeur was the only notable exception in this respect, but Charles VII took such offence that he was soon disgraced. These expedients were thus not without advantage, and other rulers, such as the duke of Milan, made use of them. The creditors, forced to make interest-free loans, nevertheless profited in some respects. The towns accumulated privileges. Above all, because his officers were also his creditors, the king could only remove them with difficulty and was virtually obliged to accept their choice of successor. The royal custom of borrowing from officers thus played a considerable part in the establishment of a hereditary and venal official class.

Although rulers virtually always preferred the short-term loan, public credit had an altogether different complexion in the towns in general and the Italian city-states in particular. Rather than levy a new direct or indirect tax, the services of creditors were called upon in times of crisis and annual interest was paid to them from the twelfth century onwards at Pisa and in the first and second halves of the thirteenth century at Venice and Florence. Once the crisis had passed the town repaid its creditors from its usual revenues, or at least those in possession of letters of credit, for their commercialization was permitted, for example, by Venice from 1262. There could thus be a sequence of loans at different rates of interest according to the state of the market. Soon they overlapped, the town being obliged to contract a new loan before it could repay the previous one. The public debt of an Italian town was thus simultaneously very complex (since it consisted of individual loans, each requiring a different rate of interest) and very large: at Genoa in 1339 annual civic income did not exceed 200,000 *livres*, but the total of loans amounted to 2,962,000 *livres*. Then the State abandoned all hope of repaying this floating debt and took the measures necessary to consolidate it. First, all creditors were paid a uniform rate of interest: 5 per cent in Venice from 1262 onwards; 5 per cent at Florence from 1345; 10 per cent at Pisa after 1348. Then, in order to administer this public debt, banks were established to pay the interest and to collect directly the resources assigned to such payments: the Camera degli Imprestiti at Venice from the first half of the thirteenth century, the Compere Capituli at Genoa in 1340; the Monte Commune at Florence in 1343–7. Other Compere were established at Genoa in the second half of the fourteenth century and they were all regrouped in 1407–8 in the Compere Sancti Georgii, otherwise known as the Casa di san Giorgio. At this stage the patricians who dominated the Italian towns might consider themselves well served: they did not pay direct taxes; they made loans to the State which brought them interest at a relatively modest but assured rate; they entirely dominated the communal banks, and since these ended by being a positive State within a State, they were able in this way to control the town very much more effectively than through the usual political institutions. But their complacency was short-lived. For since the State continued to increase its borrowing without increasing its income, the only solution was a reduction in interest. At Pisa it fell from 10 per cent in 1348 to 5 per cent in 1370; at Genoa from 10 per cent in 1368 to 8 per cent in 1381 and 7 per cent in 1407; at Venice from 5 per cent in 1262 to 4 per cent after the Chioggia war of 1379 and 1 per cent soon after that. At this level there was virtually no difference between loans and direct taxation, to which they were all soon resigned – at Florence in 1427, Pisa in 1428 and Venice in 1463.

Thus numerous economic and political factors explain the development of public credit in the States of the West. Many economic and political consequences stemmed from it, but the main point is that without this public credit, which gave governments the requisite sums when they were needed, the modern State could not have developed.

CONCLUSION

It is difficult, if not impossible, to evaluate the resources available to each of the States of the West in the late Middle Ages, or to specify their character and the sum total of revenue since both these factors varied. Some States relied essentially on indirect taxation; this was the case with

Table 1   Income of States in the West

State	Period	Annual income in national currency	Equivalent in florins
England	First half of the 14th century	30,000 *l*.st.	
	1377–89	120,000	770,000
	1433	65,000	
	Beginning of the reign of Henry VII	52,000	
	End of the reign of Henry VII	142,000	
France	*c.*1250	250,000 *l.t.*	
	temp. Charles VI	2,500,000	2,678,000
	1418	674,000	
	temp. Charles VII	1,800,000	
Flanders	1332	36,000 *l.par.*	
Brittany	*temp.* Duke Francis II	400,000 *l.*	
Burgundy	*temp.* Philip the Bold	340,000 *l.t.*	365,000
	temp. John the Fearless	355,700	
	temp. Philip the Good	345,200	
	temp. Charles the Bold	761,000	
Pisa	1335		140,000
Sicily	14th century	120,000–168,000 ounces of gold	over 230,000
Hungary	Second half of the 15th century		almost 1,000,000
Brandenburg	1488–97		between 54,000 and 66,000

Abbreviations: *l*.st. *livres* sterling   *l.t. livres tournois*   *l.par. livres parisis*

the Italian cities, with England, which still derived 50 per cent of its income from wool in the first half of the fifteenth century, and with the Rhineland States, whom river tolls provided with 60 per cent of their income in the same period. Others lived off the returns from direct taxation: France under Louis XI fell into this category and so did the Rhineland States once there was a reduction in the volume of traffic on the Rhine, when 50 per cent of their revenue was derived from taxes granted by the Estates. Others would have been lost without their royal prerogatives: the power of Bohemia in the thirteenth century, that of Hungary in the second half of the fifteenth century (when she had almost as much money at her disposal as France), that of Saxony at the end of the fifteenth century, would all be inexplicable without the profit they derived from the mines worked on their lands. Yet others, such as England in the reign of Henry VII (when wool exports had fallen), relied chiefly on their domain revenue. The figures provided in table 1 may be regarded as a guide to total income.

Since the Pope at Avignon had 180,000 florins at his disposal at the end of the fourteenth century, the relative incomes of the principal European powers can be tabulated thus:

Papacy	1
France	15
England	4, 5
Burgundy	2
Sicily	slightly more than 1
Pisa	slightly less than 1

Despite its crudity, this sequence is suggestive. Its full significance is only revealed when the expenses that each State had to meet, or undertook to meet, have also been taken into consideration.

7

The Aims of the State:
Justice and Finance

'It is the king's business', said Charles V in the ordinance which he drew up for the regency of the kingdom, 'to govern and administer wisely the entire public weal.' There was no word in thirteenth-century French to specify this political and administrative action of the State. In the fourteenth century *administration* was occasionally found, but increasing use was made of *gouvernement* and, above all, of *policie*, a word taken directly from the Latin *politia* of Nicholas Oresme. From the fifteenth century onwards *policie* gave way to *police* which, together with *gouvernement* was the word most frequently used to designate the full range of State action. '*Omnis policia* ['all policy'] is rightly the sphere of the sovereign', said an advocate in the Parlement of Paris in 1448, '. . . for policy concerns the general aspect of things and the public weal.' Now, if one were to ask the rulers of the West of what that policy consisted, they would probably all have replied in terms similar to those of Louis XI in one of his ordinances: 'The conduct and policy of the public weal in our kingdom . . . consists principally of the administration of justice and the supervision of finance.' To ensure on the one hand the rule of justice – that is, not simply to settle lawsuits equitably, but to take all necessary measures at a more general level to ensure that order and equity were supreme in the kingdom; on the other to ensure that there were sufficient resources to achieve this end; these were the two aims, inextricably intertwined, of all medieval States. In order to achieve these goals they had to build an increasingly complex and effective administration at a local and central level.

LOCAL ADMINISTRATION

English uniqueness

England is doubly unique amongst the States of the West because it was unaffected by Carolingian institutions, yet its administrative development took place at a remarkably early date. But the problems faced there were also to be found on the Continent and the solutions adopted in England were not without an echo across the Channel.

England's first individual characteristic was the appearance in the middle of the tenth century of the division into about thirty 'shires' of varying origin – called 'counties' after the Norman Conquest – which remained, with the same boundaries, the basic administrative unit of the kingdom until the administrative reorganization of the 1970s. The counties of the tenth century were divided into hundreds, variable in size and of unknown origin. In general they consisted of ten to twenty villages. The hundred was not as long-lived as the county, but it was still flourishing at the end of the thirteenth century, when there were 628 in the whole kingdom.

The life of the hundred was patterned by the three-weekly meetings of the hundred court, which might take place on a hill, near a ford, at a crossroads or beneath a tree. The life of the county was similarly patterned by sessions of the county court, convened whenever necessary in a large field or, increasingly, in a great hall. Theoretically all free men were present at these courts. They were thus closely associated with the judicial and administrative life of the county, which was completely dominated in other respects by the character and activity of the sheriff ('shire-reeve'). He first appeared in the tenth century, at the same time as the county, and attained the summit of his power in the first half of the twelfth century. At that time he presided over the county court and the most important of the hundred courts. From the royal castle where he lived he administered the king's wealth, kept the king's peace and devoted an increasing amount of time to the execution of the orders of the king addressed to him in writs. Henry I's sheriffs were certainly not perfect, but no other Western ruler had such effective agents, nor would they have for a long while.

Soon a slow process began that gradually reduced the exceptional power of the sheriff. First of all it was limited geographically by an increasing number of exemptions. On an ordinary manor the lord already enjoyed considerable authority and judicial powers, and he attempted to extend these by every possible means: the strength of the manor as an institution was a prime obstacle to the sheriff's activity. Moreover, numerous hundreds had escaped royal control by a process that frequently remains obscure and had fallen into the hands of an individual lord. The status of these private hundreds was not always the same, but the role of the sheriff was in any case very limited there. In the England of Edward I there were only 270 royal hundreds (of a total of 628), while 358 remained under private jurisdiction. Finally, above all in the twelfth and thirteenth centuries, towns developed which obtained privileges from the king. In these boroughs the sheriff had virtually no role at all. At the end of the thirteenth century there were twenty-four hundreds in the county of Suffolk. Of these eight and a half constituted the great liberty of St Edmund's, where the abbot of Bury had rights equivalent to those of a sheriff; five and a half made up the liberty of St Etheldreda, where the prior of Ely enjoyed the same rights; four others were held by individual lords; the sheriff had no part to play in the three county boroughs (Ipswich, Orford, Dunwich); that left just six royal hundreds and the lords of many manors in them exercised significant judicial rights. The sheriff's power had been reduced to a considerable extent by the proliferation of exemptions.

It was also further limited by a number of royal initiatives. The financial role of the sheriff lost much of its importance with the appearance of the escheators in 1242, whose function was to manage the royal domain and ensure that, if the heir of a deceased vassal was a minor, the king exercised his full rights of wardship and drew the considerable profits that custom permitted. In addition the king assigned two assessors to each county whenever an aid had been levied, responsible for its assessment and collection. But it was the pursuit of justice and of peace which involved the greatest number of new posts. Henry II organized judicial circuits or 'eyres' in the county, where the king's justice was brought within reach of rural inhabitants and whose courts were served by judges from Westminster, who presided over the sessions of the county court in place of the sheriff. The Grand Jury or Jury of Presentment also took its final form in the reign of Henry II, composed of twelve men from each hundred and four from each village, who had to give the names on oath of all unpunished criminals.[1] Before the end of the twelfth century there were two, three, or most frequently four coroners (*custodes placitorum corone*) in each county, whose role was essentially to conduct an enquiry when someone died, thus enabling the Grand Jury to present a suspect to the circuit judges. In the course of the thirteenth century, when circumstances demanded, the king sometimes instituted keepers of the peace (*custodes pacis*) or constables (*constabularii*) to maintain the peace of the kingdom against all internal and external enemies; their role had both police and military aspects. After various experiments in the reign of Edward III these keepers of the peace became permanent officers in 1360, endowed with administrative and executive powers; it was at this time that they were given the title 'justices of the peace'. In the fifteenth century the justice of the peace played an increasingly important administrative and judicial role until, in the reign of Henry VII, he had become the most important official in the county, trusted even with control of the sheriff. Gradually

---

[1] Petty Juries (who delivered a verdict on individual cases) appeared at a later date than Grand Juries, in the thirteenth century.

stripped of his functions, the latter was no longer the powerful figure he had once been. But he continued to play an important administrative role for it was he who communicated all the orders of the king to the relevant officers of the shire. However, bureaucratic progress had greatly increased their number. In seventeen months, between May 1333 and November 1334, the sheriff of Bedfordshire and Buckinghamshire received over 2,000 writs from the king.

English local administration in the later Middle Ages was thus carried out by a large number of officials. Some of the county officials were unsalaried royal appointments; sheriffs, escheators, assessors, keepers and justices of the peace fell into this category. Others, such as coroners, were elected by the shire courts. As for the officers of exempt jurisdictions, they were naturally only dependent on their own lords. Thus life in England at a local level – with its shire and hundred courts, its exempt jurisdictions, its Grand and Petty Juries and its elected officers – was characterized by a very marked degree of autonomy. Some historians once saw this as a survival of democratic Anglo-Saxon traditions that had been sufficiently strong to win acceptance by the country's new rulers. In reality there is nothing to prove that Anglo-Saxon traditions were democratic in the first place. All the evidence indicates that, on the contrary, these institutions were sometimes accepted but more frequently imposed by kings strong enough to hope that they would be served without having to pay their officials. English local institutions are not to be explained by a people attached to their liberties, but by the will of a king powerful enough to impose his wishes. In fact, for royal officers and even those of exempt jurisdictions, the first duty was the execution of orders from Westminster. But at the same time Westminster had to take account of their points of view. For they were not bound hand and foot to the king. As their duties were unpaid and the profits from their service small by any account, it was the moneyed classes, landholders (knightly or otherwise), those whom Bracton called the *buzones* who, while serving the king, retained their own personalities and did not lose sight of their own interests. English local administration was not the concern of the people in the late Middle Ages; it was in the hands of the landholding aristocracy alone. Nevertheless, a dialogue was by this means established between king and country which was continued in Parliament and on which English democracy was gradually founded.

Continental diversity

During the Carolingian period every country of Western Europe had itself experienced or seen at close quarters an administrative organization characterized by three main features. First of all, it was placed in a clear framework: the basic unit was the *comté*, divided into *centaines*. It made a clear distinction between the public and the private sphere: while the counts were responsible for imposing the will of the State in the county, the royal domains were administered by *villici* of modest means. Finally, the count alone did not administer justice: he was assisted by *échevins* (*scabini*), whom he recruited from within the county, and together they formed a 'collegiate' judicial system. Little of this administrative organization remained in the Europe of the year 1000. Generally speaking, the *comtés* and *centaines* had disappeared, the distinction between public and private was not upheld and collegiality was moribund.

Nevertheless, whether because of the durability of the Carolingian institutions themselves, or as a result of the initiative of new rulers inspired by old models, here and there 'colleges' reappeared in the eleventh and twelfth centuries and assisted the ruler's representative in the execution of justice: thus the *échevins* (*scabini*) of Flanders or Brabant, the *boni homines* (good men) of Castile or Aragon. Although collegial justice had lost much of its vitality in the Iberian Peninsula in the later Middle Ages, at exactly the same period the activities of the *échevinages* of the Low Countries extended well beyond the narrow confines of the administration of justice. In Brabant, for example, the nobles had associated the *échevins* to such an extent with the maintenance of order and with financial responsibilities that there, on the whole, the entire spectrum of local life was conducted by an agent paid and chosen by the lord, assisted by a body of *échevins* whom the lord also chose, but who were unpaid. Moreover, the lord's choice had never been entirely free; the *échevins* had always been chosen from amongst hereditary landholders (*viri hereditarii*). From the thirteenth century onwards the lord lost the initiative. The *échevins* themselves chose their successors and the *échevinage* thus fell into the hands of an oligarchy. More democratic methods of selection then appeared in the fourteenth and fifteenth centuries. From this point onwards the character of the *échevinage* changed completely. From being the unpaid tool of the local lord, it became the representative of the community and through the *échevinage* – as in England – a dialogue was established between ruler and country within the framework of local administration.

Elsewhere the people had no role in the administration itself. But it is important to make careful distinctions. In a certain number of countries, possibly as a more or less distant and indirect survival of the Carolingian pattern, justice and finance were administered by two different sets of individuals in the thirteenth century. In Catalonia, for example, the *viguier* was responsible for justice, while the *bailli* administered the royal domain and the roles of the two officials were quite distinct. In Flanders, on the other hand, within the same framework of the castellany, the castellan was responsible for the maintenance of order and the execution of justice, while the receiver of *briefs et espiers* collected the comital revenues.[2] In Forez a similar distinction was made between the castellans, with responsibility for order and justice and the *prévôts* (provosts), who controlled the financial administration.

But such division of function was not very common; the Carolingian model had in general sunk into oblivion and feudalism evolved a simpler method. From this period onwards a single individual was most frequently responsible for the administration of justice, order and finance in a relatively limited area. Various titles were given to this almost universal jack-of-all-trades, all initially as inexact as the rest. Twelfth-century Hainault spoke of *baillis*,[3] but in France this title was soon associated with more powerful individuals. From the first quarter of the thirteenth century the title *bailli* was replaced in Hainault by *prévôt*,[4] which had been the most common term in northern France since the eleventh century. The traditional name in Castile was *merino*.[5] As for the German principalities, local administration developed there more slowly. Between the thirteenth and the mid-fifteenth centuries officials with similar functions appeared there, with the title of *Amtmann* (whose French equivalent is *bailli*) or *Vogt* (best translated as *avoué*, 'attorney').

French *prévôtés* (the area administered by a *prévôt*) were initially less a territorial unit than an assemblage of rights in the hands of a single administrator. It was only gradually, after a slow evolution that was complete by the end of the thirteenth century, that the *prévôts* found themselves at the head of districts whose structure was stable but complex, because they were the product of a long feudal past. These districts were called either *prévôtés*, *châtellenies* or, more specifically, *prévôtés-châtellenies* to distinguish these great royal *prévôtés* centred on a castle (where royal provincial activity henceforth continued at a local level) from any other royal or noble *prévôté* or *châtellenie* of lesser importance. So the *prévôt* thus gradually assembled his *prévôté*, as the *merino* his *merindad*. These developments occurred later in Germany, but they were more rapid and less organic: when the princes provided themselves with *Amtmänner*, they also created from nothing the territory over which their activities were to extend and to which the vaguest of vague terms was given: *Amt* in German and *officium* in Latin. Everywhere, there was a new administrative

---

[2] Money payments were made at offices called either *cens, echiquiers* or *briefs*; payments in kind were centralized in stores called *espiers* (from Latin *spicarium*).

[3] Classical Latin *bajulare* ('to carry on one's back'), *bajulus* ('porter') from Old French *baillir* ('to administer'), whence *bajulus, bayle, baile* in the south, *bailli, baillivus* in the north, with the very general sense of administrator.

[4] From *praepositus*, i.e. he who is at the head of, appointed to a particular office.

[5] In Latin *majorinus* from *major*, 'mayor', he who is the premier, at the head of an administrative unit.

geography to correspond to these new administrative structures.

The rulers of the eleventh and twelfth centuries had initially given fiefs to these indispensable officers of theirs, the *prévôts* and *merinos*. This practice became unacceptable in States which sought tighter control over their officials. Soon the *merinos* were salaried officials, likewise – from the outset – the *Amtmänner* and *Vögte* in Germany. The king of France moved more slowly in this direction. In the twelfth century, when he no longer enfeoffed his *prévôts*, he sold the *prévôtés* at farm. There were advantages with this system: the king could make use of the revenues of the farm in advance, at the beginning of each period of office; he retained control of the office, whose holder changed every two or three years; but then the *prévôts* were, by definition, businessmen ready to stoop to abuses for personal gain which were rightly denounced by the king's subjects. So every time there was a great crisis and the king had to demonstrate his willingness to reform the system, the practice of farms was suppressed and the *prévôtés* entrusted to a custodian. But the king soon realized that he was the real loser with this arrangement and reforms were soon carried out. This happened after Crécy (1346), then after Poitiers (1356) and then again during the Cabochian crisis (1413). It was only at the end of the fifteenth century, as a result of the ordinances of 1493 and 1499, that the farming of *prévôtés* finally disappeared in France.

Thus many different types of local administration developed on the European Continent. But the main point is undoubtedly that, while in England and in some continental countries like Brabant a dialogue was established between the ruler and the country at the very heart of the local administration, in numerous other European States an entirely different administration took shape, where the entire responsibility for local affairs fell on the shoulders of one or two salaried servants of the ruler. This was a costly system, but, to begin with at least, it was a less troublesome one. It was a purely executive arrangement within which no communication between prince and country could take place. The importance of the dialogue established between prince and country through representative assemblies in the later Middle Ages has often been emphasized. It has perhaps not been sufficiently stressed that this only proved strong and lasting where it had been prepared and sustained by another dialogue subsisting within the very framework of local administration.

French complexity

Some countries nevertheless developed in different ways, either because the administration of very large areas required intermediate mechanisms, or because new structures were dictated by changing requirements. Local administration was most complex in France.

In the early years of the reign of Philip Augustus a new level of administrators appeared above the *prévôts*. They were suggested to the French king by the reforms of Henry II of England and in particular by that of 1176 which entrusted the judicial circuits, or eyres, to itinerant judges. At the end of the thirteenth century, therefore, members of the French royal court of justice made circuits in the regions in twos or threes; they went from the principal town of one castellany to the principal town of the next. In each of these towns they presided over the assizes and supervised the financial activities of the *prévôt*. From the outset these prestigious individuals were called *baillis*. This title was often retained, but in some regions, especially in the south, people called them seneschals (*sénéchaux*), not *baillis*. Invariably, although the exercise of justice could be adapted to the temporary and collegial intervention of the *baillis*, financial control could not be, for this had to be more personal and more stable to be effective. Slowly the travelling delegate of the king's court, with temporary functions, developed towards the middle of the thirteenth century into a permanent regional administrator, personally responsible for the control of a number of castellanies, whose activities he increasingly synchronized. Thus the *bailliage* was born of the *bailli*.

In the second half of the thirteenth and the beginning of the fourteenth century the *bailli* of the king of France was as powerful an individual as the sheriff of the English king had been a hundred and fifty years earlier. He was indeed 'king' in his *bailliage*. He presided over the assizes; organized the farming-out of revenues, supervised his own payment from this source, collected the revenues which were not farmed out and was responsible for settling some expenses at a local level; he maintained the fortresses of the *bailliage* and summoned the *ban* and the *arrière-ban* (see below, pp. 139–41); preserved law and order and generally carried out the king's orders with greater dispatch because he was directly employed by him, because theoretically he had no connection with the *bailliage*, where he had not been born and where he held no lands, and because he would generally only hold the same post for two or three years; and so he remained the ruler's faithful agent throughout a genuinely prefectoral career.

But soon an increase in the number of new officers was inevitable. After 1247 in the *sénéchaussées* and 1292 in the *bailliages*, receivers appeared who relieved *baillis* and seneschals of all financial responsibilities. From the middle of the thirteenth century the judicial functions of the seneschal were entrusted in the south to *juges-mages*. In the north the *baillis* began to appoint lieutenants in the first half of the fourteenth century, who sat in judgement on run-of-the-mill cases and sometimes even presided over the assizes. It was also at the beginning of the fourteenth century that the king began to pay an advocate and proctor to defend his interests in each *bailliage*. Finally, an ordinance of 1317 that took effect slowly was responsible for the gradual appearance of a captain-general in every *bailliage* or *sénéchaussée* who limited the military role of the *bailli* or seneschal. Eventually the *bailli* or seneschal might sometimes play an important role at national level in the entourage of the king from the fourteenth century onwards, but at local level he had become a grandiose and useless figure.

English development was thus apparently paralleled by that in France. But the French experience had very different consequences. For the officials who appeared in increasing numbers were all, with rare and occasional exceptions, appointed and paid by the king. They were thus simply instruments of the royal will. There was no area of the administration where the locality could provide a counterbalance: in 1300 the vassals of the castellany often still sat as judges in the assizes, in 1500 virtually no one was involved other than professional lawyers, advocates or attorneys closely connected with the official and administrative world. As for the councils of the *bailliages*, which historians have thought included a local and representative element, they were in fact composed of none other than the same group of professional lawyers.

The institution of the *bailliage* had scarcely reached maturity when new needs created new administrative structures. New officers, chosen initially by the Estates General, appeared in 1355 to levy the enormous *fouages* (hearth-taxes) necessitated by the English war. They became royal appointments very soon afterwards, but retained the name *élu* ('elect') from their origins. These officials operated within the only simple, stable and widespread regional division then known in France: the diocese. First the *fouages* and then the *tailles* (property taxes) were levied by the diocese. But as the dioceses were sometimes too big, and in order that they might reach the tax-payers more effectively, in about 1400 they began to be divided up, following deanery boundaries in some places and those of the castellany in others, thus forming smaller administrative units soon called *élections*. In each *élection* two or three *élus* assessed the *taille*, whilst it was levied by a receiver. In the fifteenth century general advisors on the financial situation, called *généraux des finances* (or simply *généraux*) began to control the activities of the *élus*. At first these *généraux* exercised their functions within an itinerant framework, but in order to facilitate administrative routine, they soon always supervised the same group of *élections*, given the name of *département*, then *charge* and finally *généralité*. There were five or six *généralités* in France.

France was thus covered by two different administrative networks, on the one hand by *prévôtés* grouped together into *bailliages*, on the other by *élections* grouped into *généralités*. The *prévôté* developed from the office of *prévôt*, the *bailliage* from the *bailli*, the *élection* from the *élu* and the *généralité* from the *général*. Each new administrative unit was spawned by a new administrator who himself answered new needs. However, doubtless because the king was never sufficiently powerful to persuade his subjects to serve him free of charge, he always had recourse to paid officials. This solution was very much more expensive for the State. It had, moreover, the disadvantage of preventing all communication between the ruler and his country within the administrative framework. But it provided the king with an incomparably compliant administrative machine. At the end of the Middle Ages the French administration was more complex and more costly than any other in Western Europe, but it could respond better than any other to the demands of the central administration.

CENTRAL ADMINISTRATION

In the eleventh or twelfth century a Western ruler was surrounded by a number of individuals, largely his vassals, who assisted him in the administration of his lands and the execution of justice. They constituted what was called his court. There is nothing more fluid and confusing than the composition of a court. At one time an individual is present, at another he is not; now he has this role, now that. Those who played a definable role for any length of time are rare indeed. That is nevertheless the case with a number of officers (*ministri*) who were responsible for the material welfare of the prince and his entourage and who almost always reappear in the same guise in every court. The steward (French *sénéchal*, German *Truchseß*) had many functions and was sometimes the chief domestic officer at court; the butler (French *bouteiller, échanson*; German *Schenk*) filled the prince's cup, was consequently responsible for the court's supply of wine and then, moreover, for the supply of all its food and drink; the chamberlain (French *chambrier, chambellan*; German *Kämmerer*) was concerned with the prince's clothes and moveable goods; finally the constable (from the Latin *comes stabuli*; French *connétable*), assisted by his marshals, was responsible for the horses and stables. These were all necessarily lay officers. But in order to write the documents demanded from him, or at least to affix his seal, the prince called upon a cleric who had inherited the Carolingian title of chancellor (*chancelier*) in the most important courts, but who in some continental courts in the twelfth century simply appeared amongst the less important lords with the relatively unassuming title of *notaire*. The other courtiers had no defined function; they were the prince's friends, companions, confidants and vassals, who gave their lord the advice without which no prince of that period would ever have wished to take the smallest decision. So from the twelfth century the French and English kings began to refer to them as their counsellors and their Council; and they were followed in the thirteenth century by lords of less substance. But this Council was none other than the group of men who happened to be with the prince when he made the decision; it might be no more than a few officials and a few friends; on the great feast-days of the Church or on other special occasions, it might additionally comprise several dozen vassals and was then known as the Great Council, as for example in England from the twelfth century onwards.

These imprecise structures survived for a long while in the courts of the German principalities. In the fifteenth century there were still officials there who simultaneously directed the household of the prince and affairs of state. But, for a long while, virtually everywhere else the unity of the court had been ruptured and had given way to increasingly numerous and complex administrative models. A growing distinction was made first between the domestic service of the prince and the service of the State. The first was the concern of what was soon called the Household (*Hôtel*). Before the end of the thirteenth century, written sources enable us to construct a detailed picture of the already complex structures of the royal households in England and in France. Many household offices, such as the kitchen, were dominated by the department which managed the necessary funds – in England the Chamber and in France the *Chambre aux deniers* – and by that which acquired and preserved equipment and clothing – the Wardrobe in England, the *Argenterie* in France. In England the steward, butler and constable remained within the framework of the household and played no more than a modest domestic role. In France (leaving aside for the time being the constable who became the head of the royal army) the steward disappeared in the reign of Philip Augustus; the butler presided over the *Chambre des comptes* (the chief financial office) for a while, then disappeared in the fifteenth century. So that in both France and in England only the chancellor, of all the great household officers, permanently survived this structural revolution and continued to play a part in the administration of the State after the fragmentation of the court. In effect, while the household confined itself to the personal service of the prince and his entourage, the business of administering the State fell entirely on the chancellor and his assistants, and upon the counsellors who, assembled in a purely random fashion, assisted the ruler in the exercise of justice, the reckoning of accounts or the making of any other decision. And as the chancellor was the most experienced and the most respected of counsellors, so he inevitably became the keystone of the State. Moreover, although princes continued to ask advice from the great assemblies from time to time (in which we must see the origin of the representative assemblies that played an important role in the later medieval States of the West), from the thirteenth century onwards the daily administrative routine required more than counsellors or a haphazardly assembled Council. From before 1257 in England, from before 1269 in France, and from the second half of the thirteenth century in numerous German principalities, the ruler therefore retained close to him a number of men in whom he trusted, requiring from them an oath to serve him well and keep his secrets. To them (as in France) he sometimes paid wages. It was on the chancellor and upon this Council that the most clearly defined characteristics of the life of the late medieval State depended. The eleventh and twelfth centuries were the period of the court and the great officers. The fourteenth and fifteenth centuries were the age of the chancellor and the Council.

Initially, there was a period in all States when the Council took all the decisions, while all documents emanated from the Chancery. Soon the diversity of ever more important and time-consuming tasks demanded an increasing degree of specialization on the part of the counsellors, which slowly resulted in the appearance of new administrative bodies that were gradually detached from the rudimentary Council. In England this development occurred at such an early date that it happened even before the appearance of the Council and the earliest specialist administrative departments were completely detached from the court. The Exchequer appeared at the beginning of the twelfth century; its structures were permanently established from the middle of the twelfth century; from this date onwards the English king had a financial service at his disposal that many European rulers could only dream of two centuries later. From the twelfth century onwards all the legal cases concerning the king's revenues were heard within the Exchequer itself, by the Court of the Exchequer, where the barons of the Exchequer sat in judgement. In all other cases royal justice was exercised either by means of itinerant judges who, from the reign of Henry II (1154–89) until the beginning of the fourteenth century, travelled in the king's name from county to county, or by means of the two courts which, after a slow evolution, appeared in their final form in the reign of Henry III: the Common Bench, or Court of Common Pleas, and the King's Bench. The Common Bench was the first to become separated from the person of the king and established at Westminster. As a rule it judged civil lawsuits between two individuals. The king himself appeared on the King's Bench for much longer and this court still continued to follow all his movements at the beginning of the fourteenth century. The King's Bench was generally concerned with cases in which the accused had infringed the king's peace. In the later Middle Ages the Court of the Exchequer, Court of Common Pleas and the King's Bench already constituted a sophisticated judicial machine, although not, how- ever, one that avoided conflicting or overlapping judgements. But the three courts had all to make their judgements entirely within the frame- work of the Common Law (*Lex communis*), that is the law traditionally applied by the royal courts, consisting of ancient custom supplemented by innumerable judgements in the thirteenth century, which was formulated by Bracton and established in its final form by the great statutes of Edward I. At the beginning of the fourteenth century the administration of justice and finance had already long been in the hands of traditional and routine departments which only had the most distant contacts with the Council.

Developments in France occurred a little later. The word *pallamentum* was first used in 1239 to refer to a judicial session of the Council. These *parlements* became increasingly frequent and regular towards the middle of the thirteenth century. At that time the King's Court only judged, in the first instance, lawsuits brought before it by royal ecclesiastical establishments, the king's vassals and communes within the royal domain. In 1258 the Court of Louis IX forbade the judicial duel in the royal domain and substituted instead appeal to the King's Court. Despite strong resistance the King's Court soon judged an increasing number of cases on appeal. In 1263 one of the legal officers of the Court agreed to collect together all the important earlier judgements in books of parchment. He went back as far as 1254 and then entered all new judgements. His initiative was continued, and so these useful volumes were available to the Court, to which it first referred in a judgement of 1287 and which, from 1299, it considered as its own property. In 1278 the judicial work of the Court was already intense enough to necessitate its first statutes, in which the main elements of the future Parlement can be traced: the *Grand-Chambre* which gave judgement on counsel's pleading, the *Chambre des enquêtes* which made investigations and then assessments which the *Grand-Chambre* then merely turned into formal judgements; the *Chambre des requêtes* which heard the requests of litigants and had the necessary judicial documents drawn up. In order to replace a king who was too frequently absent the Court appointed two presidents from 1296 onwards. At a *parlement* of the Court in the mid-thirteenth century there was, besides a majority of occasional counsellors, a small permanent group of *mestres de la Court le roi* who, by reason of their experience and continued presence, played a very much more active role than the rest, although they had no special status. An ordinance of 1345 gave final form to an evolution that had taken place over very many years: while the 'amateurs' were not barred from the Parlement in 1345, it was decided to pay only the 'professionals', whose number was fixed and whose names were recorded. From this date the Court of Justice was composed of a fixed personnel. Finally, in 1360, contemporaries displayed an awareness of the development that had occurred: for the first time the word *parlement* was no longer used for a session of the King's Court, but for the Court of Justice that had gradually emerged from the royal Council. Moreover, at the beginning of the reign of Philip the Fair control of receipts and expenses was still provided by members of the Court sitting on committees that met *ad compotos* ('to investigate the accounts'). The *Chambre des comptes* appeared soon afterwards with its archives, traditions and staffs, after a very rapid development in which the ordinance of Vivier-en-Brie (1320) was a crucial point. In the middle of the fourteenth century the Parlement and the *Chambre des comptes* had an independent existence and had no more links with the Council than the title of *conseiller* borne by their members.

The other States of the West followed the example of England and France some while later, although they never achieved the same degree of sophistication. In Flanders a court of justice called the Audience appeared, distinct from the Council of the count, in 1348. In Castile a Chancery or Audience staffed by professionals did not come into being until the end of the fourteenth century. In the German principalities it was only in the very last years of the fifteenth century that attempts were made to organize a supreme court of justice quite distinct from the Council.

Thus in almost the entire later medieval West the Council had produced new cogs within the administrative machine that were concerned only with matters of routine. These new departments sent out their own letters themselves. The central administration was no longer the exclusive concern of Council and Chancery. Nevertheless, it retained a very marked uniformity. This was the result, in the first place, of the personal action of the ruler, who saw the services of his Household, Council and other great administrative departments in the same light and intended to be obeyed by all, limited by none; and who reserved the right to intervene personally whenever he saw fit. It was also because of the chancellor, head of the Chancery and the ruler's confidant, an influential member of the Council and sometimes its head; he was in effect master of the administration and of internal and external policy. It was also, finally, thanks to the Council itself which, relieved of the cares of justice and daily finance, remained the privileged mouthpiece of the ruler. The permanent or great Council (as it was called in England); the limited (*étroit*), personal, secret or great Council (as it was variously known in France), the secret or great Council of Germany; Milan's secret Council; finally, the Council, as it was known everywhere, brought together a number of individuals, the number varying according to time and place, ten or twenty, rarely more. It sat at irregular intervals, but more frequently in times of crisis. Its non-procedural and informal character is reflected in the fact that in the whole of Europe there are only a few rare archival survivals. It was a flexible and effective body in the hands of the ruler, both advisory and executive, which controlled the whole administrative apparatus of the State and set it into motion; it even exercised the prerogatives of the prince and, above all, acted in that area of the judicial system which he did not intend to delegate and over which he retained personal control. In the later Middle

Ages the man who controlled the Council also controlled the State.

The ruler always appointed his own counsellors. Even in England at the beginning of the fifteenth century, in that happy period that W. Stubbs mistakenly called 'Lancastrian constitutionalism', the Commons never demanded the right to nominate the king's counsellors. But it was one thing to nominate counsellors, another to choose them. The ruler was sometimes powerful enough to fill the Council with his own supporters. That was almost always the case in France. It happened in England under the house of York and the Tudors. In Germany and in Italy it was the case with some princes, such as the margrave of Brandenburg and the duke of Milan, who even went as far as appointing foreigners to their Councils in order to control them better. But whenever the country was in a position to impose its will on the ruler, its first concern was to make him accept their choice of counsellors, so that by this means they might dominate the State. In the England of Edward II, Richard II and Henry IV the Council was, for a while, less the mouthpiece of the king than of the nobles in opposition. As for the princes of the Church in the German Rhineland or the king of Hungary, they had unquestionably lost their grip on the Council from the fourteenth century onwards. Even when the ruler was untramelled in his choice and filled the Council with his servants, he had to take account of various pressures. Thus within the Council of the king of France, the voices of such and such a prince, such and such a body or region, made themselves heard more or less powerfully, according to circumstance. In the later Middle Ages the Council was thus the engine of the State. Within it the prince retained a vital role almost everywhere. But there were few Councils that were a mere tool in the hands of the ruler. More frequently they were the occasion of a dialogue (more or less discreet in character) between the ruler and his country. The later Middle Ages was the period of the Council and of dialogue; it was also the period of dialogue within the Council itself.

In States where this development was most advanced, the final stage was already evident. First, the judicial activity of the Council gave birth to a new generation of courts of justice. In England the Court of Chancery and the Star Chamber (which appeared at the end of the fourteenth and the end of the fifteenth centuries) dealt with cases unforeseen in Common Law and in this way exercised the royal prerogative. In France, from the reign of Louis XI, it is possible to distinguish clearly a judicial section of the Council, and 1497–8 saw the official birth of the *Grand Conseil*, entrusted with exercising the judicial functions retained by the king. After these further cuts the Council itself was a purely political body.

The position of both chancellor and Council was threatened by the rise of secretaries. At the end of the thirteenth century the word *secretarius* still only meant a close friend, confidant, trusted counsellor. In Germany it retained this meaning until the end of the medieval period. In more developed States, where there was an evident gulf between ruler and principal administrative departments, there was an evident need for intermediaries, and secretaries entrusted with more specific functions appeared. In England at the beginning of the fourteenth century the secretaries were the king's closest counsellors, members of his Household and of the Council, to whom important tasks – especially diplomatic missions – were entrusted and who had charge of the privy seal by which the sovereign expressed his personal will. From the outset they were very powerful individuals. In France their origin was more modest. When king and Chancery no longer necessarily lived side by side (1291), a number of notaries were appointed to follow the king. This was the origin of the *clercs du secret* (1316), the *notaires suivant le roi*, commonly called *secrétaires* from the middle of the fourteenth century. Throughout Europe secretaries emerged in this way either from the Council or from the more modest origins of the Chancery. Their rise was more rapid if they rose from the Council. In England all the factors that gave the secretaries their power were present from the reign of Edward IV onwards: the secretary had the king's confidence; he was a member of the Council and the head of an efficiently organized administrative department, that of the signet, through which the king henceforth exercised his personal will. Cardinal Wolsey was the last chancellor to dominate the English administration; in 1533 Thomas Cromwell became the most important person in the State: he was the king's secretary. The triumph of the king's secretaries was later in France and did not take place until 1547, when they were permitted to sit in the Council. But, whatever the precise chronology, after the age of chancellor and Council the age of secretaries was thus proclaimed at the end of the Middle Ages.

THE RISE OF THE CAPITAL

The progress of centralization and bureaucracy

The story of the fragmentation of the Council cannot provide an adequate picture of the tendency towards the proliferation of offices that is characteristic of the later Middle Ages. In France, for example, the imposition of direct taxation gave rise to new provincial officers, the *élus*, who assessed the *taille* (property tax) and to *receveurs des aides*, who levied it. They could have fallen under the aegis of existing bodies, the *Chambre des comptes* and the *Trésor*. That was, moreover, what happened in England, where the Exchequer remained the only department of finance. But in France the *élus* were controlled by the *généraux des finances* and the receipts of the *receveurs des aides* centralized by receivers-general (*receveurs généraux*). Moreover, in accordance with unswerving medieval tradition, the *généraux des finances* were entrusted in a general fashion from the outset with overall control and with responsibility for contentious issues. But already before the end of the fourteenth century some degree of specialization was emerging; on the one hand there were the *généraux* concerned with the finances of direct taxation, and, on the other, *généraux* concerned with the justice of the basis of tax-assessment, who constituted the *Chambre* or *Cour des aides*. France thus possessed the unusual distinction of having two entirely distinct administrations, one for 'ordinary' and one for 'extraordinary' finances. France was undoubtedly most affected by this great movement towards the proliferation of offices that affected all European States.

The number of staff in each office was increased. There was admittedly nothing in the least regular about this tendency. There were times when it went apace, as in the first half of the fourteenth century and during the reign of Louis XI, but these periods might be followed by hesitation and even retrenchment. But of the general direction there can be no doubt. In France there were four counsellors at the *Requêtes du Palais* (forerunner of the *Chambre des requêtes*) in 1314, twenty-nine in 1343; twenty counsellors at the Parlement in 1314 and sixty-two in 1343; eight *maîtres des comptes* at the beginning of the fourteenth century, ten in 1338 and nineteen in 1484; there were ten notaries in Chancery in 1286, thirty in 1316, forty-eight in 1328, fifty-nine in 1361, seventy-nine in 1418 and 120 at the beginning of the sixteenth century. Even these figures only give a faint impression of the increase in personnel, for each official was assisted by an increasing number of clerks. It has been estimated that overall, in the middle of the fourteenth century, the English royal Chancery employed a veritable hive of more than sixty individuals. In the fifteenth century more than a hundred were employed by the Court of Common Pleas alone. England and France were undoubtedly exceptional cases. While their Chancery personnel numbered dozens, there were only six clerks in the Chancery of Mecklenburg in 1326, two in the Chancery of Ireland in 1336, and six in the Chancery of Brabant in 1436. But although the smaller States had only small administrative machines, they were affected by the same tendency: there were six clerks in the Brabançon Chancery of 1436, twelve in 1461.

The proliferation of offices and officials inevitably led to a proliferation of the documents without which State action would be impossible and on which its power was based. In order to escape the lapses of memory that affected oral tradition, to assert better its control and to satisfy the ever-increasing concern for numerical precision that characterized the later Middle Ages, the first concern of the modern State was to draw up an inventory, if not of the entire country's wealth, then at least of all the ruler's resources. In 1085 William the Conqueror's enquiry resulted in the Domesday Book, which remains remarkable both for its effectiveness and the early date at which it was drawn up. At some time or other all the princes of the West drew up similar inventories, but after a significant lapse of time. An inventory of the dauphin's resources was drawn up between 1250 and 1267 and the results of the inquiry were contained in the *Probus*. The investigators of the *Extente* of the county of Champagne (1276–8), or of the *Landbuch* of the march of Brandenburg (1373–6), had the same purpose. Moreover, the appearance of direct taxation encouraged States to make lists of hearths, of which the most famous is the inventory of parishes and hearths (*l'état des paroisses et des feux*) made by the French administration in 1328. As for the Italian States, they took this taste for statistics even further. The Doge Mocenigo knew that in the Venice of 1423 there were 1,000 nobles whose annual income varied from 70 to 4,000 ducats, and that the sum total of money in commercial circulation was 10,000,000, which produced 4,000,000 ducats annually.

But the daily administrative routine also gave rise to an increasing number of documents. In fourteenth-century France the accounting system in use at the *Trésor* required that seven different books should be kept. The number of Chancery missives grew yearly in every field. It is difficult to give precise figures because there are so many errors at source that even the best historians vary greatly in their analysis. G. Tessier has estimated that towards the middle of the fifteenth century the French Chancery was sealing between 17,000 and 18,000 letters a year, while R.-H. Bautier concluded that from the reign of Philip VI, from about 1332–3 onwards, 20,000 letters were already being issued annually by the French Chancery under the great seal and another 15,000 under the secret seal. Even if we say cautiously that in the fourteenth and fifteenth centuries some thousands of letters were being sent by an office like the French Chancery, then we are in any case far from the handful of documents sealed in the twelfth century. If we add that the modest Chancery of Saxony drew up an average of ten letters a day in March 1492, or between 3,000 and 4,000 letters a year, there was a vast proliferation of official documents throughout Europe at the end of the late Middle Ages.

Some record had also to be made of all the letters sent, accounts rendered and decisions made. The efficiency of these new administrations thus depended primarily on the copying of all these documents onto rolls or into registers. It also depended upon the preservation of all these rolls and registers, whether by the construction of a central archive, as in the Hungary of Charles-Robert of Anjou (1307–42), or by their safe-keeping within each department of the administration, in countries where the individual character of the departments was more marked. Finally, the archives had to be easily accessible, which inevitably involved the con-struction of ever more detailed series, the compilation of indexes and inventories of increasing complexity. Once again, it is not pure chance that the rolls of the English Chancery are from the thirteenth century already divided into series and sub-series (Charter Rolls; Patent Rolls, themselves divided into Norman, Gascon, Welsh, Scottish, German, Roman and Treaty Rolls; Close Rolls), while the essential documents of the German principalities were still unindexed in the second half of the fifteenth or even the sixteenth century.

Sooner or later the number of personnel and the size of these archives, as well as the dictates of public convenience, prevented these departments from accompanying the ruler on the continual journeying that he still made in the later Middle Ages. In France judicial sessions of the Council began to be held regularly in Paris about the middle of the thirteenth century, regardless of the king's whereabouts. In England the Common Bench was established at Westminster in the first half of the thirteenth century; for a long while after that the king insisted that the Court of the King's Bench should accompany him everywhere, but eventually that, too, was installed at Westminster at the end of the reign of Edward III. In Castile the Audience, established at the end of the fourteenth century, initially moved from town to town but was finally given a permanent seat under the Catholic kings. The later medieval ruler was still itinerant, his administration was not.

A ruler might sometimes situate different parts of his administration in different areas for the sake of political equilibrium. In Flanders Philip the Bold established his *Chambre des comptes* at Lille, but the *Conseil de justice* (law court) sat in the Flemish-speaking lands. For security reasons all central administrative departments might be housed in an isolated castle. The Teutonic Order transferred its seat from Venice to Marienburg in 1309. But the 'capital' of the new territorial State was no more than a fortress and its administrative position remained insecure. The most stable and efficient administrations were in fact grouped together in or near an important town, or, better still, in or near the country's most important town.

Since the twelfth century London and Paris had been rich and populous towns; their populations enjoyed a level of culture and political maturity that far surpassed those of the rural majority; within their walls or close to them the king had his principal palace and the tombs of his predecessors were to be found; their prestige was such that for the English London was 'queen of the whole country' and Paris for the French the 'head of the kingdom'. From the twelfth century London and Paris were the first towns, the 'capital' cities of England and France.

When the different departments of the central administration were

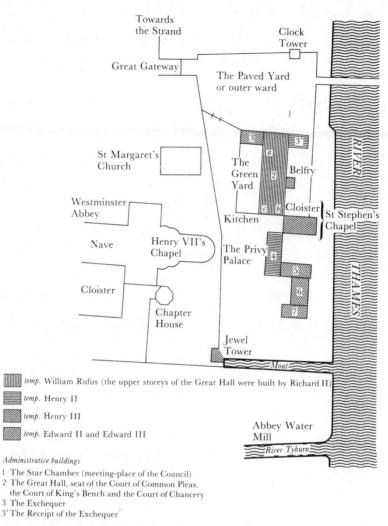

Figure 1   Westminster in the later Middle Ages (before 1540)
The Chancery was located outside the City wall, north of the Strand, near the Inns of Court, in
Chancery Lane. The Public Record Office occupies its site today. The Mint also lay outside the
City wall, near the Tower of London. After 1400 the departments of the Wardrobe were near
Ludgate, within the City.
    Source: after R.A. Brown, H.M. Colvin and A.J. Taylor, *The History of the King's Works*
(London, 1963), plan III. (Crown copyright, reproduced with permission of the Controller of
Her Majesty's Stationery Office.)

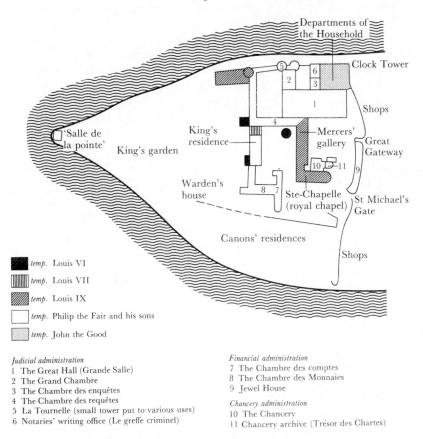

temp. Louis VI
temp. Louis VII
temp. Louis IX
temp. Philip the Fair and his sons
temp. John the Good

Judicial administration
1 The Great Hall (Grande Salle)
2 The Grand Chambre
3 The Chambre des enquêtes
4 The Chambre des requêtes
5 La Tournelle (small tower put to various uses)
6 Notaries' writing office (Le greffe criminel)

Financial administration
7 The Chambre des comptes
8 The Chambre des Monnaies
9 Jewel House

Chancery administration
10 The Chancery
11 Chancery archive (Trésor des Chartes)

Figure 2   The Palais de la Cité at Paris in the later Middle Ages (c.1360)
Source: after J. Guérout, 'Le Palais de la Cité à Paris des origines à 1417', in *Memoires de la Féderation des Sociétés historiques et archéologiques de Paris et de l'Ile-de-France,* II (1950), 21–204 and map.

established, they were naturally situated near the most important royal palace and near the town which was the only source of the educated staff that they required. From the reign of Henry III (who often resided at Westminster and undertook a considerable building programme there) Westminster could not but become the English political capital. But the wars with Scotland drew his successors towards the north; for a while York was the hub of the country. It was only in the reign of Edward III that (aided by the wars with France) the importance of London dictated the permanent establishment at Westminster of all the central administrative departments, or at least almost all, for Westminster was three kilometres from London and the warehouses of the Wardrobe and the workshops of the Mint, for example, could not be located so far from the

City (see figure 1). At Paris things were simpler. Louis IX had already built a great deal in the Palais de la Cité; the great building works of Philip the Fair and his sons provided all administrative departments with the establishments which they needed; and since the Palais de la Cité lay at the very heart of Paris there was no other centrifugal force to prevent the location there of the entire administration.

At Westminster the king's private palace was quite distinct from the administrative buildings to which the public were permitted access. At Paris the overlap between the Household and the State departments was so small that after the riots of 1358 Charles V, making no further resistance, ceded the area to his officials and installed himself on the right bank of the River Seine, retaining only State apartments in his Palais de la Cité. The divorce between service to the crown and service to the State was henceforth written in their very locations (see figure 2).

Admittedly the premises which the different departments had at their disposal were far from corresponding to our present concept of administrative comfort. We must remember that the courts that sat in the Great Hall at Westminster had only an area marked off by wooden boards at their disposal. They had to tolerate the noise of neighbouring courts and the icy north wind rushing through the great door that was always kept open. Worse still, at every coronation banquet and every solemn feast given by the king, the Great Hall had to be vacated and the courts had to seek refuge elsewhere. The judges of the seventeenth century complained bitterly about this inconvenience which was apparently scarcely noticed in the fourteenth and did not hinder their feverish labours in the least. The building of clock towers in the Palace of Westminster (1365–7), and in the Palais de la Cité (1370), whose mechanisms henceforth dictated the rhythm of central government in England and France, was in some ways the final stage in the capital's long evolutionary process.

Although the ruler's power depended primarily on the activities of the central administration, it was also affected by the closeness of the capital to the regions. This was related above all to the road network. In the twelfth and thirteenth centuries, for example, the French road system acquired its characteristic star shape, with all roads radiating from Paris, which could only assist the capital's administrative development. But the relations between the capital and the regions depended above all on the activity of messengers who provided the central administration with information and communicated their orders.

The messengers on whom the unity of the State depended are only just attracting the attention which they deserve. In the thirteenth century the king of England made use of messengers who provided their own horses and were called *nuncii*. When the matter was less urgent he made use of the less costly services of his kitchen boys, *coquini*, who travelled on foot. He called increasingly on these *coquini* so that they soon left the kitchen and in the middle of the fourteenth century adopted the more distinguished title of *cursores*. In the later Middle Ages each ruler had both pedestrian and equestrian messengers at his disposal.

The speed of a messenger on horseback depended on his mood, the state of the ground and the season. He would normally cover the 475 kilometres between Paris and Périgueux in six days in the summer, ten or eleven days in winter. But as he had to be careful not to exhaust his mount he could virtually never – no matter how urgent the business – cover more than 50 kilometres a day. So an English official knew that in average conditions an urgent order from London could only arrive in York six days later and at the northern border at the end of a week. Things were even worse in the huge kingdom of France, where Poitiers, Limoges or Mâcon were five or six days' ride away from Paris, Bordeaux or Lyon nine or ten, Toulouse or Beaucaire twelve or thirteen, and Tarbes or Carcassonne a fortnight away.

Only in an emergency would a messenger be sent with just one letter: on 4 October 1307 John Cook received a letter from the Exchequer to be carried urgently to the sheriff of Northumberland. It arrived within a week. At the same time John Cook was given less urgent letters, some of which had been waiting almost a month and did not reach the north until five weeks after they had been issued. The power of the capital was thus very closely linked to the number of messengers available to the central government (see table 2). On average the sheriffs received one communication a week from these sixty messengers, who passed through four or five counties on each journey. Although the increased number of messengers speeded up the daily administrative routine, it could not make an urgent letter travel faster. To achieve this, relays of horses had to be organized that enabled a messenger to cover about 150 kilometres a day. From the first half of the fourteenth century the English kings sometimes

Table 2   Messengers employed by the English Kings
1100–1350

	On horseback	On foot	Total
*c.*1100			1
*c.*1200			15
1236–7			18
1252–3	4	15	19
1264–5	18	19	37
1288–9	14	33	47
1340–50	21	*c.*40	*c.*60

organized relays on the two most important routes in the kingdom, London to York and London to Dover. Similarly, in France, Philip VI made use of the services of private messengers, who enabled urgent commands to reach the southern frontiers within five days. Such operations remained exceptional in the fourteenth century. It was only in the second half of the fifteenth century, in the France of Louis XI or the Aragon of John II, that the use of relays on certain routes became more frequent.

In sum then, rulers paid considerable sums for their messengers, for they knew that without them the offices of their capital were no more than legless spiders.

Limits to centralization and bureaucracy

Although bureaucratization and centralization thus quickly made great progress in the later Middle Ages, it would be erroneous to conjure up with these words images of the greatly improved government machines of the twentieth century. The process of bureaucratization and centralization had only just begun and were still contained within strict bounds. Bureaucracy suffered in the first place from its own errors. Written records were sometimes kept negligently. In Sicily, Alfonso V's treasurer did not present an account for seventeen years. In fourteenth-century France, Chancery letters were still enregistered in a way that made control virtually impossible. There were errors in the composition of documents: whether because of the wilful deceit of those who were being assessed, inadequate information or accounting errors; the inventories and lists drawn up so painstakingly by the central administration teemed with inaccuracies. Historians have already revealed many in the list of parishes and hearths of 1328; doubtless they will uncover many more. For all its efforts, the administration knew little of the real situation and had few effective means to ascertain it. There were virtually no means by which the medieval administrator could acquaint himself with the area he was administering. Although political and administrative boundaries were in fact more clearly marked on the ground than has often been admitted, maps that enabled its outline to be visualized in a distant office were still rare. In the middle of the fourteenth century the English administration drew up an admirable map of England and Scotland for the use of messengers and royal departments on a scale of 1:1,000,000, which is remarkable for the general overall accuracy of its component parts. From the second half of the fourteenth century onwards the French courts often added a more or less schematic sketch to the files of disputed boundaries. There were maps of some Italian States in the fifteenth century and the first map of France dates from 1472. However, these first attempts were still rare and, generally speaking, an administrator's picture of the area for which he was responsible was built up from lists of towns or regions that were inevitably brief or inaccurate. The medieval administrator was let down by his working methods which made him inevitably blinkered. Finally the preservation of records was chaotic. In France, in the archives of the *Chambre des comptes*, heaps of documents were to be found piled up in the offices, corridors and the attics: it was no easy task to find the document required. In the Chancery there was a completely disorganized jumble of scattered books and poorly bound registers: Louis XI ordered an inventory to be made in 1474, but a start was not even made on its execution before 1482. In short, later medieval bureaucracies still laboured under inaccurate records, inadequate control and rampant fraud.

To these internal deficiencies should be added the reluctance of the country itself. For while all England could be governed from Westminster, all the Teutonic State from Marienburg and the Papal State from Rome, in France the claims of Paris as capital sometimes foundered on the distances involved, the individual character of the provinces, and the influence and importance of towns such as Lyon, Toulouse or Bordeaux which could claim a legitimate role as provincial capitals. When he initiated the creation of provincial administrations (and provincial Parlements in particular) Charles VII and his successors simply acknowledged that it was not reasonable to attempt to govern the entire kingdom from Paris. This geographical decentralization, which filled the Parisians with apprehension and overwhelmed the inhabitants of the provinces, did not, moreover, present any threat to a king who, at the end of the Hundred Years War, was henceforth sure of himself and of the loyalty of his subjects.

So the ruler might sometimes check the process of centralization. But bureaucratization could also sometimes alarm him. After the excesses of Louis XI, Louis XII saw to it that the overcrowded ranks of officials were somewhat reduced: there were nineteen *Maîtres des comptes* in 1484, ten in 1511; 22 *Clercs des comptes* in 1487, thirteen at the beginning of the sixteenth century. Above all, the rulers maintained that although increased administrative sophistication increased their power, it also increased its burdens, that what their administration won in routine efficiency it lost in speed and spontaneity, that the administrative routine which assured their authority could soon assume a stranglehold, and that in short the growth of official departments was the first check on their personal freedom of action. Which is why, at the end of the thirteenth and the beginning of the fourteenth century, the English kings preferred to see the royal Chamber, rather than the Exchequer, responsible for the financial administration of the kingdom. After 1350, and for a hundred years afterwards, the Exchequer once more controlled English finance. But when, after the Wars of the Roses, Edward IV and Henry VII wanted to reform their finances, the ossified and antiquated machinery of the Exchequer was of no use to them, and they too had recourse to their Chamber. When Philip the Good established his *Trésor de l'Epargne* in 1444–6, when in 1465 Louis XI restored his *Epargne* (which had played a minor role in the reign of Charles VI), the purpose of both rulers was to avoid the routine and slowness of their own bureaucracies and to meet the immediate and unforeseen requirements of their policies with greater flexibility.

In the nature of things these new departments proliferated, became more complex and a burden in their turn. This time it did mark the end of the ruler's individual freedom of action. But in the fourteenth and fifteenth centuries the administrative machine had not developed to such an extent that the personality of the ruler was of no account. The administration of the States of the West in the later Middle Ages was both personal and bureaucratic.

8

The Aims of the State:
War and Diplomacy

Although in the fourteenth and fifteenth centuries the States of the West were acutely aware of the need to assert themselves within their own borders, they were no less occupied by the desire to resist the encroachments of their neighbours and indeed, for their part, to expand by every available means. Governments talked of justice and of peace, but war and diplomacy were their overriding concerns; at least half their resources were permanently consumed by them.

WAR

It is undoubtedly the noise of battles that fills the chronicles and holds universal attention. They all recount the exploits of the knights who remained the essential combatants in the fourteenth and fifteenth centuries, despite the victories secured by foot soldiers at Courtrai (1302), Bannockburn (1314) and Morgarten (1315). But battle was in fact a fairly rare occurrence in later medieval war. As it was virtually impossible to force an opponent to engage, so that a battle could in fact take place, it required the assent of both parties. However, they were often reluctant to entrust their fate to the chance outcome of a single day. The aggressor did not easily allow himself to be distracted from his true purpose, which was destruction and pillage in the course of a *chevauchée* in the fourteenth century, and in the fifteenth occupation of the land whilst he enjoyed the increased revenues available to him. The defender knew that the superiority of methods of defence over methods of attack was such that, if he refused combat, if he let the *chevauchée* pass and if he saw to it that the enemy encountered opposition at every fortress, he would undoubtedly suffer from the war, but he would ultimately be more likely to have the last word. This, then, was the secret of all those seemingly endless wars: later medieval war was defensive, a war of attrition without end.

In a defensive war walls were of paramount importance. Every town and village wanted them. Town-dwellers enclosed their entire town (save a few suburbs, which might be razed to the ground) within a strong fortification. The villagers, who seldom had the means to build a great wall, helped the neighbouring lord to fortify his castle, or the abbot his monastery, or, better still, they fortified their own village church, building a great, rough-hewn tower which was, to some extent, 'the keep of the poor'. The insecurity of the fourteenth century led to a proliferation of defensive buildings at every social level. In 1367, to the south and the south-west of the Forest of Fontainebleau within an area of forty by thirty kilometres, royal officers counted six castles, four fortified manor houses, five towers, twelve forts and twenty-eight fortified churches. Thus the invader was halted at every step by a new redoubt, which had to be conquered before further progress could be made. It is true that every stronghold captured became an operational base from which he could easily ravage the surrounding countryside and that the walls then turned against those who had built them, ultimately prolonging their suffering. Whatever the case, an increase in the number of fortified places was the main result of a deliberately defensive war. Now although the State theoretically claimed the right to authorize the building of any fortification or to order its demolition, in practice it virtually always abandoned responsibility to the inhabitants for building, maintaining and manning their walls at their own expense. Exceptionally, in the reign of Charles VI, the French monarchy kept several hundred men in some dozen places along the northern and Gascon frontiers. But this was the first and only occasion. Defensive war was generally expensive, but for the subjects rather than their ruler.

For his part the prince directed all his energies and resources to what was only a small part of the huge war effort of an entire nation; his business was the levying and supply of an operational army. In the second half of the thirteenth century no leader would have abandoned hope of securing a military contingent through the traditional ties of vassalage. This was well demonstrated by Philip the Bold in 1272 and similarly by Edward I in 1277 when he adapted the old *servitium debitum*, whose conditions had not changed since 1166, in order to make it more effective. However, it soon had to be admitted that this means of recruitment had had its day. The vassals did not necessarily have any inclination for war and the diverse and limited services they owed no longer corresponded to the needs of contemporary warfare. So that, although the English king summoned the feudal host in 1327, he ignored it afterwards. When the young Richard II assembled his vassals in 1385, this final summons of the feudal host was merely an exercise in prestige, an act more political than military. Feudalism had not, however, entirely lost its power. Through the distribution of *fief-rentes* (fiefs granted by the ruler in return for a money payment) the most important rulers of the West gained new men whose military obligations were better suited to contemporary needs. By paying their vassals they kept in the army those who positively enjoyed war. Feudalism was in any case a spent force in England and France in the second half of the fourteenth century. The existence of paid vassals in the principality of Liège in the fifteenth century or, more strikingly, of vassals in the army of the Catholic kings of Spain, strictly fulfilling their traditional obligations, at the end of the fifteenth century, were the last sparks of a fire that was already almost extinct in 1300. Rulers did not rely on their vassals to fill the ranks of the army in the later Middle Ages.

An entirely different and much more widely ranging method of recruitment was possible. Already in the thirteenth century the armies of the Italian towns were composed of citizens who were under a legal obligation to fight with arms and equipment as befitted their wealth. Elsewhere such developments occurred at a much later date. In England, after various experiments, the king, calling on the loyalty that every subject owed him, proclaimed in the Statute of Winchester (1285) that, whenever necessary, every able-bodied Englishman between the ages of fifteen and sixty should come and fight with whatever weapons his rank required. Some years later Philip the Fair had the principle of the mass levy, or *arrière-ban*, accepted. (The name is derived from the Frankish word *heriban, herban*: compare German '*Heerbann*'.) Thus the principle of a national army was established in England and in France. The mass levy – which would have paralysed the life of the entire country – was undoubtedly never applied in full. The king of France was quite prepared to accept that many individuals should pay rather than leave their homes. As for the king of England, once the principle had been established, he sent commissions of array into the counties and they recruited the ablest-bodied and best-equipped in the proportions stipulated by the administration at Westminster.

While the decline of the Italian communal militias was already apparent at the end of the thirteenth century, the first half of the fourteenth century was the golden age of the mass levy and the *arrière-ban* in France and England. It looked as if a national army was a real possibility. But the first armed encounters quickly dispelled these illusions. In the first place, these men had no experience of war. Then they did not feel sufficiently motivated not to evade these imposed military obligations on a massive scale. Above all, in a society founded entirely on the assumption that the privileged fighting classes should be distinguished from those who laboured for a living, there was a distinct risk in arming those whose depressed position was only justified by their inability to fight. Reluctance on the part of the ruler and on the part of his subjects both conspired against a national army: in 1351 Parliament forced Edward III to agree that his subjects could not be forced to serve as men-at-arms or archers without parliamentary consent; in France, after the defeat at Poitiers (1356), crying the *arrière-ban* was such an unpopular and dangerous operation that for decades the government was wary of doing so.

Moreover, the fourteenth-century army scarcely needed the foot soldiers of the *arrière-ban*. Knights, on the other hand, were in desperately short supply. Edward III therefore was particularly concerned to preserve the practice of distraint of knighthood established in the reign of Henry III: it was compulsory for every landholder with an annual income of at least forty pounds to receive knighthood and undertake politico-adminis-trative duties in the county and the military role in the army expected of that rank. Similarly, although the French king had abandoned the prac-tice of proclaiming the general *arrière-ban*, he still expected that all fief-holding nobles would continue to obey his summons. So, in the second half of the fourteenth century, compulsory knighthood in England and the summoning of nobles in France helped to provide the armies of bellicose kings with the knights they needed and to provide some degree of balance between the political and military areas of activity, at least for the privileged classes.

The concept of a national army had not entirely evaporated, however. The *arrière-ban* was called again several times in France between 1410 and 1418. Above all, in the 1440s both the obligatory military service of the *franc-archiers* (the French territorial militia) and the summoning of nobles to fight were either organized or restructured. From the reign of Louis XI the summons took the name which was henceforward traditional of *ban et arrière-ban*, alternative provision having been made for the military service of the common people. At the same time the Italian humanists, under the influence of Vegetius and a strongly patriotic perspective, were demon-strating the advantages of a national army. Their debate was so thoroughly practical that the militia ultimately re-emerged in Venice and above all in the Florence of Savonarola and Machiavelli. But the same military and political factors that had already been at work in the fourteenth century explain why the king of France hardly made use of the *franc-archiers* after 1475 or the *ban et arrière-ban* after 1494. And in Italy the defeat at Prato in 1512 buried both the Florentine republic and all discussion of a national army, at a single stroke. Ultimately the States of the West had only been able to make very little use of various concepts of military obligation to furnish their armies in the fourteenth and fifteenth centuries.

Henry II in the twelfth century, Philip Augustus at the beginning of the thirteenth and the Italian communes in the course of the fourteenth century had all found recruits for their armies by paying wages to those who had no legal obligation to serve them. But it was in the fourteenth century that the reluctance of their subjects, the growing need for experts and their increased financial resources forced governments to secure the military services of professionals with contracts and wages on a massive scale.

In England the king made an indenture with a captain, which specified the exact size of the retinue whose services he pledged to the king (an important and highly variable factor), the rate of pay and the indemnities which might be reclaimed. In his turn the captain then also drew up an indenture with each member of his retinue. The earliest surviving contract between a captain and his men dates from 1287 and the earliest indenture extant between king and captain from 1300. But the use of indentures was still limited at the beginning of Edward III's reign. This was not general practice until the first years of the Hundred Years War when engagement by indenture rapidly became so widespread that the English armies in France were essentially contract armies throughout the Hundred Years War. It was at the same time, the first half of the fourteenth century, that the *condottieri* really made their appearance in Italy. Their name was derived from the *condotta,* the contract by which – according to John of Legnano's definition – an employer (*conductor*) temporarily hired the services of another party (*locator*) under specific financial conditions for a limited period. Initially the Italian States made agreements with captains of relatively small bands of soldiers. After a while these small companies merged. The State had to deal with *societates* of considerable size, controlled by a prestigious leader and assisted by a council of the captains of the federated companies. So in 1354 the Great Company of Fra Monreale numbered 5,000 cavalry and 1,500 infantry, surrounded by a host of servants, women and merchants: in effect, a peripatetic State. At this date the employers could still play the captains off against their leader. But a little later, in the golden age of the *condottieri* (1381–1421), a company was no longer a federation but under the absolute control of one man; people no longer referred to a *societas* but to a *comitiva* commanded by a powerful *dux belli* who was now in a position to impose his wishes on anyone. For his part, the French king was somewhat slower to turn to the professionals on a huge scale. But the disasters of the mid-fourteenth century, the constraints surrounding the *arrière-ban* and the need for relatively small-scale, but experienced and permanent forces that were required to execute Charles V's novel defence policy, all explain the proliferation of *lettres de retenue* in France in the second half of the fourteenth century.

Although fifteenth-century Italy was often threatened by overpowerful mercenaries, the rulers of the West were able, although not without difficulty, to impose their will on their unruly partners and eventually to tame them. The power of the English king had never been threatened by his captains but, until 1439, a soldier who deserted his captain before the agreed date had merely broken a private contract. His only punishment was the cessation of his wages. In 1439, because of the aggravating nature of this state of affairs and because of the increased number of desertions, Parliament legislated that such a breach of contract was a crime against the king and that those guilty of it should be punished as felons. Shortly afterwards, Charles VII made the companies who then prospered in his kingdom fully conscious of his newly re-established power. In the 1440s he rid himself of the majority of the captains and formed from those whom he retained the disciplined and stable bodies of the Grande Ordonnance (cavalry in the field) and the Petite Ordonnance (bodies of authentic infantry permanently garrisoned on the frontiers). Military contractors did not appear in Germany until 1470. There, too, there were independent captains at first who recruited their men before contract and then hired themselves out to the highest bidder. At the beginning of the sixteenth century this was still the practice of Franz von Sickingen, whose army numbered as many as 3,000 lances and 12,000 *Landesknechte*. However, this type of contractor had essentially disappeared by then: after 1495, with few exceptions, in Germany there were only middlemen recruiting a company for a prince with whom he had already signed a contract and who kept him on a tight rein.

Overall, although military obligation played its part in recruitment, effective operational armies were generally made up of professional soldiers bound to their employers by formal contract. In both the military and political spheres the contractual retinue was one of the distinguishing characteristics of the fourteenth and fifteenth centuries. But already before 1500 the heyday of the contract was over. It was no longer a question of choosing one's employer and discussing terms: then you could count yourself lucky if your ruler offered you a secure position in a small but permanent army, with an assured wage. Between the age of the feudal army and that of the standing army, the fourteenth and fifteenth centuries were the era of the contract army.

The army levied by Edward III in 1346 comprised 32,000 men: this was exceptional. On other occasions the king of England set foot on the Continent with some 15,000 men, of whom perhaps 5,000 to 6,000 were paid soldiers. In 1340 his enemy, Philip VI, was able to mobilize (admittedly from the entire kingdom) as many as 80,000 men. But Charles V, with his country ravaged by the Plague, economic crises, military defeats and political difficulties, did not attempt to wage war with armies numbering more than 5,000. It was not until the second half of the fifteenth century that French military potential once more reached figures comparable to those of Philip VI: Louis XI could campaign with 25,000 men and undoubtedly raise 80,000 from the entire kingdom. Charles the Bold could draw up against him operational armies of about 20,000 combatants and totalling about, shall we say, 40,000 to 50,000 men.

Whether these troops came to the army voluntarily or because of a perceived obligation, they had to be paid. Whatever the variations and statistical difficulties of the figures advanced, paying an army undoubt-edly represented a major financial effort for the ruler. It was also a considerable administrative undertaking. First the wages had to be dis-tributed to garrisons and to field armies, then several fair copies had to be made of the accounts: in France this was the job of one or more treasurers of the king's war (*trésorier des guerres du roi*) and of one or more clerks of the crossbowmen (*clerc des arbalétriers*), assisted by several dozen subordinates. Above all, there had to be careful control over the distribution of these wages, to soldiers who were actually present and in a fit state to fight. This led to the establishment, from the fourteenth century onwards, of a system of control which, as a result of increasing precision and improve-ment, attained a kind of perfection in English-occupied Normandy in the first half of the fifteenth century. Before he could draw his company's wages, a captain had to present it to the relevant royal officers. That was the muster. This muster was periodically repeated during the time-span of the contract. In fact, to be precise, this was a review, although muster and review were then interchangeable terms. In 1424, in order to mitigate the disadvantages of possible frauds between two reviews, the English admin-istration devised the permanent appointment in the largest garrisons of an officer who would verify the comings and goings of all the men, and established a counter-roll in addition to the muster-roll: so, in 1429, nineteen garrisons in Normandy had a controller. This system of musters, reviews and controllers was complex and expensive, but effective. It achieved substantial economies for the English king.

Wages were not the end of the story, however. In theory, certainly, the combatants came with their own weapons and equipment and lived off the land. But the aggressors, above all attackers, were forced to provide an intensive support system which was only too well justified by disasters such as that which befell the French expedition against Aragon in 1285 because of shortages of food and water. So besides the recruitment and payment of soldiers, the war effort in England, for example, involved the establishment of important stocks of bows, arrows and victuals. It was, moreover, impossible for England to conduct a continental war without maintaining bridgeheads, such as Calais, which alone cost the Treasury 24,000 pounds sterling in 1378. Finally naval transport had to be provided and assured. For this purpose ships requisitioned at the relevant time generally sufficed. But Edward III and, more especially, Henry V preferred to have several dozen warships built and kept in perpetual readiness. However this was a costly exercise, which could not in any case be prolonged more than a few years on each occasion.

Artillery soon made war even more expensive. Only neuro-ballistic artillery was available to the armies of 1300. This continued to play a part throughout the fourteenth and fifteenth centuries. The Castilian armies were still using trebuchets in 1475–6. But at the beginning of the fourteenth century the first formulae for gunpowder are recorded in the West. The progress of metallurgy in general, and of the bellfounders' art in particular, enabled the manufacture of firearms from iron and bronze. The first cannon appeared at Metz in 1324, Florence in 1326 and in England in 1327. For a long while these slow and awkward weapons had no effect whatsoever in battle. They played no part in the English victory at Crécy, nor did they prevent the Castilian disaster at Aljubarrota (1385). But they quickly altered the outcome of sieges. Without them the French reconquest could not have been so quickly achieved in the reign of Charles V. Contemporaries were aware of this. Everyone who could afford to do so increased the number of his cannon. The expenses of the French artillery increased ten-fold between 1375 and 1410. In the middle of the fifteenth century Charles VII was greatly aided by his artillery in the reconquest of Normandy and Guyenne. By the end of the fifteenth century cannons had become much more numerous. The French artillery then numbered 149 pieces serviced by hundreds of men and 2,250 horses. These were the guns which broke Italian city walls and were the decisive factor in battle for the first time. Progress in artillery techniques thus changed the face of war. Defensive strategy was becoming less and less advantageous. Wars of attrition were giving way to wars on the move. But this form of warfare was increasingly expensive and within the scope of correspondingly fewer States.

War had thus forced States to resolve financial, administrative and political difficulties. Their structure had been profoundly affected by it. But in the process the balance of power within States, and between State and State, had been disturbed. For only the richest and most powerful States could afford to levy, pay, equip and supply an army, and this army then enabled them to crush all internal resistance and to threaten their neighbours. Italy's misfortunes at the end of the fifteenth century stemmed solely from the facts that she was divided into States which were each too small to maintain an effective army and that their diplomacy was unable to compensate for this military inferiority.

DIPLOMACY

At the end of the Middle Ages the theorists could still provide a noble definition of diplomacy, stating that its object was the maintenance of peace. In fact, more realistic individuals already admitted that war and diplomacy were simply different means to the same end, namely to secure and augment the State.

To negotiate with anyone, every body politic, sovereign or not, sent to them an agent whom later medieval documents call *legatus, nuncius, missus, ambasciator, ambaxator* or *orator* without distinction. Whatever their etymology all these had the same meaning in practice and meant simply one person sent by another. The only title to which the theorists occasionally gave a special meaning was *procurator* ('proctor'). Azo and Baldus made a clear distinction between a *nuncius* who was merely the bearer of a letter with a purely passive role, and the *procurator* who might exercise his own judgement and act independently. Some practical treatises also distinguish between *procurator* and *nuncius*. But in the majority of cases it is impossible to see the least difference between the two words. So until the late Middle Ages these terms were practically synonymous. However, in the fifteenth century a hierarchy was sometimes apparent here and there, and especially in Rome which was in fact the capital of Western diplomacy. The *ambaxator* or *orator* gradually acquired a position distinctly superior to that of employees of lower rank, who tended to be given the title of *nuncius* or *procurator*. The Pope increasingly distinguished between his legates and his nuncios, who were lower than the former in both rank and authority. But in 1500 there was still no universally recognized practice, far from it. There was scope for considerable confusion.

Whatever their titles, one or more ambassadors were sent on a specifically defined mission for a limited period: this was always the case at the beginning of the fourteenth century and remained the most usual practice. When these *ad hoc* embassies had to be discreet and effective they numbered only a handful of individuals; their proportions increased dramatically if it was a ceremonial occasion or a question of prestige: in 1311 Venice sent a contingent of fifty horsemen to the imperial coronation; in 1447 some of the embassies sent to Rome to pay their respects to the new Pope Nicholas V numbered 120 to 170 men; it is not unlikely that there was a total of 5,000 delegates at the peace conference of Arras in 1435. Diplomacy was consequently a costly weapon and, by force of circumstance, eventually became the exclusive preserve of wealthy powers rather than of sovereign States.

At the beginning of the fourteenth century, important embassies were always led by a pre-eminent individual, a prelate or a high-ranking noble.

In time there was inevitably an increasing preponderance of specialists, of businessmen and above all of lawyers, because they could draft or analyse the documents under discussion. To simplify, it could be said that no one in 1300 conceived of an important embassy without its great noble, no one in 1500 of one without lawyers. Moreover, those responsible for such appointments were aware that an ambassador's efficacy was directly related to his familiarity with the topic under negotiation. There was consequently a distinct tendency to turn their diplomatic agents into specialists. For a long while those responsible remained the ruler and all his Council in some cases, in others (as at Venice) the entire Senate. But, in practice, control of foreign affairs, which were becoming increasingly demanding and time-consuming, stayed in the hands of a few members of the Council or (at Venice) of that arm of the Senate called the College of the 'Wise' (Savi). Moreover, diplomacy required increasing numbers of files, archives and specialized knowledge. Those ultimately best placed to ensure effective control were therefore the clerks with a special responsibility for drafting documents and for compiling and preserving the files. So at the beginning of the fourteenth century Elias Johnston, the clerk entrusted with the safekeeping of the treaties made between the kings of England and the kings of France, managed French affairs at Westminster. With the outbreak of war the office was suppressed. But throughout Europe (particularly in England and the duchies of Brabant and Milan) there was a continued tendency, which reached a peak in the fifteenth century, to put secretaries in charge of diplomatic affairs as they were close both to the ruler and to the relevant information.

However, the establishment of permanent embassies remains for many historians the most marked characteristic in the development of diplomatic structures in this period. Who were the forebears of this permanent ambassador? Was it the consul whom some Italian States, such as Venice, sometimes had living abroad to safeguard the economic interests of their nationals? Was it the proctor whom many countries had retained since the thirteenth century at the most important courts of justice and, above all, at Rome? The permanent embassy was surely the result of the increase in the number and duration of *ad hoc* embassies, necessitated by the growing volume of business. It has always been held that the first permanent ambassadors appeared in the fourteenth century, but there were still lacking two essential characteristics of the permanent embassy, continuity and reciprocity. It was in Italy in the mid-fifteenth century, at that period of intense diplomatic activity that culminated in the peace of Lodi (1454), that the first real permanent embassies were established. Besides, these embassies were expensive; it was not clear that they provided better services than *ad hoc* missions; it was, on the contrary, unquestionable that they could be extremely indiscreet. These facts ensured that for a long while the Italian example was not followed north of the Alps. The turning-point came in the great conflagration of the Italian Wars when the Spanish kings, the Emperor Maximilian and Henry VII all established permanent embassies in some capital cities. But it was only under Henry VIII and Francis I that the most powerful European powers provided themselves with a diplomatic service with a modern structure, permanently capable of providing the government with the information which it required in despatches and reports and carrying out its orders. So, although there was some delay, diplomacy very clearly did not remain unaffected by the great movement of specialization and bureaucratization that affected all the States of the West in the later Middle Ages.

F

9

The Aims of the State: Economic Policy

Did medieval governments look beyond peace and justice, war and diplomacy? Did they have an economic policy? Historians have been discussing the issue for 150 years. Some believe that Philip of Alsace (d. 1191), Henry the Lion (d. 1195) or Frederick II (d. 1250) already operated an economic policy. Others are convinced that, although the rulers of the period had fiscal ambitions or monetary problems, none of them, not even Louis XI nor Henry VII, had either the intellectual framework nor the means to pursue an economic policy. So was there, or was there not, an economic policy? Do we have to remain locked within this dilemma? It would surely be more profitable to consider in concrete terms the kind of economic policy which the authorities might conceive and execute, carefully distinguishing between times, places and social levels, for it goes without saying that a kingdom, a principality and a town all faced different problems.

In the twelfth and thirteenth centuries Western Europe was a world essentially rooted in the countryside, whose economic progress enriched the merchants and increased the size of the towns but also produced great suffering because of problems in maintaining food supplies. The Church increased the number of charitable institutions, lords made concerted attempts at land clearance, the local authorities kept a careful watch on supplies, merchants prospered and only asked of the State that they should remain secure and go about their business unhindered. The concern for justice and the common good dictated that merchants should be protected by the ruler as no other class was. Moreover, they were far from ignoring the fact that prospering rural areas, populous towns and busy roads increased their resources and consolidated both the military security and the political unity of their lands. Consequently the most effective twelfth- and thirteenth-century rulers founded new towns, licensed markets and guaranteed the security of certain routes, and although it is only possible to attribute political, fiscal and military motives to them, their actions undoubtedly had economic consequences.

After 1250 the atmosphere gradually changed. For two centuries the West experienced a depression which aggravated the disastrous effects of war and which plagues aggravated still further. In every sector of society and every region these difficulties exaggerated the tensions that prosperity had obscured. Wage-earners in town and country demanded an increase in pay, which the employers wished to keep stable. Rural producers wanted to be able to sell their corn and wool in a free market, that is, for the highest possible price, but the towns did all they could to obtain these commodities cheaply. The workers dreamt of protection, the merchants wanted the free market control or monopoly which would enable them to maintain their interests while their competitors were ruined. Each faction sought the ruler's arbitration and attempted to dictate his decisions, making particular use of the newly formed representative institutions. But the ruler was overwhelmed by worries about the money supply and buffeted by events; subjected to the pressure of contradictory interests, without economic doctrine and, moreover, with only regulatory powers, he had repeated recourse to incoherent, ephemeral and short-term measures. The ruler continued to flounder in the economic sphere: he had no clearly thought-out policy.

However the force of circumstance imposed certain constants on this disordered activity. In order to assure social stability the supply of basic foodstuffs to the whole population was one of the authorities' perennial concerns. Salt was important but grain was the crucial issue. The government's constant worry was that there should be sufficient, and at a reasonable price. To this end the same measures were always adopted. At the first sign of possible crisis everybody's reserves were limited to what was strictly necessary; exports, even the re-export of grains, were forbidden throughout the land and imports were encouraged by the lifting of all duties. Furthermore, in Spain, Geneva and elsewhere, at least in the fifteenth century, the authorities had the foresight to accumulate stocks in granaries which they sold at the critical moment: these reserves would either save the population from famine or bring prices down. For a long while these problems of supply were left to the local urban authorities. At the very most, rulers took a personal interest in the supplies of their new capitals. But in a large State like France each town defended her sources of supply against neighbouring towns as best she could. It was only in the reign of Louis XI that the central government attempted – with considerable difficulty – to superimpose a national policy on local interests and to create a national market by encouraging the free circulation of grain within the kingdom and placing a ban only on exports. At local or national level the authorities were always concerned with the consumer's interest. The producer of grain would never profit from a time of dearth as all exports were then forbidden; when there was a surplus he was never guaranteed a minimum price. This frantic protection of the consumer was ultimately to work against him: when the Spanish government tried to tax grain in 1502, the measure had a disastrous effect; arable lands were left uncultivated; there was no work in the countryside and famine in the towns. But the spectre of famine and the later medieval peasantry's lack of political influence was such that no government (with the belated exception of fifteenth-century England) was concerned with anything other than the protection of the consumer.

The State intended to extract as much money as possible from the subjects whom it saved from starvation. Without worrying about the theoretical justification, it imposed taxes on vital goods whenever possible. The king of England taxed wool exported by the English and needed on the Continent. The French and Castilian kings imposed a salt monopoly. The king of Hungary lived off his monopoly of precious metals while the Teutonic Order grew rich from their monopoly of amber. Where possible later medieval rulers also established spice and fish monopolies for their benefit. On occasion they tried to do so. Only the fear of killing the goose that laid the golden eggs checked them in their fiscal exploitation of their State.

So fourteenth- and fifteenth-century governments had more pressing reasons than their predecessors to establish a policy on roads. Otherwise obscure aspects of the political history of southern Germany are explained by the struggle between the dukes of Bavaria, who controlled the Reichenhall salt mines and intended to secure the Western market by controlling the land route on which Munich was a vital stage, and the archbishops of Salzburg, masters of Hallein salt, who wanted to keep for themselves at least the waterway via the Inn and the Danube which gave them access to Northern and Eastern Europe. The Habsburgs similarly wanted to make Vienna a compulsory stopping-place for Westward-bound Hungarian commerce; but instead Charles IV succeeded in making the Nuremberg–Prague–Bratislava road the vital artery of the Hungarian economy, to Bohemia's greater profit.

It was the Black Death in the mid-fourteenth century which, by killing so many workers and throwing the labour and production market into total disorder, forced the principal European States to go beyond their traditional objectives and set out a genuine social and economic policy. This policy was dictated to the authorities simultaneously by the traditional medieval concept of stability and by the employers; it was expressed in statutes and ordinances which aimed at limiting wages, preventing the mobility of labour and forcing beggars and vagabonds (whose inactivity was beginning to be condemned) to work. Although the more persevering English legislation possibly succeeded in keeping wages within some bounds, the ephemeral French measures were forgotten the moment they were published, though they did at least open new perspectives for the future.

It would be unfair to claim that the thirteenth-century concept of the public weal (*utilitas publica*) confined itself to the exercise of justice and of peace and never had any positive economic element. From the first half of the thirteenth century a ruler like Frederick II was extremely concerned – or so at least he said – for the well-being of his subjects; a theorist like John of Viterbo demonstrated that justice and peace were only the means of achieving prosperity. But it must be admitted that these convictions were rarely uttered and that they had little practical outcome. From the fourteenth century onwards, in contrast, rulers asserted their desire to sustain and increase their State's prosperity more and more frequently. In 1517 Francis I surprised no one by stating that he aimed at the prosperity of the entire kingdom; by this date it was a compulsory ambition for every conscientious ruler. The pressure of circumstance and interests gradually and by degrees gave specific direction to this very generalized intention. We can praise Charles IV for developing viticulture in Bohemia, Philip the Good for concerning himself with the quality of Burgundian wines; Peter IV of Aragon for encouraging the import of chosen breeds of sheep; the duke of Milan for co-ordinating and intensifying the ·attempts of the Lombard communes to establish an irrigation and drainage system in the Po valley. But it is a fact that rural areas generally received little of their ruler's attention. Moreover they did not possess the practical means of intervention.

It was with the towns, once again, that the State was concerned. But whereas in the thirteenth century only the merchants counted for much, gradually in the fourteenth century governments were increasingly disposed to accept the viewpoint of their industrial producers – either because the trade guilds were succeeding in asserting themselves, or because rulers favoured the lower classes in order that they might more effectively dominate a balanced society, or from a genuine desire for social stability, or because of the conviction that wealth stems from industry.

Now in these times of recession what these producers most needed was protection. The European States of the fourteenth and fifteenth centuries were consequently occasionally forced to ban the export or re-export of raw materials which they needed, as well as the import of similar products made abroad. This absolute ban very quickly proved disastrous; governments reconciled the interests of their treasuries and their industries by a selective customs policy: with increasing frequenty they imposed extremely heavy duties on the export of raw materials and on the import of manufactured goods and, by contrast, levied only small sums on imported raw materials and the export of finished goods. For obvious political and military reasons States were forced to protect their naval industry in particular. The Aragonese ban on Sardinian imports of foreign cloth from ships not subject to the crown of Aragon and the Florentine ban on all exports in other than Florentine ships both had the same end, that of encouraging national ship-building. Although at an early date purely fiscal concerns had led many States to establish monopolies, in the late Middle Ages such monopolies were undoubtedly the product of a deliberately protectionist economic policy: when Ferdinand of Aragon decided in 1481 that Sardinian coral could be sold only to Aragonese subjects, the problem for Aragonese artisans was one of effective competition against their Genoese and Corsican rivals.

This increased protectionism was paralleled by the development of a genuine economic nationalism. Rulers had increasingly to make economic policy the bedrock of their State, that is, to bring about the economic unification of their lands by fostering internal trade, and encouraging their self-sufficiency. Above all, these rulers and their advisers were concerned at a very early date – from the second half of the fourteenth century in England at least – with the balance of trade and were also extremely anxious that there should be no decline in the nation's monetary reserves. These preoccupations led to regular bans on the export of metals and to sumptuary laws designed to reduce the consumption and import of luxury goods; they explain Louis XI's endeavours to establish silk manufacture at Tours and Lyon; they also explain the positive encouragement given by the French king (and many others) to the immigration of specialist textile, mining and metal workers.

And so, out of the whirlpool of ephemeral and contradictory decisions, measures appeared – isolated at first, but then repeating themselves with increasing insistence – which were undoubedly designed to enrich the State, but which were also intended to satisfy the protectionist and national aspirations of those sections of society with greatest political influence. The time came when the prince's advisers could order these scattered trends within a coherent system of ideas, and thus what we call 'mercantilism' was born. At the end of the fifteenth century the Spanish kings, profiting from earlier Aragonese experiences, introduced a coherent mercantilist system in Spain. A positive programme of mercantilist policies appeared in England between 1490 and 1530. In France, Francis I's counsellors were able to provide all the elements of a genuinely mercantilist doctrine in 1517.

In the fourteenth and fifteenth centuries the States went beyond the level of simple policy and crude fiscality. But they were not yet guided by a conscious and coherent economic doctrine. Their economic action was the result of decisions inspired both by their fiscal concerns and the influence of certain groups of their subjects. So we can call this period one of 'constructive fiscality', like U. Dirlmeier, or, like so many others, we can say that this was the pre-mercantilist period.

Part III

State and Society

One of the characteristic features of the history of the States of the West in the later Middle Ages was the continued growth of the ruler's power. Also entirely characteristic of the period was the progressive development, opposite the prince, of 'orders' or 'estates' who together created the community of the country. The country then forced the ruler to participate in a dialogue which was often unequal and always difficult, whose risks and uncertainties it is important not to underestimate. The lasting progress made by the ruler was a feature of the fourteenth and fifteenth centuries, but they were equally characterized by the achievements of the representative assemblies, organs of the country's estates. Admittedly these successes were most frequently sterile, for the future belonged to the ruler. But it would nevertheless be a grave misrepresentation of the political history of the later medieval period not to realize that they were of prime importance: it was a period of dialogue, by means of representative assemblies, between the ruler and his country.

10

The Birth of the Country

THE FORMATION OF ORDERS OR ESTATES

Legal status, wealth, profession, life-style – all these factors differentiated countless estates in Western society at the end of the Middle Ages and clerics exhausted themselves in attempts to list them in all their diversity. Whatever their estate, men were also bound together by lineage, by vassalage and economic ties. There were also more complex affiliations, such as those of the 'family clans' of Italian towns – *gente* at Florence, *albergo* at Genoa – cemented by blood-ties or the simple custom of long propinquity, whose members, whether rich or poor, bearing the same name and the same banner, might number hundreds and wielded very considerable political, military and economic power. And so various forces, pressure-groups and, occasionally, genuine parties made their presence felt in the State, and the ruler and his counsellors had either to guard against or to exploit them.

The theorists were not slow to register this complex situation. Their training had accustomed them to more straightforward categories. The old bi-partite divisions between clerics and laymen, or between freemen and serfs, no longer held good. But the notion that society was divided into three orders with different functions (prayer, war and labour), which appeared with obscure origins about the year 1000 and which was willingly supported by the theologians and disseminated by clerics, ended by being imposed more or less consciously on the whole of society. Soon everyone regarded as an incontrovertible fact the division of society into three orders or estates. With the decline of feudalism, when new social structures were being forged, what had only been an image acquired legal and institutional reality: in the majority of the States of the West society was divided – either as a result of the ruler's intervention or because of spontaneous organization by the subjects – into three orders or estates possessing a specific legal status.

The imposition of a simple tri-partite schema on a society vibrant with diversity, power-groupings and multiple influences did not take place without some difficulty. Beaumanoir distinguished between three estates, but speaks of 'two estates, namely men of noble birth and free men, and the third estate, which is composed of serfs'; in 1443 Cardinal Beaufort divided English society into three, but he saw on the one hand the prelates and magnates, on the other knights, squires and merchants, and finally the labourers, artisans and working people; in mid-fifteenth century Lyon the citizens were divided into three estates, but they were the *bourgoysie* who lived off the income from their property, the merchants (*marchandise*) and the *clergie*. The traditional tri-partite division did not so much underline reality as camouflage diversity; and the camouflage was very often inadequate.

This did not generally prevent the gradual emergence of a privileged lay order, the nobility, who formed the second estate after the clergy, who had always constituted a juridically defined group universally accorded first place. The remainder of society, the rich and poor of town and country, were grouped together in a last estate which began to be called the 'third estate' in the fifteenth century. A Namurois document of 1429 speaks of the *tiers état* for what is apparently the first time in the West. A little later Georges Chastellain speaks of the 'third member' (*tiers membre*). This expression, which seems to have originated in the Low Countries, was established in France at a specific date, since two letters of Louis XI and Charles VIII, of 1482 and 1484, appear to be the first to refer to the 'third, common and lowest estate' (*tiers, commun et bas estat*), a few months before a petition for redress of grievances made to the Estates General in 1484 speaks of the 'third and common estate' (*tiers et commun état*) and before Thomas Basin alludes to the masses in his *Histoire de Louis XI* as *tertii et inferioris status* ('the third and lowest estate').

This terminology marks the end of an evolution by which a mere concept was somehow or other transformed into an institution: in the majority of the States of the West in 1500 the clergy, nobility and third estate finally constituted three legally defined orders or estates, each with their privileges and obligations, and within which there was a place for every member of the country. For whilst these three estates were establishing their identity, they were also perforce adapting and conforming to the needs of the principality in which they lived and, by accepting certain restrictions and by allying themselves with other estates, they constituted the community of the entire country, as a counterbalance to the ruler.

THE INTEGRATION OF ORDERS OR ESTATES

The nobility

It is generally accepted that after 1300 feudalism played no real part in the 'modern' State. If this was really the case, why were so many Western lords so keen to enumerate their fiefs, to keep a record of the occasions when homage was paid to them, to provide those enormous *Lehnbücher* (books of homages) with indexes in order to facilitate daily use? In reality feudalism continued to play an active part in the Western State until the close of the Middle Ages.

In the fourteenth century rulers still intended to make positive use of the homage due to them. Charles IV attempted to establish his authority in Bohemia on a feudal basis. Homage was still a sufficiently serious issue for Edward III, for example, in 1364 and 1365, to be quite as keen to extract it from Gaston Phoebus as the latter was to withhold it. It was because it seemed important to surround themselves with vassals that rulers in the second half of the fourteenth century continued to distribute numerous annual pensions in the form of *fiefs de bourse* or *fief-rentes* for which they were owed homage. According to M. Sczaniecki the *fief-rente* was above all a political and diplomatic tool. But B. D. Lyon has convincingly demonstrated that the lords' primary expectation of these vassals was military service. In this respect they remained faithful to the original spirit of feudalism, which had so little diminished in 1373 that the archbishop of Cologne still listed his fiefs according to their military value and in 1385 the king of England called his vassals to the feudal host. What is more, in certain States, such as the duchy of Milan, we can speak of a new feudalism after 1450. The Sforza, in effect, went ahead with massive enfeoffments of huge lordships and they expected of their new vassals what a twelfth-century lord expected of his: that they maintain and defend the castles entrusted to them and fight in their lord's army whenever necessary.

Generally speaking, however, the old principles of vassalage lost most of their conviction in the last years of the fourteenth century. The concept of the subject had long been current in France and England beside that of the vassal. Things were different in Germany. But in 1379, for the first time, the bishop of Münster spoke officially not simply of his vassals but also of his subjects. In 1384 Jean Le Coq, the famous advocate at the Parlement of Paris, attached so little importance to the feudal bond that he found 'absurd' the notion (which was nevertheless widespread) that an advocate could not defend an action against a lord from whom he held a fief. After 1385 the English king never again convoked the feudal host.

Until 1388, civil servants in Parisian circles stressed that pre-eminently feudal quality, loyalty; after 1388 they preferred to underline their competence. Shortly afterwards, rulers ceased to exact a meaningless homage as a counterpart to their rents. The heritable *fief-rente* slowly died out in the fifteenth century; the last English *fief-rente* dates from 1444; there were virtually none in Germany after 1450; at Christmas 1477 the French king only allocated 160 *livres* for their payment; there were only a handful in the Low Countries in 1500. Finally, in the first half of the fifteenth century, the French king still relied as much on the bond of vassalage as that of subjection. Charles VIII always expected to be 'obeyed by his vassals and subjects' ('obéy de ses vassaulx et subjects'). At the end of his life he persisted in demanding liege-homage from the dukes of Brittany, to which they never agreed. But Louis XI – finally drawing conclusions from the theories repeated by his father's advocates in the Paris Parlement for the last twenty or so years – ignored all feudal arguments with a view to exacting the obedience of a subject from his greatest lords.

In the mid-fifteenth century, feudalism had exhausted its political strength. But it might still retain some financial importance. In the Empire, where rulers in desperate financial straits could not afford to ignore any source of income, feudal rights offered them considerable assistance. In Austria, for example, when the vassals no longer had any military value to the duke, their military service was replaced by a tax of a tenth of the annual revenue of their fief; this feudal tax (*Lehensteuer*) vanished when the duke succeeded in establishing a land tax (*Landessteuer*), but it had played a very important part in the construction of the territorial principality. Long before 1300 the English king had seen feudal institutions as little else than a source of profit. He anticipated considerable revenues, in particular from his rights of wardship (of the minor of a deceased vassal), and of marriage (of the daughter of a deceased vassal who was not yet of age). It is true that the practice of what English historians call the 'Use' (by which a vassal could transfer his fief to someone else in the interests (*ad opus*) of a third party, which English lawyers described in legal French (their technical language) as 'cestui a que use le feoffment fuit fait', always shortened to 'cestui que use') enabled the king's vassals to escape the consequences of these minorities, which were disastrous for their families, by entrusting their fief to a friend when they were about to die. The practice of the 'Use', which appeared about 1250, was widely used at the end of the thirteenth century, became common practice under Edward III and slightly reduced the profit the king would normally have had from wardship and marriage. Edward IV was the first to put in hand the restoration of royal prerogative in this area at the end of his reign. His efforts were continued by Richard III. The first two Tudors vigorously opposed the 'Use'. At the beginning of the sixteenth century a prince of the West, even though he was king of England, would not relinquish part of his feudal rights without a struggle.

Feudalism was admittedly no more than a shadow of its former self in 1500. But it would be erroneous to suppose that between 1300 and 1500 it had experienced a gradual demise whose only purpose was simply to delay the triumphs of the modern State. In practice rulers had been able to discover political support and new means of finance in feudal institutions. In the fourteenth and fifteenth centuries feudalism actively promoted the emergence of modern States. Rather than see these two centuries as a 'period of transition' when rulers were set on imposing subjection on their vassals, it would be more accurate to see it as a period when rulers based their arguments on vassalage or subjection, as circumstances dictated, in order to extract the maximum obedience from their subjects.

Whatever the case, declining feudalism cannot be expected to provide an exclusive definition of the privileged lay order. In thirteenth-century England, what might be termed the nobility comprised on the one hand the earls, that is the most powerful of the barons, the vassals who held their lands directly from the king or from his tenants-in-chief and, on the other hand, some 3,000 landholders whose estates brought in a minimum annual income of twenty pounds sterling, and who were sufficiently aware of their identity to be spoken of as the *communitas bacheleriae Angliae* ('the community of the bachelors of England') from 1259 onwards. Neither vassalage nor fief provided a definition of nobility in the fourteenth century. The only individuals of privileged status were the fifty-odd magnates, lords, peers and barons who – either because of their wealth, their power, the king's favour or bureaucratic routine – received individuals summons to Parliament and sat in the Upper Chamber; the others (knights of the shire, esquires and gentlemen) certainly played a very considerable role in the operation of the State: summoned collectively and sitting in the Lower Chamber, they were relegated to the lowest ranks of gentility and did not enjoy any special legal status. In France the outlines of the nobility crystallized slowly: possession of a fief with high justice might be one qualification, but it was far more the adoption of a noble life-style, tax exemptions and a place in the ranks of the nobility in the assemblies of estates that characterized a noble in public opinion. Before 1250 lords of comital rank in the Empire (*Herren*) and the great freeholders (*Freie Herren*) were clearly distinguished from the unfree servants of the prince (*Dienstmannen, ministeriales*). Ministeriality (their position as servants of the prince) brought the *Freie Herren* such advantages that they soon had no difficulty in grouping themselves with what remained of the *Herren* in a single noble order. In Poland the magnates alone still exercised an incontestable dominion at the beginning of the fourteenth century, but before the end of the fifteenth century the mass of knights with property (who represented a tenth of the population) were incorporated in a single privileged order, clearly outlined and with a precise legal status and this *communitas nobilium* then rose to power. In short, the privileged lay order of the nobility was everywhere defined at the very period of feudal decline by complex criteria that varied from one country to the next.

In order to maintain their position, the members of these privileged classes relied on new institutions that had no connection with feudalism and which contributed to the individuality of political societies in the fourteenth and fifteenth centuries. In England after 1300 those lords who were sufficiently powerful began to retain in their service individuals called retainers whom they maintained and whose affiliation with their lord was manifested by the wearing of his livery. As a retainer might himself engage other retainers a positive hierarchy of service was built up which might place a veritable small army at a magnate's disposal: in 1314 Thomas of Lancaster already had 600 retainers; in 1373 John of Gaunt, duke of Lancaster, had more than 200 retainers who, with their own retinues, could easily have totalled the contingent of 1,500 then available to the duke; in 1471 a hundred individuals were bound by indenture to William, Lord Hastings, and with their own retainers they undoubtedly formed the solid core of the 3,000 men whom he commanded at the battle of Barnet. Historians have vacillated between *feodalité prolongée* (M. Bloch), 'bastard feudalism' (C. Plummer, K. B. McFarlane) or 'new feudalism' (H. Cam)[1] as a name for this new form of social organization. It is more pertinent to observe that this contract system, without homage, fief or heredity, had nothing in common with feudalism and 'indenture system' is a more appropriate term. This system undoubtedly gave rise to abuses which legislation attempted to control more or less successfully. It would be absurd to hold it responsible (as Tudor propaganda did) for the turmoil of fifteenth-century England. It was no more responsible for the Wars of the Roses than it hindered the establishment of a strong Tudor monarchy. It provided the organizational basis for a hierarchy of service which was not in itself better or worse than any other, in particular than the hierarchy of feudalism. It met the deepest need of a society which could no longer rely on a feudal army and had not yet devised a permanent army. Kings themselves were glad to make use of it and the system helps to define a unique period in English political history.

At the same time many continental and especially French rulers had recourse to similar contracts. P. S. Lewis has demonstrated that the counts of Foix retained numerous *compagnons et alliés* by contract between 1375 and 1445. But the system was not as extensive as in England, at least

---

[1] Cam, *Liberties and Communities in Medieval England* (575), pp. 205–22; (1037).

in this strictly defined legal form. For the orders of chivalry which burgeoned on the Continent are very closely related to the English indentures. In 1330 Alfonso XI instituted the Order of the Sash in Castile, the first recorded secular order of chivalry. In 1348 Edward III created the Company of St George or Order of the Garter. In 1351–2 it was the turn of John the Good of France to found the Order of the Star. After this, orders of chivalry, whether they were the work of the prince or of a group of equals, proliferated for more than a century. The Order of St Michael, founded by Louis XI in 1469, was undoubtedly the last. The influence of chivalric and romance literature and the ludic element in these orders cannot be dismissed, but it would be wrong to underestimate their political and military importance. The declared aim of the Order of the Star was to reassemble and galvanize the French chivalric elite after the disaster at Crécy. As B.-A. Pocquet du Haut-Jussé says,

> the creation of the Order of the Golden Fleece by Philip the Good (1429) was also designed, beneath the wordly trappings that adorned it, to secure for the duke a devoted band of lords who were not his vassals. It had no connection with the old enfeoffed pensions; it was the flowering of an entirely different practice, that of using sealed bonds, which since the fourteenth century lords had exchanged between themselves and by which they allied themselves and promised mutual aid on the very fringe of the feudal hierarchy.[2]

Between the era of the vassal and that of the subject came the period of both vassal and subject, when society attempted political organization on foundations that were neither 'feudal' nor 'modern', and of which the indenture system and the orders of chivalry represented two parallel and complementary aspects.

Late medieval rulers were not hostile to feudal structures nor to these new institutions which were better suited to their time and played a part in the definition of the nobility in their States. They were even the first to turn them to their advantage. But it was their intention that these institutions should respect the limits of their States and even play a part in ensuring their greater stability. The Orders of the Star and the Golden Fleece were 'national' orders. The contracts agreed by the counts of Foix re-enforced their State. At the same time German princes, such as the bishop of Münster, can be observed abandoning their distant fiefs, but also forbidding the possession by foreigners of fiefs within the territorial State which they were endeavouring to construct and turning this reduced form of feudalism to their advantage in order to develop the judicial system within their lands and increase their resources. The rulers of the

[2] *Les pensionnaires fieffés des ducs de Bourgogne* (1051), p. 150.

fourteenth and fifteenth centuries were less concerned to destroy than to control, integrate and make use of forces which, left to themselves, could have blurred the limits of their States or undermined their power.

The towns

The towns presented the ruler with a similar problem. With a prosperous and long-established economic base that gave them an overwhelming superiority over the hinterland, they did not only make claims to their own autonomy (as they always had), but also demonstrated the beginnings of political horizons characteristic of the period, which suggested regroupings on a grander scale. They might, as in Italy, work for control of a considerable hinterland (*contado*) and build a city-state; or they might, like the German towns, prefer to form great urban federations. The princes, who were endeavouring to increase their own territory little by little at the same period, took umbrage at these policies. For the walled towns were an important element in their defensive network: they were undoubtedly the 'keys' of their States. Moreover, they could very quickly provide them with considerable resources. Frequent clashes between factions or social groups made the towns trouble-spots which the ruler could not afford to ignore. The rulers' policies therefore tended to absorb the towns within their States.

The clash between rulers and towns occurred throughout the West, but did not take place everywhere at the same time. We shall not discuss England, where the Norman kings never allowed their towns the least chance of any genuine autonomy. In France the problem was a thing of the past before 1300, settled in favour of the king. There had to be exceptional circumstances for Bordeaux at one point to envisage a veritable urban State, for the town was founded on the distant power of the English king as duke of Aquitaine. This State crumbled with the withdrawal of English support. In the kingdom as a whole the king of France was so sure of the support of his towns that his problem was not to subdue them, but to coerce them into some kind of autonomy. Louis XI, for example, asked his towns to provide substantial military support and subsidies on a generous scale. After which, he would willingly have granted them responsibility for law and order within their boundaries, at their own expense. But the distinguished citizens who governed the cities did not wish to shoulder these flattering but costly and difficult responsibilities. Their reluctance was so great that in France, where the towns had long been an integral part of the State, the king's problem was finally one of being unable to impose on his *bonnes villes*, despite his declared intention, the autonomy (in matters less important to him) equivalent to that which the Norman kings had been in a position to 'grant' to their English subjects soon after the Conquest.

In Germany, on the other hand, it was in the fourteenth and fifteenth centuries that the decisive clash between towns and princes occurred. The first attempts of the princes to check urban power took place in the second half of the fourteenth century. There were setbacks, however. They ran up against vigorous urban leagues which broadly overlapped the framework of a principality, such as the Hanseatic league (then at the summit of its political power), or the Union which grouped the Rhenish, Swabian, Franconian and Bavarian towns together after 1381. The rulers took up the offensive once more about the middle of the fifteenth century. The first great success amongst the rulers was that of Frederick II, elector of Brandenburg, who took advantage of internal struggles between the patriciate and the guilds to break the autonomy of Berlin in 1442. In 1448 the citizens tried to recover their former liberties, but their uprising (the *Berliner Unwille*) failed. After this, and throughout the fifty-year reign of the Emperor Frederick III, there were continual clashes. These resulted in incontestable successes for the rulers and others for the towns that were purely illusory. For even if they were victorious, the towns always emerged from the struggle ruined and deprived of their hinterland. For a long while German historians have had nothing but scorn for the deprived towns, blaming them for their egoism and for not realizing that the future lay with the territorial principalities. More recently, a few different opinions have been heard from both West Germans, who have observed that the towns were sometimes undoubtedly sincere in their proclaimed desire to defend the Empire as well as themselves, and from East Germans for whom the *Berliner Unwille* could only be a progressive phenomenon, opposing as it did a territorial State that served only the interests of the feudal nobility. Whatever the case, the great debate between the German towns and rulers, that reached its height in the second half of the fifteenth century, ended with victory for the rulers, who succeeded in integrating the towns within their principalities.

With the dazzling exceptions of a few Italian towns, such as Venice or Florence, which quite categorically secured their own existence, the victory sooner or later of the territorial State over the towns was general in the West as a whole. At the end of the fifteenth century the towns were merely the most representative element of the 'third estate'.

The Church

Difficult though it might sometimes be, the integration of the towns within the State was a small problem beside that posed by the Church. For the Church had always been an international institution. The twelfth- and thirteenth-century Popes had even made it a powerful monarchy, exercising patronage and drawing on financial resources with scant regard for the political demarcations which were gradually being established. Now the resources available to the Church and the political and judicial powers which she enjoyed were so extensive that, when they were establishing their States, the rulers had to attempt to turn the first to their own profit and gain control of the second.

They were assisted initially by an intellectual evolution that gradually distanced the best minds from any international perspective and made love of one's country an increasingly exclusive concept; the rulers were supported by all their subjects, lay and clerical, in their attempts to build a national Church. The expression *ecclesia gallicana* was never used in the twelfth century, and rarely heard in the first half of the thirteenth: the concept of the universal Church was still dominant. But in the very last years of the thirteenth century the phrases *ecclesia gallicana, patres gallicani, prelati Franciae* were constantly repeated and demonstrated that the French would be henceforth less attached to the universal Church than to their own country. For them it was the Gallican Church that was from now on the single and indivisible bride of Christ ('Ecclesia gallicana, quae tanquam una et indivisa Christi sponsa divortium non patitur'); founded on a rock ('illa, quae una est ecclesia in una petra fundata'); and it was because the 'Gallican Church' was firmly bound to the king and the kingdom of France that Philip the Fair could take a stand against the 'Roman church'. Similarly, although the expression *ecclesia anglicana* appeared as early as the twelfth century, it only referred to the Church *in* England. But as time went on the concept of an English Church became increasingly established there (*ecclesia de regno Angliae* in 1290; *seinte Eglise Dengleterre* in 1341; 'Chirche of Engelond' was in common usage at the end of the fourteenth century). Similar processes occurred throughout Europe.

It was all very well for the Pope to proclaim the advantages of the presence of strangers ('Was the blessed James, who lit the light of gospel truth amongst the Spaniards and introduced them to the sacrament of baptism, born in Spain?' demanded Clement VI of Alfonso XI of Castile): rulers and subjects agreed in the rejection of foreign bishops, priests, holders of benefices, monks and students – because the foreigners knew neither the language nor the customs of their flock, because their presence and activities might threaten the State and because they deprived the country's own sons of their legitimate income.

Furthermore there were constant problems because ecclesiastical and diocesan boundaries did not coincide with political frontiers. This enabled the archbishop of Reims, a subject of the king of France, to have a foothold in Flemish affairs, or the bishop whose seat was at Passau in Bavaria to intervene in Austria. The rulers therefore made strenuous efforts to mould the geography of the Church to that of their States. They met with some success. It was James II of Aragon who in 1318 suggested the outline of the new province of Saragossa to John XXII; Charles IV who succeeded in making Prague an archbishopric in 1344, despite the opposition of Mainz; and in 1469 Frederick III was successful in his attempts to have Vienna made a diocese on which all the lands of his Austrian duchy were dependent. Although at the end of the fifteenth century there were still great discrepancies between political and ecclesiastical boundaries, the increasing tendency of the Church to adapt itself to the framework was clear.

More specifically, this trend in the Church was evident in the oldest and most prestigious universities, which had been essentially international institutions. At the beginning of the fifteenth century the University of Paris, proud of its papal protection, claimed to be above princes and civil powers; it was even above wars, untroubled by the Hundred Years War. Distrust of this privileged body gradually increased – as much on the part of Henry VI as that of Charles VII. In the face of this hostility from the public authorities, the claims of the academics became increasingly modest. In the middle of the fifteenth century they recognized the University's royal origin. not disputing its foundation by Charlemagne; the University was subject to the law that applied to the rest of the kingdom like any other institution; they placed under the direct protection of the king an institution whose only pride was henceforth in being 'the eldest daughter of the king of France'.

The hand of the ruler lay increasingly heavily on these churches that had adapted themselves to some extent to these new political realities. The clergy might insist on recognition of their immunity to taxation in principle; the ruler nevertheless finally succeeded in extracting considerable sums from them by the expedient of tenths, most of which was granted him by the Pope, and also by directly negotiated subsidies. No one, or virtually no one, disputed the principle of ecclesiastical jurisdiction. At the end of the fifteenth century this was still a considerable factor in Spain, Italy, Hungary and Germany, though it was soon to decline. Although ecclesiastical courts were still a great problem to the French secular authorities at the time of the Assembly of Vincennes (1329), the laity completely escaped ecclesiastical jurisdiction after this date. They provided an increasingly transitory refuge for clerical criminals, and the Parlement of Paris – under pressure from churchmen themselves – ended by settling such purely ecclesiastical problems at the end of the fifteenth century as the relations between bishops and archdeacons, the authenticity of relics or the observation of the mendicants' vow of poverty.

The establishment in the second half of the fifteenth century of the *appel comme d'abus* finally submitted every sentence and every judgement by ecclesiastical authority to the scrutiny of Parlement. In 1500 the Church's jurisdiction in France was a shadow of what it had been. As for England, the problem had long since passed: since the end of the thirteenth century the dignitaries of the Church had only maintained the most modest activity in the realm of the sovereign's jurisdiction.

Neither finance nor jurisdiction was the most important issue, however. It was still more vital for the prince to make appointments to the greatest possible number of benefices, lucrative and humble. By this means he could place men devoted to him in positions of great political influence: above all, provide his servants with a livelihood without emptying his own purse. In a period when the prince's own income was uncertain it was of the utmost importance that he could rely on the Church to oil the wheels of the State. Firstly, the rulers had benefices at their disposal – like any other lord – of which they had plenary advowson because they had once been founded and endowed by one of their ancestors. But by this means, *pleno jure*, the king of England could only appoint to two or three benefices a year, and the king of Aragon had only 150 prebendaries of this kind, with a very modest income. Towards the middle of the thirteenth century the kings of England and France were strengthened by what English historians call the right of patronage and French historians the *régale spirituelle* (the royal prerogative to enjoy the rights of vacant sees and abbacies). In other words, by the extension of their temporal prerogative they had obtained the nomination to benefices normally in the gift of the bishop, should the see be empty. The exercise of this right – which required the deaths of two individuals – was extremely limited. In reality the only important problem was the general one of the granting of benefices where the ruler stumbled less against traditional practices (such as the election of a bishop by the chapter of the cathedral or the granting of minor benefices by the usual patron) than against the privileges which the popes had secured in the thirteenth and fourteenth centuries.

Throughout the fourteenth century the king of England successfully pursued a difficult but profitable policy. He took responsibility for Parliament's somewhat histrionic declarations of principle and made use of them to reach a realistic agreement with the Papacy: the Pope nominated the king's man and had some consolation in the taxes he was able to levy. In this way the king did not refuse to deal with the Pope, but he constantly adhered to the principle of 'Heads I win, tails you lose', supported by his people's sense of national identity, which was already a force to be reckoned with. Richard II's agreement with the Papacy of 1398 thus did no more than formalize what had long been a mutually satisfactory working arrangement. This first concordat had the misfortune to run up against the full force of English public opinion. The Lancastrian usurpation of 1399 made it obsolete.

On the Continent the Pope remained in control of the situation far longer. The Great Schism finally put paid to his claims. The most powerful rulers secured advantageous agreements from a weakened Papacy: in September 1417, before the election of Martin V, the College of Cardinals undertook to ensure that the Pope would henceforth nominate only individuals chosen by the successor of St Stephen (that is, the king of Hungary) to Hungarian bishoprics, archbishoprics and monasteries; on 2 May 1418 the Concordat of Constance re-established canonical elections in Germany for elective benefices and a rota system was envisaged for non-elective benefices whereby the Pope and the usual patron took it in turns to nominate to a vacancy; in the agreement with England made in July 1418 Martin V did not even secure a share in the nominations. And so began the period of concordats between princes and Popes.

In France, Charles VII – a firm supporter of Gallican personnel for the Church in France – refused to come to any agreement with the Papacy: the Pragmatic Sanction of Bourges (1438) re-established canonical elections for major benefices and the rights of the usual patron in minor benefices. But since the king's intention was to impose his nominees in every case and the Pope had not abandoned all hope of intervention, application of the Pragmatic Sanction raised countless difficulties before the king could finally congratulate himself on considerable success. Now at the same time the rulers who had decided to come to an agreement with the Pope obtained such full concessions from him that they achieved more favourable results with less trouble. In this way, after 1441, the dukes of Burgundy and Brittany had full control of the nomination of their bishops and at least partial control of the nomination of incumbents in their States, and the king of Poland (from 1447) and Francesco Sforza of Milan (after 1450) had similar powers. Louis XI took the point: he returned to papal obedience in 1461 and in 1472 concluded with him the Concordat of Amboise, whose terms were extremely conservative: the Pope would appoint to major benefices, but always in agreement with the king; he would appoint to minor benefices every other month. And so, after many other rulers had done so, the king of France made a formal agreement with the Pope with a view to exploiting the Church in his own kingdom. For a long while historians underestimated the importance of the Concordat of Amboise, which prepared the way for the Concordat of Bologna of 1516 and the French king's official seizure of the Gallican church.

And so it was that the foundations of national Churches were laid in the West in the century(1417–1516) after the Great Schism, by means of concordats that proved to be long-lasting compromises. The concordats satisfied the Pope because his spiritual authority was preserved and the dangers of conciliarism averted; they satisfied national pride and the national interests of individual peoples; and they satisfied the rulers since the Church had been successfully absorbed within the State and its powers and wealth deflected. Only a few rulers died dissatisfied, like the duke of Cleves, dreaming madly of being 'Pope in his own lands'. But Henry VIII had already succeeded to the English throne in 1509.

THE UNION OF ORDERS OR ESTATES

While each order was gradually adjusting little by little to the framework of a State, the different orders within the State were gradually accustoming themselves to a closer degree of co-existence. Historians are not in agreement on the question of whether the initiative for this grouping came from the ruler or the orders themselves. Some maintain it was the prince who forced the orders to unite so that he would no longer have to carry out protracted negotiations with each of them. Others, on the contrary, believe that the orders wished to unite in order to secure more advantageous terms from the prince. In reality each made a contribution to this unification, in proportions that varied according to time and place.

At the end of the day the community of the country was an indisputable fact. The concept of *communitas terrae* was current in England after the end of the Barons' War (1258–64). From 1283 the *universitas Cataloniae* had a sense of identity. In 1364 the 'religious, noble and good' towns of Hainault began to speak 'in the name of and for the whole body and community of this land'. In 1387, in the State of the Wettin, the various estates united to form what modern German historians term a territorial community (*gemeine Landschaft*) and what the French of the fifteenth century – following the early fifteenth-century political writer Jean de Terre Vermeille – spontaneously called a 'mystical body'.

Body or community, throughout the West the integration of the united orders within the State constituted a country (*pays*), whose dialogue with the ruler had a profound effect on contemporary political life.

11

Prince and Country

OATHS AND CONTRACTS

Merely to state that the later Middle Ages were a period of dialogue between the ruler and his country is obviously inadequate. One has to specify exactly the forms of this dialogue. For it is self-evident that neither feudalism not absolutism excludes all dialogue. In the course of their coronation, feudal monarchs such as the kings of England or France traditionally gave their oath to uphold peace and justice. In real terms this did not in the least limit their power. But the vassal who had paid homage to the king was quite convinced that by the very fact of accepting his homage the ruler was party to a contract with long-established obligations on either side. The vassals could unite in order to ensure that a ruler gave them a more specific undertaking: thus before 1250 a ruler's power was limited by his coronation oath and by his feudal contract with his vassals.

Now in the second half of the thirteenth century a new dynasty, that of the Avesnes, came to power in Hainault. No count of Hainault had ever taken any kind of oath at the beginning of his reign. The new count, Jean II, wanted to be quite sure of the loyalty of the major towns of Hainault. In return he promised to respect the laws and customs of each town. There were numerous clauses specifying the relationship between the king and his vassals in the Aragonese *Privilegio general* of 1283, but the king's relationship with the towns was also considered in many of the articles; one clause even referred to *todos del regno del Aragon* ('the whole of the kingdom of Aragon'); in 1287 the country's right to depose a king who would not respect the terms of the *Privilegio general* was acknowledged. To the coronation oath of his ancestors, Edward II had in 1308 to add an undertaking to maintain and uphold the laws and customs stated by the community of the realm. This undertaking was sufficiently important in

English eyes for failure to keep it to be cited as one of the reasons for his deposition in 1327.

So gradually the rulers of the West came to accept obligations towards their subjects, not simply towards their vassals, and obligations that were stipulated in a veritable contract with exact clauses which, if disregarded, provided justification for deposition. Most commonly this contract took the form of a solemn oath made by the ruler at the beginning of his reign: when Jeanne and Wenceslas (daughter and son-in-law of the defunct Jean III of Brabant) swore on 3 January 1356 that they would respect all the clauses of the lengthy document later known as the 'Joyeuse Entrée', they laid the first stone of the Brabançon constitution. In contrast, the foundation of the Wurtemberg constitution was laid in 1514 by the treaty of Tübingen, a copy of which was kept by both parties and which specified in detail the rights and obligations of the duke and the *Landtag* of Wurtemberg.

Admittedly not every late medieval ruler was bound by such oaths or contracts. The king of France, for example, continued to swear the same vague traditional oath. He invoked it only to escape from agreements which contemporary hardship might oblige him to make in the course of his reign. This exception notwithstanding, such oaths were very generally sworn and contracts drawn up that defined (in terms that might be more or less precise and long-lasting) the constitutional framework within which the dialogue between the ruler and his subjects should operate. These oaths and contracts had a profound effect on contemporary political life.

THE ORIGINS OF REPRESENTATIVE ASSEMBLIES

From time to time in a feudal society the lord called together his vassals to ask their advice – a duty which they willingly performed. These assemblies, variously called *colloquia, concilia, conventus, curiae, placita* or *tractatus*, were of great significance despite the fluidity of their composition and function. As time went on the lord was faced with increasingly difficult political, military, financial, economic and administrative problems. In order to solve them he took new facts into account and looked for an increasingly large measure of support. He therefore took the initiative in calling larger assemblies which, although they stemmed from the feudal council, soon acquired different characteristics.

At the same period, however, the subjects were sometimes to band together in order to defend their interests or ensure peace, and therefore themselves sometimes took the decision to convene an assembly that would speak in their name. In November 1246 the nobles of Poitou assembled as a result of their own initiative. After the fall of the Hohenstaufen, when chaos was rife in Germany, peace treaties (*Landfrieden*) were concluded which envisaged the assembly of *placita provincialia*, law courts to be attended by knights and townspeople.

It was to be expected that a period of crisis or difficulty would see the birth and development of new assemblies. The death of a ruler without a male heir, or whose son was not yet of age (as so frequently occurred in the Low Countries in the thirteenth and fourteenth centuries); wars and financial and military disasters such as prevailed in France for such a long period; financial difficulties and the division of inheritances such as were experienced by all German principalities in the fourteenth century, to which the Hussite problem and all its consequences were added in the first half of the fifteenth century; a continually enfeebled State, as was the case in Hungary after the death of Louis the Great in 1382, further exacerbated by the Turkish threat in the fifteenth century: these were some of the circumstances that (most frequently as the result of the ruler's initiative, but sometimes because of the subjects' actions) favoured the growth of the new assemblies.

In each country the assemblies took root in local soil, but they shared a common atmosphere throughout the West. In the first place this was because of the influence exerted by one country on another: Aragonese and Catalonian institutions influenced the political life of Valencia, Sardinia and Sicily; Sicily in turn influenced Italy; but the political climate in Italy crossed the Alps, reaching the Danube and the Rhône; but in Piedmont, Provence and Savoy, this Italian influence came into contact with French customs which, on the other side of the kingdom, made their way well into the Low Countries, and found there the influence of German institutions. Furthermore these areas were all influenced by ecclesiastical institutions found throughout the Church in the West. Between the thirteenth and the fifteenth centuries the development of political assemblies owed much to the experience of synods and ecclesiastical councils, to the advance of concepts of conciliarism, and even more to their outcome – the Council of Constance, which had a profound effect on contemporary thinking and also constituted one of the major political events of the period. Finally, besides or through the medium of canon law, Roman law enabled all the States of the West to recognize some fundamental principles without which these assemblies could not have existed.

Already before Justinian it was an accepted principle of procedure that, in a case of wardship or one concerning the rights to a stretch of water, 'quod omnes tangit ab omnibus approbetur': that which affects everyone should be universally approved. This principle of private law was taken up by Justinian's lawyers in 531. The twelfth century saw the rebirth of

Roman law. The canon lawyers of the second half of the twelfth century were familiar with this ancient principle which was increasingly applied in Church affairs: it is undoubtedly implied in the nineteenth canon of the Third Lateran Council (1179), concerning the taxation of the clergy; it is expressly cited in the Fourth Lateran Council (1215); in the thirteenth century it had become a classic proverb in the Church, frequently cited by the clergy to remind people that they could not be taxed without their consent. From the clerical milieu it was then an entirely natural transition to the secular world: Frederick II made specific reference to it when he called the Assembly of Verona in 1244. In the second half of the thirteenth century it permeated the atmosphere everywhere. To such an extent that when Edward I's clerks said in the summons to Parliament in 1295 that that which concerned everyone should be approved by everyone, they were certainly not being the bold innovators of the Stubbsian theory of constitutional development. At all events the principle that everyone should consent to the affairs that concerned them was admitted hundreds of times in the fourteenth and fifteenth centuries from England to Hungary, from William of Ockham to Nicholas of Cusa and from Alvaro Pelayo to Gerson.

It is self-evident, of course, that in practice it is impossible to obtain consent from everyone individually. The principle of universal consent can only be applied if there is representation. Medieval theory knew two basic forms of representation. In the first, the older and more traditional, the head 'represented' the body as the father his family, the bishop his diocese or the lord his tenants without there being any election or delegation of powers. In the political life of the late Middle Ages this form of representation was still of fundamental importance. In a second sense, representation implied the election of delegates who received precisely specified powers from their constituents. This new form of representation depended entirely on the slow progress of the practice of appointing attorneys.

It is a matter for debate whether these developments were due to improvements in judicial practice; or because it was increasingly easy to be represented at law by an attorney; or to ecclesiastical practice whereby general chapters of the religious orders and provincial and diocesan synods relied with increasing frequency on regularly appointed proctors; or, indeed, to secular attempts in this direction, such as, for example, the representation of the towns in English county courts. It is perhaps most likely that the developing concept of representation owed something to the experience of all these innovations and they undoubtedly paved the way for assemblies of chosen representatives.

At first the suspicious electorate gave their representatives only the very restricted power of *ouïr et rapporter* ('listening and reporting back'). But a mandate of this kind, which prevented an assembly from taking decisions that concerned the welfare of the constituents as a whole, obviously removed from it all practical usefulness, above all in the eyes of governments. The development of representative assemblies therefore depended on the development of appointing attorneys with full power to act (*plena potestas*) which, having its origins in the twelfth-century tribunals, was adapted to ecclesiastical institutions at the beginning of the thirteenth century, appeared in a secular context about 1250 and was common practice in 1300. By then all the theoretical obstacles to the development of representative assemblies had been removed.

But the development of these representative assemblies did not of course wait until the end of the thirteenth century. By this date they had already gradually started to increase in importance by different stages, not all of which were to be found in every case, nor in the same sequence nor at the same time. In general, however, one can safely say that only clerics and knights were present at feudal courts. The first innovation was the additional summons of townsmen by a ruler. These were at first present only in a personal and advisory capacity. Then they were elected by their peers and sat as representatives of their town. In the same way the clergy sent chosen representatives to assemblies who sat beside the prelates. Similarly, there were sometimes representatives of the nobles, who could not all claim to have received an individual summons. These developments first started in southern France. In 1168 or 1169 Count Guillaume II of Forcalquier held a plenary court to which he had summoned townsmen as well as prelates and nobles. In 1188 an assembly 'with citizens elected by each city' was held in the Spanish kingdom of Leon. In the Papal States, at the beginning of the thirteenth century, Innocent III summoned representatives of the communes to many assemblies. Similarly, it was in Castile in 1250 that representatives of the clergy first appeared in an assembly of a State in the West. Representatives of knights of the shire were first summoned in England in 1213, representatives of the townsmen in 1265, representatives of the clergy soon after 1297. In France, St Louis had called citizens to his court but only with a personal and advisory role. It was only at the beginning of the fourteenth century that the French king made a series of attempts to establish the representation of his principal towns (*bonnes villes*). Throughout the later Middle Ages, the French Estates General were composed of clergy and nobles present in an individual capacity, besides the representatives of a limited number of towns who, moreover, because they had not been granted full powers, were unable to participate. By contrast, the assembly of 1484 was truly national. Representatives of the clergy, the nobility and the third estate elected in each *bailliage* took their seats as equals. Finally, in the Empire this development occurred at an even later date: representatives of the towns appeared in Tyrol in 1362, in Austria at the end of the fourteenth century, and after 1400 in the majority of ecclesiastical principalities.

For a long while people used only the traditional terms *curiae, concilia* or *colloquia* for these increasingly large and representative assemblies. At the most they would sometimes specify a general court or assembly with words such as *curia generalis* (Agenais, 1182; Catalonia, 1283) or *congregatio generalis* (Hungary, late thirteenth century). In the twelfth century the Old French word *parlement* had only the very generalized sense of conversation, discussion, interview, conference or assembly. It was therefore the normal translation of *colloquium*. At the same time it gave rise to a new Latin word: *parlamentum* or *parliamentum*, which appeared at the end of the eleventh century with the same meaning. When Frederick I held a diet at Roncaglia in 1154, the chronicler Otto Morena spoke of a *parlamentum*. This remained an isolated example. It was only in 1236 in England and 1239 in France that *parlamentum* began to be used with the meaning which it has retained ever since. The word tended to be used in France from the outset to describe the session of a court in judgement. In England it was increasingly applied to the enlarged session of the court which sat with growing frequency in the reign of Henry III. There were references here and there in official documents, then in chronicles, until it came into general use to the advantage of the barons' cause in 1258–65. Even then it continued to be used alongside other more traditional words, and contemporaries did not register it as the hallmark of a new political reality. These things took shape and acquired permanency very gradually in the course of the fourteenth century and it was then that the word *parlamentum* (which had for a long while referred only to an occasional session) came to be used for an institution. Well before this, the word *parlamentum* had been accepted in numerous countries on the Continent: its first documented appearance in the Agenais was in 1271, in Hungary at the end of the thirteenth century, in Sweden at the beginning of the fourteenth century, in Hainault in 1314, and in Friuli in 1346.

In the first assemblies prelates, nobles and townspeople represented different communities but sat and deliberated together. In some countries, however, each estate soon began to hold separate sessions and the decision of all its assembled members counted only as one voice: the representative assembly had become an assembly of estates. The expression 'Three Estates' had appeared in Burgundy at the end of the thirteenth century to designate this new institution. The term became common in France in the first half of the fourteenth century, just when the sovereign court of justice was taking definitive shape with the name of Parlement. From France the term passed at the beginning of the fifteenth century to the Low Countries (Liège, 1420) and to Italy (Friuli, Savoy; Piedmont *c.*1430): this development was not related to institutional structure, since the term 'Three Estates' was eventually used for assemblies which were not organized in estates. French influence had also diffused the general term 'Estate' throughout almost the entire Continent, as well as the exact term, 'Three Estates'. There is no scope here for discussion of more specialized semantic developments such as the readoption of the old word *Diet* in Hungary in 1453, or *Landtag* or *Reichstag*, which were common German usage in the second half of the fifteenth century.

What general expression can the modern historian use for these assemblies which developed from the feudal courts but which were quite distinct from them? Some have used 'assemblies of estates', but not every assembly was organized in estates. Others would favour *Parlements*: this word, which is ideal for the English situation, has the disadvantage of fostering all sorts of confusion both with contemporary courts of justice and with our modern parliamentary assemblies, which are entirely different. Finally, another school of thought would prefer to adopt the term 'representative assemblies', and if by this one does not imply that all their members were elected representatives (which was not the case), but means simply that whatever their composition all these assemblies claimed to represent the country as a whole, then the term 'representative assemblies' certainly raises fewest problems. At all events these representative assemblies – whose origins are to be found well before 1300 – exerted a very considerable influence on the political life of all the States of the West in the later Middle Ages.

THE INFLUENCE OF REPRESENTATIVE ASSEMBLIES

The rulers, however, expected no more of the assemblies than that they would be united in support of the ruler's propaganda: the main importance of the assembly summoned by Frederick II in 1240 was that it enabled his subjects to contemplate the king's majesty and serenity and listen to his utterances; in 1484 the chancellor of the French king declared that the meeting of the estates gave the representatives the great privilege of seeing the king. This explains the eagerness to hold such assemblies at the beginning of a new reign. Seen from this perspective the assemblies still only had a passive role while rulers might make use of their assembly to announce their intentions and promulgate their laws. The importance of the assembly was already increasing when the prince asked for its opinion, in the best feudal tradition. The French Capetian and Valois kings, from St Louis to Louis XI, frequently summoned such consultative assemblies, and the rulers derived some advantage from this situation.

Take the case of Frederick II of Sicily: the Constitution of Messina (1234) envisaged solemn courts where two or four repreentatives from the most important towns would take their seats besides the prelates and nobles, and where complaints against royal officers would be presented to the king. Or take England under Henry III or Edward I: numerous historians have insisted on the judicial function of parliamentary sessions which made rulings on civil and criminal lawsuits either in the first instance or on appeal and, above all, communicated to the king the petitions of his subjects; as the writer of the legal treatise known as *Fleta* (*c*.1290) put it: 'Habet enim rex curiam suam in consilio in parlamentis suis' ('The king holds his court in his council in his parliaments in the presence of earls, barons and other great and experienced men; lawsuits are drawn to a close there and fresh remedies found for new misdemeanours as they appear; and justice is done to each man according to his deserts'). But the assemblies foreseen in the Constitution of Messina were undoubtedly never held and a number of historians have refused to accept the view of thirteenth-century English parliaments as exclusively judicial assemblies. Fourteenth- and fifteenth-century assemblies were all undoubtedly occasions to present grievances to the prince. But they did not assemble in the first instance to receive individual or collective complaints.

When Frederick II summoned the representatives of the Sicilian towns and castles to Foggia in 1232, it was to discuss the *utilitas regni* ('well-being of the kingdom') and the common good. When English burgesses were invited to join the Council in 1258, it was 'to consider the state of the kingdom and to discuss the common needs of the king and the kingdom'. When Pedro III of Aragon held a general court at Barcelona in 1283, it was in order to discuss the good estate and reformation of the kingdom ('del bon stament e reformatio de la terra', 'de bene statu et reformatione terre'). At the end of the Middle Ages representative assemblies were often political bodies that attempted to understand things in their full complexity.

Indeed such assemblies often met in response to specific problems – military ones above all. In a society that was essentially organized for war, where for centuries when lords had assembled their vassals and liegemen their prime intention had been to raise an army, it is not surprising that for a long while representative assemblies are to be found in a military context. About 1300 the kings of England and France viewed many of the assemblies they convened as veritable councils of war; in order to decide, at this still experimental stage, whom they should summon to these assemblies, the royal administrators often made use of lists of towns and vassals which had originally been drawn up for military purposes. Later, with the escalation of the war between England and France, military problems were amongst the most important *negotia regni* ('affairs of the kingdom') that the English Parliament had to consider in the reign of Edward III. One of the main reasons for the development of the French provincial assemblies in the second half of the fourteenth century was the need to organize the country's defence.

But in peacetime, as in war, assemblies were above all held because both the ruler and his subjects faced serious monetary problems. It seems to have been these considerations which first made such a dialogue an absolute necessity. In a feudal society the coinage was in theory the ruler's affair: he minted coins with a view to making a profit from the process. But during the thirteenth century there was a general realization that the quality of daily life in the community was dependent on the state of the coinage. This was such a dominant theme in contemporary thought that one of the first concerns of the new assemblies was to forbid rulers to revalue the coinage; in return for this concession, since the ruler had forfeited an important source of revenue, they granted him taxes, and the Aragonese *monedaje*, dating from the beginning of the thirteenth century, and the Agenais *monetagium* of 1232 were some of the earliest voted by representative assemblies.

Between 1282 and 1284 Duke Robert II of Burgundy made an even greater concession when he relinquished in perpetuity his right to devalue in exchange for the grant of a tenth from his clergy and nobility for two years only. Soon, however, it was generally realized that the ideal was not *never* to devalue, but only to devalue when it was in the interest of the community to do so. Consequently the subjects' ambition was no longer to impose a stable coinage on the prince, but to persuade him not to revalue without their consent. In 1311 Edward II agreed to seek the consent of his magnates; in 1352 Edward III promised to do nothing without the agreement of the Commons; in 1355 John the Good of France made a similar agreement dependent on the consent of the Estates; likewise in 1356 Jeanne and Wenceslas of Brabant gave an undertaking not to revalue 'without the assent of the entire country'. When Philip the Good of Burgundy effected the monetary union of all his lands in 1433, he was henceforth obliged to negotiate every currency adjustment with an assembly that represented all his lands. The monetary question was thus the origin of the Burgundian Estates General: this was the sole reason for nine assemblies between 1437 and 1461.

Nevertheless, with a few exceptions, the monetary question became of secondary importance at the end of the thirteenth century. At that time, when kings went to the trouble of summoning assemblies, it was to explain to them the 'needs of the kingdom', that is, the king's obligation to make war and request from them, in that context, the counsel and above all the financial aid traditionally provided. Philip the Fair tried vainly to win acceptance for the principle that in an emergency taxes might be levied before the subjects had given their consent. In 1321 Philip V also tried in vain to gain acceptance for the grant of a subsidy – even in peacetime – to carry out reforms. Edward III attempted to obtain the necessary subjects' consent outside Parliament – and this, too, was unsuccessful. In the mid-fourteenth century rulers had to resign themselves to the fact that they could only impose direct taxation when there was an urgent need and with the consent of the country's representatives in parliaments or Estates.

It was the same story, at least in England, with indirect taxation. England was a gross exporter of wool and the king expected considerable revenues from the taxes levied on the exported product. Consent was nevertheless still necessary. The tax of 1275 known as the *Magna et Antiqua Costuma* was established with the agreement of the *marchaunz de tot Engleterre* ('merchants throughout England'); that of 1303 (the *Parva et Nova Costuma*) with the agreement of Italian merchants; and seven times between 1303 and 1335 the Estate of Merchants consented to a new tax. This seemed a logical step, to require consent from those who would have to pay the tax. But the producers quickly realized that although merchants kept for themselves the benefits that they obtained in exchange for consenting to the tax, they would pass on the cost of these taxes to their suppliers. They therefore declared that each new practice should be accepted by the whole community of the realm. This point of view triumphed in 1362 when Edward III promised that no new tax would be levied on wool or hides without parliamentary consent.

The assemblies were soon not content merely to assent to taxation. The English Parliament of 1340 wanted to know how it was levied: it appointed commissioners to oversee the collectors' accounts. In 1348 the Estates in Normandy took the precaution of having the taxes to which they had consented levied by selected individuals in whom they could trust – those, in other words, whom they had appointed. Similarly the *élus* elected by the Estates General of 1355 assessed and levied throughout France the subsidy to which they had given their consent. In the same way, in 1356 the Estates of Provence began to play an important role in the distribution and collection of taxes.

In both England and France the mid-fourteenth century seems to have been a crucial period in the history of representative assemblies. It was at this point that they were successful in obtaining royal recognition of their prerogatives in financial matters. The success of the English Parliament in this respect was to prove long-lasting. In France, on the other hand, either as a result of royal or of provincial suspicion, the national Estates – that is, the Estates General – never succeeded in gaining recognition as the mouthpiece of the country as a whole. Where the financial role of the Estates continued, it was within a provincial framework. The Estates of

Poitou met for the first time in 1372, the three orders of the Vivarais in 1381, the Estates of Béarn in 1391, and these bodies owed their importance to the fact that they were able to give financial undertakings in the name of their region. At the same time the financial difficulties of the imperial princes favoured the development of the *Landtage* within the Empire: foreign and civil wars were a further constant drain on their resources; they sold off their domain; as a market surplus caused their revenues from mining rights to fall, direct taxation was their last resort. They were thus forced to summon the Estates and ask for their consent.

The princes listened to the grievances presented to them before the granting of subsidies. The financial importance which the assemblies had managed to acquire was thus the best guarantee of their legislative function. It was because the kings of the Spanish peninsula, since the first half of the fourteenth century, had no longer been able to levy taxes without the agreement of the *Cortes* that the latter played a crucial part in the elaboration of the *constitutiones* of Catalonia, the *fueros* of Aragon and the *furs* of Valencia. It was because the English king was financially dependent on Parliament that it gradually lost its judicial role and increased its legislative activity. In effect Parliament only received individual petitions at the end of the thirteenth century. Then collective petitions appeared which, if it thought fit, Parliament communicated to the king. In 1327 one of these petitions gave rise to a statue accepted by the king in Parliament for the first time. After this the Commons' petitions and statutes increased rapidly. Parliament had less and less time to receive individual petitions and make judgements upon them. By the 1360s litigants had abandoned Parliament. As for the king, he did not relinquish his legislative powers with good grace. For a while, once the desired subsidies had been granted and Parliament dissolved, he attempted to annul statutes by the simple expedient of an ordinance issued by his Council. But in 1341 he was forced to agree that statutes might only be annulled by another statute. At least in theory, the legislative role of the English Parliament was uncontested. In France there was never any equivalent of statutes, only ordinances. This did not mean that the Estates never played any part in their composition. In fact, all the great reforming ordinances followed an assembly of the Estates, the king's demand for a large subsidy and the presentation by the Estates of a long list of grievances. The Estates of 1439, for example, voted the king a *taille* of 100,000 *livres* and played an active part in working out the details of what became the ordinance of 2 November 1439, which was intended to re-establish discipline in the companies of men-at-arms. Some provincial Estates had scarcely less important roles: in occupied Normandy the duke of Bedford, Regent of France, relied in the best English tradition upon the Estates to legislate; similarly the Estates of Provence were accustomed to initiating legislation after 1437, when King René needed large sums for the payment of his ransom; in the mid-fifteenth century the Bretons were well aware that although the right to legislate ultimately rested with the duke, the Estates of Brittany played a very important role in the preparation of such legislation.

And so, in many countries of the West, representative assemblies, which came into being in the thirteenth century to resolve various judicial, military or monetary problems (in which they then continued to take an interest), insisted that rulers of the fourteenth century should levy no subsidy without their consent. They made use of this necessity for consent to ensure recognition of their legislative role.

The efficacy of representative assemblies cannot be judged simply by their numerous functions. Some knowledge of the circumstances in which decisions were made is also necessary. The ancient principle of unanimity for each decision was still generally accepted. Especially where voting was done by orders (as in the French Estates General, in Brabant and in Holland), unanimous consent was required from the orders on every issue. But contemporaries were perfectly well aware that the need for unanimity risked paralysing the assembly. So the principle of unanimity continued to exist but in practice a unanimity prevailed that was either confused or deliberately engineered. In the House of Commons in the middle of the fifteenth century it was still the practice to vote on bills with cries of 'aye' and 'noe', with the noisier party carrying the day by drowning the voices of their opponents; in Switzerland waverers were forced to vote ('Händ uf, liebi Landslüt'), their arms twisted if necessary; in Germany it was even legally incumbent upon the minority to regroup around the majority (*Folgepflicht*).

However, Roman law and, following it, canon law, offered another solution with the principle of the rule of the majority. From the twelfth century the Church had acceded to the notion of the *major et sanior pars* ('greater and wiser part'). The secular world had sometimes followed suit. In fact the flexible and confused concept of *major et sanior pars* was the cause of as many problems in the State as in the Church. As a result, total reliance upon numerical supremacy became fatally widespread. From 1215, the Fourth Lateran Council laid down the principle of a pure and simple numerical majority; from the middle of the thirteenth century some Orders, such as the Dominicans or Templars, elected their masters with an absolute numerical majority; finally Boniface VIII confirmed the rigorous principle that 'Non zeli ad zelum, nec meriti ad meritum, sed solum numeri ad numerum fiat collatio' ('a total should not be made by the addition of zeal or merit, but only by adding one number to another'). Following these examples secular assemblies began to count their votes. In order to avoid the difficulties they had hitherto experienced, the Diet of

Rhens (1338) decided that the election of the king of the Romans should be made *concorditer vel a majori parte* ('either unanimously or by majority vote'). The Golden Bull of 1356 gave positive confirmation of this principle. At the beginning of the fifteenth century, the House of Commons sometimes elected its speaker by a majority of only two or three. In France, Brabant and Holland unanimity between the orders might be required but decisions were made within each order by majority vote. In Germany, in the second half of the fifteenth century, the princes themselves encouraged the *Landtage* to take decisions on a majority vote which they might then impose on the dissenters. In this way the principle of the majority made gradual progress. Nevertheless, many continued to adhere to the concept of unanimity and criticized the majority principle for removing the rights of the minority and fostering the tyranny of the ruler. In Poland the weakness of the crown in the early sixteenth century was sufficient for the official practice of the principle of the majority to be stopped for good, in the face of the need for unanimity which – as in many other Western countries in the fourteenth and fifteenth centuries – had remained the rule.

The efficacy of a representative assembly also depended upon the length and frequency of its sessions. Now, although some sessions of the Estates General were exceptionally long, the majority of the Estates on the Continent sat only for a few days: a session of the Estates of Hainault, for example, lasted between one and five days; a session of the Poitevin Estates often took only a day, never longer than five. As for England, the average length of Parliament in the reign of Edward III was only three weeks.

Contemporaries were aware that this brevity had to be counterbalanced by the regularity and frequency with which sessions were held. The subjects of Pedro III of Aragon demanded that from 1283 onwards he should summon the Cortes annually at Saragossa; in 1327 the representatives of the city of London wanted Parliament to be summoned annually; at Paris in 1356–8 the leaders of the opposition (headed by Etienne Marcel) realized that the real power of the Estates General depended primarily on the frequency with which it was convened. But the French Estates General was always summoned very erratically by the king; although from the beginning of the fourteenth century regular sessions of the Cortes were accepted practice in Aragon and Catalonia, they only took place once every three years; although parliaments occurred almost annually in fourteenth-century England, nevertheless years when the king did not think it worth summoning one were far from rare. Finally, in the first half of the fifteenth century, there were almost annual sessions of representative assemblies in many countries, but these still took place at irregular intervals. It was only towards the middle of the fifteenth century that the concept of a regular annual session took root – in Hungary and Languedoc in 1445, in Normandy in 1458. The first meeting of representatives of the towns and the first vote of a subsidy are both important dates in the history of representative assemblies. Nevertheless, historians believe the crucial point occurred when assemblies began to be summoned on a fairly frequent basis for it was only then that they might participate in political affairs with any degree of continuity and were able to adopt a constitutional role.

This relative continuity was still related to the composition of successive assemblies. This partly explains the power of the English Parliament. In fact virtually the same magnates were always summoned to the Lords while, as for the Commons, although it is certainly true that the majority of the representatives of the shires and the towns only attended one session, from the beginning of the fourteenth century a good number of knights and burgesses sat in several parliaments in the course of their career, or indeed several consecutive parliaments. Moreover, this tendency became more marked in the course of the fourteenth century: under Edward I and II sixty knights sat in three consecutive parliaments, fourteen in four, five in five, one in six and one in seven; under Edward III 124 knights attended three consecutive sessions, forty-two were at four sessions, nineteen at five, nine at six and four at seven. The Commons were thus led by an increasingly influential kernel of experienced men of proven worth, who ensured institutional continuity. An essential step forward was made in 1376 when the Commons first adopted the custom of electing a speaker at the beginning of each session (referred to then as 'parlour pur les Communes'; 'commune parlour' between 1397 and 1410; 'prelocutor Communitatis in parliamento' in 1406; 'prelocutor', 'speaker for the Communes' in 1414 and 'speker' in 1445). The speaker, chosen for his experience, eloquence and courage, was for a long while to be an inconvenient partner for lords and kings.

The latter could at least rest easy in the intervals between parliamentary sessions. It was only in a very few States in the whole of the West that, in their concern for better control of the government, the assemblies succeeded in extending their sessions into a permanent commission and forcing continuous dialogue upon the ruler. A Council emerged from the Parliament in Friuli in the second half of the thirteenth century and in the fourteenth century this was simultaneously an instrument of both Parliament and government. In the realm of Aragon permanent commissions developed in the fourteenth century whose task was to supervise the collection of taxes voted by the Cortes; they were organized formally at the beginning of the fifteenth century; in 1413 for the Generalitat of Catalonia, in 1418 for that of Valencia. They played a vital political role in the fifteenth century. In the State of the Wettin in 1438, the economic situation was so grave that in order to obtain any money at all, the margraves of Brandenburg had to abandon financial control to the Estates: this involved the creation of an eight-member commission of *Zisemeister* who worked in constant collaboration with the margrave's Council.

So there were assemblies and assemblies: in some countries their sessions were so brief, rare and irregular that their role was never anything other than episodic; elsewhere more frequent and regular sessions turned them into real institutions; and sometimes they even gave birth to commissions that forced the prince into continual dialogue. Nevertheless political life with these assemblies was still very different from that of our modern parliamentary governments: the ruler's administrators, for example, were never responsible to them. Such as they were, however, they were almost everywhere sufficiently powerful to constitute a force with which the ruler had to reckon. One of the essential characteristics of the States of the West in the fourteenth and fifteenth centuries was the establishment of a dialogue between the ruler and his lands by means of assemblies that represented the entire country.

THE DECLINE OF REPRESENTATIVE ASSEMBLIES

Towards the middle of the fifteenth century the influence of representative assemblies began to decline. In some places they disappeared completely. Most frequently they survived, but with the loss of their most important characteristics. Instead of remaining the unbiddable partner capable of influencing rulers for over a century they now became little more than his adjutant. In France the Estates General of 1439 still voted taxes and played a not inconsiderable legislative role; but this was the last time they did so, after this date both Charles VII and Louis XI levied the *taille* without summoning them. When they did summon the Estates, they were generally sparse assemblies, content merely to have been consulted by the king. The Estates of 1484 were thus a quite exceptional event that did not create a precedent. As for the provincial assemblies, the Estates of Languedoc are typical: they continued to be convened regularly; they remained and institution; but no longer discussed the level of taxation; their main concern henceforth was to protect regional economic interests, to build and maintain roads, bridges and ports, and to control the export of wine and grain according to the size of the harvest. When opportunity offered they ratified treaties concluded by the king. One clause in the Treaties of Arras (1482), Etaples (1492) and Cambrai (1529) provided for their ratification by the three estates of the kingdom. The king effectively required assent from the provincial Estates, the assemblies of *bailliages* and towns – and a refusal would certainly have come as a surprise to him.

In the Empire, in the second half of the fifteenth century, the *Landtage*, which had been so powerful a short while before, tended almost everywhere to become simply tools in the hands of the territorial princes; now it was the princes themselves who, to ensure that taxes were levied without opposition, insisted that the Estates should assemble because they could represent and make pledges on behalf of the entire country: in 1472 Albert-Achilles of Brandenburg succeeded in summoning the common Estates of the whole country for the first time; in 1505 the Estates of all Bavaria first sat together. Even in England, where parliamentary traditions were so strong, the Parliament which Henry IV so greatly feared had largely lost its bite. The creation of numbers of peers assured the king of the docility of the upper house where, moreover, the Lords rarely troubled to take their seats; as for the Commons, peopled with royal officers and the retainers of magnates, it had quite lost its independence. From 1435 at the latest the Speaker was an officer paid and appointed by the crown and Parliament was now such an insignificant cog in English political life that it was not even summoned between 1456 and 1459, 1478 and 1483, and is hardly mentioned by Fortescue in his writings on English government.

What were the reasons for this general decline? Holding assemblies was expensive for his subjects and could be risky for the ruler. For them to take place it was essential that both parties thought that it was a worthwhile exercise or that they could not manage without it. Towards the middle of the fifteenth century, however, the ruler's financial position gradually became more secure: in Germany, for example, once certain technical difficulties had been overcome, mining revenues yielded a better return than ever; indirect taxes granted at an earlier date – like that on beer in the State of the Wettin – were almost sufficient to cover the State's expenses; in France direct taxation, which had been under discussion for so long, was now paid with increasing reluctance after a century of war. There was therefore less pressure on rulers to go and ask for the Estates' agreement or to accord them any importance.

Besides, countries were still too geographically diverse and the character of each province too distinct for any assembly to be truly representative. That above all was the case in France, where many provincials had always had reservations about seeing their representatives sucked into the great whirlpool of the Estates General, had always been reluctant to give them full powers and disliked being pledged to decisions made such a long way away; any agreement extracted from the Estates General was therefore only of theoretical worth if the king had to negotiate with each province, and it meant expending a great deal of time and money on a mere debate: king and subjects soon agreed to bypass the process.

For representative assemblies to be powerful, the orders of the country had above all to share common interests and opinions. The great weakness of the Estates General was undoubtedly that once the clergy and the nobility were free from taxation they took no further interest in the matter. It was the same in the Iberian peninsula, once the two first orders were able to avoid the payment of taxes and its burden fell solely upon the towns, once the king was able to play the orders off against each other and could be content with summoning an ever-decreasing number of towns, the decline of the Cortes was assured. In early sixteenth-century Sicily, parliament began to lose its drive when increasingly powerful rulers found themselves dealing with orders who had quite lost sight of the common good and were concerned only with a peevish defence of their own privileges.

Even where the country was a solid geographical and social unit, the Estates withered once the prince and his subjects chose the more discreet and effective means of direct negotiation in preference to assemblies which, despite their outward show, were cumbersome, expensive and frequently unproductive. If there is a distinction between 'absolute' and 'limited' monarchy in the fourteenth and fifteenth centuries, it must lie in the fact that some rulers found their subjects less difficult partners, and also that dialogue between them was henceforth conducted through other channels.

12

The Country:
Legal Theory and Reality

The assemblies that maintained a lively dialogue with the rulers of the West claimed to represent the community of the entire country. But that did not mean that all the inhabitants were equally represented. Very rarely did it happen that townspeople or peasants of limited means sent representatives who made their voices heard or sustained their interests. Much more frequently the ordinary people of town and country were only present in a fictitious and passive capacity, through no choice of their own; they did not lack spokesmen insofar as the lords were supposed to represent their liegemen, the bishops their faithful, the towns the dependent countryside and the rich burgesses their towns, but it goes without saying that these rich men, prelates and nobles did not take the lot of poorer men very much to heart. The legal composition of the representative assemblies reveals the extent to which these were aristocratic societies and how numerous were those excluded from the political life of the States of the West. Those who enjoyed the privilege of participation in political life did not all have the same influence. The nobility was preponderant virtually everywhere.

The preponderance of the nobility

The political and economic difficulties of the later Middle Ages have frequently been emphasized. One of the traditional themes of French historiography is that of an alliance between crown and bourgeoisie to weaken both the Church and a feudal aristocracy. More recently, writers have attempted to demonstrate how a particular combination of economic circumstances – rising prices, an agrarian crisis and rural depopulation – resulted in depressed revenues for the nobility and provoked a general crisis amongst them whose clearest symptoms were noble banditry and seigneurial reaction. There is no need to overemphasize these difficulties. Many studies will certainly be necessary before one can fully grasp the fate of the nobles and their families; no one can now deny that the nobility of this period had their fair share of worries; and it is self-evident that their position varied across the West from Spain to Poland. For all that, it is none the less true that the nobility sustained or increased their predominance throughout almost the entire West between 1300 and 1500.

The nobility remained above all masters of the land. In fifteenth-century England fifty magnates owned 10 per cent of the land. Another 10 per cent was in the hands of 183 knights of more modest means. In Castile noble ownership of land continued to grow at the expense of the king and the Church. In Germany the impecunious princes either mortgaged their inheritances, sold to their nobles, or enfeoffed them with castles, towns and villages. With landed wealth went economic power: the nobles of Eastern Europe controlled the grain trade, and, by means of the association of stockmen known as the *Mesta*, those of Castile controlled the sheep-rearing to which two-thirds of the area of the country was devoted. Landed wealth went hand in hand with lucrative judicial and administrative power which the rulers in the more westerly countries undoubtedly succeeded in undermining, but which towards the eastern frontiers continued to be built up at their expense. The nobility involved themselves in politics to increase their wealth and power and also to increase their revenues which perennially fell short of their needs. Whether they chose to serve their ruler or play their part in an assembly they had sufficient influence to make their presence felt in either case.

It was in fact the nobility who most frequently dominated the representative assemblies. In fifteenth-century Béarn the nobility and the clergy constituted the *Grand Corps*, which was superior to the *Second Corps*, composed of all the non-noble representatives. In Velay eighteen nobles of high descent sat in the same assembly as ten members of the clergy and the consuls only from the town of Le Puy. The Estates in Dauphiné comprised 270 members of the nobility, thirty-six clergy and 115 representatives of the Third Estate. Whether they relied on the greater influence of an upper chamber or on sheer force of numbers and status, the predominance of the nobility was guaranteed.

This preponderance was still more clearly marked when the prelates who represented the clergy were of noble extraction and shared their point of view. The evidence from England and France, so far as it has been studied, does not appear to suggest that this was particularly the case there. Of the eighty-five bishops of Edward III's reign only fifteen came from aristocratic families; the 'bishops of King Louis [XI]' were, in the eyes of Frenchmen, zealous servants of the crown rather than nobles. But things were very different in the Empire. The example of the Weisseneck family from Carinthia (south Germany), where in the mid-fifteenth century three brothers were archbishop of Salzburg, bishop of Passau and bishop of Seckau, demonstrates the extent to which the order of clergy was affiliated to the nobility in the Estates.

In the eastern lands of the German Empire the nobility were not merely predominant, but became exclusive representatives. In the fifteenth century both the Hungarian and Polish nobility ended by keeping their kings on a very tight rein, as they were themselves the only beneficiaries of any real freedom and the only representatives of the State: this trend was so marked that in 1444 the ambassadors of the German towns began to use the Hungarian *orszag* (which means 'country', *regnum*) to refer to the Hungarian nobility, and in Poland in the second half of the fifteenth century the two expressions *communitas nobilium* and *corpus regni* became synonymous, while the Polish *panstwo* ('State'), which appeared in the sixteenth century and remains current today, partly stems from Polish words for the nobility (*pan* = noble; *pany* = the higher nobility).

Whilst the nobility were securing their power and influence its composition altered and there were changes in the balance of power within the class itself. In the fourteenth century most countries were dominated by a few dozen noble families. This was still sometimes the case in the fifteenth century: in about 1450, for example, Castilian politics were still largely controlled by fifteen or so families. But more frequently there was positive democratization in the ranks of the nobility which sometimes resulted in the foundation of noble republics. In Hungary at the beginning of the fifteenth century it was still only the magnates who assembled to grant the king the necessary taxes. Little by little the other nobles exerted their influence. In 1453 there was a formal admission that no tax might be levied without their consent, given at a Diet. From then on, for two or three weeks every year, while the great nobles met in the castle of Buda in embryonic sessions of the future upper chamber, the great mass of the nobility who 'were' the people pitched their tents on the opposite bank of the Danube in a vast prairie called *Rakos* and held their tumultuous and colourful assemblies, or Diets.

All the nobility were by now convinced of the principle that Werböczi was to set out at the beginning of the sixteenth century, that there was but one and the same liberty for all the nobility: *una eademque libertas nobilium*. There was a similar development in Poland. In the fourteenth century the magnates alone had been influential and powerful. But during the period when they succeeded in excluding towns and peasants from the country's legal processes, they had been forced to share their privilege with the middle and the petty nobility. In 1453, for the first time, the nobles delegated by districts had sufficient sense of identity to meet separately and this custom continued until the end of the fifteenth century. From then on it was understood that Polish politics were dominated by the general Diet, where, besides the magnates sitting in the upper chamber, those who represented the entire nobility in the chamber of deputies also played their part.

England experienced an analogous development in slightly different guise. While political life had long been dominated by the fifty or so magnates entitled to sit in the upper house, the influence of the country gentry was increasingly evident in the course of the fifteenth century: they had always represented the shires in the House of Commons; a growing number now began to represent the towns as well; and when, from the mid-fourteenth century, kings adopted the practice of elevating important knights to the peerage, they began to invade the upper house itself.

Whatever its precise form – here nobility, there aristocracy; here magnates, there the whole spectrum of the noble class; here in the prince's service, there a very real presence at assemblies – virtually everywhere a privileged minority secure in its lands and military strength had the economic and political means to impose its views. That did not of course prevent the nobility from sometimes being an excellent servant of the state. According to R. Cazelles the nobility, far from being the scapegoat of the Parisian rising of 1356–8, was the dynamic force behind it. In fourteenth-century France the lengthy process of reform and political progress was that 'of a nobility fired with enthusiasm for the public good'. However, it is certainly easier to credit later medieval nobilities in the West with purely egoistical concerns and to assume that it was enough for them to avoid their share of public expenses, to escape taxation, or that they intended to use all the resources of the State which they dominated to slake their thirst for power and lands. Hence the aggrandisement and alliances characteristic of the fourteenth and fifteenth centuries. To a large extent the Aragonese nobility was responsible for the conquests of the thirteenth century upon which the king of Aragon embarked in the Mediterranean and it was also their principal beneficiary. The Polish nobility supported the Polno-Lithuanian Union of 1385 because they stood to gain from it. The Union of Kalmar (1389) accorded with the wishes of the Danish nobility, who could now establish a hold in Norway, and surely it is reasonable to suggest that the king of England was pushed by his nobles into his continental adventures? There is no question of underestimating mercantile interest in fourteenth- and fifteenth-century Europe, but it operated in a political world where the nobility most frequently succeeded in imposing their point of view.

Townsmen and peasants

Most frequently – but not always. Although the towns entered into the great majority of representative assemblies in the West by the back door, the reader will hardly need to be reminded of the Italian city-states which were dominated by merchants, or that the three towns of Ghent, Bruges and Ypres were the three first *membres* of the Estates of Flanders.

Although noble domination became increasingly exclusive in Eastern Europe, in the North it had to come to terms with new forces. In the fifteenth century the Swedish aristocracy had come to accept, little by little, that the power that they had kept to themselves throughout the fourteenth century would have to be shared with the merchants of Stockholm and with the owners of silver and copper mines who were in a position to lead the peasant population in order to make their views felt.

The peasantry were in fact generally no more than tools in the hands of one privileged class or another in times of conflict. However, there were two exceptions, in regions where nature was most inhospitable – the Alps and the hinterland bordering the North Sea near the Zuiderzee. Frisian politics were dominated by a peasant patriciate. In Guelders the treaty of 1402 marked the birth of a dualist constitution in which the bishop dealt with Estates reduced to a single order of freeholding tenants. In the Alps, the union on an equal footing of rival cantons and towns such as Zürich or Bern was what gave the Confederation its originality and its secure foundation. In some of the countries bordering Switzerland peasants were able (admittedly somewhat late in the day) to gain access to the country's legislative process by forming a fourth Estate and securing direct representation in assemblies. This was already the case in the Tyrol before 1500. It happened in the sixteenth century in the Vorarlberg and in Bresgau, where delegates of peasants from the Black Forest appeared at the *Landtag*.

These revealing exceptions prove the rule. Participation in the political life of the States of the West in the fourteenth and fifteenth centuries was confined almost exclusively to privileged classes and as a general rule the great body of townsmen and country dwellers had no place in it. For this great mass of people excluded from their country's legislative process violence was the only remaining option.

THE REVOLTS OF THE EXCLUDED

Chronic disorder and violence were part of everyday life in the later Middle Ages. On the fringes of society there was a whole world of vagabonds, brigands and those who lived beyond the law and beyond governmental control. For their part, workers in town and country were easily roused and quick to act; here, there and everywhere were riots, men were attacked or houses burnt. But on this familiar ground uprisings would flare up and revolt spread in waves with a power and intensity which terrified even their contemporaries.

In 1323 Flanders was riven by disturbances that lasted five years. A few years later the towns of southern France rebelled – Toulouse in 1322 and Cahors in 1336. Calm reigned after these local storms, but it was soon shattered by a crisis that affected both Italy and France: Cola di Rienzo was master of Rome in 1347; there were uprisings in Sienna in 1355; Lavaur and Toulouse in 1357; Parisian unrest reached its peak in 1358 a few weeks before the peasant revolt of the Jacquerie ravaged the Ile-de-France. This first crisis was nothing compared with that which affected the whole of Southern and Western Europe in 1378–82: in Florence in 1378 the *Ciompi*, unskilled paid workers without any rights, rebelled and established a regime that lasted until 1382; also in 1378 there was a revolt in Le Puy; in 1379 the unrest spread to Montpellier, Nîmes, Clermont de Lodève, Alès and Aubenas; at the same time there was manifest disaffection in the Catalan countryside and rural Languedoc was menaced by bands of 'Tuchins', unfortunates for whom brigandage was the last resort.

In 1381 the Peasants' Revolt shook the whole of southern and eastern England (above all Kent and Essex); in 1382 there was the 'Hérelle' at Rouen and, a few days later, the riot of the Maillotins in Paris. This great crisis of unrest was followed by thirty years of calm, interrupted in 1413 by renewed peasant violence in Catalonia, yet another Parisian revolt (that of the Cabochiens), and by a new wave of disturbances in the towns of southern France. There was no period of complete calm in Western Europe after this date and urban revolts were fairly common occurrences, such as the 'Rebeyne' of Lyon in 1436, the 'Tricoterie' of Angers, the 'Miquemaque' of Reims in 1461 and a dozen others in the reign of Louis XI. But the great cauldron of unrest had moved eastwards, to central Europe. In 1420 Bohemia was shattered by the formidable Hussite Revolt, which was to shake the entire Empire for fifteen years. It produced very profound effects which were to have repercussions throughout rural Germany and at least partly explain the movements that took hold there, sporadically at first and then with increasing violence until the outbreak of the Peasants' War in 1524. These included the Drummer of Niklashausen, 1476; the *Bundschuh* of Selestat in 1493, of Spier in 1502, of Lehen in Bresgau in 1513 and 'poor Konrad' in Wurtemberg in 1514.

None of these revolts lacked rational causes. It has already been observed that social structures were so dominated by the nobility that violence was the only path left open to the peasant; to such an extent that 'agrarian revolt seemed as inseparable from the seigneurial regime as the strike from capitalist enterprise' (M. Bloch). Marxist historians have gone to great lengths to link the disturbances of the fourteenth and fifteenth centuries to the 'first developments of capitalism' and the 'first crisis of feudal society' which, making the wealthy still richer and the poor yet poorer, brought about widespread social unrest. But in addition to such general trends it is important also to take account of such middle-term factors as the epidemics which affected the West periodically from the middle of the fourteenth century. These plagues killed many and created many problems and difficulties, but did not prove themselves to be such a disaster in the longer term to the survivors, for the peasant with land could cultivate it better and the hired labourer was in a position to ensure that he received higher wages. But then there were also overfrequent wars and their train of concomitant miseries. These opposing forces created societies where, side by side in varying proportions, one could find wretched creatures in a state of the most extreme destitution besides citizens and country-dwellers whose economic lot was improving imperceptibly. But the newfound prosperity of the latter did not continue unchecked. It was impossible for them to rise politically, as they had economically, without setbacks in a world where the social orders were defined with increasing rigidity. Moreover the wealthy interests of town and country reacted strongly. At first they attempted to persuade the State to prevent all wage rises. Above all, in order to maintain their revenues at the same level and to ensure that they benefited from the peasants' prosperity, the lords attacked the legal position of their tenants and threatened their liberties. This all resulted in a state of extreme unease which was periodically aggravated by poor harvests, famine and high prices. In these circumstances the announcement of a new tax was like a spark to gunpowder.

These objective causes can explain why a revolt was possible, but not why it actually took place. With comparable economic and social conditions there would be a revolt in one place and not in another. Uprisings occurred, not because things were intolerable, but because they seemed so. In the final analysis the determining cause of a revolt was a rebellious mood. In the fourteenth and fifteenth centuries this inclination to revolt stemmed primarily from a more or less vague feeling of disquiet and insecurity. The feeling of dissatisfaction amongst those who had a little and wanted more answered 'the uncertain feeling of uncertainty' (F. Graus) of the very lowest members of society. Worry and dissatisfaction quickened hostility to the agents of power such as judges or financial officials, and to the wealthy – rich lords, rich townsmen and above all rich prelates. The revolts of the fourteenth century in particular were born of hatred, which explains their spontaneous, inorganic and sporadic nature.

When the insurgents did have ideas, these were as unremarkable as their feelings were violent.

Basically their one wish was to ensure more justice in a society whose structures they did not dream of changing. They rose up against corrupt representatives of the law, the ruler's evil counsellors, but their confidence in their monarch – source of all justice – was unshaken. Their violence and hatred exploded against the wicked rich men whose greed seemed the cause of their misfortunes, but they did not question the social hierarchy of orders and estates. So, for example, the *Ciompi* were content with the creation of three new Trades to represent them and, in the face of seigneurial reaction and the progress of Roman law, peasants from Catalonia to England or Germany had essentially only the most conservative of ambitions: the suppression of unjust practices, the restoration of ancient liberties and the defence of the old law. For a long while the insurgents of the West gave violent expression to very moderate demands.

Heresy soon gave revolt an entirely different dimension. That is not simply to reduce heresy to a social problem or make it merely the reflection of a class struggle. For there were as many rich as poor men amongst the heretics. Heresy, having questioned the Church and her teaching, was initially the business of the clergy and believers. It could have stayed that way. But heresy often happened to overlap with politics, whether by virtue of its internal logic or in response to initiatives made by the State itself. For a long while the Lollards in fact only attacked the Church and not the civil powers. But when the Church finally succeeded in winning the active support of the State, the Lollards turned against it as well. And so in 1414, after thirty years, heresy also became politically subversive. In a more general way, as Church and State were closely interlinked and each supported the other, religious protest could very easily provide a cloak for social protest: a challenge to the Church might feed on social discontent and end by undermining the fabric of the State. Both on the political and the religious plane heresy seemed the only path forward in a sterile society.

Heresy and its manifestations in religious fervour, apocalyptic yearnings and milleniarist dreams made social protest infinitely more powerful and, above all, gave it fixed aims which, this time, were unquestionably revolutionary. The Church had always talked of the society without inequalities and possessions that had existed before the Fall and which should be once more at the Day of Judgement; in the meanwhile the Church defended both ownership and hierarchy. The heretics, however, wanted to realize in this world the society of which the Church had taught them to dream. They put the entire fabric of society on trial. From that very day they wanted a society in which all men should be equal and all goods held in common. Such were the ideas fostered by the Brethren of the

Free Spirit in the fourteenth century, which the Taborites put into practice for a brief period in southern Bohemia during the Hussite crisis and which penetrated rural Germany in the second half of the fifteenth century. After 1476 and the preaching of the Drummer of Niklashausen, the defence of ancient laws was only one of the peasants' demands and of ever diminishing importance. Instead stress was increasingly placed on the revolutionary hope of an egalitarian society in which the natural law would be restored.

Finally, national sentiment intensified feelings on the subject. After Wycliffe's initiative the Lollards read the Bible in English translation. A powerful nationalist current sprang up in Prague and ran through all Hussite movements; in Bohemia it was so strong that, for the first time in the West, a nation did not emerge from the State but in opposition to it. To the west of Germany social and religious feelings ran still higher as a result of the violent national reaction provoked by Charles the Bold's attacks on Alsace and Neuss. In his apocalyptic and milleniarist visions Savonarola promised power and wealth exclusively to the inhabitants of Florence.

Although the West was overrun by wave after wave of revolts, it was not because there was any agreement between the leaders of one country and another, one town and another, or even between a town and the surrounding countryside. It was simply that the infectious mixture of social resentment, religious hopes and a strong sense of national identity had played spontaneously on a common ground of social disaffection, economic crises and political mismanagement.

The disaffected were as diverse as their beliefs were complex. Marxist historians have sought to give the lowest social classes a privileged role. The world of vagrants and beggars, prostitutes and vagabonds, servants and valets, journeymen and paid workers – this, they claim, was the recruiting ground for heresy and revolt. These unfortunates were undoubtedly the rank and file of most riots. But it is equally clear that they were cheek by jowl with landholding peasantry, tradespeople and comfortably placed artisans, like shoemakers or sailors, innkeepers and, above all, butchers. Why were they all in revolt? Some historians believe it was because they felt themselves to be under economic threat. That was sometimes the case. More often their contemporaries denounced the pride of these people of low estate (*meschant estat*) and their affluence. From such comments we realize that these individuals, aware of their greatly improved economic position, were prevented from playing any part in the affairs of their town or country. They revolted because they were excluded.

Besides, these people of modest means were too weak and insufficiently educated or experienced to go far without support. 'The poor did not do it unaided', wrote Louis XI of the rising of Bourges in 1474. To be a threat to the State their revolt had to be instigated by men who were richer, better educated and more powerful. It was important for them to be powerful: the English peasants who idolized Robin Hood looked for deliverance from evil rich men and wicked judges to his knights turned outlaws who, according to legend, would punish injustice with their famous longbows. There was no lasting revolt without the support of a warrior class alienated from society. It was important for them to be rich: the 1355 uprising in Sienna was led by the rich who wanted to participate in government; at Le Puy in 1477 it was supported by wealthy individuals whom the oligarchy kept at a distance from the consulate. There were few urban revolts which did not involve rich citizens prevented from participating in civic affairs. It was important that they should be educated: there were few urban revolts without notaries, such as Cola di Rienzo at Rome in 1347 or Jean de Condeyssie whose culture sustained the course of the uprising at Lyon in 1436 and whose eloquence inspired it; and above all few revolts without the preaching of all those poor priests and vagabond clerics for whom the Church had not found the place they had dreamt of at university. The force of the revolts stemmed from the combination of those who felt themselves excluded at many levels of society.

In this also lay their weakness. For these vehement leaders were often the most timorous of reformers, quickly frightened by the turn of events, quick to submit provided their own particular grievances were set right. This loss of momentum played into the hands of the State which had only to take a firm line. Subversion, repudiated by the intellectuals and abandoned by the noble and rich, returned to its bed of sorrow and no longer affected communication between the ruler and the privileged classes.

13

Servants of the State

There were three main fields of activity in the service of the State and they required such widely differing abilities that a career in one area rarely impinged at all on another. These three were justice in general (in other words civil administration with the exception of finance), war and finance. With few exceptions it was invariably the same privileged secular order that provided vassals for the feudal army, captains for the contractual army and the permanent staff of the standing army. Military service therefore assisted in the preservation of a predominant social group but did not create one. On the other hand only merchants or businessmen dared risk involvement with the coinage or public credit. Moreover it brought them dazzling wealth. In their case the service of the State again re-enforced an existing social position without creating a new one. In contrast, advances in the judicial system and civil administration would not have been possible without men who were soon to be conscious of their originality and, in time, constituted a new force that was to modify profoundly the face of political society in the States of the West.

Service by his hereditary vassals had at first met all the prince's needs, although they had no formal education or specialized experience. Moreover he sometimes received the necessary advice without loosening his purse-strings. So, for example, the English kings had easily been able to persuade the most eminent men of each shire to administer these areas in their name, without remuneration. On the continent rulers undoubtedly also made use of their subjects' free services. In France, for example, tax assessors and collectors received nothing and there were hundreds of them: in the *vicomté* of Paris, excluding Paris itself and the castellany of Poissy, 322 collectors were appointed in 1314 to oversee the collection of the aid levied on the occasion of the knighting of Louis de Navarre. These occasional feudal duties had no effect on the country's social structure. But they did not guarantee the State the competent and reliable service that it needed. Administrative progress went hand in hand with the emergence and growth of a professional class which – given the required degree of competence – was prepared to devote an increasing proportion of its time to the State but also intended to derive considerable personal profit in the process.

There was competence and competence. A serjeant had above all to be reliable. It already bordered on the exceptional if, in addition, he could read and write and draw up brief reports. The written work of tribunals and departments that was produced by the daily operation of the government relied on men who had much more education – notaries in Italy and clerics in England or France. Italian notaries, trained at Bologna, were already very numerous in the twelfth century; in the fifteenth there were 400 in the State of Florence alone. In the England of Henry II there were already many clerks in the king's service; G. P. Cuttino has estimated that in the thirty-seven years of Edward I's reign 1,500 *clercs du roi* ('king's clerks') worked at London and Westminster. These clerks and notaries were the indispensable core of royal servants. They were soon led by legal specialists who alone were capable of taking the most finely judged decisions, drawing up or appraising the most difficult texts, and on them the whole administrative fabric ultimately depended. One of the essential characteristics of the history of the later medieval State in the West was the appearance and then the proliferation of these graduates in canon or civil law whom continental historians call respectively *légistes* and *juristes*.

In the forty-six years of his reign Philip Augustus had several dozen servants with the title 'Master', but there is no indication that they had studied law. It was Blanche of Castile (mother of St Louis and regent of France, 1226–34) who first made consistent use of councillors whom we know to have been doctors of law and who probably graduated from Bologna. In 1248 the first of many lawyers trained at Orléans entered royal service. The notorious lawyers in the service of Philip the Fair were following a long-established tradition. By contrast, law graduates did not appear in the service of the count of Flanders until 1278. Germany was still further behind and they were not found in councils of rulers there until the second half of the fourteenth century. Whether it occurred sooner or later there was universal recognition of the powerful and efficient character of an administration dependent on university graduates and thus also on the universities themselves. Hence the creation of colleges by the richest administrators and the foundation of universities by the wisest rulers.

Despite this progress these servants of the State were far from forming a new social group with a sense of identity. In the first place no one challenged the ruler's right to give offices to anyone he thought fit, to withdraw them when it pleased him and to transfer his servants at will.

Does this explain why service to the State was not the supreme ambition of the university graduate? J. R. Strayer has demonstrated that many lawyers from Languedoc preferred the profits of an advocate's career to the risks of royal service in the reign of Philip the Fair. Similarly under Charles V the most famous lawyers were advocates rather than counsellors in the Parlement. So for many who graduated in law the king was only one among many clients. As yet State service was neither distinctly preferable, nor exclusive. However, a university education was expensive. Education did sometimes enable men to rise socially within certain limits. But most frequently it remained the means of assuring the continued predominance of the privileged. And so the sons of rich burgesses featured amongst these graduates. But there were also – and from a much earlier date than is generally recognized – sons of the nobility who had no reason to seek an education in order to obscure their origins. There are recorded in Languedoc, between 1280 and 1320, 211 judges, advocates and proctors: three-quarters were of bourgeois origin but the remaining quarter were of noble birth. The proportion of nobles increases as one climbs the administrative hierarchy: all the lawyers admitted by Philip the Fair to his Council were nobles, with the sole exception of Guillaume de Nogaret whom the king ennobled. Under Philip VI the Council was exclusively noble, the great majority of the *baillis* and *sénéchaux* were nobles and the majority of counsellors in the Parlement; which is not to deny that nobles were also found in much lowlier positions. For a long while the administration remained an aristocratic milieu. These scions of the universities were all tonsured and technically clerics. At the end of their studies some simply forgot this fact, married and lived as laymen; this was what happened to the majority of the king's servants in the south of France. But in the north of France and in England there were still innumerable clerks at the beginning of the fourteenth century who remained in the Church. This actually suited the kings very well. They were able to fatten with benefices and bishoprics the servants for whom they would otherwise have been hard put to find wages. If there had been some progress in bureaucratization by the middle of the fourteenth century it was partly because God had made provision for it. In general servants of the State were increasingly numerous and able, but too many factors still prevented them from recognizing their innovatory and original social character.

The secularization which had affected the whole of society in England and France in the thirteenth century came to an end in the middle of the fourteenth century. From then on French graduates most often forgot their clerical status once their studies were completed. From the reign of Edward III young Englishmen could study law at the Inns of Court without even attending a university. The vast majority of civil servants were henceforth laymen.

Consequently they could no longer claim the protection of the ecclesiastical courts. The ruler's grip became firmer. Besides, the ambition of these officials was henceforth less to escape the ruler's control than to ensure his especial protection against the very real dangers they might encounter. The ruler granted them protection all the more willingly because it, in turn, increased his influence still further. At times French officials sometimes demanded that every attack on their person in the exercise of their duty should, because they were *pars corporis regis* ('part of the body of the king'), be considered as a case of *lèse-majesté in secunda specie* ('at one remove') and punished as such. They never succeeded in this aim. But from the fourteenth century the king of France and, later, the duke of Burgundy granted them their special safe-conduct, and letters of commission ensured that they were only answerable to the highest courts in the land. And so the first precursors of the special status of the public servant came into being, soon to be reinforced by further judicial and financial privileges.

A cleric removed from princely office retained his benefices. He could bear the ruler's disfavour or old age with equanimity. But for a layman who lived off a paid wage and had, moreover, to bring up a family, the future was more worrying. As civil disturbances greatly increased the number of arbitrary dismissals in the France of John the Good and above all Charles VI, the officials' concern for stability naturally became more and more pressing, and the ruler all the more ready to meet it because he hoped that this might be the way to paralyse intrigue and faction. In the ordinance of 1359 which brilliantly reintegrated all the officials driven away by civic disturbances, the Dauphin Charles was the first to establish that no official could be dismissed without a formal hearing in the courts of justice. The idea was to return and become widespread during the quarrel between the Armagnacs and the Burgundians in Paris at the beginning of the fifteenth century. In 1427 Odart Morchesne (a notary in the French Chancery) enunciated the principle clearly in his formulary and in 1467 Louis IX restated what had frequently been the practice for the past century.

At the same time that the ruler began to lose the freedom to dismiss his servants, his hitherto arbitrary choice of personnel also encountered limitations. In France, for example, an official had to obtain a letter of provision from the king. But the French recognized only too well the loopholes and inconsistencies of a system which definitely did not result in the appointment of the most competent individuals. So they relied increasingly on an electoral system. In many provinces in the mid-fourteenth century the assessors and collectors of taxes were appointed by the votes of the inhabitants; in 1355 they were elected (*élus* – this was also their official title) on a national scale by the Estates. In 1372 the king himself had his chancellor chosen by a vote. In 1391 the counsellors in the Paris Parlement were first elected by their peers. In 1413 the Cabochien ordinance extended the principle of election to a large proportion of public offices. This rapid progress owed much to the continuing rise of democratic ideals, a phenomenon due in part to the influence of canon and civil law, in part to the works of Marsilius of Padua and partly to the works of Aristotle through the translation of Nicholas Oresme; many individuals were convinced that an election appointed *le plus ydoine et convenable* ('the most fitting and suitable candidate'). But these elections also marked and simultaneously re-enforced a sense of corporate identity amongst civil servants which was to prove lasting.

Official elections receded in the fifteenth century with democratic ideals. The principle was still invoked by the Estates General in 1484 and envisaged in 1494 for the appointment of *prévôts en garde*. Then it disappeared. For all that, the ruler did not regain his earlier freedom of choice. That disappeared before the triumph of venality. Individuals such as Jean le Coq or the fifteenth-century historian Thomas Basin might oppose the sale of offices on principle. But although public opinion as a whole and officials in particular might deplore certain venal abuses, they did not condemn the system itself. Firstly, the practice of farming offices had accustomed people to acquiring some degree of public influence in return for money payments. Then, since the Church allowed the occupants of benefices to appoint their successor, why should the principle of *resignatio in favorem* (resignation in favour of a named individual) be forbidden to the servants of the State? And, since the State made no provision for retirement for the old men who had served so long and faithfully until their powers failed them, why should they not reclaim some money from the successor they nominated to the king? The very close connection between the secularization of the State and the venality of offices has not always been appreciated. Finally, one cannot be sure that a ruler like Charles VI, pulled hither and thither by factions and besieged by requests for offices, did not see the appointment of an official by his predecessor – even if it was for money – as conducive to order and stability. The sale of offices between individuals was always widespread in numerous states on the Continent. The case of France is particularly well known. While in the first half of the fourteenth century only the relatively unimportant office of serjeant was sold, and the reformers of 1357 did not mention the venality of offices, the ordinance of 1387 indicated that the practice was becoming widespread and at the beginning of the fifteenth century it had become general. From then on officials were increasingly inclined to view their office as personal property. We shall not consider public venality here since the French king did not make the decision to sell official posts himself until the great financial crisis of 1521–2.

Although private venality differed from appointment by election in so many respects, both methods left to civil servants the choice of their peers and further enhanced their sense of identity as a cohesive socio-professional group. Whatever method was used to appoint officials, they drew fat profits from their service to the State. Their wages had not been negligible at the end of the thirteenth century, but, as currencies were devalued and public opinion demanded stable prices, although wage levels scarcely varied in accounting terms between 1300 and 1500, their real value was continually diminishing. The State's servants were too valuable for them to be unable to recoup elsewhere what they consequently lost. But however explicable and inevitable these new resources were and however much they became standard practice, they surrounded officials with an atmosphere of doubt and suspicion. Gifts from the ruler fell into this category: in 1402 the French king wanted to revoke all the presents made to his officials, but he had to abandon this plan 'considérans leurs petits gaiges ordinaires' ('considering the low level of their regular wages'). Also in this category were the *épices*, fees paid by the litigants and officially taxed by the Court, which were paid in France, for example, to judges who had examined the documents of a case and drawn up a report upon which the tribunal's verdict was based. The rate of these fees rose spectacularly: it represented less than a third of the wages of a councillor in the Parlement of Toulouse in 1446, but was higher than his wages in 1525. Who could have convinced a litigant that the *épices* paid by his opponent were not the real cause of his own misfortune?

Apart from these established (if suspect) profits, what was the level of those which were quite simply illegal? It is impossible to know, but contemporaries were in no doubt that they pertained to every office and that no official ever failed to avail himself of them. So even without plurality of offices, it was scarcely a miserable existence and plurality was the rule. No doubt there was another side to the coin. The State was frequently in a very difficult financial position; wages were not paid and, what is more, the prince could demand loans from his servants. As there was no question of dismissing a creditor, this increased their security, if not their welfare. In sum, however, service to the State undoubtedly resulted in financial gains. Before, fortunes had above all been made in trade. In the fourteenth and fifteenth centuries the growth of the State and State bureaucracy on the one hand, and economic difficulties on the other, resulted in *marchandise* (business) being less profitable and wealth being associated above all with the State.

Even in the fifteenth century nobles from the oldest families in Germany, Burgundy and France were prepared to follow lucrative careers in the civil service. They were also still numerous in the Parlement of Toulouse in the reign of Louis XI. It was the dream, moreover, of many bourgeois officials to buy themselves lordships carrying rights of justice, to ally themselves through marriage to a noble family or obtain a grant of nobility, thereby crowning several generations of efforts to entrench themselves in the privileged order of nobility. State service consequently remained a noble milieu. But overall, if the whole spectrum of officialdom is considered, entry into the nobility was an ambition not so frequently realized. Their administrative careers had left such an imprint on this minority of new nobles that they seldom, and then only very slowly, succeeded in integrating themselves with the old military caste. They retained a distinct attitude of mind and remained, willy-nilly, a *noblesse de robe* ('nobility of office') and ultimately only represented the top rung of a career in public service.

They had the same ideas and attitudes as civil servants in general. These traits might at first cause one to suppose that their single concern was service to the State and their sole desire to increase its power. Already in the thirteenth century French lawyers wanted their king to be emperor in his own kingdom. At the beginning of the fourteenth century Guillaume de Nogaret believed himself justified in defending his lord the king and his country the kingdom of France. Like their master, the servants of Filippo Maria Visconti, duke of Milan (1412–47), were less concerned with the body than the soul, and less with the soul than with the State. The canon lawyers of Florence did not hesitate to say that 'just as the one God should be adored, so the priors should be venerated by every citizen' (1429), and that they put the prosperity of their city before the strict interpretation of Holy Writ (1501). In Germany *doctores legum* (doctors of law) incurred much hatred because they wanted to impose Roman law and 'help the rulers deprive the people of their law and liberty' (J. Wimpfeling). Everywhere civil servants at first appeared faithful instruments of the ruling power.

When the situation is considered more carefully, it is evident that these appearances are deceptive. In the first place civil and canon lawyers were not merely the executants of policies. In the councils of rulers or republics they made an important contribution to their definition. So they could put the interests of magnates who patronized them, or of the urban patriciate to which they belonged, before those of the State. Further still, their sole concern could be the egoistical defence of their interests as officials. Then the State itself ran up against a wall of class-interest and complicity.

In a State in the West in the later Middle Ages officials did not constitute a numerous social group: in the whole of the kingdom of France there were not more than 12,000 in 1505; in the fifteenth century the State of Florence was served by twenty-five civil lawyers and 400 notaries. Nevertheless, this new social group, hierarchical but cohesive, educated, powerful and rich, capable of serving the State without losing sight of their own interests, was a new professional group whose influence was out of all proportion to its size. This new body made its mark increasingly felt until, for example, at Mont-Saint-Michel in about 1400 a religious writer, attempting to explain the Dionysian theory of the heavenly hierarchy and why angels should be venerated, explained that 'they are close to God as the royal officers are near their sovereign; they surround him or are sent by him with a delegation of his powers to govern in his name.' The process continued into the sixteenth century which was quite prepared to let the *gens de justice* (royal lawyers) form a fourth Estate.

In the later Middle Ages the progress of the State gave rise to a new social group, which both served the public weal and was served by it. This group gradually developed an autonomy which changed the character of political life and also paralysed the advance of the State.

Conclusion

The transition from the medieval to the modern State, from feudal to absolute monarchy, *Lehnstaat* to *Ständestaat*, feudalism to capitalism – all these quite different perspectives share a view of the fourteenth and fifteenth centuries as a period of transition. Of course everyone would accept that 'every period is, in a certain sense, a period of transition in the course of which some old practices die and new ones appear' (F. Graus). But there seems to be a fairly general consensus that there was a far higher than average incidence of these lapses and innovations. In this book I have tried to remove this transition complex and restore the personality of the fourteenth and fifteenth centuries. Just as F. Chabod asked himself if there was such a thing as the 'Renaissance State', I asked myself whether the 'Fourteenth- and Fifteenth-century State' existed.

The State at this period seems to have been a complex entity composed of positive characteristics. On the one hand the ruler used everything that came his way to maintain and increase his power. He played the feudal role and founded chivalric orders; he exhorted his subjects to obedience and roused their patriotism; he encouraged the proliferation of officials and official posts. On the other hand, counterbalancing the ruler, the country he governed was becoming increasingly ordered, developing its personality and refining its hierarchical class structure. Both ruler and country were affected by the passage of democratic ideas which challenged neither the monarchical principle nor the accepted social order, but which within each social group played their part in establishing a new climate and a new set of relationships between the ruler and the privileged classes. The fourteenth and fifteenth centuries were a period of increasing bureaucratization, limited monarchy and a democracy of elites.

We can be more precise about the dates at which these changes occurred. At the end of the thirteenth and in the first half of the fourteenth century lawyers played a predominant role, the great departments of state crystallized and there was a spectacular growth in the number of state officials. But the misery of the period – wars, plagues, and scarcity of bullion – put an end to this galloping bureaucracy. Between 1345 and 1360 the atmosphere changed completely. While bureaucratic progress was halted the first orders of chivalry appeared, the first great wave of revolts swept across Europe, representative assemblies flexed their muscles for the first time and the people secured their most cherished privileges from their rulers. These tendencies continued in the second half of the fourteenth century. At the beginning of the fifteenth century the power of the English parliament was such that Stubbs could speak incorrectly of Lancastrian parliamentarism; a new revolutionary wave engulfed France and Catalonia; in Germany the *Stände* reached their zenith; the Council of Constance undermined the foundations of papal power; the Hussite Revolution shook the whole of the Empire and questioned the basis of Western society. After which the tide flowed in the opposite direction. Gradually Pope and rulers reasserted themselves; democratic convictions waned, the orders of chivalry died and bureaucratization – long halted by wars and disturbances, with their concomitant problems and financial difficulties – resumed its onward march.

States where the ruler's power developed and where social hierarchies acquired more precise definition, struck by a wave of democracy that started in the mid-fourteenth century, reached its highest point in the first two decades of the fifteenth century, then slowly retreated, though not without trace – this, in the last analysis, seems to me the unique character of the history of the States of the West in the fourteenth and fifteenth centuries.

Appendix

Historiographical Problems:
An Outline of some Debates

The picture that has emerged, with all its problems and uncertainties, is only a provisional assessment of vast and worthy researches which are nevertheless inevitably guided by contemporary enthusiasm and fatally enclosed within national traditions. The best way of giving the reader an idea of the dynamism and complexity of history seems to be to describe the outlines of some of the great historiographical debates which have gradually enabled us to see the later medieval States of the West more clearly. It seems that nothing could better demonstrate how an increasingly rich, complex and convincing perception of the truth emerges from the difficult dialogue between the past and the present.

I have given one of the historiographical outlines elsewhere.[1] It seems pointless to reproduce or summarize it here.

THE EMPIRE

The problem of the Empire enables us to understand better than any other the extent to which historians are more or less consciously enclosed within a national tradition and are affected by the pressures of contemporary events. With a few exceptions French historians have only looked at imperial history from afar. They have concerned themselves solely with its Carolingian history, the only period which has affected their national traditions. Italian historians have had several reasons for an interest in the creation of the Ottonian Empire, and they have been strongly influenced by contemporary political thinking. In the eighteenth century Muratori

---

[1] 'L' Histoire de l'Etat en France' (129).

was only able to publish an expurgated version of the Lucchese chronicler Giovanni Sercambi who, at the end of the fourteenth century, still emphasized that Italy was part of the Empire. And in the nineteenth century the 'romantic' school of Italian historical writing only approached the history of the Empire from an angle that was in some ways negative: it was concerned simply with the victory of the Church and the communes over the Empire. However, in the twentieth century the study of the Empire in Italy was taken in hand by the jurists, and was henceforth more positive and less biased. But in Germany the Empire remains as burning a question today as it was a hundred years ago.

It was in the mid-nineteenth century, at the time when the great conflict between Prussia and Austria was imminent, that a debate began, with Häusser proponent of *Kleine Deutsche* (1854–7) on the one hand, and Giesebrecht, proponent of *Grossdeutsche* (1859). A little later the crux of the debate occurred. In a lecture of lasting fame H. von Sybel condemned imperial policies in Italy because they had deflected energies away from German issues. J. von Ficker answered him, supporting the *grossdeutsche* viewpoint in *Das deutsche Kaiserreich in seinen universalen und regionalen Beziehungen* (1861) and in *Deutsches Königtum und Kaisertum* (1862). According to him, Germany should not be condemned for the Italian policies of the Emperor since this was a vital necessity for the kingdom of Germany and the principal source of her glory. The victory of Sadowa (1866) cut the debate short and stilled these feelings. They reappeared fifty years later in a more violent form. The arguments of Sybel and Ficker were repeated and their writings reprinted.[2]

Other viewpoints emerged. Sybel 'and Ficker had agreed that the Emperors had had to chose between an Italy-centred policy and an Eastward-looking one. A. Brackmann, however, thought on the contrary that the Emperors had necessarily had to be masters of Italy and the Papacy *in order to* be able to execute an effective German and Slavonic policy: the power of the Emperor in fact grew and declined everywhere in the same way at the same time.[3] H. Mitteis made this theory his own, and – at least for the early Holy Roman Empire – there is plenty of evidence to support it. It was also adopted with enthusiasm by German historians of the 1930s who, confusing the universal Empire with the German Empire in other respects, found justification for the world-wide ambitions of National Socialist Germany in the medieval Empire. This was such a dangerous and persistent confusion of past and present that in 1958 H. Sproemberg still thought it necessary solemnly to warn his fellow countrymen that the medieval Empire was not a German State.[4]

[2] Schneider, *Universalstaat oder Nationalstaat* (93).

[3] *Die Ostpolitik Ottos des Grossen* (67).

[4] *La naissance d'un Etat allemand* (280).

The particular problem posed by the Empire at the end of the Middle Ages is grafted on to this general debate. For a long while historians, obsessed by the birth of territorial principalities where – not without reason – they saw the States of the future, underestimated the importance of the Empire after 1250. Nevertheless, one would lay oneself open to accusations of failing to understand the nature of political life in the West if the Empire of Charles IV and Maximilian was portrayed as anything other than an anachronistic and inconsistent dream. The concept of Empire thus retained much more importance at the end of the Middle Ages than has often been admitted. But what were its relations with Germany? Reacting against earlier abuses, historians such as R. Folz have admitted that 'responsibility must be placed upon the Empire – and doubtless still more upon the interpretation given to it – for preventing Germany, above all from the thirteenth century onward, from developing into a State in the way that the other kingdoms of the West did.' According to H. Sproemberg it is not possible to say that the Empire helped to develop German national consciousness; the Hanse, for example, which was 'a decisive factor in the diffusion of German national consciousness', 'was established almost without reference to the Empire'.

This reaction seems a little extreme. Perhaps the medieval Empire was not universal in law; it certainly was not German. But it is a fact that many people dreamt of a universal Empire and spontaneously saw the Germans as masters of Europe. 'Who then has raised the Germans to be the judges of other nations?' protested John of Salisbury as early as the twelfth century. The inhabitants of the Empire, from Alexander of Roes to the Alsatian humanists, thought that the Empire was both universal and German. It would be perverse to maintain that the concept of Empire played no part in the formation of German national consciousness and did not assist the development of Germany. German national sentiment was born in the shadow of a concept of Empire that was certainly mistaken but nevertheless very real. Universal Empire, German Empire: an unhappy assimilation and a notion whose conclusions would be intolerable today, but one, it has to be admitted, that is well documented in the Middle Ages.

To understand the situation better it would be necessary to specify the attitude of each region, each social group and each body politic towards the Empire. From this precise and objective study one might expect a deepening of current historical understanding. This highly developed regional approach has already proved its worth with the study of areas like Alsace, whose humanists were the most ardent supporters of an Empire that was at the same time German and universal. But the territorial princes, who were disinclined to lend their support to foreign ventures, did much to draw the Empire back within its German borders.

H

According to Thomas Mayer the relations between Church and Empire should be deemed essential. Finally, the relationship of the German towns and their citizens to the Empire poses a further problem. According to H. Sproemberg the towns made a powerful contribution to the awakening of German consciousness, but without links with the Empire. Many other historians have placed the towns within an imperial framework. But according to some – the more numerous group – they restored the Empire in direct proportion to their own self-interests, while for others, such as H. Schmidt,[5] they preserved the vision of former imperial greatness. Perhaps these two points of view are not so essentially contradictory as at first appears if it is true, as W. Berges maintains, that 'in the Middle Ages regional and universal perspectives were remarkably and intimately mingled.'

The Empire thus poses the historian some formidable problems, complicated by national feeling and traditions. Nevertheless, it is impossible to hope to understand the political life of the West in the late Middle Ages unless one first understands what the Empire meant to the men of the fourteenth and fifteenth centuries.

THE ORIGINS OF THE SWISS CONFEDERATION

It was in the fifteenth century that written references to William Tell and the three Swiss first appeared. In the sixteenth century Giles Tschudi set down their story. And it is through the account of Giles Tschudi that the origins of the Confederation were viewed for centuries.

But in 1835 J. E. Kopp published his *Urkunden zur Geschichte der eidgenössischen Bünde*. From then on, throughout the nineteenth century, as a result of the efforts of Swiss historians like J. E. Kopp himself, J. C. Bluntschli and W. Œchsli, a great project was completed, which resulted in the publication of sources and a complete reappraisal of the history of the origins of the Confederation. At the end of this endeavour W. Œchsli published *Die Anfänge der schweizerischen Eidgenossenschaft* (1891); William Tell was relegated to the world of legend; the agreement between the cantons of 1 August 1291, almost unknown in 1760, became known as the birth of the Confederation; Switzerland celebrated her national day, 1 August, for the first time in 1891.

However, the triumph of history over legend was not complete. Firstly, because William Tell survived the hypercritical assaults of nineteenth-century historians. And above all because modern scholars only offer the public problems and uncertainties instead of the fine stories of long ago. It

---

[5] *Die deutschen Städtechroniken* (1100).

is true that these problems and uncertainties are the result of a constant enrichment of historical perspectives. The works of the Swiss historian K. Meyer have contributed much to this development since 1911. But the history of the origins of the Confederation entered a more active phase since, shortly before 1940 (and under the pressure of contemporary events), a dialogue was hammered out between Swiss historians (K. Meyer, W. Näf, B. Meyer) and German historians (T. Mayer, K. S. Bader, K. Mommsen). The debate has been difficult. In the first place because feelings ran so high; later because the Swiss historians inherited a tradition which for a long while had considered only Switzerland, and because the German historians, supporters of the Empire, failed to recognize the Confederation's profound originality. Today, as the re-assessments of K. S. Bader, B. Meyer or K. Mommsen demonstrate, these points of view have come closer, and there is at least agreement on what remains to be done for a full understanding of the origins of the Confederation.

Firstly, it is important not to be too preoccupied by the thirteenth century and to direct some attention to the fourteenth and fifteenth centuries. Then a detailed social and institutional study of the members of the Confederation is needed. Burgesses and peasant farmers are perhaps a little better known, but bishops and abbots have not yet been studied in sufficient depth. The nobles with whom the confederates clashed have scarcely been considered by the historian. These studies should be concerned with establishing the individual characteristics of these towns, nobles and regions, and also with the extent to which they resembled those around them, so that they can be better placed in the context of south-west Germany, of which they formed part. A study of neighbouring principalities is also needed. How can one hope to understand the origins of the Confederation without some knowledge of the Alemannic territories of the Habsburgs? Finally, the Confederation must be placed within the context of the Empire and its institutions related to those of the Empire. For example, the treaties concluded in the thirteenth century by the first confederates need to be seen within the general movement of territorial peace-treaties (*Landfriede*), which the Empire experienced in the last centuries of the Middle Ages. But even this broad framework of Swiss history would still be inadequate. For, as K. Meyer has shown, it is also important to take account of Italian influences; in particular, the influence of the University of Bologna and the acceptance of Roman law in Switzerland at the end of the Middle Ages form an important aspect of the history of the Confederation.

Two problems posed by medieval Swiss history particularly merit our attention because of their political character: that of the creation of the Confederation and of its place within the Empire.

All history of the Confederation is essentially rooted in the opening of the St Gotthard Pass. K. Meyer places this event at the beginning of the twelfth century. But current opinion generally agrees that the pass was opened in 1230, or very shortly before. As a result of the traffic across this new route, the inhabitants of Uri and Schwyz suddenly became rich and the Emperor Frederick II suddenly developed an interest in these regions, that were, simultaneously, threatened by the advance of the Habsburgs. Was it by the wish of the inhabitants, as K. Meyer maintained, or as a result of imperial initiative, as T. Mayer thought? (The two historians engaged in a debate made more vehement by the Second World War.) Did it not more probably stem from the common interest of the inhabitants and the Emperor against the Habsburgs? Whatever the case, in 1231 the inhabitants of Uri and in 1240 those of Schwyz obtained letters of privilege from Frederick II, assuring them of the direct protection of the Emperor. The collapse of Staufen power in 1250 impelled all the political bodies of southern and western Germany towards unity. An alliance of the towns of Lake Constance was established on the pattern of the league of Rhenish towns (1254), which still awaits its historian. Moreover – in 1273 according to K. Meyer, about 1252 according to B. Meyer – Uri, Schwyz and Unterwalden made an agreement which, in K. Meyer's opinion, was already political and directed against the Habsburgs, but which B. Meyer believes was still only a regional peace (*Landfriede*) designed to combat private war (*Fehde*). Whatever the case, this was the first union.

The period that followed was decisive for the birth of the Confederation and also has the greatest concentration of problematical issues. The traditional account was centred round two main episodes: that of William Tell and of the destruction of the castles. Nineteenth-century criticism completely rejected these traditions. The historians of the twentieth century have reappraised this wholesale condemnation. K. Meyer even believed in William Tell; few have followed him. On the other hand, the destruction of the Habsburg castles seems very probable today and the difficulties concern its dating. According to K. Meyer, it occurred in response to the threats which the policy of Rudolph of Habsburg, King of the Romans (deliberately confusing imperial possessions and domain lands), had posed to the inhabitants of Uri, Schwyz and Unterwalden. The treaty of August 1291, which would then have followed this event, therefore had great political significance and was worthy of solemn celebration in twentieth-century Switzerland. B. Meyer, on the other hand, maintains that it is mistaken to overestimate the importance of the 1291 agreement: on the death of Rudolph the inhabitants of Uri, Schwyz and Unterwalden, fearful of disturbances, were content to renew the earlier peace, adding a few clauses to it; according to this view the act of 1291 was much more a peace-treaty than a political document. But in

1309 the three cantons together obtained confirmation of their liberties from Henry VII: henceforth they enjoyed an incontestable right to the liberty of the Empire and together constituted an imperial bailliwick (*Reichslandvogtei*). Leopold of Habsburg was unable to stomach this measure which signalled the collapse of his hopes of incorporating the cantons in the territorial State which he was endeavouring to construct: this is the context in which Leopold's campaign, his defeat at Morgarten (November 1315) and the destruction of the castles must be placed. The agreement of December 1315 (which for K. Meyer was a straightforward renewal of that of 1291) becomes for B. Meyer the real occasion of the birth of the Confederation. Besides, there was as yet no State. The Swiss State was born slowly in the course of the fourteenth and fifteenth centuries. It was formed firstly by the struggle and victory against the Habsburgs and, later, against Charles the Bold. It occurred as a result of the addition of new members to the original kernel of the Confederation. The union of political bodies as different as towns, like Zürich or Bern, and the rural cantons did not take place without grave tensions that sometimes jeopardized the very existence of the Confederation. But, once the crisis was past, it was this very union of towns and rural areas on an equal footing which constituted the originality of the Confederation and ensured its stability. The essential element was perhaps the presence of common bailliwicks: Aargau from 1415 and Thurgau from 1460 were administered by all the cantons. This arrangement necessitated a federal Diet that soon became the soul of the Confederation. To these factors the birth of what we must call Swiss national sentiment must be added: it was at the beginning of the fifteenth century that the deeds of William Tell were first sung, and in 1485 – when an Argovian was elected proctor of the German nation at the University of Paris – that an enthusiastic scribe wrote in the register: 'Vivat Elvetica proles.'

What was the position of this new State within the Empire? Since Bluntschli and Œchsli the classic theory has gone as follows: the Confederates were united at first in order to obtain instant imperial protection against the Habsburgs; throughout the thirteenth and fourteenth centuries they remained very attached to the Empire and the concept of Empire. It was only when the Habsburgs were to be found permanently at the head of the Empire that the Swiss detached themselves from it. When in 1495 Maximilian attempted to restore a certain vigour to the Empire, the Confederates, their liberties threatened, did not hesitate to fight; they won, and the Peace of Basel (1499) tacitly acknowledged their independence, although this was not officially proclaimed until the Treaty of Westphalia (1648). The classic theory has been attacked on two fronts. K. Meyer attempted to show that the Confederates had been hostile to the Empire from the start; this has not proved convincing. Recently K.

Mommsén has attempted to demonstrate that in the fifteenth century the Confederates were still able to distinguish between the Habsburgs, whom they fought, and the Empire, to which they remained attached. It is an exaggeration to say that in the Treaty of Basel they intended to have nothing more to do with the Empire. The privileges which they then obtained were not after all so exceptional as to exclude them from the Empire. They escaped, for example, the jurisdiction of the Court of the Imperial Chamber (*Reichskammergericht*). But K. Mommsen observed that this exemption was also granted to the prince-electors who could not be described as outside the Empire because of this privilege. The problem of relations between the Confederation and the Empire thus needs to be re-examined by looking at the history of the Confederation itself in greater detail, and above all by relating it to that of the territorial principalities which were becoming more powerful within the Empire at this period. Comparison with the Low Countries might be particularly fruitful.

NATIONS AND NATIONAL SENTIMENT

The words *patria* and *natio* were already used by the Romans. But the word 'patriotism' did not appear until the eighteenth century, the word 'nationalism' in the nineteenth. It is difficult to be sure whether the States of the West in the late Middle Ages were the same as nations, or whether their cohesion owed something to their population's awareness of consti-tuting a nation. Did national sentiment play a role in their existence? The problem is difficult because of the complexity of the facts, and it is made more difficult by historians, excessively concerned with understanding or justifying their own time. For to resolve it one must face the question of when national sentiment appeared and one's reply to this last question essentially depends on what one understands by 'nation'. Now nothing has been more controversial for the last 200 years than the concept of nation. A nation, said the *Dictionnaire de l'Académie française* in the eight-eenth century, is 'all the inhabitants of the same State, of the same country, who live under the same laws and employ the same language'. Turgot said even more simply, 'a nation is a collection of men who speak the same mother-tongue.' Over and against this objective theory the century of Rousseau and the *Social Contract* elaborated a subjective theory, in which the nation was above all the result of a collective will to live together. Rationalism at first supported the subjective definition of the nation and romanticism the objective definition, with no regard for national boundaries. Soon the intellectual traditions of France and Ger-many, the repeated clashes of the two countries, the nature of the conflicts which set them against each other, all impelled French historians towards the subjective definition of the nation, German historians towards the objective definition. To speak in even more general terms, in countries with a Germanic culture, 'nation' was defined by race and language, in Latin countries by their collective will. From 1835, in the definition of a nation given in the new edition of the *Dictionnaire de l'Académie*, the reference to language disappeared. Later, Italian unity was established in the name of the right of peoples to decide their own lot, while the unifiers of Germany intended to gather together the peoples with a Germanic language. The drama of 1870 and the problem of Alsace-Lorraine still continues, and so, for a long while, did the opposition: Treitschke's definition of nation in 1871 and the reply to him by Renan in 1882 still echo today in France and Germany.

The historians who would define a nation by a factor as objective and as old as language naturally have a marked tendency to discover nations and national sentiment from the beginning of the Middle Ages. By contrast, those who make a nation the result of a conscious act of will would rather refuse to speak of real nations and a true national sentiment before the end of the eighteenth century. Between the Carolingian Empire and the French Revolution plenty of other solutions are possible and many dates have been singled out for the birth of national consciousness. Let us take just a few examples. According to G. Monod, P. Kirn and countless German historians, one can speak of nations from the ninth century onwards; national sentiment was first expressed at the break-up of the Carolingian Empire. For W. Holtzmann and many other German historians one is not yet justified in speaking of nations in the tenth century. After which J. Huizinga and H. Kohn are prepared to talk of nations in the twelfth century at the period when the first modern states were forged in reaction to the imperial policy of the Hohenstaufen. But F. von der Heydte does not concede this phenomenon before the end of the thirteenth century and the wave of nationalism which, in his view, then broke across Europe. But H. Hauser sees French national consciousness only as a result of the Hundred Years War. On the other hand, C. Seignobos will not talk of national consciousness at the end of the Hundred Years War. And H. Kohn tells us that it is only at the Renaissance that 'the purely organic awareness of the group developed for the first time in the national consciousness.' But F. Chabod draws our attention to the fact that this awareness only occurred in a minority and that it is only really possible to talk of national consciousness at the end of the sixteenth century.[6] Let us

---

[6] Kirn, *Aus der Frühzeit des Nationalgefühls* (448): Holtzmann, 'Imperium und Nationen' (79); Huizinga, 'Patriotism and Nationalism in European History' (440); Kohn, *The Idea of Nationalism* (450); der Heydte, *Die Geburtsstunde des souveränen Staates* (36); Chabod, 'Y a-t-il un Etat de la Renaissance?' (35).

leave the subject there and try rather to see the reasons for this strange lack of agreement.

Historians seem to have been guilty on two counts: anachronism and excessive generalization. Almost all of them have adopted the definition of nation that is valid for their own time and country; then they have applied this single definition to other times and places. Now the important thing is that there is not one sole uniform, European national sentiment, which, once it appeared, one could research in tranquillity: there are differing degrees and types of national consciousness. In the birth of French national identity, for example, a political fact – the existence of a king and a kingdom – was of primordial importance. Language certainly played a vital role in the development of German national consciousness. As for Italian national awareness, it owes much to the memory of Rome and has a historical foundation. Even without the added confusion of anachronistic hindsights, the observations of German and French historians would lead them to different conclusions, which they then make the further mistake of generalizing. Let us take the problem further. There is no single French national sentiment whose date of birth it is sufficient to note. In reality the French have known for centuries that France was their country and that they loved their country. But the precise problem is to analyse the nature of their national consciousness century after century, to measure its intensity and even to specify which group and which individuals experienced it most acutely.

Did national consciousness exist in Europe at the end of the Middle Ages? That is an open question and badly phrased. It would be better to say: what did a European understand by 'nation' at the end of the Middle Ages? In which given State did the inhabitants see themselves as part of a nation? How intense was this 'national' consciousness and what was it like? What vigour and cohesion did the State derive from this 'national' sentiment?

To reply to these precise questions, a semantic study is first necessary, and a start has fortunately been made on this in many works. The general words 'nation', 'race', 'people', 'country', the specific terms given to the country where they live – all these words deserve to be studied. When did they appear? How frequently were they used? Who used them? And above all what was the precise meaning with which they were used? All study of national consciousness should be preceded by such a semantic enquiry. Let us take one example to show what misunderstandings would have been avoided, had this approach been adopted earlier. Isidore of Seville, taking up the definitions of antiquity, distinguished between nation and people: a nation is a group of men with a common, racial origin; a people is a politically organized human group. This classical definition was maintained throughout the Middle Ages. But at the beginning of the modern period, when there was an increasing correspondence between State and nation, even the best writers ended by confusing the 'racial' and the 'political': in Seyssel the words 'nation', 'race', 'country' and 'kingdom' are interchangeable. From the eighteenth century onward when the need for the distinction reappeared, the nation was no longer a race, it was a human group politically organized, a people. This was the only way in which the late nineteenth-century publicist and historian Ernest Renan conceived it – the way in which it was then universally conceived. As proof, take this statement by a contemporary German historian: 'It is important to beware of speaking of nations in the tenth century. It is merely a question of peoples, and, more specifically, peoples with no corporate awareness, or, if they did have one, one so weak that the sources give no impression of what it was like.' To express the same idea, a contemporary of Aquinas would have said that in the tenth century there were only nations and no peoples. The problem would not be so serious if all historians were completely aware of this shift in meaning. But in practice German historians use the medieval definition of nation to the profit of their own nation, without taking account of the fact that the medieval 'nation' was none other than our 'race'. Meanwhile French historians deplore the medieval definition without registering that the Middle Ages perfectly understood the modern concept of nation, but they spoke of it as a people.

After this preliminary study, a second phase should research the constituent parts of national consciousness and determine concretely and exactly the role played by language, religion, history, and so on. Indeed numerous works, many of them excellent, enable one to make some evaluation of this aspect. This is the main aim of my chapter 'State and Nation'.

A third line of enquiry, on the other hand, is still in its infancy: that which would enable one to establish the part played by each milieu in the development of national consciousness.

These three approaches should result in a comparative history of European national awareness in the Middle Ages. But they should be conducted initially within the framework of each nation. To be really fruitful, they should begin with a survey of the historiographical traditions of each region and should endeavour to go beyond them. For historians of every country have been prone to enclose themselves within excessively narrow parameters.

The Hundred Years War virtually monopolizes the attention of French historians. It was in the course of this war, they say, that the French nation was born. At the outset there was just a simple dynastic quarrel between the Valois and Plantagenets. The defeats of the royal armies were the making of France. This theory cuts no ice with me. The semantic

studies that I have undertaken have almost invariably led to the thirteenth century. The history of French national consciousness cannot
progress unless historians escape from their obsession with the Hundred
Years War and concentrate their work on the thirteenth century.

In England the problem is still dominated by the attitudes of Bishop
Stubbs. According to Stubbs the English nation has existed since the
beginning of the thirteenth century. Magna Carta was, as it were, her
birth certificate. Pollard reacted vigorously against Stubbs in this as in
other respects. He remarked that he would take English thirteenth-
century 'nationalism' more seriously if he knew of a single copy of the
Great Charter in English, if the so-called national clergy were less peopled
with foreigners and spoke the language of their flock a little more
frequently. According to Pollard, in the course of the thirteenth century
English nationalism gradually emerged from the sessions of Parliament.[7]
The English historiographical tradition thus remains enclosed within the
magic circle of Parliament.

In Germany the most important work concerns the concept of Empire,
humanism and the Renaissance. The history of German national sentiment is too often reduced to the study of ideas expressed in the writings of
the great scholars of the second half of the fifteenth century. Some studies,
such as those of J. Wagner or P. Goerlich, do fortunately make a
distinction between different periods and locations.[8]

Dante, Petrarch and Machiavelli have been the curse of Italian historiography. For too long, Italian historians have believed they could
resolve every problem, and especially the problem of Italian national
awareness, by putting every word of these great men, with a few others,
under the microscope. There, too, the current problem (following in the
footsteps of historians like Burdach or Baron) is to study the patriotism of
Naples, Rome, Florence, Milan or Venice in depth, in order to discover –
amongst other things – the extent to which national sentiment paved the
way for the development of a more general Italian national consciousness.[9]

I should not wish to end this section without drawing attention to the
work of P. Vilar, whose excellent study of the Catalan nation provides a
sure introduction to research on any nation.[10]

[7] *The Evolution of Parliament* (1252).

[8] Wagner, *Nationale Strömungen in Deutschland* (472); Goerlich, *Zur Frage des Nationalbewusstseins in ostdeutschen Quellen* (433).

[9] Baron, *The Crisis of the Early Italian Renaissance* (1421).

[10] *La Catalogne dans l'Espagne moderne* (240).

STATES AND ASSEMBLIES OF ESTATES

It is easy to understand why the study of the Estates General and of French provincial estates was so enthusiastically pursued in the second half of the eighteenth century and why this continued throughout the nineteenth century. But in their monumental works the Romantic historians were more concerned with flattering the liberal, bourgeois and national prejudices of their readers than with extracting the truth from documents. The study of French representative assemblies began in earnest in 1872 with the appearance of G. Picot's *Histoire des Etats généraux*, the second edition of which (published in 1888) has not yet been superseded. In the next twenty years three young graduates of the *Ecole des Chartes*, A. Thomas, L. Cadier and A. Coville, published three exemplary studies of provincial assemblies, which were to establish the themes and perspectives of the French historical school in this field for a long while. First they defined the provincial Estates which were, according to L. Cadier, 'the meeting of regularly constituted assemblies of the three orders of estates, called at regular intervals and possessing certain political and administrative characteristics, of which the most important was the granting of taxes'. They then proceeded to show how their origins, organization and function should be minutely detailed. Finally, they developed some fundamental themes, of which the most important stated that assemblies of estates came into being as a result of the will of the ruler, who had called them together, with a view to solving his financial problems. Until the Second World War the example of A. Thomas, L. Cadier and A. Coville was followed by many French, Belgian and Italian historians, whose studies greatly enriched the history of the representative assemblies themselves.

The great weakness of these *parlementaristes* as E. Lousse realized, is that concerning themselves with the history of the *institution*, and only the institution, their enquiries were carried out on a superficial plane: they did not explain the assemblies at any fundamental level because they did not study 'their less direct relationships with the social and political structure of the regions which they represented'. As a result they gave no explanation as to why representative assemblies were assemblies of estates.

Contemporary with G. Picot, A. Thomas, L. Cadier and A. Coville, the German school of history was engaged in quite different lines of research, led first by O. von Gierke. In his masterly work *Das deutsche Genossenschaft* O. von Gierke showed – in four volumes, 3,500 pages and almost fifty years' work (1868–1913) – how medieval German society was composed not of isolated individuals, but of corporate bodies, estates and groups.

Gierke himself did not have time to tackle the problem of the representation of these bodies. That was the task of G. von Below and, above all,
H. Spangenberg, who in 1912 published his classic work *Vom Lehnstaat zum
Ständestaat. Ein Beitrag zur Entstehung der landständischen Verfassung*. It has
been clear to German historians ever since that medieval society was
organized in groups and that from this corporate organization (*Stände-
wesen*) stemmed the corporate structure (*Ständeverfassung*) of representative assemblies of this period. For Gierke and his successors assemblies
of estates, far from resulting from the initiative of the ruler, came into
being because of the subjects' wish to defend their interests and privileges.
In the corporate State (*Ständestaat*) 'the power of the ruler was limited by
the rights of his subjects, organized into *corpora* and represented at a
political level by assemblies of Estates.' The corporatist school undoubtedly went further to explain assemblies of estates than the *parlementariste*
school.

Already before the First World War the work of Gierke began to be
known in translation in England and France. But corporatist ideas did not
really spread outside Germany until the thirties, and then thanks to the
untiring efforts of the Belgian historian E. Lousse and to the International
Commission for the History of Assemblies of Estates which Lousse himself
launched at the International Congress in Warsaw in 1933. It saw the
light of day in 1936 and was responsible for the publication of many
important works. On the eve of the Second World War corporatist ideas
were even making inroads into the French *parlementariste* bastion. Unfortunately, the success of the corporatist school can also partly be
explained by an execrable confusion of history and politics. To assert that
medieval society was organized in groups was one thing, to assert that
twentieth-century society should also be organized in groups is another,
entirely different, matter. But it is a fact that corporatist historians were
not always able to keep their distance from the 'neocorporatism' of
Mussolini's Italy, Hitler's Germany or Vichy France. This deplorable
compromise had the unfortunate result of blinding medievalists legitimately hostile to the governments of Mussolini, Hitler and Vichy France
to the fact that the corporatist analysis of medieval society might have
been essentially right. The defeat of the Fascist powers was to some extent
the defeat of corporatist ideas which were attacked after 1945 with an
intensity of feeling quite understandable in the light of recent events.

The 'corporatist dreams' were simultaneously attacked in relation to
representative assemblies and in relation to the estates themselves. In
1950 J. Dhondt emphasized that an assembly of estates, far from being the
fruit of calm and balanced relations between estates, was nothing other
than the result of a bitter struggle between different 'forces', that is
between 'socio-economic entities'. 'The composition, competence and

authority of an assembly of estates at any one given time', he wrote, 'is the exact reflection of the balance of power between the prince, the different constituent parts and the various socio-economic forces present in the principality at that moment.'[11] As these relations were constantly changing the assemblies of estates were also in a state of perpetual evolution.

While Gierke and his disciples had believed in the profound reality of the estates and orders, for the historians who wrote in the wake of the Second World War, and above all for the Marxist historians, it was important not to be distracted by the juridical structure of the orders which only masked the social reality of the classes. To understand the political realities of the West at the end of the Middle Ages properly, it was therefore necessary to ignore the appearances which had misled even their contemporaries and make use of the concepts of class and class struggle that had been developed in the nineteenth century. 'There is no reason', wrote P. Vilar, 'for not analysing *conjunctures* [conjunctions of events] and structures, relations between State and classes, whether of the Aragonese kingdoms of the thirteenth century, nineteenth-century Spain or the Catalan revolutions of 1604 and 1705.' In the aftermath of the Second World War the class concept satisfied the great majority of historians, R. Mousnier above all.

Later R. Mousnier became convinced that if this concept, founded on a simple economic criterion, was an adequate explanation of contemporary societies, it did not permit a complete understanding of earlier societies.[12] The 'order' was no mere distraction from the historian's real work, nor even a straightforward juridical reality. An order was a social group with status, honours, privileges, rights, duties and obligations recognized by a general consensus of opinion. Ultimately the law fixed some of these regulations which were dictated by the political structure of the State. Societies composed of orders were as familiar to the fourteenth or seventeenth centuries as societies of classes to the nineteenth. It is useless to measure a society of orders by the yardstick of class. The debate between R. Mousnier and his opponents remains open and lively. Doubtless it will stay that way for a long while to come. For now, he has had the great merit of convincing historians that a political society is to be explained both by the real forces which affect it and by contemporary mental images, as well as the continual interaction of the one upon the other.

Besides, research on representative assemblies cannot be confined within the framework of this debate. The history of French general and provincial assemblies has especially benefited from the work of English-

[11] 'Ordres ou "puissances"' (995).

[12] Mousnier, Labatut and Durand, *Problèmes de stratification sociale* (1004); Mousnier, *Problèmes de stratification sociale* (1005).

speaking historians who had only received distant echoes of this debate over the Channel. The first attempt in this field was that of G. Post who was concerned with the study of the intellectual context in which assemblies were able to develop: it is above all because of his work that there has been much progress in the study of problems such as representation and consent.[13] The second endeavour was that of J. R. Strayer and C. H. Taylor who, while focusing entirely on the concrete study of the first French assemblies of about 1300, nevertheless came to conclusions of widespread interest.[14] It is not therefore surprising that under the direction of such teachers young American historians have recently been able to make significant contributions to the study of the French Estates. The third approach which has enabled us to understand these Estates better is English: for a long while English historians considered their Parliament an unique phenomenon which it was important not to confuse with representative assemblies on the Continent. Fortunately this isolationism is now at an end. Many historians realized that a comparative study of the institutions of England and the Continent was necessary and in the interest of both parties, beginning with England and France, whose destinies were so tightly intertwined in the fourteenth and fifteenth centuries. In particular, comparison of the English Parliament with the Estates General of France – a study begun by R. Fawtier, continued by A. R. Myers and above all by P. S. Lewis – now enables us to understand the failure of the French Estates General better.[15]

Historians did not only disagree about the nature of representative assemblies; at the same time they were not at one on the place they should be accorded in the political history of the fourteenth and fifteenth centuries. Did the Estates have a positive or a negative role? In France the debate goes back to an old quarrel between the Orléanists and the republicans over the events of 1356–8. While A. Thierry, writing in the time of Louis-Philippe, saw this as a lamentable moment, when France and the monarchy had all but foundered, under the Second Empire F.-T. Perrens boasted of the political intelligence displayed by the Estates in 1357, of their 'precocious instinct for liberal institutions'. He regretted the success of the Dauphin Charles: 'What progress for France', he wrote, 'if national self-government had prevailed there, at the same time that it was

---

[13] *Studies in Medieval Legal Thought* (54).

[14] Strayer and Taylor, *Studies in Early French Taxation* (822); Taylor, 'Assemblies of French Towns' (1210); 'An Assembly of French Towns' (1211); 'French Assemblies and Subsidy' (1212); 'The Assembly of 1312' (1213); 'The Composition of Baronial Assemblies in France' (1214).

[15] Fawtier, 'Parlement d'Angleterre et Etats généraux de France' (1149); Myers, 'The English Parliament and the French Estates-General' (1157); Lewis, 'The Failure of the French Medieval Estates' (1187).

established in England.' A century later, in what was admittedly an entirely different atmosphere, the same dialogue continued: while in 1945 E. Faral saw the enemies of the Dauphin as mediocre and short-sighted schemers, R. Fawtier in 1953 considered the Estates' programme of reform a model of wisdom and political perception. The debate has undoubtely not yet come to a close.[16]

In any case it arouses feelings of less intensity than that of Germany. For almost all late nineteenth-century German historians – proud of their unity, admirers of princes – there was no doubt that the Estates had played a purely negative role, had never been able to go beyond the egoistical perspectives of a *Standespolitik* and had simply prevented princes anxious to promote a *Staatspolitik* from establishing more stable States at an earlier date. These views are still those of the textbooks most frequently read and re-edited.[17] But in 1954 K. S. Bader asked whether, contrary to what had always been thought, the policy of Maximilian had been so important for the Empire, whether the Emperor had not dreamed of policies instead of executing them, and whether it was not in fact the representatives of the Estates who had attempted to reform the Empire at the end of the fifteenth century.[18] Then, in 1959, the English historian F. L. Carsten showed that the Estates had had a positive influence, both on internal and foreign policy.[19] K. S. Bader and F. L. Carsten made the German historians hesitate, led them to emphasize the differences between one principality and another and to qualify their assertions; but the traditional position has essentially been maintained either because the weight of historiographic tradition pressed too heavily, or because the evidence of the facts themselves could not be dismissed.

Positive or negative, all these historians recognized in any case that representative assemblies played a major role in the political history of the fourteenth and fifteenth centuries. By contrast Marxist historians essentially accord them little importance. Certainly, they say, these assemblies are a 'progressive' phenomenon; they reflect a new balance of forces; they translate the political role acquired by the lesser and middle nobility and by townsmen at the expense of the magnates. But they do not mark the birth of a new State; they remain part of the feudal State and even re-enforce that State in so far as they facilitate the control of internal contradictions within the dominant class.

It is easy to see that there is little common ground between the

[16] Faral, 'Robert Le Coq et les Etats généraux' (1174); Fawtier, 'Parlement d'Angleterre et Etats généraux de France' (1149); Guenée, 'L'histoire de l'Etat en France' (129).

[17] Gebhardt, *Handbuch der deutschen Geschichte* (255); Hartung, *Deutsche Verfassungsgeschichte* (257).

[18] 'Kaiserliche und ständische Reformgedanken' (61).

[19] *Princes and Parliaments in Germany* (1173).

corporatists, liberals and Marxists. Nevertheless they hold one conviction in common: these assemblies were closely linked to the societies which they represented. In the words of G. M. Trevelyan, without social history political history is unintelligible; it is essential not to separate State and society.

THE ENGLISH PARLIAMENT

The history of the English Parliament was initiated in the seventeenth century by the series of documents edited with a commentary by William Prynne in his *Brief Register, Kalendar and Survey of the several Kinds and Forms of all Parliamentary Writs* (1659–64). Nevertheless, it was in 1819 that the first *Report from the Lords Committees touching the Dignity of a Peer* undertook to give an overall view of this long and glorious history. Its themes are a little confused and indecisive. But, for example, the idea that thirteenth-century parliaments had played the role of the ordinary Council of the king or of a court of justice, or the notion that the king's Council was at least the basis of the great majority of parliaments remained generally accepted for fifty years until the great work of William Stubbs.[20]

William Stubbs (1825–1901) was thoroughly English, a cleric and a conservative of the Victorian era. His aim was to show how since the Middle Ages the English people had gradually fulfilled its 'mission, that of instituting parliamentary democracy' (C. Petit-Dutaillis), such as existed in England in the second half of the nineteenth century, to general satisfaction. The *Constitutional History*, published in three volumes between 1874 and 1878, was at once a great success. The Oxford professor had achieved such a perfect synthesis, a theory of such luminous simplicity, that it has guided generations of historians, who have been able to confirm it, document it more precisely and, above all, to destroy entire sections with works of admirable scholarship – but, a hundred years later, they have still not been able to replace it.

Stubbs saw in Parliament an assembly of an essentially political nature, prepared by the initiatives of patriotic barons in the thirteenth century, and finally realized by the will of Edward I, the English Justinian, whose main claim to fame was the summons of the 'model Parliament' of 1295. The importance of this 'model Parliament' in the eyes of the English is easier to understand if one remembers that in 1925 the English peerage still believed that their right to sit in the upper chamber was derived from the hereditary right which they held from an ancestor who had been

[20]Cam, 'Stubbs Seventy Years After' (1224); Richardson and Sayles, 'William Stubbs' (1257).

summoned in 1295. Whatever the case, Parliament – which had not been a regular event under Edward I – made dazzling progress in the fourteenth century and became institutionalized, became in fact the fundamental institution of political life. Parliament, the uncontested representative of the community of the country, saw itself recognized as the sole body with power to grant taxes, participated more and more closely in the legislative process, controlled ministers, finally played an essential role in the fall of Richard II and forced Henry IV to reckon with it willy-nilly: that was the origin of the Lancastrian constitutionalism of the fifteenth century. This triumph of Parliament was not that of the upper chamber; it was that of the Commons, of the knights of the shire whose influence and experience worked wonders at Westminster. In essence, at least, the institution of Parliament was already sketched out in fifteenth-century England.

The survival of the *Constitutional History* has been prodigious. The three fat volumes were translated into French: the last appeared in 1927, fifty years after the original work. In 1936 G. T. Lapsley declared that 'anyone who neglects Stubbs does so at his peril.' And in 1948 H. M. Cam expressed satisfaction that the *Constitutional History* was still accorded an unrivalled position amongst the books compulsory for students reading history at Cambridge. And yet no one should be surprised that a synthesis written so quickly and so long ago should teem with mistakes of detail which have been patiently uncovered over the past hundred years. But the very foundations of Stubbs's edifice have been attacked by his critics. As long ago as 1885 a German historian, L. Riess, showed that a parliament of Edward I was not a political assembly and that the king had administrative purposes in mind when he summoned it.[21] Riess's little essay disturbed neither Stubbs nor England. In 1893 the great Cambridge legal historian F. W. Maitland in his turn insisted on the fact that an Edwardian parliament was a royal, bureaucratic and judicial institution and that every parliament was essentially a session of the royal Council.[22] But when Maitland died in 1901 he too had disturbed neither Stubbs nor England. The first historians to do justice to Maitland's endeavour were C. H. McIlwain in 1910 and D. Pasquet in 1914.[23] In 1920 the *Constitutional History* was attacked directly and in its entirety: basing himself on Maitland but going beyond him, A. F. Pollard persistently undermined all the old Stubbsian myths, especially the myths of the political origin of Parliament, of the 'model Parliament' of 1295, of the peerage, of the

---

[21] *Geschichte des Wahlrechts zum englischen Parlament* (1259).

[22] 'Introduction to *Memoranda de Parliamento*' (1249).

[23] McIlwain, *The High Court of Parliament and its Supremacy* (1246); Pasquet *Essai sur les origines de la Chambre des Communes* (1251).

importance of the Commons, of 'Lancastrian constitutionalism'.[24] In short, Pollard's book made English historians rudely aware that 'the entire history of Parliament had to be rewritten.'

Thus began the impassioned revision of the Anti-Stubbsian school, which reached its goal in the works jointly written by H. G. Richardson and G. O. Sayles, in whom, according to one of their opponents, the very name of Stubbs provoked disturbing reactions. If one is to believe the Anti-Stubbsians, Parliament was *essentially* a judicial instrument in origin; it remained one afterwards in function. Because it was judicial even in the fourteenth century this body only played a minor political role. Admitting that Parliament had nevertheless a certain importance, this school of thought would argue that this significance was that of the Lords: in the Middle Ages the Commons had never been anything other than the plaything of the Lords; the representatives of the counties and the towns – chosen under pressure from the magnates, rarely re-elected, frequently absent – had neither the independence, the experience nor the enthusiasm to act as a counterbalance to the Lords. It is therefore absurd to speak of 'Lancastrian constitutionalism'. Under the first Tudors Parliament was still what it had been in the thirteenth century: a body destined by the monarchy to facilitate the exercise of royal justice and to increase its administrative efficiency, a body whose importance in English political life was negligible. It was the Council, not Parliament, whose name he scarcely mentioned, whom Fortescue placed in the centre of the English constitution. The Anti-Stubbsians produced a history of Parliament that was quite different from that of Stubbs, but just as simple. Too simple, in fact.

For there were still numerous historians (C. Stephenson, J. F. Willard, M. V. Clarke, H. M. Cam, and so on)[25] who declared themselves convinced, like Stubbs, of the essentially political nature of the English Parliament, of the importance of the representative element in its midst, and of the considerable role played by Parliament in the fourteenth century and, above all, at the end of that century. They saw Parliament as master in the name of the community of the realm, granting or withholding the taxes demanded by the king, exploiting this role in order to impose on him the legislative concessions they wished for, supported by better-informed and more decided public opinion. According to this view, Parliament was certainly a largely uncooperative partner for the ageing Edward III, for Richard II and Henry IV. And nothing could convince

[24] Pollard, *The Evolution of Parliament* (1252).

[25] Willard, *Parliamentary Taxes on Personal Property* (838); Clarke, *Medieval Representation and Consent* (1225); Cam, 'Recent Books . . . on the Parliamentary Institutions' (1223); 'Stubbs Seventy Years After' (1224).

the Stubbsians that the power of Parliament was only a reflection of the strength of the magnates.

Both Stubbsians and Anti-Stubbsians have convincing arguments. Both parties mistakenly ignore the objections of their opponents. Theory seems to force itself fatally upon factual complexity. It appears that an increasingly vigorous conciliatory stream of thought (represented by T. F. T. Plucknett, G. P. Cuttino and above all J. G. Edwards)[26] should be capable of securing considerable support and putting an end to this age-old quarrel on the origin and nature of the English Parliament. The Parliament of Edward I was neither essentially political nor essentially judicial. It was in essence unspecific, omnicompetent. Parliament was not exclusively representative, but no more was it simply the Council. Let us say that the Council was the heart of Parliament, that Parliament was the Council and something more.

As for the problems concerning the importance of Parliament in the fourteenth and fifteenth centuries, and the relative weight of the upper and lower chambers, they are not yet resolved, but well on the way towards solution as a result of the works of J. G. Edwards, K. L. Wood-Legh, N. B. Lewis and above all the numerous excellent studies of J. S. Roskell.[27] These historians in effect decided that, in order to settle the question, it was necessary first to make a systematic study of the composition of the different Parliaments. Their lengthy and concrete researches justify several important conclusions here and now: the knights of the shire did not always owe their election to a magnate; their re-election occurred much more frequently than was once believed; moreover there is no evidence to confirm their absenteeism. The evidence continues to mount and to make it increasingly difficult to question the independence, experience and enthusiasm of members of the lower chamber and thus the influence of the Commons.

It is still necessary to distinguish between different periods. For, if it is true that from roughly 1375 to 1425 Parliament had a role of prime importance in England, and the Commons in Parliament, it is also clear that from the middle of the fifteenth century there was a reaction: the

---

[26] Plucknett, *The Legislation of Edward I* (158); Cuttino, 'Mediaeval Parliament Reinterpreted' (1226); Edwards, *Historians and the Medieval English Parliament* (1231).

[27] Edwards, '"Justice" in Early English Parliaments' (1232); 'The Emergence of Majority Rule' (1233); 'The Huntingdonshire Parliamentary Election' (1234); Wood-Legh, 'Sheriffs, Lawyers and Belted Knights' (1274); 'The Knights' Attendance' (1275); Lewis, 'Re-election to Parliament' (1243); Roskell, 'Aspects and Problems of the English *Modus tenendi Parliamentum*' (1261); 'Perspectives in English Parliamentary History' (1262); *The Commons and their Speakers* (1263); *The Commons in the Parliament of 1422* (1264); 'The Parliamentary Representation of Lincolnshire' (1265); 'The Problem of the Attendance of the Lords' (1266); 'The Social Composition of the Commons' (1267).

Commons were allied increasingly closely with the nobility, Parliament increasingly gave way to the king to such an extent that, in effect, at the beginning of the sixteenth century Parliament was no more in opposition to Henry VII than it had been to Edward I at the end of the thirteenth century.

In this way, taking account of differences of time, place and character, one arrives at a history of the English Parliament considerably more complex and subtle than the Bishop of Oxford had imagined, but not one, however, that makes his opinions look ridiculously out-of-date or radically mistaken.

I am wrong to talk of an outcome. English historians doubtless hold back from giving us the synthesis to which we are legitimately entitled by the acute sense that they are still in the thick of the fray and that it is no time to draw up a balance-sheet. The study of Parliament itself, above all in the fifteenth century, is far from finished. Moreover the history of Parliament will not be properly understood − as, for example, K. B. McFarlane was well aware[28] − unless it is replaced in the general picture of late medieval English political society, whose structures have been far from adequately investigated. Above all it is striking how few, in the course of this century-long quarrel, have seen fit to make any comparison with the situation on the Continent. Now, if it is true that the history of the English Parliament can be summarized by progress in the fourteenth century, culmination about the year 1400 and decline in the fifteenth century, it was evidently not a unique phenomenon, but in step with other European representative assemblies, and its destiny, like theirs, was linked with the preparation, success and ebb of one of the major events of the political history of the West at the end of the Middle Ages, the Council of Constance.

CIVIC HUMANISM

It has been known for a long while that in the fourteenth and fifteenth centuries there was political rivalry on a dramatic scale between Florence and Milan[29] and that this struggle was accompanied by an intense propa-

[28] 'Parliament and "Bastard Feudalism"' (1425).

[29] Baron, *The Crisis of the Early Italian Renaissance* (1421); 'The Social Background of Political Liberty' (1422); Carotti, 'Un politico umanista' (1423); Garin, *L'umanesimo italiano* (1424); Herde, 'Politik und Rhetorik in Florenz' (1425); Kohl, Witt and Welles, *The Earthly Republic* (1426); Martines, *The Social World of the Florentine Humanists* (1427); Oppel, 'Peace vs. Liberty' (1428); Robey, 'P.P. Vergerio the Elder' (1429); Seigel, '"Civic Humanism" or Ciceronian Rhetoric?' (1430); *Rhetoric and Philosophy in Renaissance Humanism* (1431); Witt, 'A Note on Guelfism' (1432); 'The *De Tyranno*' (1433).

ganda war, the propaganda of Milan developing the theme of the *pax Italiae*, the propaganda of Florence that of *libertas*. In the liberal atmosphere of the nineteenth century, J. Burckhardt and G. Voigt took Florentine propaganda at its face value. In the nationalistic atmosphere of Italian unity G. Romano and many others took Milanese propaganda as gospel truth. During yet a third period, the first half of the twentieth century, scepticism developed with regard to both types of propaganda. On the one hand there were 'political' historians like N. Ottokar who animated men who did not in fact know where they were going or where they wished to go; on the other hand there were intellectual historians like P. O. Kristeller who studied humanism without doubting that humanists had been witnesses and sometimes actors in the political events of their time. This trend led to the synthesis of L. Simeoni in 1950, which displayed no interest whatsoever in humanist propaganda.[30]

However, the link between politics and literature was soon re-established. In 1949 N. Valeri attached greater importance to intellectual phenomena.[31] Nevertheless he concluded that humanism was essentially a politically neutral culture. But in his *Umanesimo italiano* of 1950, E. Garin insisted on the importance laid by many generations of humanists on political activity and made an especial study of their eulogies on the active life, demonstrating that their political commitment was not neutral and that most of them, being Florentines, had held republican opinions. This new approach in Italian historiography had been prepared by numerous articles by H. Baron that themselves led in 1955 to his great work: *The Crisis of the Early Italian Renaissance. Civic Humanism and Republican Liberty in an Age of Classicism and Tyranny*. Since 1955 civic humanism has been one of the great problems raised by fourteenth- and fifteenth-century history.

According to H. Baron the main characteristics of civic humanism were admiration for the active life (and no longer for the contemplative), the eulogy of riches as a means of political action, which replaced the eulogy of poverty traditionally made by humanists influenced by Franciscan thought, the defence of liberty and love of one's country which were easily associated with admiration for classical Rome – all these propensities found an outlet in one of the themes fundamental to civic humanism, the foundation of Florence by Sylla, a Roman republican. The poet Petrarch (1304–74), and Coluccio Salutati (1331–1406), chancellor of Florence from 1375 until his death, had at one time occasionally announced these themes. Their fleeting adoption of these attitudes had in 1400 still not changed the traditional atmosphere of humanism in the least. In 1402, at the height of Gian Galeazzo Visconti's attack that threatened the very

---

[30] *Le signorie* (232).
[31] *L'Italia nell' età dei principati* (237).

existence of Florence, Leonardo Bruni, until then a humanist in the traditional mould, was suddenly converted by an intense love of liverty and a great hatred of tyrants which then inflamed the relatively un-cultured Florentine citizens, principal among whom was Goro Dati, author of the *Istoria di Firenze*. Leonardo Bruni was the first and the most important representative of civic humanism which, forged in the struggle against Milan, used 'the classical model as a guide to create a new literature with a new language in a new nation'. This humanism flourished remarkably throughout the first half of the fifteenth century, and even later, although somewhat displaced by the rise to power of the Medicis, it re-emerged from time to time in the foreground of Florentine history, which would be inexplicable without it.

H. Baron's theories have been subjected to manifold attacks. First the 'political' historians have observed that it does not follow automatically, as H. Baron implicitly states that Milan was evil and Florence good. Some emphasize the positive facets of the lordship of the Visconti; others reveal the murky aspects of the Florentine regime, which was after all no more than the hegemony of one privileged class over a town. The Italians, above all the neighbours of Florence, preferred the tyranny of Milan to Florentine liberty.

On the other hand there are historians who admit the importance of the humanists' political role but refuse to accept the idea of a sudden turn-about in 1402. In the first place because they do not support the new chronology of the works of Leonardo Bruni proposed by H. Baron and upon which his entire thesis depends. And above all because they main-tain, following E. Garin, that the true founder of civic humanism was not Leonardo Bruni but Coluccio Salutati. It was Coluccio Salutati who first developed this scorn for contemplative literature and the eulogy of civil life which was the foundation of humanism and for a long while remained one of the traditional themes of Florentine humanism.

Quite recently P. Herde and J. E. Seigel have gone still further. Accord-ing to P. Herde the theme of liberty is a well-worn one taken from Florentine Guelphism and Coluccio Salutati's work was not original when he took it up in his letters as Chancellor of Florence. Moreover this much-paraded freedom did not prevent either Florence from seeking an alliance with some tyrants, nor Salutati from resuming his amicable correspon-dence with the Visconti chancellor once peace was established. Because their employers had been stupid enough to wage war, he wrote, there was no need for their friendship to suffer. One should not, concluded P. Herde, take the tirades of the humanists at face value. They praise the tyrant when he is the paymaster, freedom when they are in the service of the republic.

As for J. E. Seigel he has convincingly explained Leonardo Bruni's writings in terms of his education and activity as a rhetorician rather than by his political beliefs. He shows how the humanists are the heirs of the *dictatores*, that the debate between the *vita contemplativa* and the *vita activa* is purely a literary, rhetorical one, the genre having been rediscovered in the fourteenth century at the same time as Cicero's *De Oratore*. 'The history of ideas', he concluded, 'should be integrated with social history, but we should guard against the temptation of simply replacing the first with the second.'

After the enthusiasm aroused by H. Baron's theories, doubt had assailed the historians once more. Perhaps humanists were purely rhetoricians, politically neutral, whose utterances were guided by circumstance; perhaps there was nothing much left of the civic humanism of H. Baron.

At least there remains Gian Galeazzo Visconti's famous declaration that the letters of Salutati had done him more harm than a thousand cavalry. If it is difficult to discover the real feelings of the humanists in the fourteenth and fifteenth centuries, it is still quite clear that their writings played an important role in Italian political life. It might now be useful to look at the problem from a different angle, not to go on trying to untangle the origins of humanist writings, but to measure their influence. This should be done with a conviction that neither the autonomy nor the close interaction of political and intellectual history should be underestimated.

THE HUSSITE REVOLUTION

Historians have long been convinced of the complexity of the Hussite movement.[32] For more than a century no one has contested its simultaneously religious, national and social character. But Hussitism is indeed a sufficiently complex phenomenon for everyone to find his own version of the truth.

From the start Protestant historians took a great interest in Hus studies because he preceded Luther, and Hussitism because it heralded the Reformation. Catholic historians, on the other hand, tarred the heretical Wycliffe and Hus, his epigony, with the same censorious brush. With the re-emergence of Czech national consciousness in the middle of the nineteenth century a national opposition between Czech and German historians was added to the old religious polarity. F. Palacky made a fervent study, both of Hus whom he made a Czech national hero, and of the Hussite period – for him the high point of Czech history – while the Germans continued to see Hus as a narrow-minded fanatic and Hussitism

---

[32] Kalivoda, 'Seibt's *Hussitica*' (1307); Macek, 'Jean Hus et son époque' (1322); Seibt, *Hussitica* (1340).

as a period of anarchy. The addition of a national to the religious perspective forced some qualifications upon the Catholic Czech historians and the German Protestant historians, who were careful to emphasize everything which, for all that, still separated Hus from the great Luther. The more Germano-Czech relations deteriorated, the more the national viewpoint asserted itself. Whilst in the young Czechoslovak republic Hussitology became a privileged field of historical research and Czech historians tended to overestimate the national character of the Hussite movement, German historians cultivated such an aversion for Hus and Hussitism that it deterred them from this area.

The end of the Second World War imposed quite different perspectives by placing Hus and Hussitism under a Marxist light. The liberal historians of pre-1945 were not unaware of the social character of the Hussite movement. But in their eyes this was a secondary characteristic. The Marxist historians rescued Hussitology from an excessively narrow national Czech viewpoint and made their priority research into the social problems, thus adding much to our knowledge of the Hussite Revolution. Or at least the Czech Marxist historians did. For the Marxist historians of East Germany – held up this time by Engels's idea that the Peasants' War (1524–5) was the first European revolution of the capitalist period – continued, in the eyes of the Czechs, to underestimate the importance of the Hussite revolutionary movement.

The work of the Czech Marxist historians has tended to renew the image of Hus and Hussitism. They tried firstly to present John Hus not just as a cleric obsessed by the idea of sin and the decadence of the Church, but also as a man profoundly aware ˙of social problems. They worked moreover to make better known the Taborite movement, that is, the 'radical and communist movement within Hussitism itself' (J. Macek); to place Hussitism more accurately within fifteenth-century Czech society; and to place it more accurately within the European framework of the 'first crisis of feudalism' (F. Graus).[33] Thus to Hus the Protestant, Hus the liberal and Hus the patriot, was added a socio-revolutionary Hus, and the Hussite Revolution became the first revolution of the capitalist period.

It is difficult to agree that Hus must be placed first on the social plane. The Marxist revision of Hus is undoubtedly less convincing than the Marxist revision of Hussitism, whose social character had previously been underestimated. However, even the Hussitism of the Czech Marxists has met with some reservations. Firstly, they have been criticized for having overestimated the importance of Taborism in the Hussite movement, of making what was just one current the essence of Hussitism. In his *Hussitica* F. Seibt has best expressed these criticisms. Hussitism, he argues,

[33] 'Das Spätmittelalter als Krisenzeit' (40).

should not be reduced to the revolutionary Utopianism of the Taborite movement. It was in fact a mixture of various currents – religious, national and social. More precisely: although before F. Seibt it had always been thought that Hussitism had drawn these different currents together, the German historian believed that the Hussites had only been given a spurious unity by hatred of their enemy and that, far from mingling the different currents within the movement, had always remained distinct from, if not opposed to, the others. There was no synthesis but *Nebenein-ander* (juxtaposition), if not indeed *Gegeneinander* (polarity) of the aspirations of the different estates, who all wanted change in some area. To understand the Hussite Revolution it should not be made a pre-capitalist revolution, but should be placed in the context of the orders and estates of fifteenth-century society.

Another criticism of the Marxist interpretation is that it does not recognize the autonomy of heresy, but makes it simply the reflection of social unrest. Certainly a successful heresy always leaves its imprint on the social context, but there is no reason to underestimate the role of religious uncertainty in heresy, nor to fail to evaluate what Hussitism owes to the anguished doubts of the faithful at the beginning of the fifteenth century.

More than a century of intense debte, above all in the last twenty years, has remarkably enriched our knowledge of the Hussite Revolution. We are better able to appreciate its complexity; we are aware of what must be done to continue to progress towards a better understanding. We must stop explaining Hussitism by what was to follow it and place it in a contemporary context. We must stop explaining one facet crudely in terms of another, however real they both may be. In our study of Hussitism we must take account of the religious, economic, social and political problems that affected the whole of Europe at the beginning of the fifteenth century, without, however, neglecting its local aspects. For the Hussite revolution was a vital moment in Czech history, but also one of those rare phenomena in which the whole of European history appears to be encapsulated and one may legitimately wonder whether historians will ever be able to master its complexity.

REFORMATIO SIGISMUNDI

The *Reformatio Sigismundi* is a text written in German.[34] It enjoyed a wide audience since it has survived in seventeen manuscripts, was printed as

[34] Dohna, *Reformatio Sigismundi* (1289); Koller, 'Untersuchungen zur Reformatio Sigismundi (1314); Straube, 'Die Reformatio Sigismundi' (1341).

early as 1476, four further editions were produced before 1500 and it was published four times more in 1520–22. The *Reformatio Sigismundi* undoubtedly played a part in the events that led to the Peasants' War.

Historical criticism seized hold of this important text in 1876 and has not yet released its grip. It poses such formidable problems that after one hundred years of uninterrupted research we still do not know for sure the date, the author, the sources or even the meaning. That is not to say that in a century there has been no real progress – on the contrary.

One school of historians, foremost amongst them H. Koller, has seen their main task as the study of manuscripts, the sources of the treatise and the identification of the author. It would undoubtedly be difficult to take this approach beyond the conclusions which they have now reached. The author's name remains permanently irrecoverable. However, we can take comfort in the fact that a mere name would have added nothing to the affair and that, moreover, attentive study of the manuscripts demonstrates that there was not one author but four: the original redaction, written in 1439 in a milieu closely connected with the Council of Basel, was edited three times, first at Augsburg in 1440, then at Basel again before 1449 and in the Rhineland just after the middle of the century.

Without despising these scholarly researches, Marxist historians like M. Straube maintained that they did not tackle the essential question, which was to understand the work's meaning and significance. Now their task in this respect was facilitated by the fact that in his study of the Peasants' War, F. Engels had seen the *Reformatio Sigismundi* (printed the very year when the Niklashausen town-crier heralded the beginning of revolutionary disturbance in rural Germany) as a revolutionary document that had contributed very considerably to the explosion of 1524. The Marxist historians therefore set themselves the task of studying the actual content of the *Reformatio Sigismundi* and placing it in the context of German revolutionary activity on the eve of the Peasants' War. Lothar, count of Dohna, did not deny the revolutionary use to which the *Reformatio Sigismundi* was put at the end of the fifteenth and the beginning of the sixteenth century, but he believed that the text itself should be studied and that one should first perceive the intentions of the authors at the time when they were writing, towards the end of the first half of the fifteenth century. Now all the evidence would suggest that the authors were not revolutionaries but reformers concerned – like so many other medieval pamphleteers – above all with justice and with peace.

This interpretation has the merit of attempting to place the *Reformatio Sigismundi* in context. Like Langland in England three-quarters of a century earlier, the author of the *Reformatio Sigismundi* only expressed moderate ideas with great force. These would tally very well with the contemporary atmosphere, if one recalls the history of the Council of Basel and if one accepts the ideas of G. Franz, according to which peasant revolts in Germany before 1476 pursued only conservative and reforming aims. The trouble is that Lothar, count of Dohna, comes up against objections that he is unable to rebut convincingly. Even the non-Marxist reader of Lothar, count of Dohna, cannot doubt that the *Reformatio Sigismundi* speaks of the *Gemein Folck* (the common people), undoubtedly referring to the lowest orders of society. The fact remains that the *Reformatio Sigismundi* announces the second coming of the king-priest Frederick and then demands *Slach iederman zue*, 'Let every man go to'. If we admit that the *Reformatio Sigismundi* might have been a reforming text for its writers, for all its readers – and that is what matters – it was undoubtedly a revolutionary text. It is thus impossible to ignore the idea that to understand the *Reformatio Sigismundi* properly, it would make sense to look not just at the milieu of the reformers at Basel but also at Hussite revolutionary currents.

All things considered, future research will probably end by placing the *Reformatio Sigismundi* more squarely still in the reforming, prophetic and revolutionary atmosphere of the fifteenth century. However, I do not see how one can escape the conclusion that this text, written in southern Germany, then published in Augsburg, was one of the essential stages on the road leading from the Hussite Revolt to the Peasants' War.

WHEN DID THE MIDDLE AGES END IN ENGLAND?

In the *Report of the Royal Commission on the Constitution and Working of Ecclesiastical Courts* of 1883 W. Stubbs demonstrated that the canon law of the Roman Church had never really been applied in medieval England by the ecclesiastical tribunals. He thus confirmed opinions dear to the Anglican authorities: the English Church had been national throughout the Middle Ages; the establishment of an independent Anglican Church only formalized an existing situation; the measures of the 1530s were in no sense a rupture. Queen Victoria's subjects would not have been pleased to have found the end of the Middle Ages here.

On the other hand, the efficacy of Tudor propaganda had long enabled the English to recognize the father of modern England. This was the founder of the Tudor dynasty, Henry VII, who, after the period of disasters abroad and civil war, had been able to remodel English institutions and establish the power of the State on new foundations. For a long while the date of 1485 traditionally marked the end of the Middle Ages in England.

For some years there has been a tendency to admit that in many areas the Yorkist period prepared the way for the reign of Henry VII. For example, A. B. Ferguson made Fortescue the first Tudor pamphleteer; B. P. Wolffe has shown that the much-vaunted financial reorganization of Henry VII was simply an extension of the vigorous measures taken by Edward IV and Richard III. There are many, therefore, who would now bring the birth of modern England forward from 1485 to 1461.

Others would then point to numerous characteristics of Yorkist England which were already present under the Lancastrians and maintain that generally after the Wars of the Roses the kingdom under the Yorkists and the Tudors ran along lines already familiar in the fourteenth century. To follow the argument closely let us remember first how H. G. Richardson and G. O. Sayles believed – in opposition to W. Stubbs – that in the thirteenth century the English ecclesiastical courts did indeed properly apply the canon law of the Roman Catholic church and that English lawyers of this period were still very much in touch with judicial thought on the Continent. It was after Bracton, at the end of the thirteenth century, that the English jurists, trained far from the great universities in Inns of Court (practical schools with limited horizons), began to lose sight of the Continent, to be turned in upon themselves and prepare for the intellectual impoverishment and insularization of England that was to characterize the establishment of the English Church. It would be possible to take other examples of this continuity and arrive at the conclusion that the end of the Middle Ages in England is lost in the sands of time.

It was at this point that G. R. Elton abruptly shook the myth of continuity. In his analysis, although Henry VII had the great merit of restoring order and peace, he did so by using time-honoured traditional methods and especially by making use of the means offered by his household, as many of his thirteenth- and fourteenth-century predecessors had done. Moreover, Henry VII personally played a large role in this work of administrative restoration. This last characteristic provided dazzling confirmation that the England of Henry VII, and even that of the first years of Henry VIII, was still medieval.

All that changed in the 1530s when Henry VIII made use of the genius of Thomas Cromwell. There was first the break with Rome, whose daring should not be underestimated, nor the dangers into which it brought England's rulers, nor the agonies of conscience it provoked in many Catholics. It was only after this break that England could lay any claim to be a sovereign state. To ensure its success Cromwell had to manipulate English public opinion, increase the legislative power of Parliament and thus give a place such as it had not previously held to parliamentary law, the Statute. To this must be added a veritable remodelling of the central administration. The work of the king's secretary, keeper of the signet, was now the hub of administrative work; from being a fluid and informal body, the Council became a fixed and permanent organ of government; the king no longer had any personal impact on a bureaucracy that henceforth acted of its own accord. Under Henry VII and in the opening years of the reign of Henry VIII the vitality and impact of government institutions still depended on the king himself and on his household; English government was still medieval. Cromwell's reforms, on the other hand, created a bureaucratic government that was resolutely modern. Thanks to Cromwell, therefore, we may talk of a veritable revolution in England in the 1530s that killed the Middle Ages.

There has been no shortage of objections to Elton's thesis. It has been observed that, if there was a revolution, Cromwell's part in it was not so very considerable; that the England of 1547 was after all not so very different from the England of 1509; and finally that the incontestable changes which did occur in the reign of Henry VIII had in fact been prepared by a process of secular change: the national sovereign State was not a product of the Reformation, on the contrary it was an instrument of the Reformation; the legislative role of Parliament was not so negligible before 1530 and English government was bureaucratic long before that date.

These historians refuse to see English history as the unrolling of a smooth continuum unbroken by sudden events. They admit a series of even stretches and sudden breaks. But when all is said and done, they do not believe that the incontestable changes of the 1530s constitute a real revolution and deserve – more than 1485 or 1461, for example – to be considered as marking the end of the Middle Ages.

When, then, did the Middle Ages end in England? The economic or cultural historian might perhaps be able to provide a more precise answer to this question. But the historian of the State would rather not be asked. Most recent discussions have at least shown convincingly that if there is no obligation to make medieval England stop in 1485 there is also no overriding reason for extending it to 1530.

Bibliography

SOURCES

It is extremely difficult to define and review the sources required for the study of political history. At one level everything is a source for political structures. There is much valuable material for the political historian in the *Treaty Rolls* edited by P. Chaplais, the *Gascon Rolls* edited by Y. Renouard and in A. Lhotsky's edition of the *Chronica Austriae* of Thomas Ebendorfer, to mention only a few publications. But there is a risk of undue digression with this line of enquiry. It is also pointless to repeat here sources that have long been in print and are easily traced in such well known works as those of F. Lot and R. Fawtier (144), A. Marongiu (1154) and J. Favier (582). It has therefore generally seemed preferable to allow the authors of works mentioned in the bibliography to communicate their own sources. Where an edition of a text is also preceded by a substantial historical introduction it has also been included in the bibliography. The choice of sources is thus deliberately selective. Further information on primary sources is to be found in R.C. van Caenegem, *Guide to the Sources of Medieval History* (Amsterdam, 1977), whilst current work in journals is documented in the *International Medieval Bibliography*, directed by R.S. Hoyt and P.H. Sawyer, 1967– (Leeds, 1968–).

Attention must nevertheless be drawn at the outset to several collective enterprises which have contributed to progress in many areas of the study of political history. In the series *Recueil des historiens de la France* the Académie des Inscriptions et Belles-Lettres de l'Institut de France has produced several volumes of *Documents financiers* which facilitate a better understanding of both French and Burgundian finances in the works of R. Fawtier and F. Maillard and of M. Mollat. The ordinances issued by Philip the Bold and Margaret de Male between 1381 and 1393 were published by P. Bonenfant, J. Bartier and A. van Nieuwenhuysen in the *Recueil des anciennes ordonnances de la Belgique* in 1965. Also in Belgium J. Cuvelier, J. Dhondt and R. Doehard published in 1965 the *Actes de 1427 à 1477* in the series of the *Actes des Etats généraux des anciens Pays-Bas,* under the aegis of the Commission royale d'histoire. A new series of the *Monumenta Germaniae Historica, Staatsschriften des späteren Mittelalters*, was initiated (with volume II) in 1941 and the *Viridarium* of

Dietrich of Nieheim (edited by A. Lhotsky and K. Pivec, 1956), the writings of Alexander of Roes (edited by H. Grundmann and H. Heimpel, 1958), the *Reformatio Sigismundi* (edited by H. Koller, 1964) and a three-volume edition of Konrad von Megenberg's *Ökonomik* (edited by S. Krüger, 1973, 1977, 1984) have already appeared. The publication of the *Deutsche Reichstagsakten* by the Historische Kommission der Bayerischen Akademie der Wissenschaften continues to progress under the direction of H. Heimpel. By 1973 volumes I–XVII; XIX, i and XXII, i had appeared, covering the period 1376–1470. This series (*Ältere Reihe*) is to consist of twenty-four volumes up to 1485. A *Mittlere Reihe* of twelve volumes for the years 1486 to 1518 is envisaged of which three volumes (to 1490) had appeared in 1972. The Fondazione Italiana per la Storia Amministrativa has, in addition to its *Annali*, published a monograph series, *Italica: Raccolta di Documenti sulla Amministrazione Pubblica in Italia del Medioevo alla Constituzione dello Stato Nazionale*. Early volumes included A.R. Natale's edition of *I Diari di Cicco Simonetta* (1962) and (in two volumes) the *Acta in Concilio secreto in castello Portae Jovis Mediolani, 1477–1478* (1963–4), while *Stilus Cancellarie. Formulario Visconti-Sforzesco* (1979) constituted the nineteenth volume. The Neapolitan archivists B. Mazzoleni, E. Pontieri and C. Salvati have been engaged in the reconstruction of the riches of their collection destroyed in the Second World War; their work has borne fruit in the invaluable eight-volume *Fonti Aragonesi (1442–1501)* (Accademia Pontaniana di Napoli, 1957–71).

Besides these large-scale collective enterprises some monographs which provide particularly remarkable illustrations in various areas of political history are listed below:

1   Bougard, P. and Gysselivy, M., *L'impôt royal en Artois (1295–1302). Rôles du 100ᵉ et du 50ᵉ présentés et publiés avec une table anthroponymique*, Louvain, 1970.

2   Boulet, M., *Questiones Johannis Galli*, Paris, 1944.

3   Boulton, H.E., *The Sherwood Forest Book*, Nottingham, 1965.

4   Bourgain-Hemeryck, P., *Les oeuvres latines d'Alain Chartier*, Paris, 1977.

5   Casini, B., *Il catasto di Pisa del 1428–1429*, Pisa, 1964.

6   Cazelles, R., Lettres closes, lettres 'de par le roy' de Philippe de Valois, *Annuaire-Bulletin de la Société de l'Histoire de France*, 1956–1957, 61–225.

7   Chrimes, S.B. and Brown, A.L., *Select Documents of English Constitutional History, 1307–1485*, London, 1961.

8   Dupont-Ferrier, G., *Gallia Regia ou Etat des officiers royaux des bailliages et des sénéchaussées de 1328 à 1515*, 7 vols, Paris, 1942–66.

9   Elze, R., *Die 'Ordines' für die Weihe und Krönung des Kaisers und der Kaiserin*, Hanover, 1960.

10   Favier, J., *Cartulaire et Actes d'Enguerran de Marigny*, Paris, 1965.

11   Glénisson, J. and Mollat, G., *L'administration des Etats de l'Eglise au XIVᵉ siècle. Correspondance des légats et vicaires généraux*, I, *Gil Albornoz et Androin de La Roche (1353–1367)*, Paris, 1964.

12   Jones, M. (ed.), *Recueil des actes de Jean IV, duc de Bretagne*, I, nos. 1–430 (1357–1382), Paris, 1980.

13   Lewis, E., *Medieval Political Ideas*, 2 vols, London, 1954.

14 Martens, M., *Actes relatifs à l'administration des revenus domaniaux du duc de Brabant (1271–1408)*, Brussels, 1943.
15 Medici, L. de', *Lettere*, I (*1460–74*), II (*1474–8*) ed. R. Fubini, III (*1478–9*), ed. N. Rubinstein, Florence, 1977.
16 Müller, K., *Die Goldene Bulle Kaiser Karls IV, 1356*, Bern, 1957.
17 Näf, W., *Herrschaftsverträge des Spätmittelalters*, Bern, 1951.
18 Nieheim, D. von., *Historie de gestis romanorum principum. Cronica. Gesta Karoli Magni imperatoris*, ed. K. Colberg and J. Leuschner, Stuttgart, 1980.
19 Paravicini Bagliani, A., Eine Briefsammlung für Rektoren des Kirchenstaates (1250–1320), *DA*, 35 (1979), 138–208.
20 Pocquet du Haut-Jussé, B.-A., *La France goûvernée par Jean sans Peur. Les dépenses du receveur général du royaume*, Paris, 1959.
21 Quillet, J., *Marsile de Padoue. Le défenseur de la paix*, Paris, 1968.
22 Richardson, H.G. and Sayles, G.O., *Parliaments and Councils of Mediaeval Ireland*, Dublin, 1947.
23 Sayles, G.O., *Select Cases in the Court of King's Bench under Edward I, Edward II and Edward III*, 6 vols, London, 1936–65.
24 Schneider, J. (ed.), *Lorraine et Bourgogne (1473–8)*, Nancy, 1982.
25 Schultze, J., *Das Landbuch der Mark Brandenburg von 1375*, Berlin, 1940.
26 Thielemans, M.R., Les Croÿ, conseillers des ducs de Bourgogne. Documents extraits de leurs archives familiales, 1337–1487, *Bulletin de la Commission royale d'Histoire*, 124 (1959), 1–141.
27 Timbal, P.-C. et al., *La Guerre de Cent Ans vue à travers les registres du Parlement (1337–1369)*, Paris, 1961.
28 Vernet, A., *Le Tragicum argumentum de miserabili statu regni Francie* de Francois de Monte-Belluna (1357), *Annuaire-Bulletin de la Société de l'Histoire de France*, 1962–73, 101–163; repr. in Vernet, A., *Etudes médiévales*, Paris, 1981, 251–311.
29 Wilkinson, B., *Constitutional History of England in the Fifteenth Century (1399–1485), with illustrative documents*, London, 1964.
30 Wilkinson, B., *Constitutional History of Medieval England, 1216–1399*, 3 vols, London, 1948–58.

THE CONCEPT OF THE WEST

31 Hay, D., *Europe. The Emergence of an Idea*, new edn, Edinburgh, 1968.

ETYMOLOGY AND SEMANTICS OF THE LATER MEDIEVAL STATE

32 Baszkiewicz, J., *Panstwo suwerenne w feudalnej doktrynie politycznej do poczatkow XIV w.* [The supremacy of the State in early fourteenth-century feudal theory] (with French summary), Warsaw, 1964.

J

33 Bossuat, A., La formule 'le roi est empereur en son royaume'. Son emploi au
    XVᵉ siècle devant le Parlement de Paris, *RHDFE* (1961), 371–81.

34 Chabod, F., Alcune questioni di terminologia: stato, nazione, patria nel
    linguaggio del Cinquecento, *L'idea di nazione*, Bari, 1962, 141–86.

35 Chabod, F., Y a-t-il un Etat de la Renaissance?, in *De Pétrarque à Descartes*.
    III, *Actes du Colloque sur la Renaissance* . . ., Paris, 1958, 57–78.

36 Der Heydte, F.A. von, *Die Geburtsstunde des souveränen Staates*, Ratisbonne,
    1952.

37 Ehler, S.Z., On applying the modern term 'State' to the Middle Ages, in
    Medieval Studies presented to Aubrey Gwynn, S.J., ed. J.A. Watt, J.B. Morrall and
    F.X. Martin, Dublin, 1961, 492–501.

38 Ferguson, W.K., *Europe in Transition, 1300–1520*, Boston, 1962.

39 Geremek, B. La notion d'Europe et la prise de conscience européenne au bas
    Moyen Age, in *La Pologne au XVe Congrès International des Sciences Historiques à
    Bucarest*, Wroclaw, 1980, 69–94.

40 Graus, F., Das Spätmittelalter als Krizenzeit. Ein Literaturberich als
    Zwischenbilanz, *Mediaevalia Bohemica*, I (1969), suppl.

41 Guenée, B., Y a-t-il un Etat des XIVᵉ et XVᵉ siècles?, *Ann.* (1971), 399–406.

42 Guenée, B., *Politique et Histoire au Moyen Age. Recueil d'articles sur l'histoire
    politique et l'historiographie médiévales (1956–1981)*, Paris, 1981.

43 Hale, J.R., Highfield, J.R.L. and Smalley, B. (eds) *Europe in the Late Middle
    Ages*, London, 1965.

44 Hassinger, E., *Das Werden des neuzeitlichen Europa, 1300–1600*, Brunswick,
    1959.

45 Horalkova, Z. et al., Die Aussagen der alttschechischen Sprache über die
    mittelalterliche Auffassung des Staates in Böhmen, *Zeitschrift für Slawistik*, 18
    (1973), 838–52.

46 Jordan, W.C., McNab, B. and Ruiz, T.F. (eds) *Order and Innovation in the
    Middle Ages. Essays in Honor of Joseph R. Strayer*, Princeton, 1976.

47 Lyon, B.D., Medieval Constitutionalism: a Balance of Power, in *Album H.M.
    Cam. Studies presented to the international commission for the history of representative
    and parliamentary institutions*, 24, Louvain/Paris, 1961, 155–83.

48 Maravall, J.A., The Origins of the Modern State, *Cahiers d'Histoire mondiale*,
    6 (1961), 788–808.

49 Maravall, J.A. *Estado moderno y mentalidad social, siglos XV a XVII*, 2 vols,
    Madrid, 1972.

50 Mitteis, H., *Der Staat des hohen Mittelalters. Grundlinien einer vergleichenden
    Verfassungsgeschichte des Lehnzeitalters*, 8th edn, Darmstadt, 1968.

51 Mochi Onory, S., *Fonti canonistiche dell'idea moderna dello Stato (imperium
    spirituale, jurisdictio divisa, sovranità)*, Milan, 1951.

52 Näf, W., Frühformen des 'modernen Staates' im Spätmittelalter, *HZ*, 171
    (1951), 225–43.

53 Näf, W. and Hofmann, H.H. (eds), *Die Entstehung des modernen souveränen
    Staates*, Cologne/Berlin, 1967, 101–14.

54 Post, G., *Studies in Medieval Legal Thought. Public Law and the State, 1100–1322*,
    Princeton, 1964.

55 Powicke, F.M., Reflections on the Medieval State, *TRHS*, 4th ser., 19 (1936), 1–18.

56 *Les Principautés au Moyen Age* (Actes des Congrès de la Société des Historiens médiévistes de l'Enseignement supérieur public. Communications du Congrès de Bordeaux en 1973), Bordeaux, 1979.

57 Rotelli, E. and Schiera, P. (eds), *Lo Stato moderno*, I, *Dal Medioevo all'età moderna*, Bologna, 1971.

58 Schneider, J., Le problème des principautés en France et dans l'Empire (X^e–XVe siècles), in *Principautés et territoires et études d'histoire lorraine: Actes du CIII^e Congrès national des Sociétés savantes, Nancy-Metz, 1978*, Paris, 1979, 9–39.

59 Schnith, K., Gedanken zu den Königsabsetzungen im Spätmittelalter, *Historisches Jahrbuch*, 91 (1971), 309–26.

60 Strayer, J.R., *On the Medieval Origins of the Modern State*, Princeton, 1970.

THE EMPIRE: CONCEPT AND REALITY

61 Bader, K.S., Kaiserliche und ständische Reformgedanken in der Reichsreform des endenden 15. Jahrhunderts, *HJ*, 73 (1954), 74–94.

62 Baethgen, F., Zur Geschichte der Weltherrschaftsidee im späteren Mittelalter; in *Festschrift P.E. Schramm*, I, Wiesbaden, 1964, 189–203.

63 Barraclough, G., *The Mediaeval Empire. Idea and Reality*, London, 1950.

64 Bauer, R., *Sacrum Imperium* et *Imperium Germanicum* chez Nicolas de Cues, *Archives d'histoire doctrinale et littéraire du Moyen Age*, 29 (1954), 207–40.

65 Becker, H.J., Das Mandat *Fidem Catholicam* Ludwigs des Bayern von 1338, *DA*, 26 (1970), 454–512.

66 Bock, F., *Reichsidee und Nationalstaaten vom Untergang des alten Reiches bis zur Kündigung des deutsch-englischen Bündnisses im Jahre 1341*, Munich, 1943.

67 Brackmann, A., Die Ostpolitik Ottos des Grossen, *HZ*, 134 (1926), 242–56.

68 David, M., Le contenu de l'hégémonie impériale dans la doctrine de Bartole, in *Bartolo da Sassoferrato. Studi e documenti per il vi centenario*, ed. D. Segolini II, Milan, 1962, 199–216.

69 Dempf, A., *Sacrum Imperium. Geschichts- und Staatsphilosophie des Mittelalters und der politischen Renaissance*, 3rd edn, Munich, 1962.

70 Diehl, A., Heiliges Römisches Reich Deutscher Nation, *HZ*, 156 (1937), 457–84.

71 Engels, O., Der Reichsgedanke auf dem Konstanzer Konzil, *HJ*, 86 (1966), 80–106.

72 Folz, R., Der Brief des italienischen Humanisten Niccolo dei Beccari an Karl IV. Ein Beitrag zur Kaiseridee im 14. Jahrhundert, *HJ*, 82 (1963), 148–62.

73 Folz, R., *L'idée d'Empire en Occident du Ve au XIVe siècle*, Paris, 1953.

74 Folz, R., Le Saint Empire romain germanique, *Recueils da la Société Jean Bodin*, XXXI *Les Grands Empires*, Brussels, 1973, 309–55.

75 Graus, F., Kaiser Karl IV. Betrachtungen zur Literatur eines Jubiläumsjahres (1378/1978), *Jahrbücher für Geschichte Osteuropas*, 28 (1980), 71–88.

76 Hesslinger, H., *Die Anfänge des Schwäbischen Bundes. Ein Beitrag zur Geschichte des Einungswesens und der Reichsreform unter Kaiser Friedrich III*, Stuttgart, 1970.

77 Hödl, G., Reichsregierung und Reichsreform unter König Albrecht II. Eine Bestandsaufnahme, *ZHF*, I (1974), 129–45.

78 Hödl, G., *Albrecht II. Königtum, Reichsregierung und Reichsreform (1438–1439)*, Vienna/Cologne/Graz, 1978.

79 Holtzmann, W., Imperium und Nationen, in *Relazioni del X Congresso Internazionale di Scienze Storiche, Roma, 1955*, III, *Storia del Medioevo*, Florence, 1955, 273–303.

80 Kaiser Karl IV. (1316–1378), *Blätter für deutsche Landesgeschichte*, 114 (1978).

81 Kampers, F., *Kaiserprophetieen und Kaisersagen im Mittelalter. Ein Beitrag zur Geschichte der deutschen Kaiseridee*, Munich, 1895.

82 Koch, G., Die mittelalterliche Kaiserpolitik im Spiegel der bürgerlichen deutschen Historiographie des 19. und 20. Jahrhunderts, *ZGW*, 10 (1962), 1837–70.

83 Kölmel, W., Petrarca und das Reich. Zum historisch-politischen Aspekt der *studia humanitatis*, *Historisches Jahrbuch*, 90 (1970), 1–30.

84 Koller, H., Kaiserliche Politik und die Reformpläne des 15. Jahrhunderts, in *Festschrift für Hermann Heimpel, den Mitarbeiten des Max-Planck-Instituts für Geschichte*, II, Göttingen, 1972, 61–79.

85 Laufs, A., Reichsstädte und Reichsreform, *Zeitschrift der Savigny-Stiftung für Rechtsgeschichte*, 84 (1967), Germanistische Abteilung, 172–201.

86 Löwe, H. Dante und das Kaisertum, *HZ*, 190 (1960), 517–52.

87 McCready, W.D., The Problem of the Empire in Augustinus Triumphus and Late Medieval Papal Hierocratic Theory, *Traditio*, 30 (1974), 325–49.

88 Moraw, P., Kaiser Karl IV. im deutschen Spätmittelalter, *HZ*, 229 (1979), 1–24.

89 Most, R., Der Reichsgedanke des Lupold von Bebenburg, *DA*, 4 (1940), 444–85.

90 Müller-Mertens, E., Kaiser Karl IV, 1346–1378. Herausforderung zur Wertung einer geschichtlicher Persönlichkeit, *Zeitschrift für Geschichtswissenschaft*, 27 (1979), 340–56.

91 Post, G., Two Notes on Nationalism in the Middle Ages, *Traditio*, 9 (1953), 281–320.

92 Rowan, S.W. A Reichstag in the Reform Era: Freiburg im Breisgau, 1497, in *The Old Reich. Essays on German Political Institutions, 1495–1806*, eds J.A. Vann and S.W. Rowan, Brussels, 1974, 31–57.

93 Schneider, F., *Universalstaat oder Nationalstaat*, Innsbruck, 1941.

94 Schröcker, A., *Unio atque concordia. Reichspolitik Bertholds von Henneberg, 1484 bis 1504*, Würzburg, 1970.

95 Schröcker, A., Maximilians I. Auffassung vom Königtum und das ständische Reich, Beobachtungen an ungedruckten Quellen italienischer Herkunft, *Quellen und Forschungen aus italienischen Archiven und Bibliotheken*, 50 (1971), 181–204.

96 Schubert, E., Königswahl und Königtum im spätmittelalterlichen Reich, *ZHF*, 4 (1977), 257–338.

97 Schubert, E., *König und Reich: Studien zur spätmittelalterlichen deutschen Verfassungsgeschichte*, Göttingen, 1979.

98 Seibt, F., *Karl IV. Ein Kaiser in Europa, 1346–1378*, Munich, 1978.

99 Seibt, F., Zum Reichsvikariat für den Dauphin, 1378, *ZHF*, 8 (1981), 129–58.

100 Sproemberg, H., Contribution à l'histoire de l'idée d'Empire au Moyen Age, *RBPH*, 39 (1961), 309–33.

101 Toews, J.B., Dream and Reality in the Imperial Ideology of Pope Pius II, *Medievalia et Humanistica*, 16 (1964), 77–93.

102 Trautz, F., Die Reichsgewalt in Italien im Spätmittelalter, *Heidelberger Jahrbücher*, 7 (1963), 45–81.

103 Walther, H., *Imperiales Königtum, Konziliarismus und Volkssouveränität. Studien zu den Grenzen des mittelalterlichen Souveränitätsgedankens*, Munich, 1976.

NATIONAL STUDIES: THE BRITISH ISLES,
FRANCE AND THE LOW COUNTRIES

104 Autrand, F., *Pouvoir et société en France, XIVe–XVe siècles*, Paris, 1974.

105 Barrow, G.W.S., *Robert Bruce and the Community of the Realm of Scotland*, London, 1965.

106 Bautier, R.-H., Diplomatique et histoire politique: ce que la critique diplomatique apprend sur la personnalité de Philippe le Bel, *RH*, 525 (1978), 3–27.

107 Bonenfant, P., *Du meurtre de Montereau au traité de Troyes*, Brussels, 1958.

108 Bonenfant, P., *Philippe le Bon*, 3rd edn, Brussels, 1955.

109 Bossuat, A., Le Parlement de Paris pendant l'occupation anglaise, *RH*, 229 (1963), 19–40.

110 Cazelles, R., *La société politique et la crise de la royauté sous Philippe de Valois*, Paris, 1958.

111 Cazelles, R., Jean II le Bon: Quel homme? Quel roi?, *RH*, 509 (1974), 5–26.

112 Cazelles, R., Charles V et le fardeau de la couronne, *Ann. Bull. de la Société de l'Histoire de France, Années 1978–1979–1980* (1981), 67–75.

113 Cazelles, R., *Société politique, noblesse et couronne sous Jean le Bon et Charles V*, Geneva/Paris, 1982.

114 Chaplais, P., *Essays in Medieval Diplomacy and Administration*, London, 1981.

115 Chrimes, S.B. *Henry VII*, Berkeley/Los Angeles, 1973.

116 Chrimes, S.B., Ross, C.D. and Griffiths, R.A. (eds), *Fifteenth-Century England, 1399–1509. Studies in Politics and Society*, Manchester, 1972.

117 Davies, R.R. *Lordship and Society in the March of Wales, 1282–1400*, Oxford, 1978.

118 Demotz, B., La géographie administrative médiévale: l'exemple du Comté de Savoie, Début XIIIe – début XVe siècle, *MA*, 80 (1974), 261–300.

119 Du Boulay, F.R.H. and Barron, C.M. (eds), *The Reign of Richard II. Essays in Honour of May McKisack*, London, 1971.

120 Favier, R.J., *Philippe le Bel*, Paris, 1978.

121 Frame, R., English officials and Irish chiefs in the fourteenth century, *EHR*, 90 (1975), 748–77.

122 Fryde, N.M., Edward III's removal of his ministers and judges, 1340–1341, *BIHR*, 48 (1975), 149–61.

123 Fryde, N., *The Tyranny and Fall of Edward II, 1321–1326*, Cambridge, 1979.

124 Gaussin, P.-R., *Louis XI, roi méconnu*, Paris, 1976.

125 Girardot, A., Les Angevins, ducs de Lorraine et de Bar, *Le Pays lorrain*, 1978, 1–18.

126 Griffiths, R.A. and Thomas, R.S., *The Principality of Wales in the Later Middle Ages: the Structure and Personnel of Government*, I, *South Wales, 1277–1536*, Cardiff, 1972.

127 Guenée, B., Les limites de la France, in *La France et les Français*, M. François (ed.), Paris, 1972, 50–69.

128 Guenée, B., Les tendances actuelles de l'histoire politique du Moyen Age français, in *Actes du C^e Congres national des Sociétés savantes, Paris, 1975*, I, Paris, 1977, 45–70 and bibliography.

129 Guenée, B., L'histoire de l'Etat en France à la fin du Moyen Age vue par les historiens français depuis cent ans, *RH*, 232 (1964), 331–60.

130 Heinze, R.W., *The Proclamations of the Tudor Kings*, Cambridge, 1976.

131 Highfield, J.R.L. and Jeffs, R. (eds), *The Crown and Local Communities in England and France in the Fifteenth Century*, Gloucester, 1981.

132 Higounet, C. (ed.), *Histoire de Bordeaux*, III, Bordeaux, 1965, 1966.

133 Jacob, E.F., *The Fifteenth Century*, Oxford, 1961.

134 Jones, R.H., *The Royal Policy of Richard II: Absolutism in the Later Middle Ages*, Oxford, 1968.

135 Kirby, J.L., *Henry IV of England*, London, 1970.

136 Lander, J.R., *Conflict and Stability in Fifteenth-Century England*, London, 1969.

137 Lander, J.R., *Government and Community. England, 1450–1509*, London, 1980.

138 Leguai, A., Les 'Etats' princiers en France à la fin du Moyen Age, *AFISA*, 4 (1967), 133–57.

139 Leguai, A., *De la seigneurie à l'Etat. Le Bourbonnais pendant la Guerre de Cent Ans*, Moulins, 1969.

140 Lejeune, J., *Liège et son pays. Naissance d'une patrie (XIIIe–XIVe siècles)*, Liège, 1948.

141 Lewis, A.W., The Capetian apanages and the nature of the French kingdom, *Journal of Medieval History*, 2 (1976), 119–34.

142 Lewis, P.S., *Later Medieval France. The Polity*, London, 1968.

143 Lewis, P.S. (ed.), *The Recovery of France in the Fifteenth Century*, London, 1971.

144 Lot, F. and Fawtier, R., *Histoire des institutions françaises au Moyen Age*, 3 vols, Paris, 1957–62.

145 Lydon, J.F., *The Lordship of Ireland in the Middle Ages*, Dublin, 1972.

146 Lyon, B.D., *A Constitutional and Legal History of Medieval England*, New York, 1960.

147 Lyon, B.D., What Made a Medieval King Constitutional?, in *Essays in Medieval History presented to Bertie Wilkinson*, T.A. Sandquist and M.R. Powicke (eds), Toronto, 1969, 157–175.

148 McKisack, M., *The Fourteenth Century*, Oxford, 1959.
149 Maddicott, J.R., *Thomas of Lancaster, 1307–1322. A Study in the reign of Edward II*, Oxford, 1970.
150 Morgan, D.A.L., The King's Affinity in the Polity of Yorkist England, *TRHS*, 23 (1973), 1–25.
151 Nicholson, R., *Scotland: The Later Middle Ages*, Edinburgh, 1974.
152 Olivier-Martin, F., *Histoire du droit français des origines à la Révolution*, repr. Paris, 1951.
153 Otway-Ruthven, A.J., *A History of Medieval Ireland*, London, 1968.
154 Ouy, G., L'humanisme et les mutations politiques et sociales en France aux XIV⁰ et XV⁰ siècles, *De Pétrarque à Descartes, XXIX, L'humanisme français au début de la Renaissance*, Paris, 1973, 27–44.
155 Paravicini, W., *Karl der Kühne. Das Ende des Hauses Burgund*, Göttingen, 1976.
156 Perroy, E., Feudalism or Principalities in Fifteenth-Century France, *BIHR*, 20 (1943–45), 181–85.
157 Perroy, E., *La Guerre de Cent Ans*, Paris, 1945.
158 Plucknett, T.F.T., *The Legislation of Edward I*, Oxford, 1949.
159 Pollard, A.J., The tyranny of Richard III, *Journal of Medieval History* 3 (1977), 147–65.
160 Ross, C., *Edward IV*, London, 1974.
161 Ross, C. (ed.), *Patronage, Pedigree and Power in Later Medieval England*, Gloucester, 1979.
162 Strayer, J.R., Philip the Fair. A 'Constitutional' King, *AHR*, 62 (1956–7), 18–32.
163 Strayer, J.R., The Laicization of French and English Society in the Thirteenth Century, *Spec.*, 15 (1940), 76–86.
164 Strayer, J.R., *Medieval Statecraft and the Perspectives of History*, Princeton, 1971.
165 Strayer, J.R., *The Reign of Philip the Fair*, Princeton, 1980.
166 Tricard, J., Jean, duc de Normandie et héritier de France. Un double échec?, *Annales de Normandie*, 29 (1979), 23–44.
167 Tucoo-Chala, P., *La vicomté de Béarn et le problème de sa souveraineté des origines à 1620*, Bordeaux, 1961.
168 Tucoo-Chala, P., *Gaston Fébus. Un grand prince d'Occident au XIVᵉ siècle*, Pau, 1976.
169 Vale, M.G.A., *English Gascony, 1399–1453. A Study of War, Government and Politics during the Later Stages of the Hundred Years War*, Oxford, 1970.
170 Vale, M.G.A., *Charles VII*, London, 1974.
171 Vallez, A., La construction du comté d'Alençon (1269–1380). Essai de géographie historique, *Annales de Normandie*, 1972, 11–45.
172 Vaughan, R., *Philip the Bold. The Formation of the Burgundian State*, London, 1962.
173 Vaughan, R., *John the Fearless. The Growth of Burgundian Power*, London, 1966.
174 Vaughan, R., *Philip the Good. The Apogee of Burgundy*, London, 1970.
175 Vaughan, R., *Charles the Bold. The Last Valois Duke of Burgundy*, London, 1973.
176 Vaughan, R., *Valois Burgundy*, London, 1975.

NATIONAL STUDIES: ITALY AND THE IBERIAN PENINSULA

177 Alessandro, V.d', *Politica e Società nella Sicilia Aragonese*, Palermo, 1963.

178 Battle, C., La ideologia de la *Busca*. La crisis municipal de Barcelona en el siglo XV, *EHM*, 5 (1955), 165–96.

179 Becker, M.B., *Florence in transition*, 2 vols, Baltimore, 1967–8.

180 Black, C.F., The Baglioni as Tyrants of Perugia, 1488–1540, *EHR*, 85 (1970), 245–81.

181 Boscolo, G., Riforme e Provvedimenti di Pietro IV d'Aragona per la Sardegna, *NRS*, 62 (1978), 121–26.

182 Bowsky, W.M., The *Buon Governo* of Siena (1287–1355): a Mediaeval Italian Oligarchy, *Spec.*, 37 (1962), 368–81.

183 Brucker, G.A., *Florentine Politics and Society, 1343–1378*, Princeton, 1962.

184 Brucker, G., *The Civic World of Early Renaissance Florence*, Princeton, 1977.

185 Bueno de Mesquita, D.M., *Giangaleazzo Visconti, Duke of Milan (1351–1402). A Study in the Political Career of an Italian Despot*, Cambridge, 1941.

186 Cessi (R.), *Politica ed Economia di Venezia nel Trecento. Saggi*, Rome, 1952.

187 Chittolini, G., La crisi della libertà comunali e le origini dello stato territoriale, *RSI*, 82 (1970), 99–120.

188 Chittolini, G., *La formazione dello stato regionale e le istituzioni del contado. Secoli XIV–XV*, Turin, 1979.

189 Chittolini, G. (ed.) *La crisi degli ordinamenti comunali e le origini dello stato del Rinascimento*, Bologna, 1979.

190 Colliva, P., *Il Cardinale Albornoz, lo stato della Chiesa, le 'Constitutiones Aegidianae' (1353–57)*, Bologna, 1977.

101 Cracco, G., *Società e Stato nel medioevo veneziano (secoli XII–XIV)*, Florence, 1967.

192 De Vergottini, G., *Lezioni di storia del diritto italiano. Il diritto pubblico italiano nei secoli XII–XV*, 3rd edn, 2 vols, Milan, 1959–60.

193 Dufourcq, C.-E. and Gautier Dalché, J., Economies, sociétés et institutions de l'Espagne chrétienne du Moyen Age. Essai de bilan de la recherche d'après les travaux des quelque vingt dernières années. III. A travers les Etats de la Couronne d'Aragon des origines au XVᵉ siècle, *MA*, 80 (1973), 285–319.

194 Duprè Theseider, E., *Roma dal Comune di popolo alla signoria pontificia (1252–1377)*, Bologna, 1952.

195 Erler, A., *Aegidius Albornoz als Gesetzgeber des Kirchenstaates*, Berlin, 1970.

196 Font Rius, J.M., *Instituciones Medievales Españolas. La organización política, económica y social de los reinos cristianos de la Reconquista*, Madrid, 1949.

197 Font Rius, J.M., *Las instituciones de la Corona de Aragón en la primera mitad del siglo XV*, Palma, 1955.

198 França, E. d'Oliveira, *O poder real em Portugal e as origens do absolutismo*, São Paulo, 1946.

199 Gama Barros, H. de, *Historia de administração publica em Portugal nos seculos XII a XV*, T. de Souza Soares (ed.), 2nd edn, II vols, Lisbon, 1945–54.

200 Gimeno Casalduero, J., *La imagen del monarca en la Castilla del siglo XIV. Pedro el Cruel, Enrique II y Juan I*, Madrid, 1972.

201 Gundersheimer, W.L., *Ferrara. The Style of a Renaissance Despotism*, Princeton, 1973.

202 Hyde, J.K., *Padua in the Age of Dante*, Manchester, 1966.

203 Kohl, B.G., Government and society in Renaissance Padua, *Journal of Medieval and Renaissance Studies*, 2 (1972), 205–21.

204 Ladero Quesada, M.A., *Andalucia en el siglo XV. Estudios de historia politica*, Madrid, 1973.

205 Lalinde Abadia, J., *Las instituciones de la Corona de Aragón en el siglo XIV*, Valencia, 1967.

206 Larner, J., *The Lords of Romagna. Romagnol Society and the Origins of the Signorie*, London, 1965.

207 Law, J.E., Verona and the Venetian State in the Fifteenth Century, *BIHR*, 52 (1979), 9–22.

208 Leicht, P.S., Staatsformen in der italienischen Renaissance, *Scritti vari di storia del diritto italiano*, I, Milan, 1943, 519–33.

209 Léonard, E.G., *Les Angevins de Naples*, Paris, 1954.

210 MacKay, A., *Spain in the Middle Ages. From frontier to Empire, 1000–1500*, London/Basingstoke, 1977.

211 Marongiu, A., *Storia del diritto pubblico. Principi e instituti di governo in Italia dalla metà del IX alla metà del XIX secolo*, Milan, 1956.

212 Marongiu, A., Sui giuramenti tra re e sudditi in Aragona e Navarra, in *Storiografia e storia. Studi in onore di Eugenio Duprè Theseider*, II, Rome, 1974, 809–34.

213 Marques, A.H. de Oliveira, *History of Portugal*, I: *From Lusitania to Empire*, New York, 1972.

214 Meek, C., *Lucca, 1369–1400. Politics and Society in an Early Renaissance City-State*, Oxford, 1978.

215 Menendez Pidal, R., et al., *Historia de España*, XIV, XV, XVII, Madrid, 1966, 1964, 1969.

216 Mitre Fernandez, E., La frontière de Grenade aux environs de 1400, *MA*, 78 (1972), 489–522.

217 Mitre Fernandez, E., Mecanismos institucionales y poder real en la Castilla de Enrique III, *En la España medieval*, Madrid, 1981, 317–28.

218 Molho, A., Politics and the Ruling Class in Early Renaissance Florence, *NRS*, 52 (1968), 401–20.

219 Najemy, J.M., Guild Republicanism in Trecento Florence: The Successes and Ultimate Failure of Corporate Politics, *American Historical Review*, 84 (1979), 53–71.

220 Osheim, D.J., *An Italian Lordship: The Bishopric of Lucca in the Late Middle Ages*, Berkeley/Los Angeles, 1977.

221 Perez Bustamante, R., *Sociedad, economia, fiscalidad y gobierno en las Asturias de Santillana (S. XIII–XV)*, Santander, 1979.

222 Phillips, W.D. Jr., *Enrique IV and the Crisis of Fifteenth-Century Castile, 1425–1480*, Cambridge, Mass., 1978.

223 Piur, P., *Cola di Rienzo*, Vienna, 1931.

224 Regla, J., *Introducció a la historia de la Corona d'Aragó (dels origens a la Nova Planta)*, Palma, 1969.

225 Rubinstein, N., *The Government of Florence under the Medici (1434–94)*, Oxford, 1966.

226 Rubinstein, N. et al., *Florentine Studies. Politics and Society in Renaissance Florence*, London, 1968.

227 Ruggiero, G., Modernization and the Mythic State in Early Renaissance Venice: the *Serrata* Revisited, *Viator*, 10 (1979), 245–56.

228 Queller, D.E. and Swietek, F.R., *Two Studies on Venetian Government*, Geneva, 1977.

229 Romiti, A., Riforme politiche e amministrative a Lucca nei primi mesi di libertà (aprile-uglio 1369), *Archivio storico italiano*, 135 (1977), 165–201.

230 Ryder, A., *The Kingdom of Naples under Alfonso the Magnanimous: the making of a modern state*, Oxford, 1976.

231 Shneidman, J.L., *The Rise of the Aragonese-Catalan Empire, 1200–1350*, 2 vols, New York, 1970.

232 Simeoni, L., *Le signorie*, 2 vols, Milan, 1950.

232a *Storia di Milano* (Fondazione Treccani degli Alfieri per la storia di Milano), V, VI, VII, Milan, 1955, 1956.

233 Tramontana, S., *Michele da Piazza e il potere baronale in Sicilia*, Messine, 1963.

234 Trexler, R.C., Florence, by the Grace of the Lord Pope . . ., *Studies in Medieval and Renaissance History*, 9 (1972), 115–215.

235 Trexler, R.C., *Public Life in Renaissance Florence*, New York, 1980.

236 Valdeavellano, L.G., *Curso de historia de las instituciones españolas de los origines al final de la Edad Media*, Madrid, 1968.

237 Valeri, N., *L'Italia nell'età dei principati dal 1343 al 1516*, Milan, 1949.

238 Valeri, N., *Storia d'Italia*, I, *Il Medioevo*, 2nd edn, Turin, 1965.

239 Vicens Vives, J., *Juan II de Aragón (1398–1479). Monarquia y revolución en la España del siglo XV*, Barcelona, 1953.

240 Vilar, P., *La Catalogne dans l'Espagne moderne. Recherches sur les fondements économiques des structures nationales*, 3 vols, Paris, 1962.

NATIONAL STUDIES: GERMANY, SWITZERLAND,
HUNGARY, POLAND AND SCANDINAVIA

241 Andreas, W., *Deutschland vor der Reformation. Eine Zeitenwende*, 6th edn, Stuttgart, 1959.

242 Angermeier, H., *Königtum und Landfriede im deutschen Spätmittelalter*, Munich, 1966.

243 Bader, K.S., *Der deutsche Südwesten in seiner territorialstaatlichen Entwicklung*, Stuttgart, 1950.

244 Bardach, J., *Historia państwa i prawa Polski do rokn 1795*, I, 3rd edn, Warsaw, 1966.

245 Baszkiewicz, J., *Powstanie zjednoczonego panstwa polskiego (na przelomie XIII i XIV w.)* [The reunification of the Polish state at the end of the thirteenth and beginning of the fourteenth centuries], Warsaw, 1954.

246 Beck, M., Wilhelm Tell: Sage oder Geschichte?, *DA*, 36 (1980), 1–24.

247 Bergier, J.-F., Les Alpes et la démocratie. Sur le problème des origines de la Confédération suisse, *Il Pensiero Politico*, 4 (1971), 230–5.

248 Brunner, O., *Land und Herrschaft. Grundfragen der territorialen Verfassungsgeschichte Œsterreichs im Mittelalter*, 4th edn, Vienna/Wiesbaden, 1959.

249 Carsten, F.L., *The Origins of Prussia*, Oxford, 1954.

249a Dabrowski, J., *Kazimierz Wielki [Casimir the Great]*, Wroclaw, 1964.

250 Dollinger, P., *La Hanse (XIIe–XVIIe siècles)*, Paris, 1964.

251 Dralle, L., *Der Staat des deutschen Ordens in Preussen nach dem II. Thorner Frieden*, Wiesbaden, 1975.

252 Du Boulay, F.R.H., *Germany in the later Middle Ages* (London, 1983).

253 Eszlary, C.d', *Histoire des institutions publiques hongroises*, 2 vols, Paris, 1959–63.

254 Fiala, Z., *Predhusitske Cechy, 1310–1419. Cesky stat pod vladou Lucemburku, 1310–1419* [Pre-Hussite Bohemia, 1310–1419. The Bohemian state under the Luxemburgs], Prague, 1968.

255 Beghardt, B., *Handbuch der deutschen Geschichte*, I, *Frühzeit und Mittelalter*, 8th edn revised by H. Grundmann, repr. Stuttgart, 1956.

256 Gieysztor, A. et al., *Histoire de Pologne*, Warsaw, 1971.

257 Hartung, F., *Deutsche Verfassungsgeschichte vom 15. Jahrhundert bis zur Gegenwart*, 7th edn, Stuttgart, 1959.

258 Heymann, F.G., *George of Bohemia, King of Heretics*, Princeton, 1965.

259 Hoffmann, E., *Königserhebung und Thronfolgeordnung in Dänemark bis zum Ausgang des Mittelalters*, Berlin, 1976.

260 Homan, B., *Gli Angioini di Napoli in Ungheria, 1290–1403*, Rome, 1938.

261 Kaczmarczyk, Z. and Lesnodorski, B., *Historia państwa i prawa Polski do roku 1795*, II, 3rd edn, Warsaw, 1968.

262 Koller, H., *Das 'Königreich' Oesterreich*, Graz, 1972.

263 Koller, H., Zur Bedeutung des Begriffs 'Haus Œsterreich', *MIÖG*, 78 (1970), 338–46.

264 La Roche, E.P., *Das Interregnum und die Entstehung der Schweizerischen Eidgenossenschaft*, Bern/Frankfurt, 1971.

265 Leist, W., *Landesherr und Landfrieden in Thüringen im Spätmittelalter, 1247–1349*, Cologne/Vienna, 1975.

266 Lhotsky, A., *Aufsätze und Vorträge*, II, *Das Haus Oesterreich*, Vienna, 1971.

267 Meyer, B., *Die Bildung der Eidgenossenschaft im 14. Jahrhundert. Vom Zugerbund zum Pfaffenbrief*, Zurich, 1972.

268 Meyer, B., Die Entstehung der Eidgenossenschaft. Der Stand der heutigen Anschauungen, *SZ*, 2 (1952), 153–205.

269 Mohrmann, W.-D., *Der Landfriede im Ostseeraum während des späten Mittelalters*, Kallmünz, 1972.

270 Mommsen, K., *Eidgenossen, Kaiser und Reich. Studien zur Stellung der Eidgenossenschaft innerhalb des heiligen römischen Reiches*, Basel, 1958.

271 Musset, L., *Les peuples scandinaves au Moyen Age*, Paris, 1951.

272 Pamlenyi, E. (ed.), *Histoire de la Hongrie des origines à nos jours*, Budapest, 1974.
273 Patze, H. (ed.), *Der deutsche Territorialstaat im 14 Jahrhundert*, I, Sigmaringen, 1970.
274 Riis, T., *Les institutions politiques centrales du Danemark, 1100–1332*, Odense, 1977.
275 Russocki, S., Structures politiques dans l'Europe des Jagellon, *Acta Poloniae Historica*, 39 (1979), 101–42.
276 Schmidt, R., AEIOU. Das 'Vokalspiel' Friedrichs III. von Oesterreich, *Archiv für Kulturgeschichte*, 55 (1973), 391–431.
277 Seibt, F., Die Zeit der Luxemburger und der hussitischen Revolution, 1306 bis 1471, in *Handbuch der Geschichte der böhmischen Länder*, K. Bosl (ed.), I, 2, Stuttgart, 1966, 349–568.
278 Spěváček, J., Lucemburské koncepce českého státu a jijich přemyslovské kořeny [concepts of the Bohemian state under the Luxemburgs and their origins under the Premysl dynasty] *Sborník historický*, 24 (1976), 5–51.
279 Spindler, M., *Handbuch der bayerischen Geschichte*, II, Munich, 1966.
280 Sproemberg, H., La naissance d'un Etat allemand au Moyen Age, *MA*, 64 (1958), 213–48.
281 Stettler, B., Habsburg und die Eidgenossenschaft um die Mitte des 14. Jahrhunderts, *Revue suisse d'histoire*, 23 (1973), 750–64.
282 Vasella, O., Vom Wesen der Eidgenossenschaft im 15. und 16. Jahrhundert, *HJ*, 71 (1952), 165–83.
283 Wackernagel, H.G., Fehdewesen, Volksjustiz und staatlicher Zusammenhalt in der alten Eidgenossenschaft, *SZ*, 15 (1965), 289–313.
284 Wernli, F., *Die Entstehung der schweizerischen Eidgenossenschaft. Verfassungsgeschichte und politische Geschichte in Wechselwirkung*, Uznach, 1972.
285 Wojciechowski, Z., *L'Etat polonais au Moyen Age. Histoire des institutions*, Paris, 1949.

INFORMATION AND PROPAGANDA

286 Abel, A. et Martens, M., Le rôle de Jean de Vesale, médecin de la ville de Bruxelles, dans la propagande de Charles le Téméraire, *Cahiers bruxellois*, I (1956), 41–86.
287 Armstrong, C.A.J., Some Examples of the Distribution and Speed of News in England at the Time of the Wars of the Roses, in *Studies in Medieval History presented to F.M. Powicke*, R.W. Hunt, W.A. Pantin and R.W. Southern (eds), Oxford, 1948, 429–54.
288 Autrand, E., Géographie administrative et propagande politique. Le 'Rôle des assignations' du Parlement aux XIVᵉ et XVᵉ siècles, *Histoire comparée de l'administration (IVᵉ-XVIIIᵉ siècles)*, W. Paravicini and K.F. Werner (eds), Munich, 1980, (Francia suppl. 9), 264–81.
289 Barber, M., Propaganda in the Middle Ages: the charges against the Templars, *Nottingham Medieval Studies*, 17 (1973), 42–57.

290 Bossuat, A., La littérature de propagande au XV^c siècle. Le mémoire de Jean de Rinel, secrétaire du roi d'Angleterre, contre le duc de Bourgogne (1435), *CH*, I (1956), 129–46.

291 Cazelles, R., Peinture et actualité politique sous les premiers Valois, Jean le Bon ou Charles, dauphin, *Gazette des Beaux-Arts*, Sept. 1978, 53–65.

292 Chastel, A., La légende médicéenne, *Revue d'Histoire moderne et contemporaine*, 6 (1959), 161–80.

293 Diederichs, P.,*Kaiser Maximilian I als politischer Publizist*, Jena, 1931.

294 Eheim, F., Ladislaus Sunthaym. Ein Historiker aus dem Gelehrtenkreis um Maximilian I., *MIÖG*, 67 (1959), 53–91.

295 Gill, P.E., Politics and Propaganda in Fifteenth-Century England: The Polemical Writings of Sir John Fortescue, *Spec.*, 46 (1971), 333–47.

296 Gransden, A., Propaganda in English medieval historiography, *Journal of Medieval History*, I (1975), 363–82.

297 Graus, F., Přemysl Otakar II. Sein Ruhm und sein Nachleben. Ein Beitrag zur Geschichte politischer Propaganda und Chronistik, *MIÖG*, 79 (1971), 57–110.

298 Leclercq, J., Un sermon prononcé pendant la guerre de Flandre, *RMAL*, I (1945), 165–72.

299 Lewis, P.S., War-Propaganda and Historiography in Fifteenth-Century France and England, *TRHS*, 5th ser., 15 (1965), 1–21.

300 McKenna, J.W., Henry VI of England and the Dual Monarchy: Aspects of Royal Political Propaganda, 1422–1432, *JWCI*, 28 (1965), 145–62.

301 McKenna, J.W., Popular Canonization as Political Propaganda: The Cult of Archbishop Scrope, *Spec.*, 45 (1970), 608–23.

302 Maddicott, J.R., The County Community and the Making of Public Opinion in Fourteenth-Century England, *TRHS*, 28 (1978), 27–43.

303 Maïer, I., *Ange Politien. La formation d'un poète humaniste (1469–1480)*, Geneva, 1966.

304 Ouy, G., Humanisme et propagande politique en France au début du XV^c siècle: Ambrogio Migli et les ambitions impériales de Louis d'Orléans, in *Atti del Convegno su 'Culture et politique en France à l'époque de l'Humanisme et de la Renaissance'. Accademia delle Scienze di Torino, 29 marzo–3 aprile 1971*, Turin, 1974, 13–42.

305 Rubinstein, N., Political Ideas in Sienese Art, *JWCI*, 21 (1958), 179–207.

306 Samaran, C., Chanteurs ambulants et propagande politique sous Louis XI, *BEC*, 100 (1939), 233–4.

307 Scattergood, V.J., *Politics and Poetry in the Fifteenth Century, 1399–1485*, 2nd edn, New York, 1972.

308 Seguin, J.-P., *L'information en France de Louis XII à Henri II*, Geneva, 1961.

309 Walsh, R.J., Charles the Bold and the Crusade: politics and propaganda, *Journal of Medieval History*, 3 (1977), 53–86.

310 Willard, C.C., The Manuscripts of Jean Petit's *Justification*. Some Burgundian Propaganda Methods of the Early Fifteenth Century, *Studi francesi*, 38 (1969), 271–80.

See also: 476, 489, 509, 514, 518.

POLITICAL THOUGHT

311 Barbey, J., *Les* Tractatus *de Jean de Terrevermeille*, unpubl. thesis, Univ. de Paris II, 1979.

312 Baudry, L., *Guillaume d'Occam, sa vie, ses œuvres, ses idées sociales et politiques*, I, *L'homme et les œuvres*, Paris, 1949.

313 Belch, S.F., *Paulus Vladimiri and his Doctrine Concerning International Law and Politics*, 2 vols, The Hague, 1965.

314 Beneyto, J., *Los origenes de la ciencia politica en España*, Madrid, 1949.

315 Black, A.J., *Monarchy and Community. Political Ideas in the Later Conciliar Controversy, 1430–1450*. Cambridge, 1970.

316 Boockmann, H., *Johannes Falkenberg, der Deutsche Orden und die polnische Politik. Untersuchungen zur politischen Theorie des späteren Mittelalters. Mit einem Anhang: Die* 'Satira' *des Johannes Falkenberg*, Göttingen, 1975.

317 Carlyle, R.W. and A.J., *A History of Mediaeval Political Theory in the West*, 6 vols, London 1903–36.

318 Chrimes, S.B., *English Constitutional Ideas in the Fifteenth Century*, Cambridge, 1936.

319 Condren, C., Democracy and the *Defensor Pacis*: on the English Language Tradition of Marsilian Interpretation, *Il Pensiero Politico*, 13 (1980), 301–16.

320 Contamine, P., La théologie de la guerre à la fin du Moyen Age: la Guerre de Cent Ans fut-elle une guerre juste? in *Jeanne d'Arc. Une époque, un rayonnement. Colloque d'histoire médiévale, Orléans, octobre 1979*, Paris, 1982, 9–21.

321 Costa, P., *Jurisdictio. Semantica del potere politico nella pubblicistica medievale (1100–1433)*, Milan, 1969.

322 Daly, L.J., *The Political Theory of John Wyclif*, Chicago, 1962.

323 Daly, L.J., Wyclif's Political Theory: A Century of Study, *Medievalia et Humanistica*, 4 (1973), 177–87.

324 Damiata, M., *Guglielmo d'Ockham: provertà e potere. I: Il problema della povertà evangelica e francescana nel sec. XIII e XIV. Origine del pensiero politico di Guglielmo d'Ockham; II: Il otere come servizio. Dal 'Principatus dominativus' al 'Principatus ministrativus'*, Florence, 1978–9.

325 Delle Piane, M., *Vecchio e Nuovo nelle idee politiche di Pietro Dubois*, Florence, 1959.

326 De Mattei, R., *Il sentimento politico del Petrarco*, Florence, 1944.

327 Dolcini, C., *Il pensiero politico di Michele da Cesena, 1328–1338*, Faenza, 1977.

328 Duntham, W.H. and Wood, C.T., The Right to Rule in England: Depositions and the Kingdom's Authority, 1327–1485, *American Historical Review*, 81 (1976), 738–61.

329 Elias de Tejada, F., *Historia del pensiamento politico catalan*, 3 vols, Seville, 1963–5.

330 Feenstra, R., *Philip of Leyden and his Treatise. 'De Cura Reipublicae et Sorte Principantis'*, Glasgow, 1970.

331 Gauvard, C., Christine de Pisan a-t-elle eu une pensée politique? A propos d'ouvrages récents, *RH*, 508 (1973), 417–80.

332 Genet, J.-P., Les idées sociales de Sir John Fortescue, in *Economies et Sociétés au Moyen Age. Mélanges offerts à Edouard Perroy*, J.-P. Genet (ed.), Paris, 1973, 446–61.

333 Gewirth, A., *Marsilius of Padua, the Defender of Peace*, 2 vols, New York, 1956.

334 Gillespie, J.L., Sir John Fortescue's Concept of Royal Will, *Nottingham Medieval Studies*, 23 (1979), 47–65.

335 Gilmore, M.P., *Argument from Roman Law in Political Thought, 1200–1600*, Cambridge, Mass., 1941.

336 Gorski, K., Un traité polonais de politique au XVe siècle et l'influence de Buridan en Pologne, *APAE*, 39 (1966), 65–83.

337 Greenleaf, W.H., The Thomasian Tradition and the Theory of Absolute Monarchy, *EHR*, 79 (1964), 747–60.

338 Grignaschi, M., Nicolas Oresme et son commentaire à la *Politique* d'Aristote, *Album H.M. Cam*, I, Louvain/Paris, 1960, 95–152.

339 Grignaschi, M., Un commentaire nominaliste de la *Politique* d'Aristote: Jean Buridan, *APAE*, 19 (1960), 123–42.

340 Gross, H., Lupold of Bebenburg: National Monarchy and Representative Government in Germany, *Il Pensiero Politico*, 7 (1974), 3–14.

341 Hamman, A., Saint Augustin dans le *Breviloquium de principatu tyrannico* d'Occam, *Augustinus magister*, Congrès international augustinien, III, Paris, 1954, 1019–27.

342 Herde, P., *Dante als Florentiner Politiker*, Wiesbaden, 1976.

343 Kantorowicz, E.H., *The King's Two Bodies. A Study in Mediaeval Political Theology*, 2nd edn, Princeton, 1966.

344 Kölmel, W., Einheit und Zweiheit der Gewalt im *Corpus mysticum*. Zur Souveränitätslehre des Augustinus Triumphus, *HJ*, 82 (1963), 103–47.

345 Krynen, J., Le pouvoir monarchique selon Francesch Eiximenis. Un aspect du *Regiment de Princeps e de Comunitats*, *Annales de l'Université des Sciences Sociales de Toulouse*, 27 (1979), 339–66.

346 Krynen, J., *Idéal du prince et pouvoir royal en France à la fin du Moyen Age (1380–1440). Etude sur la littérature politique du temps*, Toulouse, 1980.

347 Lagarde, G. de, *La naissance de l'esprit laïque du Moyen Age*, revised edn, Louvain/Paris, 1956–70.

348 Leupen, P., The Emperor's Precedence. Jacobus de Middelburg and his Treatise *De Praecellentia Potestatis Imperatorie* (1500), *Revue d'Histoire du Droit*, 48 (1980), 227–42.

349 Leupen, P., *Philip of Leyden: A Fourteenth-Century Jurist. A Study of His Life and Treatise 'De cura reipublicae et sorte principantis'*, The Hague, 1981.

350 Lewis, E., The 'Positivism' of Marsiglio of Padua, *Spec.*, 38 (1963), 541–82.

351 Lewis, P.S. (ed.), *Ecrits politiques de Jean Juvénal des Ursins*, I, Paris, 1978.

352 Litzen, V., *A War of Roses and Lilies. The Theme of Succession in Sir John Fortescue's Works*, Helsinki, 1971.

353 McCready, W.D., Papal *Plenitudo Potestatis* and the source of temporal authority in late medieval papal hierocratic theory, *Spec.*, 48 (1973), 654–74.

354 McGrade, A.S., *The Political Thought of William of Ockham. Personal and Institutional Principles*, Cambridge, 1974.

355 MacIlwain, C.H., *The Growth of Political Thought in the West from the Greeks to the End of the Middle Ages*, New York, 1932.

356 Maravall, J.A., *Estudios de historia del pensiamento español. Edad media*. Serie primera, Madrid, 1967.

357 Mariani, U., *Chiesa e Stato nei teologi agostiniani del secolo XIV*, Rome, 1957.

358 Mazzone, U., *'El buon governo': un progetto di riforma generale nella Firenze Savonaroliana*, Florence, 1978.

359 Marongiu, A., Momenti ed aspetti del *Quod omnes tangit*, *Il Pensiero Politico*, 14 (1981), 441–52.

360 Miethke, J., Ein neuer Text zur Geschichte der politischen Theorie im 14. Jahrhundert: Der *Tractatus de Potestate Summi Pontificis* des Guillelmus de Sarzano aus Genua, *Quellen und Forschungen aus italienischen Archiven und Bibliotheken*, 54 (1974), 509–38.

361 Morel, H., La place de la *lex regia* dans l'histoire des idées politiques, in *Etudes offertes à J. Macqueron*, Aix, 1970, 545–55.

362 Oakley, F., Celestial Hierarchies Revisited: Walter Ullmann's Vision of Medieval Politics, *PP*, 60 (1973), 3–48.

363 Oexle, O.G., Utopisches Denken im Mittelalter: Pierre Dubois, *HZ*, 224 (1977), 293–339.

364 Passerin d'Entrèves, A., *Dante as a Political Thinker*, London, 1952.

365 Peterman, L., Dante's *Monarchia* and Aristotle's Political Thought, *Studies in Medieval and Renaissance History*, 10 (1973), 1–40.

366 Pilot, G., *Comunità politica e comunità religiosa nel pensiero di Guglielmo di Ockham*, Bologna, 1977.

367 Pincin, C., *Marsilio*, Turin, 1967.

368 Posthumus Meyjes, G.H.M., *Jean Gerson et l'Assemblée de Vincennes (1329). Ses conceptions de la juridiction temporelle de l'Eglise. Accompagné d'une édition critique du De Jurisdictione Spirituali et Temporali*, Leiden, 1978.

369 Preiser, W., Girolamo Savonarola als Staatsmann und politischer Denker, *Mitteilungen des österreichischen Staatsarchivs*, 25 (1972), 549–64.

370 Quaglioni, D., Per una edizione critica e un commento moderno del *Tractatus de regimine civitatis* di Bartolo de Sassoferrato, *Il Pensiero Politico*, 9 (1976), 70–93.

371 Quaglioni, D., Un *Tractatus de tyranno*. Il commento di Baldo degli Ubaldi (1327?–1400) alla *Lex Decernimus*, c. de Sacrosanctis Ecclesiis (c. 1, 2, 16), *Il Pensiero Politico*, 13 (1980), 64–83.

372 Quillet, J., *La philosophie politique de Marsile de Padoue*, Paris, 1970.

373 Quillet, J., *La philosophie politique du 'Songe du Vergier' (1378). Sources doctrinales*, Paris, 1977.

374 Renna, T., Aristotle and the French Monarchy, 1260–1303, *Viator*, 9 (1978), 309–24.

375 Romano, A., *Giuristi Siciliani dell'età Aragonese. Berardo Medico, Guglielmo Perno, Gualtiero Paterno, Pietro Pitrolo*, Milan, 1979.

376 Royer, J.-P., *L'Eglise et le royaume de France au XIVe siècle d'après le 'Songe du Vergier' et la jurisprudence du Parlement*, Paris, 1969.

377 Scheidgen, H., *Die französische Thronfolge (987–1500): Der Ausschluss der Frauen und das salische Gesetz*, Bonn, 1976.

378 Schmugge, L., *Johannes von Jandun (1285/89-1328). Untersuchungen zur Biographie und Sozialtheorie eines lateinischen Averroisten*, Stuttgart, 1966.

379 Schneider, R., Karls IV. Auffassung vom Herrscheramt, *HZ*, 2, neue Folge (1973), 122–50.

380 Scholz, R., *Wilhelm von Ockham als politischer Denker und sein* 'Breviloquium de principatu tyrannico', Leipzig, 1944.

381 Segall, H., *Der 'Defensor Pacis' des Marsilius von Padua. Grundfragen der Interpretation*, Wiesbaden, 1959.

382 Shahar, S., *Morale et politique en France au temps de Charles V*, Paris, 1965.

383 Sigmund, P.E., *Nicholas of Cusa and Medieval Political Thought*, Cambridge, Mass., 1963.

384 Smalley, B. (ed.), *Trends in Medieval Political Thought*, Oxford, 1965.

385 Spiegel, G.M., 'Defense of the realm': evolution of a Capetian propaganda slogan, *Journal of Medieval History*, 3 (1977), 115–33.

386 Spunar, P., *Rex, regnum a regnare* ve sbirce sentenci a prislovi Jana z Letovic [*Rex, regnum* and *regnare* in the sentences and proverbs of Jean of Letovice] (with French summary), *Studie o rukopisech*, 14 (1975), 167–81.

387 Stickler, F., Concerning the Political Theories of the Medieval Canonists, *Traditio*, 7 (1949–1951), 450–63.

388 Struve, T., *Die Entwicklung der organologischen Staatsauffassung im Mittelalter*, Stuttgart, 1978.

389 Tierney, B., *Foundations of the Conciliar Theory. The Contribution of the Medieval Canonists from Gratian to the Great Schism*, Cambridge, 1955.

390 Tierney, B., The Canonists and the Mediaeval State, *The Review of Politics*, 15 (1953), 378–88.

391 Tierney, B. and Linehan, P. (eds), *Authority and Power. Studies on Medieval Law and Government Presented to Walter Ullmann on his seventieth birthday*, Cambridge, 1980.

392 Touchard, J. et al., *Histoire des idées politiques*, I, *Des origines au XVIIIe siècle*, Paris, 1959.

393 Ullmann, W., *Principles of Government and Politics in the Middle Ages*, 2nd edn, London, 1966.

394 Ullmann, W., The Development of the Medieval Idea of Sovereignty, *EHR*, 64 (1949), 1–33.

395 Ullmann, W., *The Individual and Society in the Middle Ages*, Baltimore, 1966.

396 Ullmann, W., The Influence of John of Salisbury on Medieval Italian Jurists, *EHR*, 59 (1944), 384–92.

397 Ullmann, W., *The Medieval Idea of Law as Represented by Lucas de Penna. A Study in Fourteenth-Century Legal Scholarship*, London, 1946.

398 Ullmann, W., *Law and Politics in the Middle Ages: an introduction to the sources of medieval political ideas*, London, 1975.

399 Ullmann, W., John of Salisbury's *Policraticus* in the later Middle Ages, in *Geschichtsschreibung und geistiges Leben im Mittelalter. Festschrift für Heinz Löwe zum 65. Geburtstag*, K. Hauck, H. Mordek (eds), Cologne/Vienna, 1978, 519–45.

400 Van den Auweele, D., Un abrégé flamand du *De regimine principum* de Gilles de Rome, in *'Sapientiae Doctrina'. Mélanges de théologie et de littérature médiévales*

offerts à Dom Hildebrand Bascour O.S.B., Louvain, 1980, 327–58.

401 Wahl, J.A., Immortality and Inalienability: Baldus de Ubaldis, *Mediaeval Studies*, 32 (1970), 308–28.

402 Wahl, J.A., Baldus de Ubaldis and the Foundation of the Nation-State, *Manuscripta*, 21 (1977), 80–96.

403 Wilks, M.J., *The Problem of Sovereignty in the Later Middle Ages. The Papal Monarchy with Augustinus Triumphus and the Publicists*, Cambridge, 1963.

404 Woolf, C.N.S., *Bartolus of Sassoferrato. His Position in the History of Medieval Political Thought*, Cambridge, 1913.

405 Woš, J.W., *Dispute giuridiche nella lotta tra la Polonia e l'Ordine teutonico*, Florence, 1979.

406 Wyduckel, D., *Princeps Legibus Solutus. Eine Untersuchung zur frühmodernen Rechts- und Staatslehre*, Berlin, 1979.

407 Wyrwa, T., *La pensée politique polonaise à l'époque de l'Humanisme et de la Renaissance*, Paris/London, 1978.

See also: 54, 444, 1421–33.

PROPHETS AND PROPHECIES

408 Charmasson, T., Sciences et techniques divinatoires au XVᵉ siècle: Roland l'Ecrivain, médecin, astrologue et géomancien, *PTEC*, 1973, 27–31.

409 Chaume, M., Une prophétie relative à Charles VI, *RMAL*, 3 (1947), 27–42.

410 Cohn, N., *The Pursuit of the Millenium*, rev. edn, London, 1970.

411 De Maio, R., Savonarola, Alessandro VI e il mito de l'Anticristo, *RSI*, 82 (1970), 533–59.

412 Kurze, D., Nationale Regungen in der spätmittelalterlichen Prophetie, *HZ*, 202 (1966), 1–23.

413 Poulle, E., Horoscopes princiers des XIVᵉ et XVᵉ siècles, *Bulletin de la Société nationale des Antiquaires de France*, 1969, 63–77.

414 Reeves, M., *The Influence of Prophecy in the Later Middle Ages. A Study in Joachimism*, Oxford, 1969.

415 Rusconi, R., *L'attesa della fine. Crisi della società, profezia ed Apocalisse in Italia al tempo del grande scisma d'Occidente (1378–1417)*, Rome, 1979.

416 Sandquist, T.A., The Holy Oil of St Thomas of Canterbury, in *Essays in Medieval History presented to Bertie Wilkinson*, Toronto, 1969, 330–44.

417 Taylor, R., *The Political Prophecy in England*, New York, 1911.

418 Valois, N., Conseils et prédictions adressés à Charles VII, en 1445, par un certain Jean du Bois, *Annuaire-Bulletin de la Société de l'Histoire de France*, 1908–1909, 201–38.

419 Weinstein, D., Millenarianism in a Civic Setting: The Savonarola Movement in Florence, in *Millenial Dreams in Action. Essays in Comparative Study*, S.L. Thrupp (ed.), The Hague, 1962, 187–203.

420 Zumthor, P., *Merlin le Prophète. Un thème de la littérature polémique de l'historiographie et des romans*, Lausanne, 1943.

See also: 81, 286.

STATE AND NATION

421 Amelung, P., *Das Bild des Deutschen in der Literatur der italienischen Renaissance (1400–1559)*, Munich, 1964.

422 Beardwood, A., Mercantile Antecedents of the English Naturalization Laws, *Medievalia et Humanistica*, 16 (1964), 64–76.

423 Beumann, H. et Schröder, W. (eds), *Aspekte der Nationenbildung im Mittelalter. Ergebnisse der Marburger Rundgespräche, 1972–75*, Sigmaringen, 1978.

424 Blaschka, A., *Kaiser Karls Jugendleben und St. Wenzelslegende*, Weimar, 1956.

425 Borst, A., *Der Turmbau von Babel. Geschichte der Meinungen über Ursprung und Vielfalt der Sprachen und Völker*, 6 vols, Stuttgart, 1957–63.

426 Bossuat, R., Traditions populaires relatives au martyre et à la sépulture de saint Denis, *MA*, 62 (1956), 479–509.

427 Chadraba, R., Kaiser Karls IV. Devotio Antiqua, *Mediaevalia Bohemica*, I (1969), 51–68.

428 Davis, G., The Incipient Sentiment of Nationality in Mediaeval Castile: the *Patrimonio Real*, *Spec.*, 12 (1937), 351–8.

429 Dupont-Ferrier, G., Le sens des mots 'patria' et 'patrie' en France au Moyen Age et jusqu'au début du XVIIe siècle, *RH*, 188 (1940), 89–104.

430 *L'Etranger*, 2 vols, Brussels, 1958 (Recueils de la Société Jean-Bodin, IX, X).

431 François, M., Les rois de France et les traditions de l'abbaye de Saint-Denis à la fin du XVe siècle, in *Mélanges dédiés à la mémoire de Félix Grat*, E.-A. van Moé, J. Vielliard and P. Marot (eds), I, Paris, 1946, 367–82.

432 Gieysztor, A., Gens Polonica: aux origines d'une conscience nationale, in *Etudes de civilisation médiévale, IXe–XIIe siècles. Mélanges offerts à E.-R. Labande*, Poitiers, 1974, 351–62.

433 Görlich, P., *Zur Frage des Nationalbewusstseins in ostdeutschen Quellen des 12. bis 14. Jahrhunderts*, Marburg, 1964.

434 Graus, F., Die Bildung eines Nationalbewusstseins im mittelalterlichen Böhmen (Die vorhussitische Zeit), *Historica*, 13 (1966), 5–49.

435 Graus, F., Die Entwicklung der Legenden der sogenannten Slaven-apostel Konstantin und Method in Böhmen und Mähren, *Jahrbücher für Geschichte Osteuropas*, 19 (1971), 161–211.

436 Graus, F., *Die Nationenbildung der Westslawen im Mittelalter*, Sigmaringen, 1980.

437 Grévy-Pons, N., Propagande et sentiment national pendant le règne de Charles VI: l'example de Jean de Montreuil, *Francia*, 8 (1980), 127–45.

438 Grodecki, R., *Powstanie polskiej swiadomosci narodowej* [The origins of Polish national consciousness], Katowice, 1946.

439 Guenée, B., Etat et nation en France au Moyen Age, *RH*, 237 (1967), 17–30.

440 Huizinga, J., Patriotism and Nationalism in European History, in *Men and Ideas*, J.S. Holmes and T. van Marle (eds), London, 1960, 97–155.

441 Jones, M., *Mon Pais et ma Nation*: Breton Identity in the Fourteenth Century, in *War, Literature and Politics in the Late Middle Ages. Essays in honour of G.W. Coopland*, Liverpool, 1976, 144–68.

442 Jones,M., 'Bons Bretons et Bons Francoys': The Language and Meaning of Treason in Later Medieval France, *Transactions of the Royal Historical Society*, 5th ser., 32 (1982), 91–112.

443 Jouet, R., *La résistance à l'occupation anglaise en Basse-Normandie (1418–1450)*, Caen, 1969.

444 Kantorowiz, E.H., *Selected Studies*, New York, 1965.

445 Keeney, B.C., Military Service and the Development of Nationalism in England, 1272–1327, *Spec.*, 22 (1947), 534–49.

446 Kerhervé J., Aux origines d'un sentiment national. Les chroniqueurs bretons de la fin du Moyen Age, *Bull. de la Société archéologique du Finistère*, 108 (1980), 165–206.

447 Kibre, P., *The Nations in the Mediaeval Universities*, Cambridge, Mass., 1948.

448 Kirn, P., *Aus der Frühzeit des Nationalgefühls*, Leipzig, 1943.

449 Kirshner, J., *Civitas sibi faciat civem:* Bartolus of Sassoferrato's Doctrine on the Making of a Citizen, *Spec.*, 48 (1973), 694–713.

450 Kohn, H., *The Idea of Nationalism. A Study in its Origins and Background*, 2nd edn, New York, 1956.

451 Lanhers, Y., Deux affaires de trahison défendues par Jean Jouvenel des Ursins (1423–1427), *Recueil de mémoires et travaux de la Société d'Histoire du Droit écrit*, 7 (1970), 317–28.

452 Lejeune, J., Les notions de 'patria' et d' 'episcopatus' dans le diocèse et le pays de Liège du XIᵉ au XIVᵉ siècle, APAE, 8 (1955), 1–53.

453 Linder, A., *Ex mala parentela bona sequi seu oriri non potest*; the Trojan Ancestry of the Kings of France and the *Opus Davidicum* of Johannes Angelus de Legonissa, *Bibliothèque d'Humanisme et Renaissance. Travaux et documents*, XL, Geneva, 1978, 497–512.

454 Lügge, M., *Gallia und Francia im Mittelalter. Untersuchungen über den Zusammenhang zwischen geographisch-historischer Terminologie und politischen Denken vom 6.-15. Jahrhundert*, Bonn, 1960.

455 Mann, N., Humanisme et patriotisme en France au XVᵉ siècle, *Cahiers de l'Association internationale des Etudes françaises*, 23 (1971), 51–66.

456 Maravall, J.A., *El concepto de España en el Edad Media*, Madrid, 1954.

457 Marchello-Nizia, Chr., *Histoire de la langue française aux XIVᵉ et XVᵉ siècles*, Paris, 1979.

458 Müller, W., Deutsches Volk und deutsches Land im späteren Mittelalter. Ein Beitrag zur Geschichte des nationalen Namens, *HZ*, 132 (1925), 450–65.

459 Nonn, U., Heiliges Römisches Reich Deutscher Nation. Zum Nationen-Begriff im 15. Jahrhundert, *ZHF*, 9 (1982), 129–42.

460 Paul, U., *Studien zur Geschichte des deutschen Nationalbewusstseins im Zeitalter des Humanismus und der Reformation*, Berlin, 1936.

461 Peyer, H.C., *Stadt und Stadtpatron im mittelalterlichen Italien*, Zurich, 1955.

462 Rickard, P., *Britain in Medieval French Literature, 1100–1500*, Cambridge, 1956.

463 Robin, F., La politique religieuse des princes d'Anjou-Provence et ses manifestations littéraires et artistiques (1360–1480), in *La littérature angevine médiévale. Actes du colloque du samedi 22 mars 1980*, Angers, 1981, 155–75.

464 Schröcker, A., *Die Deutsche Nation. Beobachtungen zur politischen Propaganda des ausgehenden 15. Jahrhunderts*, Lübeck, 1974.

465 Seibt, F., Die böhmische Nachbarschaft in der österreichischen Historiographie des 13. und 14. Jahrhunderts, *Zeitschrift für Ostforschung*, 14 (1965), 1–26.

466 Šmahel, F., The Idea of the 'Nation' in Hussite Bohemia. An Analytical Study of the Ideological and Political Aspects of the National Question in Hussite Bohemia from the End of the 14th Century to the Eighties of the 15th Century, *Historica*, 16 (1969), 143–247; 17 (1969), 93–197.

467 Stelling-Michaud, S., Les influences universitaires sur l'éclosion du sentiment national allemand aux XVe et XVIe siècles, *SB*, 3 (1945), 62–73.

468 Stloukal, C., *Saint Venceslas dans l'histoire et dans la tradition du peuple tchécoslovaque*, Prague, 1929.

469 Strayer, J.R., France: the Holy Land, the Chosen People, and the Most Christian King, in *Action and Conviction in Early Modern Europe*, T.K. Rabb and J.E. Seigel (eds), Princeton, 1969, 3–16.

470 Suggett, H., The Use of French in England in the Later Middle Ages, *TRHS*, 4th ser., 28 (1946), 61–83.

471 Szücs, J., 'Nationalität' und 'Nationalbewusstsein' im Mittelalter. Versuch einer einheitlichen Begriffssprache, *Acta historica Academiae Scientiarum Hungaricae*, 18 (1972), 1–38, 245–66.

472 Wagner, J., *Nationale Strömungen in Deutschland am Ausgange des Mittelalters*, Weida, 1929.

473 Weinstein, D., *Savonarola and Florence. Prophecy and Patriotism in the Renaissance*, Princeton, 1970.

474 Zientara, B., Foreigners in Poland in the 10th–15th Centuries: their Role in the Opinion of Polish Medieval Community, *Acta Poloniae Historica*, 29 (1974), 5–28.

475 Zientara, B., Konflikty narodowościowe na pograniczu niemiecko-słowiańskim w XIII–XIV w. i ich zasięg społeczny [Ethnic conflicts in the Germano-Slav frontier territories in the 13th and 14th centuries and their social implications], *Przegląd Historyczny*, 59 (1968), 197–213.

See also: 34, 91, 412.

NATION AND HISTORY

476 Anglo, S., The 'British History' in Early Tudor Propaganda, *BJRL*, 44 (1961), 17–48.

477 Bodmer, J.-P., Die französische Historiographie des Spätmittelalters und die Franken, *Archiv für Kulturgeschichte*, 45 (1963), 91–118.

478 Bossuat, A., Les origines troyennes: leur rôle dans la littérature historique au XVe siècle, *Annales de Normandie*, 1958, 187–97.

479 Braunfels, W. and Schramm, P.E. (eds), *Karl der Grosse, IV, Das Nachleben*, Düsseldorf, 1967.

480 Carolus-Barré, L., Contribution à l'étude de la légende carolingienne. Les armes de Charlemagne dans l'héraldique et l'iconographie médiévales,

Mémorial du voyage en Rhénanie de la Société nationale des Antiquaires de France, Paris, 1953, 289–308.

481 Faral, E., *La légende arthurienne*, 3 vols, Paris, 1929.

482 Folz, R., *Le souvenir et la légende de Charlemagne dans l'Empire germanique médiéval*, Paris, 1950.

483 Grau, A., *Der Gedanke der Herkunft in der deutschen Geschichtsschreibung des Mittelalters. Trojasage und Verwandtes*, Leipzig, 1938.

484 Guenée, B., *Histoire et Culture historique dans l'Occident médiéval*, Paris, 1980, esp. bibliography.

485 Loomis, R.S., Edward I, Arthurian Enthusiast, *Spec.*, 28 (1953), 114–27.

486 Matter, H., *Englische Gründungssagen von Geoffrey of Monmouth bis zur Renaissance*, Heidelberg, 1922.

487 Monfrin, J., La figure de Charlemagne dans l'historiographie du XVᵉ siècle, *ABSHF*, 1964–5, 67–78.

488 Runge, K., *Die fränkisch-karolingische Tradition in der Geschichtsschreibung des späten Mittelalters*, Hamburg, 1965.

See also: 294, 299.

THE IMAGE OF THE PRINCE

489 Anglo, S., *Spectacle, Pageantry and Early Tudor Policy*, Oxford, 1969.

490 Bak, J.M., Medieval Symbology of the State: Percy E. Schramm's Contribution, *Viator*, 4 (1973), 33–63.

491 Bak, J.M., Coronation Orders in Hungarian Liturgical Manuscripts, *Manuscripta*, 21 (1977), 4–5.

492 Beaune, C., Costume et pouvoir en France à la fin du Moyen Age: les devises royales vers 1400, *Revue des sciences humaines*, 55 (1981), 125–46.

493 Begrich, U., *Die fürstliche 'Majestät' Herzog Rudolfs IV. von Œsterreich. Ein Beitrag zur Geschichte der fürstlichen Herrschaftszeichen im späten Mittelalter*, Vienna, 1965.

494 Berges, W., *Die Fürstenspiegel des hohen und späten Mittelalters*, Leipzig, 1938.

495 Benna, A.H., Zu den Kronen Friedrichs III, *Mitteilungen des österreichischen Staatsarchivs*, 27 (1974), 22–60.

496 Bloch, M., *The royal touch, sacred monarchy and scrofula in England and France*, tr. J.E. Anderson, London, 1973.

497 Bonime, S., Music for the Royal Entrée into Paris, 1483–1517, *Le Moyen Français*, 5 (1979), 115–29.

498 Brather, H.S., Die Verwaltungsreformen am kursächsischen Hofe im ausgehenden 15. Jahrhundert, in *Archivar und Historiker. Studien zur Archiv- und Geschichtswissenschaft. Zum 65. Geburtstag von H.O. Meisner*, Berlin, 1956, 254–87.

499 Bréjon de Lavergnée, J., L'Emblématique d'Anne de Bretagne, d'après les manuscrits à peintures (XVᵉ–XVIᵉ siècles), *Mémoires de la Société d'Histoire et d'Archéologie de Bretagne*, 55 (1978), 83–95.

500 Brinkhus, G., *Eine bayerische Fürstenspiegelkompilation des 15. Jahrhunderts. Untersuchungen und Textausgabe*, Munich, 1978.

501 Brown, E.A.R., The Ceremonial of Royal Succession in Capetian France. The Double Funeral of Louis X, *Traditio*, 34 (1978), 227–71.

502 Brown, E.A.R., The Ceremonial of Royal Succession in Capetian France. The Funeral of Philip V, *Spec.*, 55 (1980), 266–93.

503 Brown, V., Portraits of Julius Caesar in Latin Manuscripts of the Commentaries, *Viator*, 12 (1981), 319–54.

504 Byrne, D., *Rex Imago Dei*: Charles V of France and the *Livre des propriétés des choses, Journal of Medieval History*, 7 (1981), 97–113.

505 Cibulka, J., *Les joyaux du couronnement du royaume de Bohéme*, Prague, 1969.

506 Collin, H., Le train de vie d'Edouard Iᵉʳ, comte der Bar (1302–36), *BPH*, 1969, 793–817.

507 Coulet, N., Les entrées solennelles en Provence au XIVᵉ siècle. Aperçus nouveaux sur les entrées royales françaises au bas Moyen Age, *Ethnologie française*, 7 (1977), 63–82.

508 Dotzauer, W., Die Ankunft des Herrschers. Der fürstliche 'Einzug' in die Stadt (bis zum Ende des Alten Reichs), *Archiv für Kulturgeschichte*, 55 (1973), 245–88.

509 Drabek, A.M., *Reisen und Reisezeremoniell der römisch-deutschen Herrscher im Spätmittelalter*, Vienna, 1964.

510 Durliat, M., *La cour de Jacques II de Majorque (1324–49) d'après les 'Lois palatines'*, unpubl. thesis, Paris, 1962.

511 Epstein, M.J., *Ludovicus decus regnantium*: Perspectives on the Rhymed Office, *Spec.*, 53 (1978), 283–334.

512 Filarete, F. and Manfidi, A., *The Libro and cerimoniale of the Florentine Republic*, R.C. Trexler (ed.), Geneva, 1978.

513 Forstreuter, K., Die Hofordnungen der letzten Hochmeister in Preussen, *Beiträge zur preussischen Geschichte im 15. und 16. Jahrhundert*, Heidelberg, 1960, 29–34.

514 Giesey, R.E., *The Royal Funeral Ceremony in Renaissance France*, Geneva, 1960.

515 Gieysztor, A., *Non habemus Caesarem nisi regem*: la couronne fermée des rois de Pologne à la fin du XVᵉ et au XVIᵉ siècle, *BEC*, 126 (1969), 5–26.

516 Grandeau, Y., La mort et les obsèques de Charles VI, *BPH*, 1970, 133–86.

517 Grunzweig, A., Le Grand Duc du Ponant, *MA*, 62 (1956), 119–165.

518 Guenée, B. and Lehoux, F., *Les entrées royales françaises de 1328 à 1515*, Paris, 1968.

519 Heers, J., La cour de Mahaut d'Artois en 1327–28: solidarités humaines, livrées et mesnies, *Anales de Historia antigua y medieval*, 20 (1977–9), 7–43.

520 Hlaváček, I., Studi k Dvoru Václava IV (Studien zum Hof Wenzels IV.), I (with German summary), *Folia Historica Bohemica*, 3 (1981), 135–93.

521 Hofmann, H.H., Serenissimus. Ein fürstliches Prädikat in fünfzehn Jahrhunderten. *HJ*, 80 (1961), 240–51.

522 Hye, F.-H., Der Doppeladler als Symbol für Kaiser und Reich, *MIÖG*, 81 (1973), 63–100.

523 Jackson, R.A., The *Traité du sacre* of Jean Golein, *Proceedings of the American Philosophical Society*, 113 (1969), 305–24.

524 Jackson, R.A., Peers of France and Princes of the Blood, *French Historical Studies*, 7 (1971), 27–46.

525 Jackson, R.A., Les manuscrits des *ordines* de couronnement de la bibliothèque de Charles V, roi de France, *MA*, 82 (1976), 67–88.

526 Jackson, R.A., De l'influence du cérémonial byzantin sur le sacre des rois de France, *Byzantion*, 51 (1981), 201–10.

527 Lecoq, A.-M., La *Città festiggiante*. Les fêtes publiques aux XVe et XVIe siècles, *Revue de l'Art*, 33 (1976), 83–100.

528 Lewis, A.W., *Royal Succession in Capetian France: Studies on Familial Order and the State*, Cambridge, Mass., 1981.

529 Lopez, G. (ed.), *Festa di Nozze per Ludovico il Moro. Nelle testimonianze di Tristano Calco, Giacomo Trotti, Isabella d'Este, Gian Galeaszo Sforza, Beatrice de' Contrari e altri*, Milan, 1976.

530 Mateu y Llopis, F., Sacra Regia Aragonum ` Majestas. Notas sobre la diplomática y simbología real, in *Consejo Superior de Investigaciones cientificas Homenaje a Johannes Vincke*, Madrid, 1962–3, 201–20.

531 Mehl, J.-M. Le roi de l'échiquier. Approche du mythe royal à la fin du Moyen Age, *Revue d'Histoire et de Philosophie religieuses*, 58 (1978), 145–61.

532 Mertes, K., The *Liber Niger* of Edward IV: a New Version, *BIHR*, 54 (1981), 29–39.

533 Mitteis, H., *Die deutsche Königswahl und ihre Rechtsgrundlagen bis zur Goldenen Bulle*, 2nd edn, Vienna, 1944.

534 Moro, G. et al., Neue Arbeiten über den Kärntner Herzogstuhl, *Carinthia I*, 157 (1967), 420–68.

535 Muir, E., Images of Power: Art and Pageantry in Renaissance Venice, *American Historical Review*, 84 (1979), 16–52.

536 Myers, A.R., *The Household of Edward IV. The Black Book and the Ordinance of 1478*, Manchester, 1959.

537 Palacios Martín, B., *La coronación de los reyes de Aragón, 1204–1410: Aportación al estudio de las estructuras politicas medievales*, Valencia, 1975.

538 Pastoureau, M., La Fleur de lis, emblème royal, symbole marial ou thème graphique?, *La monnaie, miroir des rois, catalogue de l'exposition, Hôtel de la Monnaie, février-avril 1978*, Paris, 1878, 251–71.

539 Pertusi, A., Quedam regalia insignia. Ricerche sulle insegne del potere ducale a Venezia durante il Medioevo, *Studi Veneziani*, 7 (1965), 3–123.

540 Peyronnet, G., Rumeurs autour du sacre de Charles VII, *Annales de l'Est*, 33 (1981), 151–65.

541 Pinoteau, H., *L'ancienne couronne française dite 'de Charlemagne' 1180?–1794*, Paris, 1972.

542 Pinoteau, H., Tableaux français sous les premiers Valois, *Cahiers d'héraldique*, 2 (1975), 119–76.

543 Piponnier, F., *Costume et vie sociale. La cour d'Anjou, XIVe–XVe siècle*, Paris/The Hague, 1970.

544 Pocquet du Haut-Jussé, B.-A., Couronne fermée et cercle ducal en Bretagne, *BPH*, 1951–2, 103–12.

545 Runnals, G.A., René d'Anjou et le théâtre, *Annales de Bretagne*, 88 (1981), 157–80.

546 Schaller, H.M., Der heilige Tag als Termin mittelalterlicher Staatsakte, *DA*, 30 (1974), 1–24.

547 Schramm, P.E., *Der König von Frankreich. Das Wesen der Monarchie vom 9. zum 16. Jahrhundert. Ein Kapitel aus der Geschichte des abendländischen Staates*, 2nd edn, 2 vols, Darmstadt, 1960.

548 Schramm, P.E., *A History of the English coronation*, tr. L.G.W. Legg, Oxford, 1937.

549 Schramm, P.E., *Herrschaftszeichen und Staatssymbolik*, 3 vols, Stuttgart, 1954–6.

550 Schramm, P.E., *Sphaira, Globus, Reichsapfel. Wanderung und Wandlung eines Herrschaftszeichens von Caesar bis zu Elisabeth II. Ein Beitrag zum 'Nach-leben' der Antike*, Stuttgart, 1958.

551 Schramm, P.E. and Fillitz, H., in collaboration with F. Müterich, *Denkmale der deutschen Könige und Kaiser*, 2. *Ein Beitrag zur Herrschergeschichte von Rudolf I. bis Maximilian I. (1273–1519)*, Munich, 1978.

552 Schwarzkopf, U., Zum höfischen Dienstrecht im 15. Jahrhundert. Das burgundische Beispiel, in *Festschrift für Hermann Heimpel*, II, Göttingen, 1972, 422–42.

553 Sherman, C.R., Representations of Charles V of France (1338–1380) as a Wise Ruler, *Medievalia et Humanistica*, new series, 2 (1971), 83–96.

554 Sherman, C.R., The Queen in Charles V's 'Coronation Book': Jeanne de Bourbon and the *Ordo Reginam Benedicendam*, *Viator*, 8 (1977), 255–98.

555 Sobczyk, B., *Rex imperator in regno suo*. Suwerennośč króla polskiego w końcu XV wieku w miniaturach *Gradualu Jana Olbrachta* [The sovereignty of the king of Poland at the end of the 15th century illustrated by the miniatures of the *Gradual of Jan Albert*] (with French summary), *Folia Historiae Artium*, 10 (1974), 81–106.

556 Spiegel, G.M. and Hindman, S., The Fleur-de-lis Frontispieces to Guillaume de Nangis's *Chronique abrégée*: Political iconography in Late Fifteenth-Century France, *Viator*, 12 (1981), 381–407.

557 Steinmann, U., Die älteste Zeremonie der Herzogseinsetzung und ihre Umgestaltung durch die Habsburger, *Carinthia I*, 157 (1967), 469–97.

558 Trexler, R.C., *Public Life in Renaissance Florence*, New York, 1980.

559 Tucoo-Chala, P., Les honneurs funèbres chez les Foix-Béarn au XVe siècle, *Annales du Midi*, 90 (1978), 331–51.

560 Van Leeuwen, C.G., *Denkbeelden van een vliesridder, de* Instruction d'un jeune prince *van Guillebert Van Lannoy*, Amsterdam, 1975.

561 Vauchez, A., *Beata Stirps*: sainteté et lignage en Occident aux XIIIe et XIVe siècles, in *Famille et parenté dans l'Occident médiéval*, G. Duby and J. Le Goff (eds), Rome, 1977, 397–407.

562 Vauchez, A., Canonisation et politique au XIVe siècle. Documents inédits des Archives du Vatican relatifs au procès de canonisation de Charles de Blois, duc de Bretagne († 1364), *Miscellanea in onore di Monsignor Martino Giusti* (Collectanea Archivi Vaticani, 5, 6), II, Vatican City, 1978, 381–404.

KING AND TYRANT

563 Dabrowski, J., Corona regni Poloniae au XIVe siècle, *Bulletin international de l'Académie polonaise des Sciences et des Lettres. Classe de philologie, d'histoire et de philosophie*, suppl. 7 (1953), 41–64.

564 David, M., *La souveraineté et les limites juridiques du pouvoir monarchique du IXe au XVe siècle*, Paris, 1954.

565 David, M., Le serment du sacre du IXe au XVe siècle. Contribution à l'étude des limites juridiques de la souveraineté, *RMAL*, 6 (1950), 5–272.

566 Deér, J., *Die heilige Krone Ungarns*, Vienna, 1966.

567 Hellmann, M. (ed.), *Corona regni. Studien über die Krone als Symbol des Staates im späteren Mittelalter*, Weimar, 1961.

568 Hoffmann, H.; Die Unveräusserlichkeit der Kronrechte im Mittelalter, *DA*, 20 (1964), 389–474.

569 Hoyt, R.S., The Coronation Oath of 1308, *EHR*, 71 (1956), 353–83.

570 Lewis, P.S., Jean Juvenal des Ursins and the Common Literary Attitude towards Tyranny in Fifteenth-Century France, *Medium Aevum*, 34 (1965), 103–21.

571 Ullmann, W., Schranken der Königsgewalt im Mittelalter, *Historisches Jahrbuch*, 91 (1971), 1–21.

THE ADMINISTRATION OF THE STATE: GENERAL STUDIES

572 Bossuat, A., *Le bailliage royal de Montferrand (1425–1556)*, Paris, 1957.

573 Bruwier, M., Aux origines d'une institution: baillis et prévôts de Hainaut du XIIe au XIVe siècle, *APAE*, 3 (1952), 91–124.

574 Cam, H.M., *The Hundred and the Hundred Rolls. An Outline of Local Government in Medieval England*, London, 1930.

575 Cam, H.M., *Liberties and Communities in Medieval England. Collected Studies in Local Administration and Topography*, 2nd edn, New York, 1963.

576 Cazelles, R., Un problème d'évolution et d'intégration: les grands officiers de la Couronne de France dans l'administration nouvelle au Moyen Age, *AFISA*, 1 (1964), 183–9.

577 Chrimes, S.B., *An Introduction to the Administrative History of Mediaeval England*, 3rd edn, Oxford, 1966.

578 Cohn, H.J., *The Government of the Rhine Palatinate in the Fifteenth Century*, Oxford, 1965.

579 Demurger, A., Guerre civile et changements du personnel administratif dans le royaume de France de 1400 à 1418: l'exemple des baillis et sénéchaux, *Francia*, 6 (1978), 151–298.

580 Dupont-Ferrier, G., *Les officiers royaux des bailliages et sénéchaussées et les institutions monarchiques locales en France à la fin du Moyen Age*, Paris, 1902.

581 *Etudes sur l'Histoire de Paris et de l'Ile-de-France*. Actes du C^c Congrès national des Sociétés savantes, Paris, 1975, II, Paris, 1978.

582 Favier, J., L'histoire administrative et financière du Moyen Age depuis dix ans, *BEC*, 126 (1968), 427–503.

583 Garcia Marin, J.M., *El ofico público en Castilla durante la Baja Edad Media*, Seville, 1974.

584 Gerics, J., Beiträge zur Geschichte der Gerichtsbarkeit im ungarischen königlichen Hof und der Zentralverwaltung im 14. Jahrhundert, *Annales Universitatis Scientiarum Budapestinensis, Sectio historica*, 7 (1965), 3–28.

585 Gonzalez Alonso, B., *El Corregidor Castellano (1348–1808)*, Madrid, 1970.

586 Gorissen, P., *De Raadkamer van de Hertog van Bourgondië te Maastricht (1473–77)*, with French summary, Louvain, 1959.

587 Guenée, B., La géographie administrative de la France à la fin du Moyen Age: élections et bailliages, *MA*, 67 (1961), 293–323.

588 Homem, A.L. de Carvalho, *Subsidios para o Estudo da Administração Central no Reinado de D. Pedro I*, Porto, 1978.

589 Hudry-Bichelonne, Fr, L'administration du comté de Bar sous Edouard Ier (1302–1336), *Bulletin des Sociétés d'Histoire et d'Archéologie de la Meuse*, 3 (1966), 3–24; 4 (1967), 3–15.

590 Jewell, H.M., *English Local Administration in the Middle Ages*, Newton Abbot, 1972.

591 Lalindè Abadia, J., *La Gobernación General en la Corona de Aragon*, Madrid, 1963.

592 Leguai, A., Un aspect de la formation des Etats princiers en France à la fin du Moyen Age: les réformes administratives de Louis II, duc de Bourbon, *MA*, 70 (1964), 49–72.

593 Molho, A., The Florentine Oligarchy and the Balie of the Late Trecento, *Spec.*, 43 (1968), 23–51.

594 Monier, R., *Les institutions centrales du comté de Flandre de la fin du IXe siècle à 1384*, Paris, 1943.

595 Paravicini, W. and Werner, K.F. (eds), *Histoire comparée de l'administration (IVe–XVIIIe siècles). Actes du XIVe Colloque historique franco-allemand, Tours, 27 Mars–1er avril 1977*, Munich, 1980 (*Francia*, suppl. 9).

596 Partner, P., *The Papal State under Martin V. The Administration and Government of the Temporal Power in the Early Fifteenth Century*, London, 1958.

597 Perez Bustamanate R., *El gobierno y la administración territorial de Castilla (1230–1474)*, 2 vols, Madrid, 1976.

598 Polonio, V., *L'amministrazione della 'res publica' genovese fra Tre e Quattrocento. L'archivio 'Antico Comune'*, Genoa, 1977.

599 Potkowski, E., Ecriture et société en Pologne du bas Moyen Age (XIVe–XVe siècles), *Acta Poloniae Historica*, 39 (1979), 47–100.

600 Redoutey, J.-P., Le comté de Bourgogne de 1295 à 1314. Problèmes d'administration, *MSHD*, 33 (1975–6), 7–65.

601 Reydellet-Guttinger, C., *L'administration pontificale dans le duché de Spolète (1305–1352)*, Florence, 1975.

602 Richard, J., Les débats entre le roi de France et le duc de Bourgogne sur la

frontière du royaume à l'ouest de la Saône: l'enquête de 1452, *BPH*, 1964, 113–32.

603 Richard, J., Problèmes de ressort au XVe siècle: l'enquête de 1451–52 sur la situation de Fontaine-Française, *MSHD*, 26 (1965), 217–27.

604 Richardson, H.G. and Sayles, G.O., *The Administration of Ireland, 1172–1377*, Dublin, 1963.

605 Rogozinski, J., The Counsellors of the Seneschal of Beaucaire and Nimes, 1250–1350, *Spec.*, 44 (1969), 421–39.

606 Rogozinski, J., The First French Archives, *French Historical Studies*, 7 (1971), 111–16.

607 Rück, P., Die Ordnung der herzoglich savoyischen Archiv unter Amadeus VIII (1398–1451), *Archivalische Zeitschrift*, 67 (1971), 11–101.

608 Santoro, C., *Gli Uffici del Dominio Sforzesco (1450–1500)*, Milan, 1948.

609 Storey-Challenger, S.B. and Petit, R., *L'administration anglaise du Ponthieu après le traité de Brétigny (1361–69)*, Abbeville, 1975.

610 Strayer, J.R., Viscounts and Viguiers under Philip the Fair, *Spec.*, 38 (1963), 242–55.

611 Theuerkauf, G., Zur Typologie spätmittelalter Territorialverwaltung in Deutschland, *AFISA*, 2 (1965), 37–76.

612 Thielen, P.G., *Die Verwaltung des Ordensstaates Preussen vornehmlich im 15. Jahrhundert*, Cologne/Graz, 1965.

613 Trabut-Cussac, J.-P., *L'administration anglaise en Gascogne sous Henry III et Edouard Ier de 1254 à 1307*, Geneva, 1972.

614 Uytterbrouck, A., *Le gouvernement du duché de Brabant au bas Moyen Age (1355–1430)*, 2 vols, Brussels, 1975.

615 Willard, J.F. and Morris, W.A., *The English Government at Work, 1327–36*, 3 vols, Cambridge, Mass., 1940–7.

616 Zabalo Zabalegui, J., *La administración del reino de Navarra en el siglo XIV*, Pamplona, 1973.

THE ADMINISTRATION OF THE STATE: JUSTICE

617 Avery, M.E., The History of the Equitable Jurisdiction of Chancery before 1460, *BIHR*, 42 (1969), 129–44.

618 Autrand, F., Rétablir l'Etat: l'année 1454 au Parlement, in *Actes du 104e Congrès national des Sociétés savantes, Bordeaux, 1980*, I, Paris, 1981, 7–23.

619 Battenberg, F., *Gerichtsschreiberamt und Kanzlei am Reichshofgericht, 1235–1451*, Cologne/Vienna, 1974.

620 Bautier, R.-H., Origine et diffusion du sceau de juridiction, *Comptes rendus de l'Académie des Inscriptions et Belles-Lettres*, 1971, 304–21.

621 Bellamy, J.G., *The Law of Treason in England in the Later Middle Ages*, Cambridge, 1970.

622 Bellamy, J., *Crime and Public Order in England in the Later Middle Ages*, London, 1973.

623 Bellamy, J., *The Tudor Law of Treason: An Introduction*, London, 1979.

624 Benton, J.F., Philip the Fair and the Jours of Troyes, *SMRH*, 6 (1969), 279–344.

625 Bertényi, I., Zur Gerichtstätigkeit des Palatins und des Landesrichters (Judex Curiae Regiae) in Ungarn im XIV. Jahrhundert, *Annales Universitatis Scientiarum Budapestinensis, Sectio historica*, 7 (1965), 29–42.

626 Bisson, T.N., Consultative Functions in the King's Parlements (1250–1314), *Spec.*, 44 (1969), 353–73.

627 Blatcher, M., *The Court of King's Bench, 1450–1550: A Study in Self-Help*, London, 1978.

628 Bowsky, W.M., The Medieval Commune and Internal Violence: Police Power and Public Safety in Siena, 1287–1355, *American Historical Review*, 73 (1967), 1–17.

629 Brissaud, Y.-B., *Le droit de grâce à fin du Moyen Age (XIVe–XVe siècles). Contribution à l'étude de la restauration de la souveraineté monarchique*, unpubl. thesis, Poitiers, 1971.

630 Byl, R., *Les juridictions scabinales dans le duché de Brabant (des origines à la fin du XVe siècle)*, Brussels, 1965.

631 Chevrier, G., Les débuts du Parlement de Dijon (1477–87), *Annales de Bourgogne*, 15 (1943), 93–124.

632 Cheyette, F.L., La justice et le pouvoir royal à la fin du Moyen Age français, *RHDFE*, 4th ser., 40 (1962), 373–94.

633 Cheyette, F.L., The Royal Safeguard in Medieval France, *Studia Gratiana*, 15 (1972), 631–52.

633a *Consilium Magnum, 1473–1973. Commémoration du 500e anniversaire de la création du Parlement et Grand Conseil de Malines. Colloque du 8–9 décembre 1973*, Brussels, 1977.

634 Constant, M., La justice dans une châtellenie savoyarde au Moyen Age: Allinges-Thonon, *RHDFE*, 50 (1972), 374–97.

635 Growley, D.A., The Later History of Frankpledge, *BIHR*, 48 (1975), 1–15.

636 Cuttler, S.M., *The Law of Treason and Treason Trials in Later Medieval France*, Cambridge, 1982.

637 De Craecker-Dussart, C., L'évolution du sauf-conduit dans les principautés de la Basse-Lotharingie, du VIIIe au XIVe siècle, *MA*, 80 (1974), 185–243.

638 Elton, G.R. (ed.), *The Law Courts of Medieval England*, London, 1973.

639 Gilles, H., Les ordonnances judiciaires de Jean de Mauquenchy, sénéchal de Toulouse. *Actes du XCVI^e Congrès national des Sociétés savantes, Toulouse, 1971*. II, Paris, 1978, 231–67.

640 Grava, Y., Justice et pouvoirs à Martigues au XIVe siècle, *Provence historique*, 28 (1978), 305–22.

641 Guenée, B., *Tribunaux et gens de justice dans le bailliage de Senlis à la fin du Moyen Age (vers 1380–vers 1550)*, Paris, 1963.

642 Hanawalt, B.A., *Crime and Conflict in English Communities, 1300–48*, Cambridge, Mass., 1979.

643 Hastings, M., *The Court of Common Pleas in Fifteenth-Century England. A Study of Legal Administration and Procedure*, New York, 1947.

644 Hunnisett, R.F., *The Medieval Coroner*, Cambridge, 1961.

645 Jones, W.R., Relations of the Two Jurisdictions. Conflict and Cooperation in England during the Thirteenth and Fourteenth Centuries, *SMRH*, 7 (1970), 77–210.

646 Kaeuper, R.W., Law and Order in 14th Century England: The Evidence of Special Commissions of Oyer and Terminer, *Spec.*, 54 (1979), 734–84.

647 Lavoie, R., Les statistiques criminelles et le visage du justicier: justice royale et justice seigneuriale en Provence au Moyen Age, *Provence historique*, 29 (1979), 3–20.

648 Leclercq, P., Délits et répression dans un village de Provence (fin XVe–début du XVIe siècle), *MA*, 82 (1976), 539–55.

649 Lehmberg, S.E., Star Chamber: 1485–1509, *The Huntington Library Quarterly*, 24 (1961), 189–214.

650 Liva, A., *Notariato e documento notarile a Milano, dall'Alto Medioevo alla fine del Settecento*, Rome, 1979.

651 Lombard-Jourdan, A., Fiefs et justices parisiens au quartier des Halles, *BEC*, 134 (1976), 301–88.

652 Lorcin, M.-T., Les paysans et la justice dans la région lyonnaise aux XIVe et XVe siècles, *MA*, 74 (1968), 269–300.

653 Nicholas, D.M., Crime and Punishment in Fourteenth-Century Ghent, *RBPH*, 48 (1970), 289–334, 1141–76.

654 Ortalli, G., *Pingatur in Palatio: la pittura infamante nei secoli XIII–XVI*, Rome, 1979.

655 Pugh, B., *Imprisonment in Medieval England*, Cambridge, 1968.

656 Putnam, B.H., *The Place in Legal History of Sir William Shareshull, Chief Justice of the King's Bench, 1350–61. A Study of Judicial and Administrative Methods in the Reign of Edward III*, Cambridge, 1950.

657 Roger, J.-M., Gardes du scel et notaires dans la prévôté de Bar-sur-Aube (fin du XIIIe–milieu du XVIe siècle), *BPH*, 1974, 11–72.

658 Rogozinski, J., Ordinary and Major Judges, *Studia Gratiana*, 15 (1972), 589–612.

659 Schuler, P.-J., *Geschichte des südwestdeutschen Notariats. Von seinen Anfängen bis zur Reichsnotariatsordnung von 1512*, Bühl, 1976.

660 Small, C.M., Appeals from the Duchy of Burgundy to the Parlement of Paris in the Early Fourteenth Century, *Mediaeval Studies*, 39 (1977), 350–68.

661 Stocker, C.W., Office and Justice: Louis XI and the Parlement of Paris (1465–67), *Mediaeval Studies*, 37 (1975), 360–86.

662 Van Herwaarden, J., *Opgelegde Bedevaarten. Een studie over de praktijk van opleggen van bedevaarten (met name in de stedelijke rechtspraak) in de Nederlanden gedurende de late middeleeuwen*, Amsterdam, 1978.

663 Van Rompaey, J., *De Grote Raad van de Hertogen van Bourgondie en het Parlement van Mechelen* (with French summary), Brussels, 1973.

664 Viala, A., *Le Parlement de Toulouse et l'administration royale laïque, 1420–1525 environ*, 2 vols, Albi, 1953.

665 Wohlgemuth, H., *Das Urkundenwesen des deutschen Reichshofgerichts, 1273–1378. Eine kanzleigeschichtliche Studie*, Cologne/Vienna, 1973.

THE ADMINISTRATION OF THE STATE: FINANCE

666 Arnould, M.-A., Une estimation des revenus et des dépenses de Philippe le Bon en 1445, *Recherches sur l'histoire des finances publiques en Belgique*, III, Brussels, 1973, 131–219.

667 Baker, R.L., *The English Customs Service, 1307–43: A Study of Medieval Administration*, Philadelphia, 1961.

668 Baratier, E., *La démographie provençale du XIIIe au XVIe siècle*, Paris, 1961.

669 Barbadoro, B., *Le finanze della Repubblica fiorentina. Imposta diretta e debito pubblico fino all'istituzione del Monte*, Florence, 1929.

670 Bartier, J., Une crise de l'Etat bourguignon: la réformation de 1457, in *Hommage au Pr P. Bonenfant, 1899–1965*, G. Despy, M.A. Arnould and M. Martens (eds), Brussels, 1965, 501–11.

671 Bompaire, M., L'atelier monétaire royal de Montpellier et la circulation monétaire en Bas Languedoc jusqu'au milieu du XVe siècle, *PTEC*, 1980, 23–8.

672 Bossuat, A., Etude sur les emprunts royaux au début du XVe siècle. La politique financière du connétable Bernard d'Armagnac (1416–18), *RHDFE*, 1950, 351–71.

673 Bowsky, W.M., The Impact of the Black Death upon Sienese Government and Society, *Spec.*, 39 (1964), 1–34.

674 Bowsky, W.M., *The Finances of the Commune of Siena, 1287–1355*, Oxford, 1970.

675 Broussolle, J., Les impositions municipales de Barcelone de 1328 à 1462, *EHM*, 5 (1955), 3–164.

676 Brown, E.A.R., Gascon Subsidies and the Finances of the English Dominions, 1315–24, *SMRH*, 8 (1971), 33–163.

677 Brown, E.A.R., *Cessante Causa* and the Taxes of the Last Capetians: the Political Application of a Philosophical Maxim, *Studia Gratiana*, 15 (1972), 565–88.

678 Brown, E.A.R., Taxation and Morality in the Thirteenth and Fourteenth Centuries: Conscience and Political Power and the Kings of France, *French Historical Studies*, 8 (1973), 1–28.

679 Brown, E.A.R., Customary Aids and Royal Fiscal Policy under Philip VI of Valois, *Traditio*, 30 (1974), 191–258.

680 Brown, E.A.R., Royal Salvation and Needs of State in Late Capetian France, in *Order and Innovation in the Middle Ages. Essays in Honor of Joseph R. Strayer*, W.C. Jordan, B. McNab and T.F. Ruiz (eds), Princeton, 1976, 365–83.

681 Brühl, C.R., *Fodrum, Gistum, Servitium Regis: Studien zu den wirtschaftlichen Grundlagen des Königtums im Frankenreich und in den fränkischen Nachfolgestaaten – Deutschland, Frankreich und Italien – vom 6. bis zur Mitte des 14. Jahrhunderts*, 2 vols, Cologne/Graz, 1968.

682 Buongiorno, M., *Il bilancio di uno stato medievale, Genova, 1340–1529*, Genoa, 1973.

683 Carolus-Barré, L., Ordonnance inédite du 24 juin 1396 transférant à Compiègne le grenier à sel de Noyon, *BPH*, 1974, 73–80.

684 Cazelles, R., La stabilisation de la monnaie par la création du franc (décembre 1360). Blocage d'une société, *Traditio*, 32 (1976), 293–311.

685 Cazelles, R., Quelques réflexions à propos des mutations de la monnaie royale française (1295–1360), *MA*, 72 (1966), 83–105, 251–78.

686 Cazelles, R., Les trésors de Charles V, *Comptes rendus de l'Académie des Inscriptions et Belles-Lettres*, 1980, 214–26.

687 Chiancone Isaacs, A.K., Fisco e politica a Siena nel Trecento, *RSI*, 85 (1973), 22–46.

688 Chomel, V., Un censier dauphinois inédit. Méthode et portée de l'édition du *Probus*, *BPH*, 1964, 319–407.

689 Chomel, V., Ressources domaniales et subsides en Dauphiné (1355–64), *Provence historique*, 25 (1975), 179–92.

690 Cockshaw, P., Heurs et malheurs de la recette générale de Bourgogne, *Annales de Bourgogne*, 41 (1969), 247–71.

691 Cockshaw, P., Un compte de la recette générale de Jean sans Peur retrouvé à Dijon, *Annales de Bourgogne*, 49 (1977), 24–30.

692 Collet, D., A propos du domaine du duc de Bretagne, *Annales de Bretagne*, 76 (1969), 355–405.

693 Courcelle, P., *Huit rôles des tailles inédits de Sully-sur-Loire (1440–84)*, Paris, 1973 (Mémoires de l'Académie des Inscriptions et Belles-Lettres, XLV).

694 Courcelle, P., *Nouveaux documents inédits de Sully-sur-Loire (1364–1500)*, Paris, 1978 (Mémoires de l'Académie des Inscriptions et Belles-Lettres, new series, III).

695 Day, J., *Les douanes de Gênes, 1376–77*, 2 vols, Paris, 1963.

696 Day, J., The Great Bullion Famine of the Fifteenth Century, *PP*, 79 (1978), 3–54.

697 Delmaire, B. (ed.), *Le compte général du receveur d'Artois pour 1303–04*, Brussels, 1977.

698 De Moxó, S., Exenciones tributarias en Castilla a fines de la Edad Media, *Hispania*, 21 (1961), 163–88.

699 Deneuville, D., Quelques aspects des finances bourguignonnes en 1437, *Revue du Nord*, 61 (1979), 571–79.

700 Dickstein-Bernard, C., *La gestion financiére d'une capitale à ses débuts: Bruxelles, 1334–1467*, Brussels, 1977.

701 Dietz, F.C., *English Public Finance, 1485–1641*, 2 vols, London, 1964.

702 Dossat, Y., La lutte contre les usurpations domaniales dans la sénechaussée de Toulouse sous les derniers Capétiens, *Annales du Midi*, 1961, 129–64.

703 Dralle, L., Die Einkünfte des Deutschenordenshochmeisters Friedrich von Sachsen (1498 bis 1510). Ein Beitrag zur Finanzgeschichte der ostdeutschen Territorien, *Zeitschrift für Ostforschung*, 28 (1979), 626–40.

704 Droege, G., Die finanziellen Grundlagen des Territorialstaates in West- und Ostdeutschland an der Wende vom Mittelalter zur Neuzeit, *VSWG*, 53 (1966), 145–61.

705 Droege, G., *Verfassung und Wirtschaft in Kurköln unter Dietrich von Moers (1414–63)*, Bonn, 1957.

706 *Etudes sur la fiscalité au Moyen Age*, Actes du CII^e Congrès national des Sociétés savantes, Limoges, 1977, I, Paris, 1979.

707 Favier, J., *Les contribuables parisiens à la fin de la Guerre de Cent Ans, Les rôles d'impôt de 1421, 1423 et 1438*, Geneva/Paris, 1970.

708 Favier, J., *Finance et fiscalité au bas Moyen Age*, Paris, 1971.

709 Favier, J., Les rôles d'impôt parisiens du XVe siècle (à propos d'un article récent), *BEC*, 130 (1972), 467–91.

710 Favreau, R., Comptes de la sénéchaussée de Saintonge (1360–62), *BEC*, 117 (1959), 73–88.

711 Fédou, R., L'administration royale des Eaux et Forêts en Lyonnais aux XIVe et XVe siècles, *AFISA*, 4 (1967), 117–32.

712 *Finances et comptabilité urbaines du XIIIe au XVIe siècle. Colloque international de Blankenberge, 1962*, Brussels, 1964.

713 Fiumi, E., L'imposta diretta nei communi medioevali della Toscana, in *Studi in onore di A. Sapori*, I, Milan, 1957, 327–53.

714 Fournial, E., Enquêteurs, réformateurs et visiteurs généraux dans la comté de Forez au XIVe siècle, *Bulletin de la Diana*, 36 (1959), 22–35.

715 Fournial, E., *Histoire monétaire de l'Occident médiéval*, Paris, 1970.

716 Fournial, E., *Les mémoriaux de la Chambre des Comptes de Forez. Restitution du registre des années 1349–56*, Mâcon, 1964.

717 Fourquin, G., *Le domaine royal en Gâtinais d'après la prisée de 1332*, Paris, 1963.

718 Fourquin, G., La part de la forêt dans les ressources d'un grand seigneur d'Ile-de-France à la fin du XIIIe siècle, *Paris et Ile-de-France. Mémoires publiés par la Fédération des Sociétés historiques et archéologiques de Paris et de l'Ile-de-France*, 18–19 (1967–8), 7–36.

719 Fryde, E.B., The financial policies of the royal governments and popular resistance to them in France and England, c.1270–c.1420, *RBPH*, 57 (1979), 824–60.

720 Fryde, M.M., Studies in the History of Public Credit of German Principalities and Towns in the Middle Ages, *SMRH*, I (1964), 221–92.

721 Gilles, H., Autorité royale et résistances urbaines. Un exemple languedocien: l'échec de la réformation générale de 1434–35, *BPH*, 1961, 115–46.

722 Girard, A., Un phénomène économique: la guerre monétaire (XIVe–XVe siècles), *Ann.*, 1940, 207–18.

723 Glasscock, R.E. (ed.), *The Lay Subsidy of 1334*, London, 1975.

724 Gresser, P., Les terriers comtaux de Franche-Comté rédigés sous Philippe le Bon et Charles le Téméraire, *MSHD*, 33 (1975–6), 67–165.

725 Gresser, P. and Hintzy, J., Les étangs du domaine comtal en Franche-Comté d'après les comptes de gruerie du XIVe siècle, *Société d'émulation du Jura. Travaux, 1975–6*, Dole, 1978, 129–56.

726 Grunzweig, A., Les incidences internationales des mutations monétaires de Philippe le Bel, *MA*, 59 (1953), 117–72.

727 Guerreau, A., L'atelier monétaire royal de Mâcon (1239–1421), *Ann.*, 1974, 369–92.

728 Guy, J.A., A Conciliar Court of Audit at Work in the Last Months of the Reign of Henry VII, *BIHR*, 49 (1976), 289–95.

729 Harriss, G.L., 'Fictitious Loans', *The Economic History Review*, 2nd ser., 8 (1955), 187–99.

730 Harriss, G.L., Preference at the Medieval Exchequer, *BIHR*, 30 (1957), 17–40.

731 Harriss, G.L., *King, Parliament and Public Finance in Medieval England to 1369*, Oxford, 1975.

732 Heers, J., Fiscalité et politique: le péage de Crépy-en-Valois et la conflit Orléans-Bourgogne (1393–8), in *Studi in memoria di Federigo Melis*, 5 vols, II, Rome, 1978, 395–430.

733 Henneman, J.B., *Enquêteurs-Réformateurs* and Fiscal Officers in Fourteenth-Century France, *Traditio*, 24 (1968), 309–49.

734 Henneman, J.B., Financing the Hundred Years' War: Royal Taxation in France in 1340, *Spec.*, 42 (1967), 275–98.

735 Henneman, J.B., The Black Death and Royal Taxation in France, 1347–51, *Spec.*, 43 (1968), 405–28.

736 Henneman, J.B., *Royal Taxation in Fourteenth-Century France. The Development of War Financing, 1322–56*, Princeton, 1971.

737 Henneman, J.B., The French Ransom Aids and Two Legal Traditions, *Studia Gratiana*, 15 (1972), 613–30.

738 Henneman, J.B., *Royal Taxation in Fourteenth-Century France. The Captivity and Ransom of John II, 1356–70*, Philadelphia, 1976.

739 Henwood, P., Le Trésor royal sous le règne de Charles VI (1380–1422). Etude sur les inventaires, les orfèvres parisiens et les principaux artistes du roi, *PTEC*, 1978, 91–8.

740 Henwood, P., Administration et vie des collections d'orfèvrerie royales sous le règne de Charles VI (1380–1422), *BEC*, 138 (1980), 179–215.

741 Hesse, P.-J., *La mine et les mineurs en France de 1300 à 1550*, 3 vols, dactylographié, Paris, 1968.

742 Hesse, P.-J., La formation d'une administration minière royale dans la France médiévale et au début du XVIᵉ siècle, *Actes du XCVIIIᵉ Congrès national des Sociétés savantes, Saint-Etienne, 1973*, I: *Mines et métallurgie (XIIᵉ–XVIᵉ siècle)*, Paris, 1975, 7–22.

743 Higounet-Nadal, A., *Les comptes de la taille et les sources de l'histoire démographique de Périgueux au XIVᵉ siècle*, Paris, 1965.

743a *L'Impôt dans le cadre de la Ville et de l'Etat. Colloque international de Spa, 1964*, Brussels, 1966.

744 Isenmann, E., Reichsfinanzen und Reichssteuern im 15. Jahrhundert, *ZHF*, 7 (1980), 1–76, 129–218.

745 Jones, M., Les finances de Jean IV, duc de Bretagne (1364–99), *Mémoires de la Société d'Histoire et d'Archéologie de Bretagne*, 52 (1972–4), 27–53.

746 Kaeuper, R.W., *Bankers to the Crown. The Riccardi of Lucca and Edward I*, Princeton, 1973.

747 Kaeuper, R.W., Royal Finance and the Crisis of 1297, *Order and Innovation in the Middle Ages. Essays in Honor of Joseph R. Strayer*, W.C. Jordan, B. McNab and T.F. Ruiz (eds), Princeton, 1976, 103–10.

748 Kauch, P., Le Trésor de l'Epargne, création de Philippe le Bon, *RBPH*, II (1932), 703–19.

749 Kirby, J.L., The Issues of the Lancastrian Exchequer and Lord Cromwell's Estimates of 1433, *BIHR*, 24 (1951), 121–51.

750 Kirchgässner, B., *Das Steuerwesen der Reichsstadt Konstanz, 1418-1490*, Constance, 1960.

751 Kirby, J.L., The English Exchequer of Receipt in the Later Middle Ages, *AFISA*, 4 (1967), 78–98.

752 Kirshner, J., The Moral Theology of Public Finance. A Study and Edition of Nicholas de Anglias's *Quaestio Disputata* on the Public Debt of Venice, *Archivum Fratrum Praedicatorum*, 40 (1970), 47–72.

753 Kögl, W., Studien über das niederösterreichische Regiment unter Maximilian I. Mit besonderer Berücksichtigung der Finanzverwaltung (1490 bis 1506), *MIÖG*, 83 (1975), 48–74.

754 Lacroix, J.-B., Les fermiers du fisc à Paris dans la seconde moitié du XVe siècle, *PTEC*, 1974, 137–48.

755 Ladero Quesada, M.A., *La Hacienda Real Castellana entre 1480 y 1492*, Valladolid, 1967.

756 Ladero Quesada, M.A., Les finances royales de Castille à la veille des temps modernes, *Ann.*, 1970, 775–88.

757 Ladero Quesada, M.A., *La Hacienda Real de Castilla en el siglo XV*, Laguna, 1973.

758 Lapeyre, H., Alphonse V et ses banquiers, *MA*, 67 (1961), 93–136.

759 Lebecq, S., Vaucelles et la rançon de Jean le Bon: la crise d'une abbaye à la lumière d'une enquête de 1358, *Revue du Nord*, 58 (1976), 383–401.

760 Le Goff, J., La fiscalité du sel dans les finances des communes italiennes du Moyen Age, *XIe Congrès international des Sciences historiques, Stockholm, 1960. Communications*, Stockholm, 1960, 107–8.

761 Le Goff, J., Le sel dans la politique française à l'égard de la Savoie au XVe et au début du XVIe siècle, *BPH*, 1960, 303–14.

762 Luciński, J., Les propriétés foncières du souverain en Petite-Pologne jusqu'en 1385. *RHDFE*, 1970, 64–73.

763 Luzzatto, G., *Il debito pubblico della Repubblica di Venezia dagli ultimi decenni del XII secolo alla fine del XV*, Milan/Varese, 1963.

764 Luzzatto, G., L'oro e l'argento nella politica monetaria veneziana dei secoli XIII e XIV, *RSI*, 5th ser., 2 (1937), 17–29.

765 Lydon, J.F., Edward II and the Revenues of Ireland in 1311–12, *Irish Historical Studies*, 14 (1964), 39–57.

766 McFarlane, K.B., Loans to the Lancastrian Kings: the Problem of Inducement. *The Cambridge Historical Journal*, 9 (1947), 51–68.

767 MacKay, A., Documentos para la historia de los financieros castellanos de la Baja Edad Media. I: una 'información' del 23 de septiembre de 1466, *Historia, Instituciones, Documentos*, 5 (1978), 321–7.

768 Martens, M., *L'administration du domaine ducal en Brabant au Moyen Age (1250-1406)*, Brussels, 1954.

769 Martin, J.L., Nacionalización de la sal y aranceles extraordinarios en Cataluna (1365–7), *Anuario de Estudios Medievales*, 3 (1966), 515–25.

770 Mateu y Llopis, F., *De mutatione monetae* en el reino de Valencia, in *Studi in onore di A. Fanfani*, III, Milan, 1962, 183–216.

771 Mayhew, N. (ed.), *Edwardian Monetary Affairs (1279–1344). A Symposium held in Oxford* (British Archaeological Reports, 36), Oxford, 1977.

772 Menjot, D., L'impôt royal à Murcie au début du XVe siècle: un cas de 'pratique' financière, *MA*, 82 (1976), 477–516.

773 Menjot, D., L'incidence sociale de la fiscalité directe des Trastamares de Castille au XIVe siècle, *Historia, Instituciones, Documentos*, 5 (1978), 329–71.

774 Miskimin, H.A., The Last Act of Charles V: the Background of the Revolts of 1382, *Spec.*, 38 (1963), 433–42.

775 Mitchell, S.K., *Taxation in Medieval England*, New Haven, 1951.

776 Molho, A., *Florentine Public Finances in the Early Renaissance, 1400–33*, Cambridge, Mass., 1971.

777 Mollat, M., Recherches sur les finances des ducs Valois de Bourgogne, *RH*, 219 (1958), 285–321.

778 Mollat, M. et al., *Le rôle du sel dans l'histoire*, Paris, 1968.

779 Monier, R., *Les institutions financières du comté de Flandre du XIe siècle à 1384*, Paris, 1948.

780 Morard, N., Contribution à l'histoire monétaire du pays de Vaud et de la Savoie: la 'bonne' et la 'mauvaise' monnaie de Guillaume de Challant, *Revue d'Histoire vaudoise*, 1975, 103–33.

781 Mouradian, G., La rançon de Jean II le Bon, *PTEC*, 1970, 151–6.

782 Moxó, S. de, Los Cuadernos de alcabala. Orígenes de la legislación tributaria castellana, *Anuario de Historia del Derecho español*, 39 (1969), 317–450.

783 Munro, J.H., An Economic Aspect of the Collapse of the Anglo-Burgundian Alliance, 1428–42, *EHR*, 85 (1970), 225–44.

784 Munro, J.H., *Wool, Cloth and Gold. The Struggle for Bullion in Anglo-Burgundian Trade, 1340–1478*, Toronto, 1973.

785 Nau, E., Stadt und Münze im späten Mittelalter und beginnender Neuzeit, *Blätter für deutsche Landesgeschichte*, 100 (1964), 145–58.

786 Neirinck, D., L'impôt direct à Albi de 1236 à 1450, *PTEC*, 1969, 113–22.

787 Palmer, J.J.N., Prêts à la couronne (1385), *BEC*, 126 (1968), 419–25.

788 Pastor de Togneri, R., La sal en Castilla y León. Un problema de la alimentación y del trabajo y una politica fiscal (siglos X–XIII), *Cuadernos de Historia de España*, 37–8 (1963), 42–87.

789 Pocquet du Haut-Jussé, B.-A., Les emprunts de la duchesse Anne à Julien Tierry (1489–91), *Annales de Bretagne*, 69 (1962), 269–93.

790 Postan, M.M., Rich, E.E. and Miller, E. (eds), *The Cambridge Economic History of Europe III, Economic Organization and Policies in the Middle Ages*, Cambridge, 1965.

791 Power, E., *The Wool Trade in English Medieval History*, Oxford, 1941.

792 Prestwich, M., Edward I's Monetary Policies and their Consequences, *Economic History Review*, 2nd ser., 22 (1969), 406–16.

793 Prestwich, M.C., Exchequer and Wardrobe in the Later Years of Edward I, *BIHR*, 46 (1973), 1–10.

794 Prince, A.E., The Payment of Army Wages in Edward III's Reign, *Spec.*, 19 (1944), 137–60.

795 Pugh, R.B., Some Mediaeval Moneylenders, *Spec.*, 43 (1968), 274–89.

796 Radding, C., Royal Tax Revenues in Later Fourteenth-Century France, *Traditio*, 32 (1976),361–8.

797 Reddaway, T.F., The King's Mint and Exchange in London, 1343–1453, *EHR*, 82 (1967), 1–23.

798 Rey, M., *Le domaine du roi et les finances extraordinaires sous Charles VI, 1388–1413*, Paris, 1965.

799 Rey, M., *Les finances royales sous Charles VI. Les causes du déficit, 1388–1413*, Paris, 1965.

800 Rey, M., Aux origines de l'impôt: les premiers comptes des aides dans l'élection de Langres, in *Economies et Sociétés au Moyen Age. Mélanges offerts à Edouard Perroy*, J.-P. Genet (ed.), Paris, 1973, 498–517.

801 Richard, J., Les archives et les archivistes des ducs de Bourgogne dans le ressort de la Chambre des Comptes de Dijon, *BEC*, 105 (1944), 123–69.

802 Richardson, H.G. and Sayles, G.O., Irish Revenue, 1278–1384, *Proceedings of the Royal Irish Academy*, 62 C (1961), 87–100.

803 Richardson, W.C., *Tudor Chamber Administration, 1485–1547*, Baton Rouge, 1952.

804 Rigaudière, A., *L'assiette de l'impôt direct à la fin du XIVe siècle. La livre d'estimes des consuls de Saint-Flour pour les années 1380–5*, Paris, 1977.

805 Rogers, A., Clerical Taxation under Henry IV, 1399–1413, *BIHR*, 46 (1973), 123–44.

806 Rolland, H., *Monnaies des comtes de Provence (XIIe–XVe siècle). Histoire monétaire, économique et corporative, description raisonnée*, Paris, 1956.

807 Romefort, J. de, Le sel en Provence du Xe siècle au milieu du XIVe. Production, exportation, fiscalité, *BPH*, 1958, 169–80.

808 Romestan, G., La gabelle des draps en Languedoc (1318–33), in *Hommage à André Dupont, 1897–1972. Etudes médiévales languedociennes*, G. Barruol et al. (ed.), Montpellier, 1974, 197–237.

809 Rondinini, G.S., Politica e teoria monetarie dell'età viscontea, *NRS*, 59 (1975), 288–330.

810 Roover, R. de, A Florence: un projet de monétisation de la dette publique au XVe siècle, in *Mélanges en l'honneur de Fernand Braudel, I: Histoire économique du monde méditerranéen, 1450–1650*, Toulouse, 1973, 511–19.

811 Rosen, J., Prices and Public Finance in Basle, 1360–1535, *Economic History Review*, 2nd ser., 25 (1972), 1–17.

812 Roustit, Y., La consolidation de la dette publique à Barcelone au milieu du XIVe siècle, *EHM*, 4 (1954), 15–156.

813 Rubner, H., *Untersuchungen zur Forstverfassung des mittelalterlichen Frankreichs*, Wiesbaden, 1965.

814 Schubert, E., Das Königsland: zu Konzeptionen des Römischen Königtums nach dem Interregnum, *Jahrbuch für fränkische Landesforschung*, 39 (1979), 23–40.

815 Schwarzkopf, U., *Die Rechnungslegung des Humbert de Plaine über die Jahre 1448 bis 1452. Eine Studie zur Amtsführung des burgundischen maître de la chambre aux deniers*, Göttingen, 1970.

816 Senkowski, J., *Skarbowosc Mazowska od konka XIV wieku do 1526 roku* [Maz-

ovian finances from the fourteenth century to 1526] (with French summary), Warsaw, 1965.

817 Shatzmiller, J., La perception de la *tallia Judeorum* en Provence au milieu du XIVe siècle, *Annales du Midi*, 82 (1970), 221–36.

818 Spufford, P., *Monetary Problems and Policies in the Burgundian Netherlands, 1433–96*, Leiden, 1970.

819 Steel, A., The Financial Background of the Wars of the Roses, *History*, 40 (1955), 18–30.

820 Steel, A., *The Receipt of the Exchequer, 1377–1485*, Cambridge, 1954.

821 Strayer, J.R., Pierre de Chalon and the Origins of the French Customs Service, in *Festschrift P.E. Schramm*, P. Classen and Scheckert (eds), 2 vols, Wiesbaden, 1964, 334–9.

822 Strayer, J.R. and Taylor, C.H., *Studies in Early French Taxation*, Cambridge, Mass., 1939.

823 Strayer, J.R., Notes on the Origin of English and French Export Taxes, *Studia Gratiana*, 15 (1972), 399–422.

824 Stromer, W. von, Das Zusammenspiel Oberdeutscher und Florentiner Geldleute bei der Finanzierung von König Ruprechts Italienzug, 1401–2, *Oeffentliche Finanzen und privates Kapital im spätem Mittelalter und in der ersten Hälfte des 19. Jahrhunderts. Forschungen zur Sozial- und Wirtschaftsgeschichte*, XVI, Stuttgart, 1971, 60–86.

825 Sutherland, D.W., *Quo Warranto Proceedings in the Reign of Edward I, 1278–94*, Oxford, 1963.

826 Thielemans, M.-R., Un emprunt brabançon sur la place de Bruges en 1425, in *Hommage au Pr P. Bonenfant, 1899–1965*, G. Despy (ed.), Brussels, 1965, 453–65.

827 Torrella Niubo, F., El impuesto textil de 'la Bolla' en la Cataluña medieval, *Hispania*, 14 (1954), 339–64.

828 Trasselli, C., Sul debito pubblico in Sicilia sotto Alfonso V d'Aragona, *EHM*, 6 (1956–9), 69–112.

829 Uyttebrouck, A., Notes et réflexions sur la structure des premiers comptes conservés à la recette de Brabant (années 1363–4 et séq.) *Centenaire du Séminaire d'histoire médiévale de l'Université libre de Bruxelles, 1876–1976*, Brussels, 1977, 219–57.

830 Van der Wee, H. and Van Cauwenberghe, E., Histoire agraire et finances publiques en Flandre du XIVe au XVIIe siècle, *Ann.*, 1973, 1051–65.

831 Van Nieuwenhuysen, A., L'organisation financière des Etats du duc de Bourgogne Philippe le Hardi, *Acta Historica Bruxellensia*, I, Brussels, 1967, 215–47.

832 Van Nieuwenhuysen, A., La comptabilité d'un receveur de Philippe le Hardi, in *Hommage au Pr P. Bonenfant, 1899–1965*, G. Despy, M.A. Arnould and M. Martens (eds), Brussels, 1965, 409–19.

833 Van Nieuwenhuysen, A., Le transport et le change des espèces dans la recette générale de toutes les finances de Philippe le Hardi, *RBPH*, 35 (1957), 55–65.

834 Van Werveke, H., Currency Manipulation in the Middle Ages: the Case of Louis de Male, Count of Flanders, *TRHS*, 4th ser., 31 (1949), 115–27.

835 Vidal, J., *L'équivalent des aides en Languedoc*, Montpellier, 1963.

836 Vignier, F., L'organisation forestière du duché de Bourgogne au XIVe siècle. Son application dans le bailliage de la Montagne, *BPH*, 1959, 481–92.

837 Violante, C., Per la storia economica e sociale di Pisa nel Trecento. La riforma della zecca del 1318, *Bulletino dell'Istituto Storico Italiano per il Medio Evo*, 66 (1954), 129–205.

838 Willard, J.F., *Parliamentary Taxes on Personal Property, 1290–1334. A Study in Mediaeval English Financial Administration*, Cambridge, Mass., 1934.

839 Wolff, P., *Les 'estimes' toulousaines des XIVe et XVe siècles*, Toulouse, 1956.

840 Wolffe, B.P., Henry VII's Land Revenues and Chamber Finance, *EHR*, 79 (1964), 225–54.

841 Wolffe, B.P., The Management of English Royal Estates under the Yorkist Kings, *EHR*, 71 (1956), 1–27.

842 Wolffe, B.P., *The Royal Demesne in English History. The Crown Estate in the Governance of the Realm from the Conquest to 1509*, London, 1971.

843 Wyrozumski, J., *Panstowa Gospodarka Solna w Polsce do Schyku XIV Wieku* [Polish salt policy and the manufacture of salt until the end of the fourteenth century], Cracow, 1968.

844 Young, C.R., *The Royal Forests of Medieval England*, Leicester, 1979.

THE ADMINISTRATION OF THE STATE:
CHANCERY, COUNCIL AND SECRETARIES

845 Bansa, H., *Studien zur Kanzlei Kaiser Ludwigs des Bayern vom Tag der Wahl bis zur Rückkehr aus Italien (1314–29)*, Kallmünz, 1968.

846 Bautier, R.H., Recherches sur la chancellerie royale au temps de Philippe VI, *BEC*, 122 (1964), 89–176; 123 (1965), 313–459.

847 Bayne, C.G. and Dunham, W.H., *Select Cases in the Council of Henry VII*, London, 1958.

848 Brown, A.L., The Commons and the Council in the Reign of Henry IV, *EHR*, 79 (1964), 1–30.

849 Brown, A.L., The King's Councillors in Fifteenth-Century England, *TRHS*, 5th ser., 19 (1969), 95–118.

850 Cazelles, R., Les mouvements révolutionnaires du milieu du XIVe siècle et le cycle de l'action politique, *RH*, 228 (1962), 279–312.

851 Cazelles, R., Une chancellerie privilégiée: celle de Philippe VI de Valois, *BEC*, 124 (1966), 355–81.

852 Chaplais, P., The Chancery of Guyenne, 1289–1453, in *Studies presented to Sir H. Jenkinson*, J. Conway-Davis (ed.), 1957, 61–96.

853 Cockshaw, P., Un rapport sur la chancellerie royale française du milieu du XIVe siècle, *MA*, 75 (1969), 503–28.

854 Courtel, A.-L., La chancellerie et les actes d'Eudes IV, duc de Bourgogne (1315–49), *BEC*, 135 (1977), 23–71, 255–311.

855 Elton, G.R., Why the History of the Early-Tudor Council remains unwritten, *AFISA*, 1 (1964), 268–296.

856 Guttinger, C., La chancellerie d'Humbert II, dauphin de Viennois (1333–49), *PTEC*, 1966, 57–64.

857 Harsgor, M., *Recherches sur le personnel du Conseil du Roi sous Charles VIII et Louis XII (1483–1515)*, unpubl. thesis, University of Paris IV, 1972.

858 Hlaváček, I., Die Geschichte der Kanzlei König Wenzels IV. und ihre Beamten in den Jahren 1376–1419, *Historica*, 5 (1963), 5–69.

859 Hlaváček, I., Das Urkunden und Kanzleiwesen des böhmischen und römischen Königs Wenzel (IV), 1376–1419. Ein Beitrag zur spätmittelalterlichen Diplomatik, Stuttgart, 1970.

860 Kirby, J.L., Councils and Councillors of Henry IV, 1399–1413, *TRHS*, 14 (1964), 35–65.

861 Kraus, A., Secretarius und Sekretariat. Der Ursprung der Institution des Staatssekretariats und ihr Einfluss auf die Entwicklung moderner Regierungsformen in Europa, *RQ*, 55 (1960), 43–84.

862 Lander, J.R., Council, Administration and Councillors, 1461–85, *BIHR*, 32 (1959), 138–80.

863 Malyusz, E., La chancellerie royale et la rédaction des chroniques dans la Hongrie médiévale, *MA*, 75 (1969), 51–86, 219–54.

864 Moraw, P., Kanzlei und Kanzleipersonal König Ruprechts, *Archiv für Diplomatik*, 15 (1969), 428–531.

865 Nüske, G. Fr., Untersuchungen über das Personal der päpstlichen Kanzlei, 1254–1304, *Archiv für Diplomatik*, 20 (1974), 39–240; 21 (1975), 249–431.

866 Otway-Ruthven, J., *The King's Secretary and the Signet Office in the Fifteenth Century*, Cambridge, 1939.

867 Otway-Ruthven, J., The Mediaeval Irish Chancery, in *Album H.M. Cam. II, Studies presented to the international commission for the history of representative and parliamentary institutions*, 24, Louvain/Paris, 1961, 117–38.

868 Pocquet du Haut-Jussé, B.-A., Le Conseil du duc en Bretagne d'après ses procès-verbaux (1459–63), *BEC*, 116 (1958), 136–69.

869 Renoz, P., *La chancellerie de Brabant sous Philippe le Bon (1430–67). Histoire et organisation, rédaction et expédition des actes*, Brussels, 1955.

870 Reydellet-Guttinger, C., La chancellerie d'Humbert II, dauphin de Viennois (1333–49), *Archiv für Diplomatik*, 20 (1974), 241–83.

871 Richardson, M., Henry V, the English Chancery, and Chancery English, *Spec.*, 55 (1980), 726–50.

872 Scheurer, R., La chancellerie de France et les écritures royales au temps de Charles VIII et de Louis XII (1483–1515), *PTEC*, 1962, 107–12.

873 Scheurer, R., L'enregistrement à la chancellerie de France au cours du XVe siècle, *BEC*, 120 (1962), 104–29.

874 Schück, H., Kansler och capella regis under folkungatiden, *Historisk Tidskrift*, Stockholm, 1963, 133–87 (with German summary).

875 Schwarz, B., *Die Organisation kurialer Schreiberkollegien von ihrer Entstehung bis zur Mitte des 15. Jahrhunderts*, Tübingen, 1972.

876 Suzkowska-Kurasiowa, I., *Dokumenty króslewskie i ich funkcje w państwie polskim za Andegawenow i pierwszych Jagiellonów, 1370–1444* [Royal documents and their function in the Polish kingdom during the Angevin and early Jagellonian dynasties], Warsaw, 1977.

877 Tessier, G., *Diplomatique royale française*, Paris, 1962.

878 Tessier, G., La chancellerie royale française d'après l'ordonnance cabochienne (1413), *MA*, 69 (1963), 679–90.

879 Uyttebrouck, A., Les origines du Conseil de Brabant: la Chambre du Conseil du duc Jean IV, *RBPH*, 36 (1958), 1135–72.

879a Virgoe, R., The Composition of the King's Council, 1437–61, *BIHR*, 43 (1970), 134–60.

880 Witt, R.G., *Coluccio Salutati and His Public Letters*, Geneva, 1976.

See also: 617.

THE ADMINISTRATION OF THE STATE:
THE RISE OF THE CAPITAL

881 Bautier, R.-H., Recherches sur les routes de l'Europe médiévale, *BPH*, 1960, 99–143; 1961, 277–308.

882 Brown, R.A., Colvin, H.M. and Taylor, A.J., *The History of the King's Works. The Middle Ages*, 2 vols, and plates, London, 1963.

883 Cauchies, J.-M., Messageries et messagers en Hainaut au XVᵉ siècle, *MA*, 82 (1976), 89–123, 301–41.

884 Chevalier, B., *Tours, ville royale (1356–1520). Origine et développement d'une capitale à la fin du Moyen Age*, Louvain/Paris, 1975.

885 Coulet, N., *Aix-en-Provence. Espace et relations d'une capitale (milieu XIVᵉ s.–milieu XVᵉ s.)*, unpubl. thesis, Aix, 1979.

886 Elekes, L., *Essai de centralisation de l'Etat hongrois dans la seconde moitié du XVᵉ siècle*, Budapest, 1960.

887 Favreau, R., Voyages et messageries en Poitou à la fin du Moyen Age, *Bulletin de la Société des Antiquaires de l'Ouest et des Musées de Poitiers*, 4th ser., XIII (1975), 31–53.

888 Favreau, R., *La ville de Poitiers à la fin du Moyen Age. Une capitale régionale*, 2 vols, Poitiers, 1978.

889 Fawtier, R., Comment le roi de France, au début du XIVᵉ siècle, pouvait-il se représenter son royaume?, in *Mélanges offerts à P.-E. Martin*, Geneva, 1961, 65–77.

890 Fey, H.-J., *Reise und Herrschaft der Markgrafen von Brandenburg (1134–1319)*, Cologne/Vienna, 1981.

891 Graus, F., Prag als Mitte Böhmens, 1346–1421, in *Zentralität als Problem der mittelalterlichen Stadtgeschichtsforschung*, F. Meynen (ed.), Vienna/Cologne, 1979, 22–47.

892 Guérout, J., Le Palais de la Cité à Paris des origines à 1417. Essai topographique et archéologique, *Mémoires de la Fédération des Sociétés historiques et archéologiques de Paris et de l'Ile-de-France*, 1 (1949), 57–212; 2 (1950), 21–204; 3 (1951), 7–101.

893 *Das Hauptstadtproblem in der Geschichte*, Tübingen, 1952.

894 Hill, M.C., *The King's Messengers, 1199–1377. A Contribution to the History of the Royal Household*, London, 1961.

895 Mályusz, E., *Die Zentralisationsbestrebungen König Sigismunds in Ungarn*, Budapest, 1960.

895a *Paris, fonctions d'une capitale*, Paris, 1962.

896 Peyer, H.C., Das Reisekönigtum des Mittelalters, *VSWG*, 51 (1964), 1–21.

897 Renouard, Y., Information et transmission des nouvelles, in *L'histoire et ses méthodes*, C. Samaran (ed.), Paris, 1961, 95–142.

898 Timbal, P.C., Civitas Parisius, communis patria, in *Economies et sociétés au Moyen Age. Mélanges offerts à Edouard Perroy*, J.-P. Genet (ed.), Paris, 1973, 661–5.

899 Tout, T.F., The Beginnings of a Modern Capital: London and Westminster in the Fourteenth Century, *The Collected Papers of T.F. Tout*, III, Manchester, 1934, 249–75.

900 Weber, R.E.J., The Messenger-Box as a Distinctive of the Foot-Messenger, *Antiquaries Journal*, 46 (1966), 88–101.

WAR

901 Allmand, C.T. (ed.), *War, Literature and Politics in the Late Middle Ages. Essays in honour of G.W. Coopland*, Liverpool, 1976.

902 Balard, M., A propos de la bataille du Bosphore. L'expedition génoise de Paganino Doria à Constantinople (1351–2), *Travaux et mémoires du Centre de recherches d'histoire et civilisation byzantines*, Paris, 1970, 431–69.

903 Bayley, C.C., *War and Society in Renaissance Florence. The 'De Militia' of Leonardo Bruni*, Toronto, 1961.

904 Bécet, M., Comment on fortifiait une petite ville pendant la guerre de Cent Ans. Les fortifications de Chablis au XVe siècle, *Annales de Bourgogne*, 21 (1949), 7–30.

905 Bruand, Y., De l'importance historique et de la valeur militaire des ouvrages fortifiés en Vieille-Castille au XVe siècle, *MA*, 63 (1957), 59–86.

906 Brusten, C., *L'armée bourguignonne de 1465 à 1468*, Brussels, 1954.

906a Cheyette, F.L., The Sovereign and the Pirates, 1332, *Spec.*, 45 (1970), 40–68.

907 Chomel, V., Chevaux de bataille et roncins en Dauphiné au XIVe siècle, *Cahiers d'Histoire*, 7 (1962), 5–23.

908 Contamine, P., L'artillerie royale française à la veille des guerres d'Italie, *Annales de Bretagne*, 71 (1964), 221–61.

909 Contamine, P., Batailles, Bannières, Compagnies. Aspects de l'organisation militaire française pendant la première partie de la Guerre de Cent Ans, *Les Cahiers vernonnais*, 4 (1964) (Actes du Colloque international de Cocherel, 16, 17 et 18 mai 1964), 19–32.

910 Contamine, P., *Guerre, Etat et société à la fin du Moyen Age. Etudes sur les armées des rois de France* (1337–1494), Paris, 1972.

911 Contamine, P., *War in the Middle Ages*, tr. M. Jones (Oxford, 1984).

912 Fournier, G., La défense des populations rurales pendant la Guerre de Cent Ans en Basse-Auvergne, *Actes du XC^e Congrès national des Sociétés savantes, Nice, 1905, Section d'archéologie*, Paris, 1966, 157–99.

913 Fowler, K., Les finances et la discipline dans les armées anglaises en France au XIVᵉ siècle, *Les Cahiers vernonnais*, 4 (1964) (Actes du Colloque international de Cocherel, 16, 17 et 18 mai 1964), 55–84.

914 Freeman, A.Z., A Moat Defensive: the Coast Defense Scheme of 1295, *Spec.*, 42 (1967), 442–62.

915 Gaier, C., Analysis of Military Forces in the Principality of Liège and the County of Looz from the Twelfth to the Fifteenth Century, *SMRH*, 2 (1965), 205–61.

916 Gaier, C., *Art et organisation militaires dans la principauté de Liège et dans le comté de Looz au Moyen Age*, Brussels, 1968.

917 Gaier, C., La fonction stratégico-défensive du plat pays au Moyen Age dans la région de la Meuse moyenne, *MA*, 69 (1963), 753–71.

918 Goodman, A., *The Wars of the Roses. Military activity and English society, 1452–97*, London, 1981.

919 *La guerre et la paix. Frontières et violences au Moyen Age*, Paris, 1978 (Comité des Travaux historiques et scientifiques, Section de Philologie et d'Histoire jusqu'à 1610. Actes du CIᵉ Congrès national des Sociétés savantes, Lille, 1976).

920 Gutierrez de Velasco, A., La financiación aragonesa de la 'Guerra de los Dos Pedros', *Hispania*, 19 (1959), 3–43.

921 Hale, J., War and Public Opinion in the Fifteenth and Sixteenth Centuries, *PP*, 22 (1962), 18–35.

922 Hay, D., The Division of the Spoils of War in Fourteenth-Century England, *TRHS*, 5th ser., 4 (1954), 91–109.

923 Hewitt, H.J., *The Organization of War under Edward III, 1338–62*, Manchester, 1966.

924 Jones, M., The Defence of Medieval Brittany: a survey of the establishment of fortified towns, castles and frontiers from the Gallo-Roman period to the end of the Middle Ages, *The Archeological Journal*, 138 (1981), 149–204.

925 Keen, M.H., *The Laws of War in the Late Middle Ages*, London, 1965.

926 Keen, M., *Chivalry*, New Haven and London, 1984.

927 Kepler, J.S., The Effects of the battle of Sluys upon the administration of English naval impressment, 1340–3, *Spec.*, 48 (1973), 70–7.

928 Ladero Quesada, M.A., *Castilla y la conquista del reino de Granada*, Valladolid, 1967.

929 Ladero Quesada, M.A., *Milicia y economia en la guerra de Granada: el cerco de Baza*, Valladolid, 1964.

930 Leguay, J.-P., *La ville de Rennes au XVᵉ siècle à travers les comptes des Miseurs*, Paris, 1969.

931 Lewis, N.B., The Recruitment and Organization of a Contract Army, May to November 1337, *BIHR*, 37 (1964), 1–19.

932 Lewis, N.B., The Summons of the English Feudal Levy, 5 April 1327, in *Essays in Medieval History presented to Bertie Wilkinson*. T.A. Sandquist and M.R. Powicke (eds), Toronto, 1969, 236–49.

933 Lot, F., *L'art militaire et les armées au Moyen Age en Europe et dans le Proche-Orient*, 2 vols, Paris, 1946.

934 Lot, F., *Recherches sur les effectifs des armées françaises des guerres d'Italie aux guerres de religion, 1494–1562*, Paris, 1962.

935 McFarlane, K.B., England and the Hundred Years' War, *PP*, 22 (1962), 3–13.

936 Martens, M., Du *Vestgeld* aux droits d'usage concédés sur les premiers remparts des grandes villes brabançonnes au Moyen Age, in *Miscellanea Mediaevalia in memoriam J.F. Niermeyer*, Groningen, 1967, 283–92.

937 Merlin-Chazelas, P. (ed.), *Documents relatifs au Clos des galées de Rouen et aux armées de mer du roi*, 2 vols, Paris, 1977–8.

938 Mesqui, J., Enceintes urbaines et fortification au Moyen Age. Un exemple: Provins (IXe–XV^{e}s), *Ecole pratique des Hautes Etudes, IVe section. Positions de thèses d'école de l'année 1978–9 et positions de thèses de IIIe cycle*, Paris, 1982, 30–6.

939 Mollat, M., De la piraterie sauvage à la course réglementée (XIVe–XVe siècle), *Mélanges de l'Ecole française de Rome. Moyen Age, Temps modernes*, 87 (1975), 7–25.

940 Newhall, R.A., *Muster and Review. A Problem of English Military Administration, 1420–40*, Cambridge, Mass., 1940.

941 Perroy, E., L'artillerie de Louis XI dans la campagne d'Artois (1477), *Revue du Nord*, 26 (1943), 171–96, 293–315.

942 Pescador, C., La caballeria popular en León y Castilla, *Cuadernos de Historia de España*, 33–4 (1961), 101–228; 35–6 (1962), 56–201; 37–8 (1963), 88–198; 39–40 (1964), 169–260.

943 Pieri, P., *Il Rinascimento e la crisi militare italiana*, 1934; 2nd edn, Turin, 1952.

944 Postan, M.M., The Costs of the Hundred Years' War, *PP*, 27 (1964), 34–53.

945 Powicke, M.R., Lancastrian Captains, in *Essays in Medieval History presented to Bertie Wilkinson*, T.A. Sandquist and M.R. Powicke (eds), Toronto, 1969, 371–82.

946 Powicke, M.R., *Military Obligation in Medieval England. A Study in Liberty and Duty*, Oxford, 1962.

947 Prestwich, M., *War, Politics and Finance under Edward I*, London, 1972.

948 Prestwich, M., English castles in the reign of Edward II, *Journal of Medieval History*, 8 (1982), 159–78.

949 Richmond, C.F., English Naval Power in the Fifteenth Century, *History*, 52 (1967), 1–15.

950 Schmidtchen, V., *Die Feuerwaffen des Deutschen Ritterordens bis zur Schlacht bei Tannenberg, 1410. Bestände, Funktion und Kosten, dargestellt anhand der Wirtschafts-bücher des Ordens von 1374 bis 1410*, Lüneburg, 1977.

951 Sherborne, J.W., The Cost of English Warfare with France in the Later Fourteenth Century, *BIHR*, 50 (1977), 135–50.

952 Sherborne, J.W., Indentured Retinues and English Expeditions to France, 1369–80, *EHR*, 79 (1964), 718–46.

953 Sherborne, J.W., The Hundred Years' War. The English Navy: Shipping and Manpower, 1369–89, *PP*, 37 (1967), 163–75.

954 Strayer, J.R., The Costs and Profits of War: the Anglo-French Conflict of 1294–1303, in *The Medieval City*, H.A. Miskimin, D. Herlihy and A.L. Udovitch (eds), New Haven, 1977, 269–91.

956 Vale, M., *War and Chivalry. Warfare and aristocratic culture in England, France and Burgundy at the end of the Middle Ages*, London, 1981.

957 Verbruggen, J.F., *Het leger en de vloot van de graven van Vlanderen vanaf het outstaan tot in 1305*, Brussels, 1960.

See also: 445.

DIPLOMACY

958 Brill, R., The English Preparations before the Treaty of Arras: A New Interpretation of Sir John Falstolf's 'Report', September 1435, *SMRH*, 7 (1970), 211–47.

959 Cheyette, F., Paris BN ms. latin 5954: The Professional Papers of an English Ambassador on the Eve of the Hundred Years War, in *Economies et sociétés au Moyen Age. Mélanges offerts à Edouard Perroy*, J.-P. Genet (ed.), Paris, 1973, 400–13.

960 Cuttino, G.P., *English Diplomatic Administration, 1259–1339*, Oxford, 1971.

961 Dickinson, J.G., *The Congress of Arras, 1435. A Study in Medieval Diplomacy*, Oxford, 1955.

962 Ferguson, J., *English Diplomacy, 1422–61*, Oxford, 1972.

963 Forstreuter, K., *Die Berichte der Generalprokuratoren des Deutschen Ordens an der Kurie*, I, *Die Geschichte der Generalprokuratoren von den Anfängen bis 1403*, Göttingen, 1961.

964 Forstreuter, K., Die deutsche Sprache im auswärtigen Schriftverkehr des Ordenslandes und Herzogtums Preussen, *Beiträge zur preussischen Geschichte im 15. und 16. Jahrhundert*, Heidelberg, 1960, 7–28.

965 Ganshof, F.-L., *Histoire des relations internationales*, I, *Le Moyen Age*, Paris, 1953.

966 Höflechner, W., *Die Gesandten der europäischen Mächte, vornehmlich des Kaisers und des Reiches, 1490–1500*, Vienna/Cologne, 1972.

967 Höflechner, W., Anmerkungen zu Diplomatie und Gesandtschaftswesen am Ende des 15. Jahrhunderts, *Mitteilungen des Oesterreichischen Staatsarchivs*, 32 (1979), 1–23.

968 Jones, M., The Diplomatic Evidence for Franco-Breton Relations, *c*.1370–2, *EHR*, 93 (1978), 300–19.

969 Kyer, C.I., *Legatus* and *nuntius* as Used to Denote Papal Envoys: 1245–1378, *Mediaeval Studies*, 40 (1978), 473–7.

970 Mattingly, G., *Renaissance Diplomacy*, London, 1955.

971 Perrin, J.W., *Legatus* in Medieval Roman Law, *Traditio*, 29 (1973), 357–78.

972 Queller, D.E., *The Office of Ambassador in the Middle Ages*, Princeton, 1967.

973 Rondinini, G.S., Ambasciatori e embascerie al tempo di Filippo Maria Visconti (1412–26), *NRS*, 49 (1965), 313–44.

974 Schneider, J., Des rives de la Meurthe au lac de Constance. Le voyage d'une ambassade lorraine en 1496, *Le Pays Lorrain*, 1980, 109–24.

975 Thomas, H., Französische Spionage im Reich Ludwigs des Bayerns, *Zeitschrift für historische Forschung*, 5 (1978), 1–21.

ECONOMIC POLICY

976 Bergier, J.-F., Commerce et politique du blé à Genève aux XVe et XVIe siècles, *Revue suisse d'Histoire*, 14 (1964), 521–50.

977 Bergier, J.-F., Port de Nice, sel de Savoie et foires de Genève. Un ambitieux projet de la seconde moitié du XVe siècle, *MA*, 69 (1963), 857–65.

978 Bergier, J.-F., De nundinis rehabendis frivola prosecutio. La politique commerciale de Genève devant la crise des foires de Lyon, 1484–94, in Lyon et l'Europe: hommes et sociétés, in *Mélanges d'histoire offerts à R. Gascon*, Lyon, 1980, 33–46.

979 Coornaert, E., La politique économique de la France au début du règne de François Ier, *Annales de l'Université de Paris*, 8 (1933), 414–27.

980 Dias, M. Nunes, *O capitalismo monárquico portugués (1415–1549). Contribuçào para o estudo das origens do capitalismo moderno*, 2 vols, Coimbra, 1963–4.

981 Dirlmeier, U., *Mittelalterliche Hoheitsträger im wirtschaftlichen Wettbewerb*, Wiesbaden, 1966.

982 Gandilhon, R., *Politique économique de Louis XI*, Rennes, 1941.

983 Gascon, R., Nationalisme économique et géographie des foires. La querelle des foires de Lyon (1484–94), *CH*, 1 (1956), 253–87.

984 Glénisson, J., Une administration médiévale aux prises avec la disette. La question des blés dans les provinces italiennes de l'Etat pontifical en 1374–5, *MA*, 57 (1951), 303–26.

985 Ibarra y Rodriguez, E., *El problema cerealista en España durante el reinado de los Reyes Católicos (1475–1516)*, Madrid, 1944.

986 Lesportes, F., Droit économique et police des métiers en France du Nord (milieu du XIIIe–début du XVe siècle), *Revue du Nord*, 63 (1981), 321–36.

987 McGovern, J.F., The Rise of New Economic Attitudes – Economic Humanism, Economic Nationalism – during the Later Middle Ages and the Renaissance, AD 1200–1550, *Traditio*, 26 (1970), 217–53.

988 Pistono, S.P., Flanders and the Hundred Years War: the Quest for the *Trêve marchande*, *BIHR*, 49 (1976), 185–97.

989 Verlinden, C., A propos de la politique économique des ducs de Bourgogne à l'égard de l'Espagne, *Hispania*, 10 (1950), 681–715.

990 Vicens Vives, J., El 'redreç' de la economia catalana de 1481. Origines del mercantilismo en España, in *Studi in onore di Armando Sapori*, II, Milan, 1956, 897–909.

See also: 790.

SOCIETY AND THE STATE: GENERAL STUDIES

991 Bachmann, S., *Die Landstände des Hochstifts Bamberg. Ein Beitrag zur territorialen Verfassungsgeschichte*, Bamberg, 1962.

992 Brewer, D.S., Class Distinction in Chaucer, *Spec.*, 43 (1968), 290–305.

993 Brown, J. (ed.), *Scottish Society in the Fifteenth Century*, London, 1977.

994 Capra, P., Les bases sociales du pouvoir anglo-gascon au milieu du XIVe siècle, *MA*, 81 (1975), 273–99, 447–73.

995 Dhondt, J., Ordres ou 'puissances'. L'exemple des Etats de Flandre, *Ann.*, 1950, 289–305.

996 Elekes, L., Désaccord entre les états et ordres dans la Hongrie du XVe siècle et les problèmes de recherche y relatifs, *Nouvelles Etudes historiques publiées à l'occasion du XIIe Congrès international des Sciences historiques par la Commission nationale des historiens hongrois*, Budapest, 1965, 105–36.

997 Elekes, L., Système diétal des Ordres et centralisation dans les Etats féodaux (Problèmes concernant les recherches ayant trait à l'Europe orientale et particulièrement à la situation de la Hongrie au XVe siècle), *Studia Historica*, 53, *La Renaissance et la Réformation en Pologne et en Hongrie, 1450–1650*, Budapest, 1963, 331–95.

998 Frame, R., Power and Society in the Lordship of Ireland, 1272–1377, *PP*, 76 (1977), 3–33.

999 Heers, J., Partis politiques et clans familiaux dans l'Italie de la Renaissance, *Revue de la Méditerranée*, 20 (1960), 259–79.

1000 Heinemann, W., Zur Ständedidaxe in der deutschen Literatur des 13.–15. Jahrhunderts, *Beiträge zur Geschichte der deutschen Sprache und Literatur*, 88 (1966), 1–90; 89 (1967), 290–403.

1001 Helbig, H., *Der Wettinische Ständestaat. Untersuchungen zur Geschichte des Ständewesens und der landständischen Verfassung in Mitteldeutschland bis 1485*, Cologne, 1955.

1002 Laurent, J.K., The signory and its supporters: the Este of Ferrara, *Journal of Medieval History*, 3 (1977), 39–52.

1003 Lousse, E., *La société d'Ancien Régime. Organisation et représentation corporatives*, 2nd edn, Louvain, 1952.

1004 Mousnier, R., Labatut, J.-P. and Durand, Y., *Problèmes de stratification sociale. Deux cahiers de la noblesse (1649–51)*, Paris, 1965.

1005 Mousnier, R. (ed.), *Problèmes de stratification sociale. Actes du Colloque international (1966)*, Paris, 1968.

1006 Palme, S., Les impôts, le statut d'Alsnö et la formation des ordres en Suède (1250–1350), in *Problèmes de stratification sociale*, R. Mousnier (ed.), Paris, 1968, 55–71.

1007 Prevenier, W., *De Leden en de Staten van Vlaanderen (1384–1405)* (with French summary), Brussels, 1961.

1008 Prevenier, W., Réalité et Histoire. Le quatrième Membre de Flandre, *Revue du Nord*, 43 (1961), 5–14.

1009 Schubert, E., *Die Landstände des Hochstifts Würzburg*, Würzburg, 1967.

SOCIETY AND THE STATE: NOBILITY AND FEUDALISM

1010 Autrand, F., L'image de la noblesse en France à la fin du Moyen Age. Tradition et nouveauté, *Comptes rendus de l'Académie des Inscriptions et Belles-Lettres*, 1979, 340–54.

1011 Bean, J.M.W., *The Decline of English Feudalism, 1215–1540*, Manchester, 1968.

1012 Bueno de Mesquita, D.M., Ludovico Sforza and his vassals, in *Italian Renaissance Studies. A Tribute to the Late C.M. Ady*, E.F. Jacob (ed.), London, 1960, 184–216.

1013 Carpenter, C., The Beauchamp affinity: a study of bastard feudalism at work, *EHR*, 95 (1980), 514–32.

1014 Contamine, P., L'ordre de Saint-Michel au temps de Louis XI et de Charles VIII, *Bulletin de la Société nationale des Antiquaires de France*, 1976, 212–38.

1015 Contamine, P., De la puissance aux privilèges: doléances de la noblesse française envers la monarchie aux XIVe et XVe siècles, *La noblesse au Moyen Age, XIe–XVe siècles. Essais à la mémoire de Robert Boutruche*, P. Contamine (ed.), Paris, 1976, 235–57.

1016 Cuvillier, J.-P., Noblesse sicilienne et noblesse aragonaise en 1392–1408. Collusions et rivalités de deux groupes de privilégiés, d'après les registres *Tractarum* (n. 2104 et 2324) de l'Archivio de la Corona de Aragón, *Mélanges de l'Ecole française de Rome. Moyen Age, Temps modernes*, 85 (1973), 381–420.

1017 Dunham, W.H., Lord Hastings' Indentured Retainers, 1461–83. The Lawfulness of Livery and Retaining under the Yorkists and Tudors, *Transactions of the Connecticut Academy of Arts and Sciences*, 39 (1955), 1–175.

1018 Ellis, S.G., The destruction of the liberties: some further evidence, *BIHR*, 54 (1981), 150–61.

1019 Gerbet, M.-C., *La noblesse dans le royaume de Castille. Etude sur ses structures sociales en Estrémadure de 1454 à 1516*, Paris, 1979.

1020 Gerbet, M.-C., La population noble dans le royaume de Castille vers 1500: la répartition géographique de ses différentes composantes, *Anales de Historia Antigua y Medieval*, 1977–9, 78–99.

1021 Goodman, A., *The Loyal Conspiracy. The Lords Appellant under Richard II*, London, 1971.

1022 Harsgor, M., L'essor des bâtards nobles au XVe siècle, *RH*, 514 (1975), 319–54.

1023 Hicks, M.A., The Beauchamp Trust, 1439–87, *BIHR*, 54 (1981), 135–49.

1024 Jalland, P., The Influence of the Aristocracy on Shire Elections in the North of England, 1450–70, *Spec.*, 47 (1972), 483–507.

1025 Jansen, H.P.H., *Hoekse en Kabeljauwse twisten*, Bussum, 1966.

1026 Klassen, J.M., *The Nobility and the Making of the Hussite Revolution*, New York, 1978.

1027 Klebel, E., Territorialstaat und Lehen, in *Vorträge und Forschungen*, V, *Studien zum mittelalterlichen Lehenswesen*, T. Mayer (ed.), Lindau/Constance, 1960, 195–228.

1028 Konetzke, R., Territoriale Grundherrschaft und Landesherrschaft im spanischen Spätmittelalter. Ein Forschungsproblem zur Geschichte des spanischen Partikularismus, in *Mélanges en l'honneur de Fernand Braudel*, I: *Histoire économique du monde méditerranéen, 1450–1650*, Toulouse, 1973, 299–310.

1029 Ladewig Petersen, E., Monarchy and Nobility in Norway in the Period around 1500, *Mediaeval Scandinavia*, 7 (1974), 126–55.

1030 Lander, J.R., *Crown and Nobility, 1450–1509*, London, 1976.

1031 Lewis, N.B., Indentures of Retinue with John of Gaunt, Duke of Lancaster, Enrolled in Chancery, 1367–99, *Camden Miscellany*, 22 (1964), 77–112.

1032 Lewis, N.B., The Last Medieval Summons of the English Feudal Levy, 13 June 1385, *EHR*, 73 (1958), 1–26.

1033 Lewis, P.S., Decayed and Non-Feudalism in Later Medieval France, *BIHR*, 37 (1964), 157–84.

1034 Lucas, R.H., Ennoblement in Late Medieval France, *Mediaeval Studies*, 39 (1977), 239–60.

1035 Lyon, B.D., *From Fief to Indenture. The Transition from Feudal to Non-feudal Contract in Western Europe*, Cambridge, Mass., 1957.

1036 McFarlane, K.B., Bastard Feudalism, *BIHR*, 20.(1943–5), 161–80.

1037 McFarlane, K.B., The English Nobility in the Later Middle Ages, *XIIe Congrès international des Sciences historiques, Vienna, 1965, Rapports*, I, Vienna, 1965, 337–45.

1038 McFarlane, K.B., *The Nobility of Later Medieval England. The Ford Lectures for 1953 and Related Studies*, Oxford, 1973.

1039 Martinez Sopena, P., *El estado senorial de Medina de Rioseco bajo el almirante Alfonso Enriquez (1389–1430)*, Valladolid, 1977.

1040 Menzel, J.J., *Jura Ducalia. Die mittelalterlichen Grundlagen der Domanialverfassung in Schlesien*, Würzburg, 1964.

1041 Mitre Fernandez, E., *Evolución de la Nobleza en Castilla bajo Enrique III (1396–1406)*, Valladolid, 1968.

1042 Moxó, S. de, De la nobleza vieja a la nobleza nueva. La transformación nobiliaria castellana en la Baja Edad Media, *Cuadernos de Historia*, anexos de la revista *Hispania*, III, Madrid, 1969, 1–210.

1043 Naughton, K.S., *The Gentry of Bedfordshire in the Thirteenth and Fourteenth Centuries*, Leicester, 1976.

1044 Paravicini, W., *Guy de Brimeu. Der burgundische Staat und seine adlige Führungsschicht unter Karl dem Kühnen*, Bonn, 1975.

1045 Paravicini, W., Expansion et intégration. La noblesse des Pays-Bas à la cour de Philippe le Bon, *Bijdragen en mededelingen betreffende de geschiedenis der Nederlanden*, 95 (1980), 298–314.

1046 Paravicini, W., Die Preussenreisen des europäischen Adels, *HZ*, 232 (1981), 25–38.

1047 Pascoe, L.B., Nobility and Ecclesiastical Office in Fifteenth-Century Lyons, *Mediaeval Studies*, 38 (1976), 313–31.

1048 Pastoureau, M., *Traité d'héraldique*, Paris, 1979.

1049 Peña, N. de, Vassaux gascons au service du roi d'Angleterre dans la première moitié du XIVe siècle: fidélité ou esprit de profit?, *Annales du Midi*, 88 (1976), 5–21.

1050 Philipps, J.R.S., *Aymer de Valence, Earl of Pembroke, 1307–24. Baronial Politics in the Reign of Edward II*, Oxford, 1972.

1051 Pocquet du Haut-Jussé, B.-A., Les pensionnaires fieffés des ducs de Bourgogne de 1352 à 1419, *MSHD*, 8 (1942), 127–50.

1052 Pocquet du Haut-Jussé, B.-A., Une idée politique de Louis XI: la sujétion éclipse la vassalité, *RH*, 226 (1961), 383–98.

1053 Podehl, W., *Burg und Herrschaft in der Mark Brandenburg. Untersuchungen zur*

L

mittelalterlichen Verfassungsgeschichte unter besonderer Berücksichtigung von Altmark, Neumark und Havelland, Cologne/Vienna, 1975.

1054 Rawcliffe, C., *The Staffords, Earls of Stafford and Dukes of Buckingham, 1394–1521,* Cambridge, 1978.

1055 Ruser, K., Zur Geschichte der Gesellschaften von Herren, Rittern und Knechten in Süddeutschland während des 14. Jahrhunderts, *Zeitschrift für württembergische Landesgeschichte,* 34/5 (1975–6), 1–100.

1056 Renouard, Y., L'Ordre de la Jarretière et l'Ordre de l'Etoile. Etude sur la genèse des Ordres laïcs de chevalerie et sur le développement progressif de leur caractère national, *MA,* 55 (1949), 281–300, repr. in Y. Renouard, *Etudes d'histoire médiévale,* I, Paris, 1968, 93–106.

1057 Reynaud, M., Le service féodal en Anjou et Maine à la fin du Moyen Age, *CH,* 16 (1971), 115–59.

1058 Richmond, C., The Nobility and the Wars of the Roses, 1459–61, *Nottingham Medieval Studies,* 21 (1977), 71–86.

1059 Rogozinski, J., Ennoblement by the Crown and Social Stratification in France, 1285–1322: A Prosopographical Survey, in *Order and Innovation in the Middle Ages. Essays in Honour of Joseph R. Strayer,* W.C. Jordan, B. McNab and T.F. Ruiz (eds), Princeton, 1976, 273–91.

1060 Scufflaire, A., *Les fiefs directs des comtes de Hainaut de 1349 à 1504. Essai d'inventaire statistique et géographique,* Brussels, 1978.

1061 Sczaniecki, M., *Essai sur les fiefs-rentes,* Paris, 1946.

1062 Spiess, K.-H., *Lehnsrecht, Lehnspolitik und Lehnsverwaltung der Pfalzgrafen bei Rhein im Spätmittelalter,* Wiesbaden, 1978.

1063 Suarez Fernandez, L., *Nobleza y monarquia. Puntos de vista sobre la historia castellana del siglo XV,* Valladolid, 1959.

1064 Suarez Fernandez, L., Nobleza y monarquia en la estructura politica castellana del siglo XV, *XIᵉ Congrès international des Sciences historiques, Stockholm, 1960, Résumés des Communications,* Stockholm, 1960, 116–18.

1065 Suarez Fernandez, L., Nobleza y monarquia en la politica de Enrique III, *Hispania,* 12 (1953), 323–400.

1066 Tuck, A., *Richard II and the English Nobility,* London, 1973.

1067 Theuerkauf, G., *Land und Lehnswesen vom 14. bis zum 16. Jahrhundert. Ein Beitrag zur Verfassung des Hochstifts Münster und zum nordwestdeutschen Lehnrecht,* Cologne/Graz, 1961.

1068 Val Valdivieso, M.I. del, Los bandos nobiliarios durante el reinado de Enrique IV, *Hispania,* 35 (1975), 249–93.

1069 Vale, M.G.A., A Fourteenth-Century Order of Chivalry: the 'Tiercelet', *EHR,* 82 (1967), 332–41.

1070 Ventura, A., *Nobiltà e popolo nella società veneta del' 400 e' 500,* Bari, 1964.
See also: 273, 931, 932, 952.

SOCIETY AND THE STATE: TOWN AND COUNTRY

1071 Bader, K.S., Staat und Bauerntum im deutschen Mittelalter, *Adel und Bauern im deutschen Staat des Mittelalters,* T. Mayer (ed.), Leipzig, 1943, 109–29.

1072 Bader, K.S., *Studien zur Rechtsgeschichte des mittelalterlichen Dorfes*, I, *Das mittelalterliche Dorf als Friedens- und Rechtsbereich*, Weimar, 1957; II, *Dorfgenossenschaft und Dorfgemeinde*, Weimar, 1962.

1073 Batany, J., Le 'bonheur des paysans': des *Géorgiques* au bas Moyen Age, *Présence de Virgile. Actes du Colloque des 9, 11 et 12 décembre 1976*, R. Chevallier (ed.), Paris, 1978, 233–48.

1074 Benito Ruano, E., *Toledo en el siglo XV. Vida politica*, Madrid, 1961.

1075 Bonachia Hernando, J.A., *El concejo de Burgos en la Baja Edad Media (1345–1426)*, Valladolid, 1978.

1076 Carmen Carlé, M. del, *Del concejo medieval castellano-leonés*, Buenos Aires, 1968.

1077 Chevalier, B., La politique de Louis XI à l'égard des bonnes villes. Le cas de Tours, *MA*, 70 (1964), 473–504.

1078 Chevalier, B., Pouvoir royal et pouvoir urbain à Tours pendant la guerre de Cent ans, *Annales de Bretagne*, 81 (1974), 365–92.

1079 Chevalier, B., *Les bonnes villes de France du XIVᵉ au XVIᵉ siècle*, Paris, 1982.

1080 Coornaert, E., L'Etat et les villes à la fin du Moyen Age. La politique d'Anvers, *RH*, 207 (1952), 185–210.

1081 Favier, J., Autonomie municipale et tutelle royale au XVᵉ siècle: les élections à Paris, *Cultus et cognitio*, Warsaw, 1976, 145–98.

1082 François, M., Les bonnes villes, *Comptes rendus de l'Académie des Inscriptions et Belles-Lettres*, 1975, 551–60.

1083 Füchtner, J., *Die Bündnisse der Bodenseestädte bis zum Jahre 1390. Ein Beitrag zur Geschichte des Einungswesens, der Landfriedenswahrung und der Rechtsstellung der Reichsstädte*, Göttingen, 1970.

1084 Gautier-Dalché, J., Sepulveda à la fin du Moyen Age: évolution d'une ville castillane de la Meseta, *MA*, 69 (1963), 805–28.

1085 Heers, J., *Le clan familial au Moyen Age. Etude sur les structures politiques et sociales des milieux urbains*, Paris, 1974.

1086 Heers, J., *Parties and Political Life in the Medieval West*, Amsterdam/New York and Oxford, 1977.

1087 Le Goff, J. (ed.), *La ville médiévale, des Carolingiens à la Renaissance* (Histoire de la France médiévale, II), Paris, 1980.

1088 Koller, H., Die Aufgaben der Städte in der *Reformatio Friderici* (1442), *Historisches Jahrbuch*, 100 (1980), 198–216.

1089 McKisack, M., London and the Succession to the Crown during the Middle Ages, in *Studies in Medieval History presented to F.M. Powicke*, R.W. Hunt, W.A. Pantin and R.W. Southern (eds), Oxford, 1948, 76–89.

1090 Maddicott, J.R., *The English Peasantry and the Demands of the Crown, 1294–1341*, Oxford, 1975.

1091 Maire-Vigueur, J.-C., Classe dominante et classes dirigeantes à Rome à la fin du Moyen Age, *Storia della Città*, 1 (1976), 4–26.

1092 Moraw, P., Deutsches Königtum und bürgerliche Geldwirtschaft um 1400, *VSWG*, 55 (1968–9), 289–328.

1093 Moraw, P., Reichstadt, Reich und Königtum im späten Mittelalter, *ZHF*, 6 (1979), 385–424.

1094 Morel, H., Seigneur et cité à la fin du Moyen Age: le comte d'Armagnac et Lectoure en 1418, *Annales du Midi*, 64 (1952), 49–58.

1095 Müller-Mertens, E., Zur Städtepolitik der ersten märkischen Hohenzollern und zum Berliner Unwillen, *ZGW*, 4 (1956), 525–44.

1096 Petit-Dutaillis, G., *Les communes françaises. Caractères et évolution des origines au XVIIIe siècle*, Paris, 1947.

1097 Raiser, E., *Städtische Territorialpolitik im Mittelalter. Eine vergleichende Untersuchung ihrer verschiedenen Formen am Beispiel Lübecks und Zürichs*, Lübeck/ Hamburg, 1969.

1098 Roughol, D., Quelques aspects originaux du 'Tiers Etat' au royaume d'Ecosse, *Etudes sur l'histoire des assemblées d'états*, Paris, 1966, 73–94.

1099 Ruiz, T.F., The Transformation of the Castilian Municipalities. The Case of Burgos, 1248–1350, *PP*, 77 (1977), 3–32.

1100 Schmidt, H., *Die deutschen Städtechroniken als Spiegel des bürgerlichen Selbstverständnisses im Spätmittelalter*, Göttingen, 1958.

1101 Stromer, W. von, *Oberdeutsche Hochfinanz, 1350–1450*, 2 vols, Wiesbaden, 1970.

1102 Toubert, P., Les statuts communaux et l'histoire des campagnes lombardes au XIVe siècle, *MAH*, 1960, 397–508.

1103 Vaillant, P., Les origines d'une libre confédération de vallées: les habitants des communautés briançonnaises au XIIIe siècle, *BEC*, 125 (1967), 301–48.

1104 Vicens Vives, J., *Historia de los remensas en el siglo XV*, Barcelona, 1945.

1105 Wolff, P., Pouvoir et investissements urbains en Europe occidentale et centrale du XIIIe au XVIIe siècle, *RH*, 524 (1977), 277–311.

SOCIETY AND THE STATE: THE CHURCH

1106 Baldwin, J.W. and Goldthwaite, R.A. (eds), *Universities in Politics. Case Studies from the Late Middle Ages and Early Modern Period*, Baltimore, 1972.

1107 Bauer, C., Studien zur spanischen Konkordatsgeschichte des späten Mittelalters. Das spanische Konkordat von 1482, *Gesammelte Aufsätze zur Wirtschafts- und Sozialgeschichte*, Fribourg/Basel/Vienna, 1965, 186–232.

1108 Becker, M.B., Some Economic Implications of the Conflict between Church and State in 'Trecento' Florence, *Mediaeval Studies*, 21 (1959), 1–16.

1109 Betcherman, L.R., The Making of Bishops in the Lancastrian Period, *Spec.*, 41 (1966), 397–419.

1110 Buisson, L., *Potestas und Caritas. Die päpstliche Gewalt im Spätmittelalter*, Cologne/Graz, 1958.

1111 Contamine, P., The Contents of a French Diplomatic Bag in the Fifteenth Century: Louis XI, Regalian Rights and Breton Bishoprics, 1462–5, *Nottingham Medieval Studies*, 25 (1981), 52–72.

1112 Davies, R.G., The Episcopate and the Political Crisis in England of 1386–8, *Spec.*, 51 (1976), 659–93.

1113 Denton, J., Walter Reynolds and Ecclesiastical Politics, 1313–16: a Postscript to 'Councils and Synods, II', in *Church and Government in the Middle*

Ages. Essays presented to C.R. Cheney on his 70th birthday, C.N.L. Brooke, D.E. Luscombe, G.H. Martin and D. Owen (eds), Cambridge, 1976, 247–74.

1114 Donaldson, G., The Rights of the Scottish Crown in Episcopal Vacacies, *The Scottish Historical Review*, 45 (1966), 27–35.

1115 Edwards, K., The Political Importance of the English Bishops during the Reign of Edward II, *EHR*, 59 (1944), 311–47.

1116 Flieder, V., *Stephansdom und Wiener Bistumsgründung, eine diözesan- und rechts-geschichtliche Untersuchung*, Vienna, 1968.

1117 Fumi, L., Chiesa e Stato nel dominio di Francesco I Sforza, *Archivio Storico Lombardo*, 51 (1924), 1–74.

1118 Gazzaniga, J.-L., *L'Eglise du Midi à la fin du règne de Charles VII (1444–61) d'après la jurisprudence du Parlement de Toulouse*, Paris, 1976.

1119 Grass, N., *Der Wiener Dom, die Herrschaft zu Oesterreich und das Land Tirol*, Innsbruck, 1968.

1120 Haines, R.M., *The Church and Politics in Fourteenth-Century England: The Career of Adam Orleton, c.1275–1345*, Cambridge, 1978.

1121 Hay, D., The Church of England in the Later Middle Ages, *History*, 53 (1968), 35–50.

1122 Highfield, J.R.L., The English Hierarchy in the Reign of Edward III, *TRHS*, 5th ser., 6 (1956), 115–38.

1123 Howell, M., *Regalian Right in Medieval England*, London, 1962.

1124 Jones, W.R., Bishops, Politics, and the Two Laws: the Gravamina of the English Church, *Spec.*, 41 (1966), 209–45.

1125 Koller, G., *Princeps in Ecclesia. Untersuchungen zur Kirchenpolitik Herzog Albrechts V. von Œsterreich*, Vienna, 1964.

1126 Le Goff, J., Les Universités et les pouvoirs publics au Moyen Age et à la Renaissance, *XIIᵉ Congrès international des Sciences historiques, Vienna, 1965, Rapports*, III, Vienna, 1965, 189–206.

1127 Mályusz, E., *Das Konstanzer Konzil und das königliche Patronatsrecht in Ungarn*, Budapest, 1959.

1128 Ourliac, P., Eglise et Etats, in Delaruelle, E., Labande, E.-R. and Ourliac, P., *L'Eglise au temps du Grand Schisme et de la crise conciliaire (1378–1449)*, Paris, 1962, 293–447.

1129 Ourliac, P., L'Eglise du XVᵉ siècle, in *Etudes d'histoire du droit médiéval*, P. Ourliac (ed.), Paris, 1979, 329–634.

1130 Pacaut, M., *La théocratie. L'Eglise et le pouvoir au Moyen Age*, Paris, 1957.

1131 Perroy, E., *L'Angleterre et le Grand Schisme d'Occident. Etude sur la politique religieuse de l'Angleterre sous Richard II (1378–99)*, Paris, 1933.

1132 Rankl, H., *Das vorreformatorische landesherrliche Kirchenregiment in Bayern (1378–1526)*, Munich, 1971.

1133 Rosenthal, J.T., The Training of an Elite Group. English Bishops in the Fifteenth Century, *Transactions of the American Philosophical Society*, 9th ser., LX, 1970.

1134 Strnad, A.A., Libertas Ecclesiae und fürstliche Bistumspolitik. Zur Lage der Kirche in Œsterreich unter Herzog Rudolf IV, *Römische Historische Mittei-lungen*, 6, 7 (1962–3, 1963–4), 72–112.

1135 Verger, J., *Les universités au Moyen Age*, Paris, 1973.

1136 Verger, J., Les universités françaises au XVe siècle: crise et tentatives de réforme, *CH*, 21 (1976), 43–66.

1137 Vincke, J., Kirche und Staat in Spanien während des Spätmittelalters, *RQ*, 43 (1935), 35–53.

1138 Vencke, J., *Staat und Kirche in Katalonien und Aragon während des Mittelalters*, Münster, 1931.

1139 Watt, J.A., *The Church and the Two Nations in Medieval Ireland*, Cambridge, 1970.

1140 Wright, J.R., *The Church and the English Crown, 1305–34. A Study based on the Register of Archbishop Walter Reynolds*, Leiden, 1980.
See also: 357, 376, 467.

REPRESENTATIVE ASSEMBLIES: GENERAL STUDIES

1141 *Album François Dumont* (Etudes présentées à la Commission internationale pour l'Histoire des Assemblées d'Etats, 60), Brussels, 1977.

1142 *Assemblées d'Etats*, Louvain/Paris, 1965 (*APAE*, XXXIII).

1143 Bisson, T.N., The Military Origins of Medieval Representation, *AHR*, 71 (1966), 1199–1218.

1144 Black, A., *Council and Commune: the Conciliar Movement and the Fifteenth-Century Heritage*, London, 1979.

1145 Blockmans, W.P., A typology of representative institutions in late medieval Europe, *Journal of Medieval History*, 4 (1978), 189–215.

1146 Cam, H.M., Marongiu, A. and Stökl, G., Recent Work and Present Views on the Origins and Development of Representative Assemblies, *Relazioni del X Congresso Internazionale di Scienze Storiche*, I, Florence, 1955, 1–101.

1147 Congar, Y.-M.-J., Quod omnes tangit ab omnibus tractari et approbari debet, *RHDFE*, 1958, 210–59.

1148 Elsener, F., Zur Geschichte des Majoritätsprinzips (Pars major und Pars sanior), insbesondere nach schweizerischen Quellen, *Zeitschrift der Savigny-Stiftung für Rechtsgeschichte*, 73 (1956), Kanonistische Abteilung, 73–116.

1149 Fawtier, R., Parlement d'Angleterre et Etats généraux de France au Moyen Age, *Comptes rendus de l'Académie des Inscriptions et Belles-Lettres*, 1953, 275–84.

1150 Hintze, O., Typologie der ständischen Verfassungen des Abendlandes, *HZ*, 141 (1929), 229–48.

1151 Hintze, O., Weltgeschichtliche Bedingungen der Repräsentativverfassung, *HZ*, 143 (1931), 1–47.

1152 Koranyi, K., Zum Ursprung des Anteils der Städte an den ständischen Versammlungen und Parlamenten im Mittelalter, in *Album H.M. Cam*, I, *Studies presented to the international commission for the history of representative and parliamentary studies*, 23, Louvain/Paris, 1960, 37–53.

1153 Marongiu, A., *Medieval Parliaments. A Comparative Study*, London, 1968.

1154 Marongiu, A., Q.o.t., principe fondamental de la démocratie et du consentement, au XIVe siècle, in *Album H.M. Cam*, II, *Studies presented to the inter-*

national commission for the history of representative and parliamentary studies, 24, Louvain/Paris, 1961, 101–15.

1155 Marongiu, A., Pré-parlements, parlements, états, assemblées d'états. Une mise au point, *RHDFE*, 57 (1979), 631–44.

1156 Myers, A.R., The English Parliament and the French Estates-General in the Middle Ages, in *Album H.M. Cam*, II, *Studies presented to the international commission for the history of representative and parliamentary studies*, 24, Louvain/Paris, 1961, 139–53.

1151 Näf, W., Herrschaftsverträge und Lehre vom Herrschaftsvertrag, *SB*, 7 (1949), 26–52.

1158 Russocki, S., Typologie des assemblées pré-représentatives en Europe, *XIII⁰ Congrès international des Sciences historiques, Moscow, 1970. Etudes présentées à la Commission internationale pour l'Histoire des Assemblées d'Etats*, LII, Warsaw, 1975, 27–38.

1159 Spangenberg, H., *Vom Lehnstaat zum Ständestaat. Ein Beitrag zur Entstehung der landständischen Verfassung*, new edn, Aalen, 1964.

1160 Spufford, P, Assemblies of Estates, Taxation and Control of Coinage in Medieval Europe, *XII⁰ Congrès international des Sciences historiques, Vienna, 1965. Etudes présentées à la Commission internationale pour l'Histoire des Assemblées d'Etats*, XXXI, Louvain/Paris, 1966, 113–30.

1161 Wilkinson, B., *The Creation of Medieval Parliaments*, New York, 1972.
See also: 54, 1003.

REPRESENTATIVE ASSEMBLIES: THE CONTINENT

1162 Angenmeier, H., Bayern und der Reichstag von 1495, *HZ*, 224 (1977), 580–614.

1163 Bák, J.M., *Königtum und Stände in Ungarn im 14.–16. Jahrhundert*, Wiesbaden, 1973.

1164 Bardach, J., Gouvernants et gouvernés en Pologne au Moyen Age et aux Temps modernes, *APAE*, 36 (1965), 255–85.

1165 Bisson, T.N., *Assemblies and Representation in Languedoc in the Thirteenth Century*, Princeton, 1964.

1166 Bisson, T.N., The General Assemblies of Philip the Fair: their character reconsidered, *Studia Gratiana*, 15 (1972), 537–64.

1167 Blockmans, W.P., *De Volksvertegenwoordiging in Vlaanderen in de Overgang van Middeleeuwen naar Nieuwe Tijden (1384–1506)*, Brussels, 1978.

1168 Bónis, G., The Hungarian Feudal Diet (Thirteenth–Fourteenth Centuries), *APAE*, 36 (1965), 287–307.

1169 Brown, E.A.R., Assemblies of French Towns in 1316: Some New Texts, *Spec.*, 46 (1971), 282–301.

1170 Brown, E.A.R., Subsidy and Reform in 1321: the Accounts of Najac and the Policies of Philip V, *Traditio*, 27 (1971), 399–430.

1171 Brown, E.A.R., Representation and Agency Law in the Later Middle Ages:

the Theoretical Foundations and the Evolution of Practice in the Thirteenth- and Fourteenth-Century Midi, *Viator*, 3 (1972), 329–64.

1172 Brown, E.A.R., Royal Necessity and Noble Service and Subsidy in Early Fourteenth-Century France: the Assembly of Bourges of November 1318, *Paradosis*, 32 (1976), 135–68.

1173 Carsten, F.L., *Princes and Parliaments in Germany from the Fifteenth to the Eighteenth Century*, Oxford, 1959.

1174 Faral, E., Robert le Coq et les Etats généraux d'octobre 1356, *RHDFE*, 1945, 171–214.

1175 Folz, R., Les assemblées d'états dans les principautés allemandes (fin XIIIe–début XVIe siècles), *SB*, 20 (1962–3), 167–87.

1176 Garillot, J., *Les Etats généraux de 1439. Etude de la coutume constitutionnelle au XVe siècle*, Nancy, 1947.

1177 Giesey, R.E., The French Estates and the Corpus Mysticum Regni, in *Album H.M. Cam*, I, *Studies presented to the international commission for the history of representative and parliamentary studies*, Louvain/Paris, 1960, 153–71.

1178 Gilissen, J., *Le régime représentatif avant 1790 en Belgique*, Brussels, 1952.

1179 Gilles, H., *Les Etats du Languedoc au XVe siècle*, Toulouse, 1965.

1180 Gorissen, P., *Het Parlement en de Raad van Kortenberg* (with French summary), Louvain, 1956.

1181 Gorski, K., *Communitas, Princeps, Corona Regni. Studia selecta*, Warsaw/Poznan/Torun, 1976.

1182 Hartung, F., Herrschaftsverträge und ständischer Dualismus in deutschen Territorien, *SB*, 10 (1952), 163–77; repr. in *Staatsbildende Kräfte der Neuzeit. Gesammelte Aufsätze*, Berlin, 1961.

1183 Hébert, M., Guerre, finances et administration: les Etats de Provence de novembre 1359, *MA*, 83 (1977), 103–30.

1184 Helbig, H., Fürsten und Landstände im Westen des Reiches im Uebergang vom Mittelalter zur Neuzeit, *Rheinische Vierteljahrsblätter*, 29 (1964), 32–72.

1185 Khatchatourian, N.A., *L'apparition des états généraux en France* (in Russian with French summary), Moscow, 1976.

1186 Khatchatourian, N.A., Du rôle restrictif des ordres dans les états généraux de France au début du XIVe siècle, *XIIIe Congrès international des Sciences historiques, Moscow, 1970. Etudes présentées à la Commission internationale pour l'Histoire des Assemblées d'Etats*, LII, Warsaw, 1975.

1187 Lewis, P.S., The Failure of the French Medieval Estates, *PP*, 23 (1962), 3–24.

1188 Lönnroth, E., Representative Assemblies of Mediaeval Sweden, *Etudes présentées à la Commission internationale pour l'Histoire des Assemblées d'Etats*, 18 (1958), 123–31.

1189 Lousse, E., La Joyeuse Entrée brabançonne du 3 janvier 1356, *SB*, 10 (1952), 139–62.

1190 Major, J.R., *Representative Institutions in Renaissance France, 1421–1559*, Madison, 1960.

1191 Major, J.R., *The Deputies to the Estates General in Renaissance France*, Madison, 1960.

1192 Major, J.R., *Representative Government in Early Modern France*, New Haven, 1980.

1193 Málvusz, E., Les débuts du vote de la taxe par les ordres dans la Hongrie féodale, *Nouvelles études historiques publiées à l'occasion du XIIᵉ Congrès international des Sciences historiques par la Commission nationale des Historiens hongrois*, I, Budapest, 1965, 55–82.

1194 Marongiu, A., *Il Parlamento in Italia nel medio evo e nell'età moderna*, new edn, Rome, 1962.

1195 Menjot, D., Un moment dans 'le temps du dialogue'. Murcie et les premiers Trastamares entre 1374 et 1425, *Les Communications dans la Péninsule ibérique au Moyen Age. Actes du colloque tenu à Pau les 28 at 29 mars 1980*, P. Tucoo-Chala (ed.), Bordeaux, 1971, 131–54.

1196 Pocquet du Haut-Jussé, B.-A., La genèse du législatif dans le duché de Bretagne, *RHDFE*, 1962, 351–72.

1197 Richard, J., Les Etats de Bourgogne, *SB*, 20 (1962–3), 230–48.

1198 Russocki, S., *Protoparlamentaryzm czech do poczatku XV wieku (Der Protoparlamentarismus Böhmens bis zum Beginn des XV. Jahrhunderts)* (with German summary), Warsaw, 1973.

1199 Russocki, S., Les assemblées préreprésentatives en Europe centrale. Préliminaires d'une analyse comparative, *Acta Poloniae Historica*, 30 (1974), 33–52.

1200 Russocki, S., The Parliamentary Systems in Fifteenth-Century Central Europe, *Poland at the 14th International Congress of Historical Sciences in San Francisco. Studies in Comparative History*, Warsaw, 1975, 7–21.

1201 Russocki, S., Prémices d'un 'Constitutionnalisme' médiéval: le *Jus resistendi* dans le centre-est de l'Europe, in *Album Elemér Mályusz*, 1976, 185–97.

1202 Russocki, S., Le système représentatif de la 'République nobiliaire' de Pologne, *Der moderne Parlamentarismus und seine Grundlagen in der ständischen Repräsentation . . .*, K. Bosl (ed.), Berlin, 1977, 279–96.

1203 Rycraft, P., The role of the catalan *Corts* in the later middle ages, *EHR*, 89 (1974), 241–69.

1204 Santamaria, A., Sobre la institucionalizacion de las asambleas representativas de Mallorca. Dal sistema de 'Franquesa' de 1249 al sistema de 'Vida' de 1373, *Anuario de Historia del Derecho Español*, 50 (1980), 265–302.

1205 Sarasa Sanchez, E., *Las Cortes de Aragon en la Edad Media*, Saragossa, 1979.

1206 Schubert, F.H., *Die deutschen Reichstage in der Staatslehre der frühen Neuzeit*, Göttingen, 1966.

1207 Scufflaire, A., Les serments d'inauguration des comtes de Hainaut (1272–1427), *APAE*, I, Louvain, 1950, 79–132.

1208 Sobrequés Vidal, S., Los orígines de la Revolución catalana del siglo XV. Las Cortes de Barcelona de 1454–8, *EHM*, 2 (1952), 1–96.

1209 Spufford, P., Coinage, Taxation and the Estates General of the Burgundian Netherlands, *APAE*, 40 (1966), 61–88.

1210 Taylor, C.H., Assemblies of French Towns in 1316, *Spec.*, 14 (1939), 275–99.

1211 Taylor, C.H., An Assembly of French Towns in March 1318, *Spec.*, 13 (1938), 295–303.

1212 Taylor, C.H., French Assemblies and Subsidy in 1321, *Spec.*, 43 (1968), 217–44.

1213 Taylor, C.H., The Assembly of 1312 at Lyons-Vienne, *Etudes d'histoire dédiées à la mémoire de Henri Pirenne*, Brussels, 1937, 337–49.

1214 Taylor, C.H., The Composition of Baronial Assemblies in France, 1315–20, *Spec.*, 29 (1954), 433–59.

1215 Tyrrell, J.M., *A History of the Estates of Poitou*, The Hague/Paris, 1968.

1216 Valdeón Baruque, J., Las Cortes de Castilla y las luchas políticas del siglo XV (1419–30), *Anuario de Estudios Medievales*, 3 (1966), 293–326.

1217 Van Bragt, R., *De Blijde Inkomst van de Hertogen van Brabant Johanna en Wenceslas (3 januari 1356). Een inleidende studie en tekstuitgave*, Louvain, 1956.

1218 Van Der Straeten, J., *Het charter en de raad van Kortenberg* (with French summary), 2 vols, Louvain, 1952.

1219 Wellens, R., *Les Etats généraux des Pays-Bas des origines à la fin du règne de Philippe le Beau (1464–1506)*, I, Heule, 1974.

1220 Wellens, R., Les instructions des députés de Douai aux Etats Généraux des Pays-Bas en 1488, *Revue du Nord*, 62 (1980), 573–7.
See also: 991, 1001, 1007, 1009.

REPRESENTATIVE ASSEMBLIES: THE BRITISH ISLES

1221 Bellamy, J.G., Appeal and Impeachment in the Good Parliament, *BIHR*, 39 (1966), 35–46.

1222 Bryant, W.N., The Financial Dealings of Edward III with the County Communities, 1330–60, *EHR*, 83 (1968), 760–71.

1223 Cam, H.M., Recent Books in English on the Parliamentary Institutions of the British Isles in the Middle Ages, *Bulletin of the International Committee of Historical Sciences*, 9 (1937), 413–18.

1224 Cam, H.M., Stubbs Seventy Years After, *The Cambridge Historical Journal*, 9 (1948), 129–47.

1225 Clarke, M.V., *Medieval Representation and Consent. A Study of Early Parliaments in England and Ireland, with Special Reference to the 'Modus Tenendi Parliamentum'*, 2nd edn, New York, 1964.

1226 Cuttino, G.P., Mediaeval Parliament Reinterpreted, *Spec.*, 41 (1966), 681–7.

1227 Davies, R.G. and Denton, J.H. (eds), *The English Parliament in the Middle Ages*, Manchester, 1981.

1228 Denton, J.A., The *Communitas Cleri* in the Early Fourteenth Century, *BIHR*, 51 (1978), 72–8.

1229 Duncan, A.A.M., The Early Parliaments of Scotland, *The Scottish Historical Review*, 45 (1966), 36–58.

1230 Dunham, W.H., 'The Books of the Parliament' and 'The Old Record', 1396–1504, *Spec.*, 51 (1976), 694–712.

1231 Edwards, J.G., *Historians and the Medieval English Parliament*, Glasgow, 1960.

1232 Edwards, J.G., 'Justice' in Early English Parliaments, *BIHR*, 27 (1954), 35–53.

1233 Edwards, J.G., The Emergence of Majority Rule in English Parliamentary Elections, *TRHS*, 5th ser., 14 (1964), 175–96.

1234 Edwards, J.G., The Huntingdonshire Parliamentary Election of 1450, in *Essays in Medieval History presented to Bertie Wilkinson*, T.A. Sandquist and M.R. Powicke (eds), Toronto, 1969, 383–95.

1235 Edwards, J.G., *The Second Century of the English Parliament*, Oxford, 1979.

1236 Fryde, E.B. and Miller, E. (eds), *Historical Studies of the English Parliament*, 2 vols, Cambridge, 1970.

1237 Goodman, A., Sir Thomas Hoo and the Parliament of 1376, *BIHR*, 41 (1968), 139–49.

1238 Goutnova, E.V., list and summary of his writings in E.A. Kosminsky, Les ouvrages des historiens soviétiques sur l'histoire des assemblées représentatives de l'Europe occidentale, *APAE*, 18 (1959), 175–96.

1239 Harriss, G.L., War and the Emergence of the English Parliament, 1294–1360, *Journal of Medieval History*, 2 (1976), 35–56.

1240 Holmes, G., *The Good Parliament*, Oxford, 1975.

1241 Illsley, J.S., Parliamentary Elections in the Reign of Edward I, *BIHR*, 49 (1976), 24–40.

1242 Lapsley, G.T., *Crown, Community and Parliament in the Later Middle Ages. Studies in English Constitutional History*, Oxford, 1951.

1243 Lewis, N.B., Re-election to Parliament in the Reign of Richard II, *EHR*, 48 (1933), 364–94.

1244 Lydon, J.F., William of Windsor and the Irish Parliament, *EHR*, 80 (1965), 252–67.

1245 McFarlane, K.B., Parliament and 'Bastard Feudalism', *TRHS*, 4th ser., 26 (1944), 53–79.

1246 McIlwain, C.H., *The High Court of Parliament and its Supremacy. An Historical Essay on the Boundaries between Legislation and Adjudication in England*, repr., Hamden, 1962.

1247 McKenna, J.W., The Myth of Parliamentary Sovereignty in Late Medieval England, *EHR*, 94 (1979), 481–506.

1248 McKisack, M., *The Parliamentary Representation of the English Boroughs during the Middle Ages*, repr., Oxford, 1963.

1249 Maitland, F.W., Introduction to *Memoranda de Parliamento*, 1305, in *Selected Historical Essays of F.W. Maitland*, H.M. Cam (ed.), Cambridge, 1957, 52–96.

1250 Palmer, J.J.N., The Parliament of 1385 and the Constitutional Crisis of 1386, *Spec.*, 46 (1971), 477–90.

1251 Pasquet, D., *Essai sur les origines de la Chambre des Communes*, Paris, 1914.

1252 Pollard, A.F., *The Evolution of Parliament*, 2nd edn, London, 1926.

1253 Post, G., The Two Laws and the Statute of York, *Spec.*, 29 (1954), 417–32.

1254 Pronay, N. and Taylor, J., The Use of the *Modus tenendi parliamentum* in the Middle Ages, *BIHR*, 47 (1974), 11–23.

1255 Pronay, N. and Taylor, J. (eds), *Parliamentary Texts of the Later Middle Ages*, Oxford, 1980.

1256 Richardson, H.G. and Sayles, G.O., *The Irish Parliament in the Middle Ages*, Philadelphia, 1952.

1257 Richardson, H.G., and Sayles, G.O., William Stubbs, the Man and the Historian, *The Governance of Medieval England*, Edinburgh, 1963, 1–21.

1258 Richardson H.G. and Sayles, G.O., *The English Parliament in the Middle Ages*, London, 1981.

1259 Riess, L., *Geschichte des Wahlrechts zum englischen Parlament im Mittelalter*, Leipzig, 1885; tr. with additional notes K.L. Wood-Legh, Cambridge, 1940.

1260 Rogers, A., Parliamentary Elections in Grimsby in the Fifteenth Century, *BIHR*, 42 (1969), 212–20.

1261 Roskell, J.S., A Consideration of Certain Aspects and Problems of the English *Modus Tenendi Parliamentum*, *BJRL*, 50 (1967–8), 411–42.

1262 Roskell, J.S., Perspectives in English Parliamentary History, *BJRL*, 46 (1963–4), 448–75.

1263 Roskell, J.S., *The Commons and their Speakers in English Parliaments, 1376–1523*, Manchester, 1965.

1264 Roskell, J.S., *The Commons in the Parliament of 1422. English Society and Parliamentary Representation under the Lancastrians*, Manchester, 1954.

1265 Roskell, J.S., The Parliamentary Representation of Lincolnshire during the Reigns of Richard II, Henry IV and Henry V, *Nottingham Mediaeval Studies*, 3 (1959), 53–76.

1266 Roskell, J.S., The Problem of the Attendance of the Lords in Medieval Parliaments, *BIHR*, 29 (1956), 153–204.

1267 Roskell, J.S., The Social Composition of the Commons in a Fifteenth-Century Parliament, *BIHR*, 24 (1951), 152–72.

1268 Sayles, G.O., *The King's Parliament of England*, London, 1975.

1269 Strayer, J.R. and Ruddishall, G., Taxation and Community in Wales and Ireland, 1272–1327, *Spec.*, 29 (1954), 410–16.

1270 Tout, T.F., The English Parliament and Public Opinion, 1376–88, *The Collected Papers of T.F. Tout*, II, Manchester, 1934, 173–90.

1271 Tuck, J.A., The Cambridge Parliament, 1388, *EHR*, 84 (1969), 225–43.

1272 Virgoe, R., The Parliamentary Subsidy of 1450, *BIHR*, 55 (1982), 125–37.

1273 Wood, C.T., Celestine V, Boniface VIII and the Authority of Parliament, *Journal of Medieval History*, 8 (1982), 45–62.

1274 Wood-Legh, K.L., Sheriffs, Lawyers and Belted Knights in the Parliaments of Edward III, *EHR*, 46 (1931) 372–88.

1275 Wood-Legh, K.L., The Knights' Attendance in the Parliaments of Edward III, *EHR*, 47 (1932), 398–413.

See also: 848.

REVOLTS OF THE EXCLUDED

1276 Arnold, K., *Niklashausen, 1476. Quellen und Untersuchungen zur sozialreligiösen Bewegung des Hans Behem und zur Agrarstruktur eines spätmittelalterlichen Dorfes*, Baden-Baden, 1980.

1277 Aston, M.E., Lollardy and Sedition, 1381–1431, *PP*, 17 (1960), 1–44.

1278 Baerten, J., Les mouvements paysans au Moyen Age. Comparaison entre deux ouvrages récents, *MA*, 87 (1981), 455–63.

1279 Barth, R., *Argumentation und Selbstverständnis der Bürgeropposition in städtischen Auseinandersetzungen des Spätmittelalters. Lübeck, 1403–8, Braunschweig, 1374–6, Mainz, 1444–6, Köln, 1396–1400,* Cologne/Vienna, 1974.

1280 Becker, M.H., Florentine Politics and the Diffusion of Heresy in the Trecento: a Socioeconomic Inquiry, *Spec.*, 34 (1959), 60–75.

1281 Bessmertniy, Y., Réflexions sur les soulevements paysans du XIVe siècle en France, *La France dans les recherches des historiens soviétiques*, Moscow, 1977, 23–9.

1282 Blickle, P. (ed.), *Revolte und Revolution in Europa. Referate und Protokolle des Internationalen Symposiums zur Erinnerung an den Bauernkrieg 1525 (Memmingen, 24–27 März 1975)*, Munich, 1975 (*HZ*, Beiheft 4, Neue Folge).

1283 Blickle, P. (ed.), *Aufruhr und Empörung? Studien zum bäuerlichen Widerstand im alten Reich*, Munich, 1980.

1284 Brock, P., *The Political and Social Doctrines of the Unity of Czech Brethren in the Fifteenth and Sixteenth Centuries*, The Hague, 1957.

1285 Cazelles, R., La Jacquerie fut-elle un mouvement paysan?, *Comptes rendus de l'Académie des Inscriptions et Belles-Lettres*, 1978, 654–66.

1286 Cohen, E., Le vagabondage à Paris au XIVe siècle. Analyse conceptuelle, *MA*, 88 (1982), 293–313.

1287 Congar, Y., Deux facteurs de la sacralisation de la vie sociale au Moyen Age (en Occident), *Concilium*, 47 (1969), 53–63.

1288 Dobson, R.B., *The Peasants' Revolt of 1381*, London, 1970.

1289 Dohna, L. Graf zu, *Reformatio Sigismundi. Beiträge zum Verständnis einer Reformschrift des fünfzehnten Jahrhunderts*, Göttingen, 1960.

1290 Durvin, P., Les origines de la Jacquerie à Saint-Leu-d'Esserent en 1358, in *La guerre et la paix. Frontières et violences au Moyen Age*, Paris, 1978 (Comité des Travaux historiques et scientifiques, Section de Philologie et d'Histoire jusqu'à 1610. Actes du CI^e Congrès national des Sociétés savantes, Lille, 1976).

1291 Erbtösser, M. and Werner, E., *Ideologische Probleme des mittelalterlichen Plebejertums. Die freigeistige Häresie und ihre sozialen Wurzeln*, Berlin, 1960.

1292 Favreau, R., La Praguerie en Poitou, *BEC*, 129 (1971), 277–301.

1293 Fédou, R., Une révolte populaire à Lyon au XVe siècle: la Rebeyne de 1436, *CH*, 3 (1958), 129–49.

1294 Fédou, R., Le cycle médiéval des révoltes lyonnaises, *CH*, 18 (1973), 233–47.

1295 Fourquin, G., *The anatomy of popular rebellion in the Middle Ages*, tr. A. Chesters, Amsterdam, 1978.

1296 Franz, G., *Der deutsche Bauernkrieg*, 11th edn, Darmstadt, 1977.

1297 Geremek, B., La lutte contre la vagabondage à Paris aux XIVe et XVe siècles, *Ricerche storiche ed economiche in memoria di Corrado Barbagallo*, II, Naples, 1970, 213–36.

1298 Geremek, B., *Ludzie marginesu w sredniowiecznym Paryzu XIV–XV wiek* [Fringe areas of medieval Paris, XIV–XVth centuries] (with French summary), Warsaw, 1971.

1299 Geremek, B., Criminalité, vagabondage, paupérisme: la marginalité à l'aube des temps modernes, *Revue d'Histoire moderne et contemporaine*, 21 (1974), 337–75.

1300 Graus, F., Au bas Moyen Age: pauvres des villes et pauvres des campagnes, *Ann.*, 1961, 1053–65.

1301 Graus, F., *Struktur und Geschichte. Drei Volksaufstände im mittelalterlichen Prag*, Sigmaringen, 1971.

1302 Graus, F., Ketzerbewegungen und soziale Unruhen im 14. Jahrhundert, *Zeitschrift für historische Forschung*, 1 (1974), 3–21.

1303 Gonon, M., Quelques aspects de la violence au Moyen Age en Forez, *Université de Saint-Etienne. Bulletin du Centre d'Histoire régionale*, 1 (1977), 7–16.

1304 Hilton, R., *Bond Men Made Free: Medieval Peasant Movements and the English Rising of 1381*, London, 1973.

1305 Hugenholtz, F.W.N., *Drie Boerenopstanden uit de Veertiende Eeuw, Vlanderen, 1323–8, Frankrijk, 1358, Engeland, 1381. Onderzoek naar het opstandig Bewustzijn* (with French summary), Haarlem, 1949.

1306 Joos, E., Die Unruhen der Stadt Konstanz, 1300–1400, *Zeitschrift für die Geschichte des Oberrheins*, 116 (1968), 31–58.

1307 Kalivoda, R., Seibt's *Hussitica* und die hussitische Revolution, *Historica*, 14 (1967), 225–46.

1308 Kalivoda, R., *Revolution und Ideologie. Der Hussitismus*, Cologne/Vienna, 1976.

1309 Kaminsky, H., *A History of the Hussite Revolution*, Berkeley, 1967.

1310 Kaminsky, H., The Free Spirit in the Hussite Revolution, *Millenial Dreams in Action. Essays in Comparative Study*, S.L. Thrupp (ed.), The Hague, 1962, 166–86.

1311 Kieckhefer, R., Radical tendencies in the flagellant movement of the mid-fourteenth century, *Journal of Medieval and Renaissance Studies*, 4 (1974), 157–76.

1312 Keen, M., Robin Hood, Peasant or Gentleman?, *PP*, 19 (1961), 7–18.

1313 Keen, M., *The Outlaws of Medieval Legend*, London, 1961.

1314 Koller, H., Untersuchungen zur Reformatio Sigismundi, *DA*, 13 (1957), 482–524; 14 (1958), 418–68; 15 (1959), 137–62.

1315 Leff, G., *Heresy in the Later Middle Ages, The Relation of Heterodoxy to Dissent, c.1250–c.1450*, 2 vols, Manchester, 1967.

1316 Le Goff, J. (ed.), *Hérésies et sociétés dans l'Europe préindustrielle, XIe–XVIIIe siècles*, Paris/The Hague, 1968.

1317 Leguai, A., Emeutes et troubles d'origine fiscale pendant le règne de Louis XI, *MA*, 73 (1967), 447–87.

1318 Leguai, A., Troubles et révoltes sous le règne de Louis XI: les résistances des particularismes, *RH*, 506 (1973), 285–324.

1319 Leguai, A., Les troubles urbains dans le nord de la France à la fin du XIIIe et au début du XIVe siècle, *Revue d'Histoire économique et sociale*, 54 (1976), 281–303.

1320 Leguai, A., Les oppositions urbaines à Louis XI en Bourgogne et en Franche-Comté, *Ann. de Bourgogne*, 53 (1981), 31–7.

1321 Leguai, A., Les révoltes rurales dans le royaume de France du milieu du XIVe siècle à la fin du XVe, *MA*, 88 (1982), 49–76.

1322 Macek, J., Jean Hus et son époque, *Historica*, 13 (1966), 51–80.

1323 Macek, J., Racines sociales de l'insurrection de Cola di Rienzo, *Historica*, 6 (1963), 45–107.

1324 Macek, J., *Jean Hus et les traditions hussites*, Paris, 1973.

1325 Macek, J., Die böhmische und die deutsche radikale Reformation bis zum Jahre 1525, *Zeitschrift für Kirchengeschichte*, 2 (1974), 5–29.

1326 MacKay, A., Popular Movements and Pogroms in Fifteenth-Century Castile, *PP*, 55 (1972), 33–67.

1327 Maddicott, J.R., The birth and setting of the ballads of Robin Hood, *EHR*, 93 (1978), 276–99.

1328 Martines, L. (ed.), *Violence and Civil Disorder in Italian Cities, 1200–1500*, Berkeley/Los Angeles, 1972.

1329 Mollat, M. and Wolff, P., *Ongles bleus, Jacques et Ciompi. Les révolutions populaires en Europe aux XIVe et XVe siècles*, Paris, 1970.

1330 Mommsen, K., Die 'Reformatio Sigismundi', Basel und die Schweiz, *Revue suisse d'Histoire*, 20 (1970), 71–91.

1331 Pavan, E., Recherches sur la nuit vénitienne à la fin du Moyen Age, *Journal of Medieval History*, 7 (1981), 339–56.

1332 Platelle, H., Une révolte populaire à Saint-Amand en 1356, *La guerre et la paix* (919), 349–63.

1333 Radding, C.M., The Estates of Normandy and the Revolts in the Towns at the Beginning of the Reign of Charles VI, *Spec.*, 47 (1972), 79–90.

1334 Rapp, F., Les paysans de la vallée du Rhin et le problème de l'autorité civile (1493–1525), *Recherches germaniques*, 4 (1974), 161–79.

1335 Rotz, R.A., Urban Uprisings in Germany: Revolutionary or Reformist? The Case of Brunswick, 1374, *Viator*, 4 (1973), 207–23.

1336 Rotz, R.A., Investigating Urban Uprisings with Examples from Hanseatic Towns, 1374–1416, *Order and Innovation in the Middle Ages. Essays in Honor of Joseph R. Strayer*, W.C. Jordan, B. McNab and T.F. Ruiz (eds), Princeton, 1976, 215–33.

1337 Ruggiero, G., *Violence in Early Renaissance Venice*, New Brunswick, NJ, 1980.

1338 Rutenburg, V.I., La vie et la lutte des Ciompi de Sienne, *Ann.*, 1965, 95–109.

1339 Rutenburg, V.I., *Les mouvements populaires dans les villes d'Italie, au XIVe et au début du XVe siècle* [Russian text], Moscow/Leningrad, 1958.

1340 Seibt, F., *Hussitica: Zur Struktur einer Revolution*, Cologne/Graz, 1965.

1341 Straube, M., Die Reformatio Sigismundi als Ausdruck der revolutionären Bewegungen im 15. Jahrhundert, *Die frühbürgerliche Revolution in Deutschland*, G. Brendler (ed.), Berlin, 1961, 108–15.

1342 Tillotson, J.H., Peasant unrest in the England of Richard II: some evidence from Royal Records, *Historical Studies*, 16 (1974), 1–16.

1343 Valdeón Baruque, J., *Los conflictos sociales en el reino de Castilla en los siglos XIV y XV*, Madrid, 1975.

1344 Waugh, S.L., The Profits of Violence: the Minor Gentry in the Rebellion of 1321–2 in Gloucestershire and Herefordshire, *Spec.*, 52 (1977), 843–69.

1345 Wolff, P., Les luttes sociales dans les villes du Midi français XIIIe–XIVe siècles, *Ann.*, 1947, 443–54.

See also: 223, 410.

SERVANTS OF THE STATE

1346 Autrand, F., Offices et officiers royaux en France sous Charles VI, *RH*, 242 (1969), 285–338.

1347 Autrand, F., *Naissance d'un grand corps de l'Etat: les gens du Parlement de Paris, 1345–1454*, Paris, 1981.

1348 Autrand, F., Naissance illégitime et service de l'Etat: les enfants naturels dans le milieu de robe parisien, XIVe–XVe siècle, *RH*, 542 (1982), 289–303.

1349 Balbi, G., *L'epistolario di Jacopo Bracelli*, Genoa, 1969.

1350 Bartier, J., *Légistes et gens de finances au XVe siècle. Les conseillers des ducs de Bourgogne Philippe le Bon et Charles le Téméraire*, Brussels, 1955.

1351 Bautier, R.-H., Guillaume de Mussy, bailli, enquêteur royal, panetier de France sous Philippe le Bel, *BEC*, 105 (1944), 64–98.

1352 Boockmann, H., *Laurentius Blumenau. Fürstlicher Rat-Jurist-Humanist (ca. 1415-84)*, Göttingen, 1965.

1353 Bresc, H., Les livres et la culture à Palerme sous Alphonse le Magnanime, *MAH*, 81 (1969), 321–86.

1354 Brown, A., *Bartolomeo Scala, 1430–97, Chancellor of Florence. The Humanist as Bureaucrat*, Princeton, 1979.

1355 Cazelles, R., Pierre de Becoud et la fondation du Collège de Boncourt, *BEC*, 120 (1962), 55–103.

1356 Cazelles, R., Robert de Lorris et la liquidation des Bouteiller de Senlis, *Comptes rendus et Mémoires de la Société d'Histoire et d'Archéologie de Senlis*, 1975 (1977), 17–54.

1357 Cheney, C.R., *Notaries Public in England in the Thirteenth and Fourteenth Century*, Oxford, 1972.

1358 Clough, C. (ed.), Profession, Vocation and Culture in Later Medieval England, *Essays dedicated to the memory of A.R. Myers*, Liverpool, 1982.

1359 Contamine, P., Un serviteur de Louis XI dans sa lutte contre Charles le Téméraire: Georges de la Trémoille, sire de Craon (vers 1437–81), *Annuaire-Bulletin de la Société de l'Histoire de France*, années 1976–7, 63–80.

1360 Costamagna, G., *Il notaio a Genova tra prestigio e potere*, Rome, 1970.

1361 Cuttino, G.P., King's Clerks and the Community of the Realm, *Spec.*, 29 (1954), 395–409.

1362 De Frede, C., *Studenti e uomini di leggi a Napoli nel Rinascimento. Contributo alla storia della borghesia intellettuale nel Mezzogiorno*, Naples, 1957.

1363 De Rosa, D., *Coluccio Salutati: il cancelliere e il pensatore politico*, Florence, 1980.

1364 Derville, A., Pots-de-vin, cadeaux, racket, patronage. Essai sur les mécanismes de décision dans l'Etat bourguignon, *Revue du Nord*, 56 (1974), 341–64.

1365 Favier, J., Les légistes et le gouvernement de Philippe le Bel, *Journal des Savants*, 1969, 92–108.

1366 Favier, J., *Un conseiller de Philippe le Bel: Enguerran de Marigny*, Paris, 1963.

1367 Favier, J., Service du prince et service des administrés. Les voies de la fortune et les chemins de l'opulence dans la France médiévale, *Domanda e consumi. Livelli e strutture (nei secoli XIII–XVIII). Atti della 'sesta settimana di studio' (27 aprile–3 maggio 1974)*. Istituto F. Datini, Prato, Florence, 1978, 237–46.

1368 Fédou, R., *Les hommes de loi lyonnais à la fin du Moyen Age. Etude sur les origines de la classe de robe*, Paris, 1964.

1369 Fédou, R., Les sergents à Lyon aux XIVe et XVe siècles: une institution, un type social, *BPH*, 1964, 283–92.

1370 Gilissen, J., Les légistes en Flandre aux XIIIe et XIVe siècles, *Bulletin de la Commission royale des Anciennes Lois et Ordonnances de Belgique*, 15, 3 (1939), 117–231.

1371 Gilomen-Schenkel, E., *Henman Offenburg (1379–1459). Ein Basler Diplomat im Dienste der Stadt, des Konzils und des Reichs*, Basel, 1975.

1372 Gouron, A., Le rôle social des juristes français et allemands à la fin du Moyen Age, *RHDFE*, 1971, 700–1.

1373 Griffiths, R.A., Public and Private Bureaucracies in England and Wales in the Fifteenth Century, *TRHS*, 30 (1980), 109–30.

1374 Guillot, R., *Le procès de Jacques Cœur (1451–7)*, Bourges, n.d.

1375 Guenée, B., *Tribunaux et gens de justice dans le bailliage de Senlis à la fin du Moyen Age (vers 1380–vers 1550)*, Paris, 1963.

1376 Guillemain, B., *La Cour pontificale d'Avignon, 1309–76. Etude d'une société*, repr., Paris, 1966.

1377 Guillemain, B., Les carrières des officiers pontificaux au XIVe siècle, *MA*, 69 (1963), 565–81.

1378 Hausmann, Fr., *Georg von Neudegg. Humanist und Staatsmann der Zeit Maximilians I.*, *MIÖG*, 71 (1963), 333–53.

1379 Ives, E.W., Promotion in the Legal Profession of Yorkist and Early Tudor England, *The Law Quarterly Review*, 75 (1959), 348–63.

1380 Ives, E.W., Some Aspects of the Legal Profession in the Late Fifteenth and Early Sixteenth Century, *BIHR*, 31 (1958), 98–103.

1381 Ives, E.W., The Common Lawyers in Pre-Reformation England, *TRHS*, 5th ser., 18 (1968), 145–73.

1382 Ives, E.W., The Reputation of the Common Lawyers in English Society, 1450–1550, *University of Birmingham Historical Journal*, 7 (1959), 130–61.

1383 Jones, M., Education in Brittany during the Later Middle Ages: a Survey, *Nottingham Mediaeval Studies*, 22 (1978), 58–77.

1384 Kaminsky, H., The Early Career of Simon de Cramaud, *Spec.*, 49 (1974), 499–534.

1385 Kerhervé, J., Une famille d'officiers de finances bretons au XVe siècle: les Thomas de Nantes, *Annales de Bretagne*, 83 (1976), 7–33.

1386 Kirshner, J., Paoli di Castro on *Cives ex privilegio*. A Controversy over the Legal Qualifications for Public Office in Early Fifteenth-Century Florence, *Renaissance Studies in Honor of H. Baron*, 1971, 227–64.

1387 Kubler, J., *Recherches sur la fonction publique sous l'Ancien Régime. L'origine de la perpétuité des offices royaux*, Nancy, 1958.

1388 Lanhers, Y., Crimes et criminels au XIVe siècle, *RH*, 240 (1968), 325–38.

1389 Lapeyre, A. et Scheurer, R., *Les notaires et secrétaires du roi sous les règnes de Louis XI, Charles VIII et Louis XII (1461–1515). Notices personnelles et généalogies*, 2 vols, Paris, 1978.

1390 Leone, A., *Il notaio nella società del quattrocento meridionale*, Salerno, 1979.

1391 Lieberich, H., Die gelehrten Räte. Staat und Juristen in Baiern in der Frühzeit der Rezeption, *Zeitschrift für bayerische Landesgeschichte*, 27 (1964), 120–89.

1392 McNamara, J.A., *Gilles Aycelin. The Servant of Two Masters*, Syracuse, 1973.

1393 Maddicott, J.R., *Law and Lordship: Royal Justices as Retainers in Thirteenth- and Fourteenth-Century England*, Oxford, 1978.

1394 Maillard, F., Mouvements administratifs des baillis et des sénéchaux sous Philippe le Bel, *BPH*, 1959, 407–30.

1395 Maillard, F., Les mouvements administratifs des baillis et des sénéchaux de 1314 à 1328, *BPH*, 1963, 899–912.

1396 Maillard, F., Les mouvements administratifs des baillis et des sénéchaux sous Philippe VI, *BPH*, 1966, 623–38.

1397 Martines, L., *Lawyers and Statecraft in Renaissance Florence*, Princeton, 1968.

1398 Mate, M., A Mint of Trouble, 1279–1307, *Spec.*, 44 (1969), 201–12.

1399 Moxó, S. de, La promocion politica y social de los 'letrados' en la corte de Alfonso XI, *Hispania*, 35 (1975), 5–29.

1400 Paravicini, W., Soziale Schichtung und soziale Mobilität am Hof der Herzöge von Burgund, *Francia*, 5 (1977), 127–82.

1401 Paravicini, W., Zur Biographie von Guillaume Hugonet, Kanzler Herzog Karls des Kühnen, *Festchrift für Hermann Heimpel*, II, Göttingen, 1972, 443–81.

1402 Pegues, F.J., *The Lawyers of the Last Capetians*, Princeton, 1962.

1403 Post, J.B., King's Bench Clerks in the Reign of Richard II, *BIHR*, 47 (1974), 150–63.

1404 Poulon, M.-E., Guillaume de Varye, facteur de Jacques Cœur et général des finances de Louis XI, *PTEC*, 1972, 161–6.

1405 Prevenier, W., Officials in Town and Countryside in the Low Countries. Social and Professional Developments from the Fourteenth to the Sixteenth Century, *Acta Historiae Neerlandicae*, 7 (1974), 1–17.

1406 Radding, C.M., The Administrators of the Aids in Normandy, 1360–80, in *Order and Innovation in the Middle Ages. Essays in Honour of Joseph R. Strayer*, W.C. Jordan, B. McNab and T.F. Ruiz (eds), Princeton, 1976, 41–53.

1407 Richard, J., Finances princières et banquiers au XIVᵉ siècle. L'affaire des Bourgeoise et la réformation de 1343 en Bourgogne, *Annales de Bourgogne*, 27 (1955), 7–32.

1408 Ringel, I.H., *Studien zum Personal der Kanzlei des Mainzer Erzbischofs Dietrich von Erbach (1434–59)*, Mainz, 1980.

1409 Sainty, J.C., The Tenure of Offices in the Exchequer, *EHR*, 80 (1965), 449–75.

1410 Slavin, A.J., Profitable Studies: Humanists and Government in Early Tudor England, *Viator*, 1 (1970), 307–25.

1411 Smith, W.E.L., *The Register of Richard Clifford, Bishop of Worcester, 1401–7*, Leiden, 1976.

1412 Stelling-Michaud, S., *L'Université de Bologne et la pénétration des droits romain et canonique en Suisse aux XIIIᵉ et XIVᵉ siècles*, Geneva, 1955.

1413 Stones, E.L.G., Sir Geoffrey le Scrope (c.1285–1340), Chief Justice of the King's Bench, *EHR*, 69 (1954), 1–17.

1414 Strayer, J.R., *Les gens de justice du Languedoc sous Philippe le Bel*, Toulouse, 1970.

1415 Tessier, G., Le formulaire d'Odart Morchesne (1427), in *Mélanges dédiés à la mémoire de Félix Grat*, E.-A. van Moé Nielliard and P. Marot (eds), I, Paris, 1949, 75–102.

1416 Tessier, G. and Ouy, G., Notaires et secrétaires du roi dans la première moitié du XVᵉ siècle d'après un document inédit, *BPH*, 1963, 861–90.

1417 Tout, T.F., The English Civil Service in the Fourteenth Century, *The Collected Papers of T.F. Tout*, III, Manchester, 1934, 191–221.

1418 Trusen, W., *Die Anfänge des gelehrten Rechts in Deutschland*, Wiesbaden, 1962.

1419 Vercauteren, F., Henri de Jodogne, légiste, clerc et conseiller des princes (mort en 1352), *Bulletin de l'Institut historique belge de Rome*, 27 (1952), 451–505.

1420 Vercauteren, F., Maître Jean Ventura de Florence: un conseiller de Guillaume Iᵉʳ de Hainaut (1308–33), *Economies et Sociétés au Moyen Age. Mélanges offerts à Edouard Perroy*, Paris, 1973, 538–52; repr. in F. Vercauteren, *Etudes d'histoire médiévale*, Brussels, 1979, 611–25.

See also: 605.

CIVIC HUMANISM

1421 Baron, H., *The Crisis of the Early Italian Renaissance. Civic Humanism and Republican Liberty in an Age of Classicism and Tyranny*, Princeton, 1966.

1422 Baron, H., The Social Background of Political Liberty in the Early Italian Renaissance, *Comparative Studies in Society and History*, 2 (1959–60), 440–51.

1423 Carotti, N., Un politico umanista del Quattrocento: Francesco Barbaro, *RSI*, 54 (1937), 18–37.

1424 Garin, E., *L'umanesimo italiano. Filosofia e vita civile nel Rinascimento*, Bari, 1952.

1425 Herde, P., Politik und Rhetorik in Florenz am Vorabend der Renaissance. Die ideologische Rechtfertigung der Florentiner Aussenpolitik durch Coluccio Salutati, *Archiv für Kulturgeschichte*, 47 (1965), 141–220.

1426 Kohl, B.G., Witt, R.G. and Welles, E.B. (eds), *The Earthly Republic: Italian Humanists on Government and Society*, Philadelphia, 1978.

1427 Martines, L., *The Social World of the Florentine Humanists, 1390–1460*, Princeton, 1963.

1428 Oppel, J.W., Peace vs. Liberty in the Quattrocento: Poggio, Guarino and the Scipio-Caesar controversy, *Journal of Medieval and Renaissance Studies*, 4 (1974), 221–65.

1429 Robey, D., P.P. Vergerio the Elder: Republicanism and Civic Values in the Work of an Early Humanist, *PP*, 58 (1973), 3–37.

1430 Seigel, J.E., 'Civic Humanism' or Ciceronian Rhetoric? The Culture of Petrarch and Bruni, *PP*, 34 (1966), 3–48.

1431 Seigel, J.E., *Rhetoric and Philosophy in Renaissance Humanism. The Union of Eloquence and Wisdom, Petrarch to Valla*, Princeton, 1968.

1432 Witt, R.G., A Note on Guelfism in Late Medieval Florence, *NRS*, 53 (1969), 134–45.

1433 Witt, R.G., The *De Tyranno* and Coluccio Salutati's View of Politics and Roman History, *NRS*, 53 (1969), 434–74.

Index

Aachen 61,62
Ableiges, Jacques d' 34
Absolutism 19–21, 35, 171, 187
Accurso, Francesco 33
Acre 2
Adalbero, bishop of Laon 5
Æneas 60–1
Agenais, the 176, 179
Agincourt, battle of 84
Ailly, Pierre d' 47
Aix-la-Chappelle, *see* Aachen
Albi 103
Alès 193
Alexander of Roes 7, 16, 60
Aljubarrota, battle of 74, 144
Alsace, county of 196
Philip of, *see* Flanders
Alvaro Pelayo 10, 174
Amboise, Concordat of 169
Anagni, deposition of 10, 55
Andlau, Peter of 60
Andrea, Giovanni d' 35
Angers, 'Tricoterie' of 193
Anjou, house of, *see* Naples and Sicily;
    Hungary
Aquinas, St Thomas 5, 33–4, 37, 39,
    42, 53, 85
Aquitaine, duke of 164
Aragon, kingdom of 7–9, 11, 14, 49, 74,
    77, 78, 115, 143, 152, 171, 173,
    179, 181, 183–4, 191

Ferdinand and Isabella, king and
    queen of Castile and 49, 57–8, 61,
    75, 152
James II 167
John II 134
Pedro III 178, 183
Pedro (Peter) IV (the
    Ceremonious) 79, 151
Arbitration 11
Archives 128–9
Aristotle 29, 37–9, 40–1, 53, 83, 85, 202
Arles, lord of 100
Armagnacs 201
Arras, conference of 145
    treaty of 185
Arthur, prince of Wales 63
Astrology, astrologers 47–8
Aubenas 193
Augsburg 105
Aunis 100
Austria, duchy of 160, 166–7, 176
    Frederick (the Fair), duke of 74
Autun, cathedral church of 92
Auxerre 92
Averroists 53
Avesnes, house of 171
Avignon, Papacy at 10, 78, 110

Bacon, Roger 53
Baldus de Ubaldis 145
Bannockburn, battle of 137

311

Barcelona 178
  count of 51
Bardi, company of the 106–7
Barnet, battle of 162
Barons' War, the 170
Bartolus of Sassoferrato 5, 13, 33–4, 37
Basin, Thomas 3, 36, 64–5, 88, 158,
  202
Bavaria:
  duke(s) of 14, 150, 166
  Estates of 186
Béarn:
  Estates of 181
  vicomté of 18, 189
Beatus Rhenanus 63
Beaucaire 133
Beaufort, Cardinal Henry 158
Beaumanoir, Philippe de 83, 158
Beauvais, Vincent de 44
Bebenberg, Lupold of 16
Beccari, Niccolo dei 8
Bedfordshire and Buckinghamshire,
  sheriff of 114
Belleperche, Pierre de 7, 34
Benefices, ecclesiastical 168–70,
  200–2
Berlin 165
Berliner Unwille 165
Bern 192
Bible 38–9, 40, 42, 45, 85
Black Death 142, 150
Blanot, Jean de 7, 55
Bocaccio, Giovanni 85
Bohemia, duchy then kingdom of 5, 7,
  14–17, 56, 77, 83–4, 95, 110,
  150–1, 193, 196
  Charles IV *see* Holy Roman
    Empire
  Premysl I 15
  Premysl (Premysl Ottokar) II 56,
    75
  Wenceslas, duke of 56
  Wenceslas IV, king of the Romans
    and king of 8, 76, 86
Bologna 34, 199
  Concordat of 169
Bordeaux 133, 135, 164

Bourgeois, bourgeoisie 20–1, 28,
  175–6, 192, 200
Bourges 197
  Pragmatic Sanction of 169–70
Bouvines, battle of 61
Brabant, duchy of 62, 115, 117, 172,
  182–3
  rulers of 92, 106
  Jean III, duke of 172
  Jeanne and Wenceslas, co-rulers
    of 172, 179
Bracton 71, 114, 123
Braga, Martin of 69
Brandenburg, margravate of 109
  Estates of the margravate 186
  Landbuch of the margravate 128
  margrave of 125, 185
  Albert-Achilles, elector of 186
  Frederick II, elector of 165
Bratislava 150
Bresgau 192
Brethren of the Free Spirit 195–6
Bridlington, John of 45
Bristol 104
Britain, Britons 3, 60
Brittany, duchy of 18, 65, 100, 182
  Estates of the 182
  dukes of 76, 109, 160
  Francis II, duke of 77
Bruges 106, 107, 192
Bruni, Leonardo 36, 38
Brutus 60–1, 63
Buda, castle of 190
Budé, Guillaume 69
Bull, Golden 15–16, 183
Buonaccorsi, Filippo 45
Burgos 46, 100
  ordinance of 100
Burgundy 11, 49, 51, 69, 80, 92,
  109–10, 151, 176, 200, 201, 203
  duke(s) of 76, 78, 92, 107
  Estates General of 179
  kingdom of 11
  Charles (the Bold, the Rash), duke
    of 34, 48, 51, 72, 76, 107, 143, 196
  John (the Fearless), duke of 9, 72, 107
  Mary, duchess of 49

Philip (the Bold), duke of 49, 72, 96, 105, 107, 129, 138
Philip (the Good), duke of 57, 72, 76, 136, 151, 179
Robert II, duke of 179
Buridan, Jean 85
Bury, abbot of 113

Caen, *bailliage* of 104
Cahors 53, 193
Calais 98, 143
Camaldolesi, Venetian 44
Cambrai, treaty of 185
Canterbury, *see* Peckham
Caramanico, Marino da 7
Carcassone 100, 133
  viscount of 100
Carinthia 190
Castile, kingdom of 10, 49, 74–5, 93, 101, 115–6, 124, 129, 144, 163, 175, 189–90
  Alfonso X 64, 71
  Alfonso XI 100, 163, 166
  Enrique IV 75
  Ferdinand and Isabella, king and queen of Aragon and, *see* Aragon
Catalonia, *Catalani* 50–1, 115, 170, 173, 176, 181, 183–4, 193, 195, 208
Cato 54
Châlon 92
Champagne, *Extente* of the county of 128
Chancellor, Chancery 28, 30–1, 39, 98, 124–8, 134–5, 177
Charles, the Dauphin, *see* France
Chartres 25
Chastellain, Georges 3, 54, 158
Chioggia:
  salt marshes of 99
  War 108
Christendom 1–4, 9, 53
Cicero 38–9, 52, 54, 72, 85
Clermont de Lodève 193
Cleves, duke of 170
Clovis, king of the Franks 59
Cluny, abbey of 92
Coeur, Jacques 107

Coinage, currency 92–6, 179
Cologne, archbishop of 159
Common weal, concept of 42, 82, 148, 151, 178
Commynes, Philippe de 3, 45
Conciliar movement 8, 17, 21, 32, 35, 148, 169–70, 173, 208
Concordats 168–9
Condeyssie, Jean de 197
Constance:
  concordat of 169
  council of 8, 173, 208
Constantine, emperor 1
  donation of 12
Coronation 26–7, 29, 67–9, 84, 171–2
Corsica 152
Cosenza, Telesphore de 45
Council, counsellors 37, 73, 87, 120–6, 129, 146, 172, 178, 180–2, 184–5, 195, 199, 200
Councils, Lateran, Third and Fourth 174, 182
Court 79–80, 120–3
Courtrai, battle of 137
Cracow *see* Saints
Crécy, battle of 117, 144, 163
Credit, public 107–8
Cromwell, Thomas 22, 126
Crown 4–5, 12, 46, 67–8, 74–8, 83–4, 106
Crusade 2, 9, 46, 51, 101
Customs dues 96–9, 152

Dagobert, king of the Franks 30
Dante Alighieri 3, 7, 13, 39, 67
Dauphiné 11
  Estates of 189
Débat des Hérauts de France et d'Angleterre, Le 3, 60
Debate of the Heralds of England and France 3
Decretists, the 35, 39
Democracy 32, 36, 82–3, 114, 190, 201–2, 207–8
Denmark, nobility of 191
Dialects 53
Dijon 92

Dionysius the Areopagite (Pseudo-Dionysius) 38–9
Diplomacy 126, 145–7
Domain 12, 14, 84, 91–2, 101, 106, 109–10, 181
Domesday Book 128
Dominicans, Order of the 182
Dover 134
Du Bois, Jean 45
Dubois, Pierre 7, 37, 47
Dunwich, borough of 113
Durant, Guillaume 7

Economy, economic policy 38, 72, 148–53, 179, 184–5
Einhard 69
Elector Palatine 91
Ely, prior of 113
Empire, emperors:
  Byzantine 1–3, 76
  Carolingian 1
  Roman (imperium romanum) 2, 4, 38, 55
  Salian and Saxon 2, 6
  universal, principle of 2, 7–9, 17
  see also Holy Roman Empire
Engelbert of Admont 7, 40
England 4, 8, 11, 16–18, 26, 49, 57, 60, 63, 65, 68, 77, 80, 83–4, 87–8, 91–4, 97–9, 101, 103–5, 107, 109–10, 112, 114–15, 117–18, 120–2, 124–7, 129, 132–5, 139–44, 150–2, 158–62, 164–6, 171, 174–6, 178, 180–1, 183, 185–6, 189, 191, 193, 195, 197–200
  Edward I 19, 22, 54, 57, 60, 63, 68, 75, 84, 96–7, 103, 106, 112, 123, 138, 174, 178, 184, 199
  Edward II 44, 68, 84, 86–7, 125, 171, 179, 184
  Edward III 44, 49, 57, 64, 75, 79, 97–8, 107, 113, 129–30, 140–3, 159–60, 163, 179–81, 182–3, 183–4, 189, 200
  Edward IV 44, 79, 126, 136, 160
  Henry I 6, 112

Henry II 46, 74, 113, 118, 122, 140, 199
  Henry III 22, 75, 130, 140, 176, 178
  Henry IV 28, 44, 46, 125, 186
  Henry V 59, 143
  Henry VI 70, 78, 167
  Henry VII 19, 27, 63, 70, 92, 110, 113, 136, 148
  Henry VIII 22, 27, 77, 88, 170
  John 9
  Richard II 26, 43–4, 84, 86, 125, 138
  Richard III 160
  William the Conqueror 128
Entries, royal and princely 27–9
Erasmus 38, 69, 70, 72
Essex, county of 193
Etaples, treaty of 185
Ewiger Landfriege 17
Extente, see Champagne

Faits des Romains, Les 59
Ferrara 13
Feu, Jean 9
Feudalism, fiefs 9–10, 19–20, 22, 37, 64, 101–2, 112–13, 116, 138–9, 159–64, 171–2, 178, 188–9, 198, 207
Fiore, Joachim de 45–6
Flanders:
  count of 199
  county of 28, 49, 59, 75, 109, 115, 124, 129, 166, 192–3
  Louis de Male, count of 49
  Philip of Alsace, count of 148
Florence 12–13, 36, 59, 66, 101–4, 107–8, 140, 144, 152, 157, 164, 193, 196, 199, 204
  church of Santa Maria del Fiore in 30
  revolt of the Ciompi at 193, 195
Foggia 178
Foix:
  counts of 163
  Gaston Phoebus, count of 159
Fontainebleau, Forest of 138
Forcalquier, Guillaume II, count of 175

Forez 43
Fortescue, Sir John 186
Foulechat, Denis 29, 39
France:
Constable of 77–8
Estates General of 39, 119, 158, 175,
180–3, 185–7, 202
kingdom and kings of 3, 7–11, 14,
16–18, 26, 28, 33, 44, 46, 48–9,
58–65, 68–9, 74, 76–8, 84, 87–8,
91, 93, 96, 99–101, 103–5, 107,
109–10, 116–30, 132–5, 138–41,
143, 149–52, 158–64, 166–7,
170–3, 175–81, 183–6, 189, 191,
193, 198, 199, 200–4, 208
Adela of Champagne, queen of 61
Anne, queen of 29
Blanche of Castile, queen and regent
of 199
Charles IV (the Fair) 8, 49, 62, 75,
78, 150, 167
Charles V (the Wise) 8–9, 26,
29–30, 38–9, 57, 62, 69, 71–3,
75–6, 93, 95, 103, 111, 132, 141–2,
144, 200–1
Charles VI 27, 47, 51, 69, 78–9, 87,
136, 201–2
Charles VII 22, 33, 45, 47, 54, 69,
76, 107, 135, 138, 142, 144, 167,
185
Charles VIII 26–7, 44, 47, 69, 158,
160
Francis I 9, 16, 18, 22, 62, 77, 151–2
Isabella of Hainault, queen of 61
John, duke of Bedford, regent of 181
John II (the Good) 72, 99–100, 163,
179, 201
Louis VI 6, 57, 69
Louis IX (St Louis) 22, 44, 54, 68,
70, 77, 94, 123, 132, 175, 177, 199,
201
Louis X 51, 140
Louis XI 27–8, 47–8, 51, 57, 62, 69,
77, 84, 87, 107, 109, 111, 125–6,
134–6, 143, 148–9, 152, 158, 160,
163–4, 177, 185, 189, 193, 197, 203
Louis XII 27, 29, 57, 61, 101, 135

Marie, queen of 29
Philip III (the Brave) 72
Philip IV (the Fair) 8, 10, 22, 28–9,
49, 56–7, 68, 72, 87, 94–5, 106,
123, 132, 139, 166, 179, 199–200
Philip V 179
Philip VI 28, 64, 83, 100, 102, 134,
142–3, 200
Philip Augustus 51, 61, 118, 121,
140, 199
Francia, Franci 50–1, 60–1
Franciscans, Spiritual 44–5
Frankfurt 17
Franks 60–3, 65
Franzesi, Albizi and Musciatto 106
Frescobaldi, company of the 106
Frisia 192
Friuli 176, 184
Froissart, Jean 54
Frontiers 20, 64, 96–9, 138, 142, 166–7
Fugger:
company of the 62
Jacob 105
Funerals 26–7

Galbert of Bruges 6
Gallia, Galli 50, 52
Garter, Order of the 163
Gaul, Gauls 3, 56, 60, 65
Geneva 149
Genoa 66, 96–8, 101, 108, 152, 157
Gerald of Wales 64
Gerbert of Reims 55
Germania, Germani 50, 52, 60
Germany 3, 7, 9, 12, 15–18, 46, 52, 61,
63, 79, 86, 95, 106, 116–17, 121,
124–5, 129, 142, 150, 159, 160,
164, 167, 170, 172, 182–3, 189,
193, 195–6, 199, 203–4, 208
kingdom and kings of 2, 11, 14,
16–17, 62, 68, 74
principalities and princes of 116,
121–2, 124, 163–5, 173, 183
Gerson, Jean 47, 85, 88, 174
Ghent 192
Ghibellines 11, 13, 83
Giotto 30

Glastonbury, abbot and monks of 63
Glossators, the 33, 38
Gniezno 57
Golden Fleece, Order of the 163
Golein, Jean 29
Grandes Chroniques de France, Les 54, 58–9, 76
Gratian 34
Grenada, Moorish kingdom of 2
Grossetto, salt marshes of 99
Guelders, duchy of 192
Guelphs 11
Guyenne, duchy of 144

Habsburg:
  house of 49, 58, 150
  Rudolf of, king of the Romans 12, 15–16
  see also Austria, Holy Roman Empire
Hainault:
  county of 116, 170–1, 176
  Estates of 183
  Jean II, count of 171
Hallein, salt mines of 150
Hanse, Hanseatic League 16, 52, 165
Hastings, Lord William 162
Heresy 195–6
Hierarchy 43–4
Historia Britonum 60
Historia regum Francorum 58
Hohenstaufen, imperial house of 6, 12, 16, 173
Holland, county of 182–3
Holy Roman Emperors, Empire 2, 4, 6–18, 26, 30–1, 34, 40, 52, 59, 61–2, 76–8, 81, 85, 160–1, 190, 193, 208
  institutions of 17, 30
  Landtage of 181, 183, 186
  prince-electors of 15
  vicariate of 11–13, 16
Charlemagne 1, 46, 51, 61–3, 69, 74, 76, 167
Charles the Bald 7, 77
Charles IV 8, 12–17, 47, 56, 76, 84, 151, 159

Charles V 9, 14, 16, 19, 22, 49, 62, 94, 100
Conrad II 2, 74
Conrad III 76
Frederick I (Barbarossa) 2, 61, 76, 176
Frederick II (also king of Sicily) 6, 10, 15, 19, 46, 68, 148, 151, 174, 177–8
Frederick III 9, 13, 15–16, 22, 46, 105, 167
Henry II 122
Henry VII 8, 12–13
Louis (the Pious) 76
Lewis of Bavaria 8, 12, 14, 29, 62, 74
Maximilian I 14, 16–17, 29–30, 45, 47, 49, 75, 105
Otto I 1, 76
Otto III 61, 76
Sigismund 8, 12–13, 74–5
Holy See, *see* Papacy
Horace 54
Household, Black Book of the 79
Households, princely 78–80, 121, 132
Hugues Capet, king of the Franks 30
Humanism, humanist 3, 23, 25, 30, 36–7, 66, 71
Hundred Years War 65, 119, 135, 141, 167, 174
Hungary 3–4, 7, 11, 49, 58, 74, 77, 83–4, 95, 109–10, 125, 150, 167, 173, 176–7, 183, 188, 190
  Rakos of 190
  Albert II 74
  Béla IV 75
  Charles-Robert of Anjou 74, 128
  Elisabeth, queen of 74
  Lewis (Louis) I the Great, Poland and 49, 173
  Mathias Corvinus 74
Hus, Jan 56
Hussite movement(s) and revolts 173, 193, 196, 208

Ile-de-France 193
Indentures 141–2, 162–3

Inns of Court 34, 200
Insignia 6, 7, 9, 14, 57, 61, 74–8
  see also crown
Ipswich, borough of 113
Ireland, lordship of 127
Isidore of Seville 39, 52, 71
Islam 2
Italian Wars 29, 44
Italy 3, 10–14, 23, 46–7, 50, 61, 63,
    66–7, 69, 85, 98, 102–3, 107–9,
    125, 128, 134, 139, 140–1, 144,
    157, 164–5, 167, 173, 176, 192–3,
    199
  kingdom of 2, 11
  merchants of 106, 180

Jacobus Alemannus 85
Jacquerie, revolt of the 88, 193
James of Viterbo 40
Janow, Matthew of 46
Jerusalem 47
Jews 58, 65, 106
Joan of Arc 45, 56–7, 69
John of Salisbury 6, 29, 39, 43, 52, 69,
    81, 85
Joinville 69
Julius Caesar 59, 63
Justice 41–2, 77–8, 178
Justinian 40, 173
  Code of (Codex) 33–4

Kalmar, union of 191
Kenilworth 63
Kent, county of 193
Kings and queens, legendary 46,
    59–63

Lampugnano, Uberto de 8
Lancaster:
  John of Gaunt, duke of 162
  Thomas, earl of 162
Landbuch, see Brandenburg
Landino, Cristoforo 30
Language(s):
  Catalan 53, 79
  English 54
  French 54, 111, 160, 176–7

Germanic 4, 16, 53, 116, 129, 177
  Latin 1, 2, 4, 16, 53–4, 111, 116, 176
  Romance 53
  Slavonic 4, 53
Languedoc 97, 100, 184–5, 193, 200
  'Tuchins' of 193
Lannoy, Ghillebert de 73
Latinity 2–4
Lavaur 193
Law 41, 81–2
  canon 6–7, 34–6, 182
  civil 33–4
  common 122
  Roman 12, 33–6, 39–40, 81–3, 99,
    173–4, 182, 195, 204
Le Breton, Güillaume 61
Le Coq, Jean 159, 202
Legists 199–200
Legnano, John of 12, 141
Lehen in Bresgau, Bundschuh of 193
Leon, kingdom of 175
Le Puy 93, 189, 193, 197
Le Roi, Adenet 61
lèse-majesté 8, 15, 88, 201
Liège, archbishopric of 55, 139, 176
Lille 129
  Alain de 46
Limoges 133
Lippi, Filippino 30
Literature, heroic and chivalric 30, 51,
    61, 197
Lithuania, duchy of 2
  Ladislas Jagellon II, king of Poland
    and duke of 49, 50
  Ladislas Jagellon III, duke of 74
Loans 105–8, 203
Lollards, Lollardy 195–6
Lombard communes 151
London 54, 75, 106, 129–34, 183, 199
London, Tower of 26, 59
Lorenzetti, Ambrogio 25
Low countries, the 16, 115, 158, 160,
    173, 176
Lübeck, council of 14
Lucca 102
Luxemburg, John, duke of 47

Lyon 102, 133, 135, 152, 197
'Rebeyne' of 193
Lytlington, Nicholas, abbot of
Westminster 26

Machiavelli, Niccolo 3, 5, 38, 69, 73,
140
Mâcon 92, 133
Mainz, archbishop of 167
Majorca, James II, king of 78–9
Male, Louis de, see Flanders
Malines 106
Manetti, Giannozzo 66
Mantua, marquis of 13
Manutius, Aldus 38
Maps 134–5
Marcel, Etienne 183
Marienburg 129
Marsilius of Padua 32–3, 37, 39–40,
85, 202
Martinus 81
Mecklenburg, duchy of 127
Medici 30, 66
bank of the 107
Cosimo de 30
Juliano de 30
Lorenzo de 30
Melgueil 93
Merlin 44–7
Messengers, royal 132–4
Messina, Constitution of 178
Metz 144
Meung, Jean de 43
Middelburg, Paul, bishop of 47
Milan 13, 66, 124, 159
basilica of St Ambrose in 12
duke of 106, 125, 151
Sforza, Francesco, duke of 66
Visconti, Bernabo, lord of 13, 15
Visconti, Filippo Maria, duke of 66,
204
Visconti, Gian Galeazzo, duke of 13,
30
Mines, mining 94–5, 184, 186, 192
Mirandola, Pico della 47
Mirrors of princes 69–74, 87
Modena, duke of 13

Molinet, Jean 39
Monmouth, Geoffrey of 46, 54, 58, 60,
62
Monopolies 97–100, 149–50, 152
Montpelier 193
, lord of 100
Montreuil, Jean de 51
Mont-Saint-Michel 57, 205
Morchesne, Odart 201
More, Thomas 38
Morena, Otto 176
Morgarten, battle of 137
Mühldorf, battle of 74
Munich 74, 150
Münster, bishop of 159, 163
Murcia 53

Namur, county of 158
Nantes 28
Naples 10–12, 34
king of 78
Naples and Sicily:
Charles of Anjou, titular king of 12,
47, 100
René of Anjou, king of 182
Nassau, Adolf, king of the Romans and
count of 86
Nation 49–65
National sentiment 48–9, 51–2, 64–5
Navarre, Louis de 198
Neuss 196
Nicholas of Cusa 8, 17, 43, 174
Niklashausen, the drummer of 193,
196
Nîmes 193
Nobles, nobility, ennoblement 21,
139–40, 145–6, 159–66, 176–7,
188–91, 200, 203–4
Nogaret, Guillaume de 55, 200, 204
Nominalism 32, 36, 42
Norman Conquest 112
Normandy, duchy and inhabitants
of 64, 143–4, 181, 184
Northumberland, sheriff of 133
Notaries 8, 13, 35–6, 120, 127, 197,
199
Nuremberg 14, 17, 51, 75, 150

Office, officers 202–5
Orders of chivalry 162–3, 208
  see also Garter, Golden Fleece, St
    Michael
Oresme, Nicholas 29, 38, 47, 72, 83,
  94–5, 111, 202
Orford, borough of 113
Orléans 33, 54, 199
  Jonas d' 69
  Charles, duke of 55
  Louis, duke of 85
Orosius 4
Ostia, salt marshes of 99
Oxford, council of 57

Padua 34, 38
Papacy, Papal States 1–3, 6–7, 9–12,
  16, 32, 37, 40, 45, 77, 85, 101, 135,
  145, 166, 168, 175, 208
  see also Popes
Paris 8, 25–8, 33, 46, 48, 53–4, 56,
  59–60, 106, 129, 132–3, 135, 160,
  183, 193, 198, 201
  chronicle of the Bourgeois of 54, 87
  government departments at 129, 132
  Palais de la Cité 25, 132
  Parlement of 9, 41, 59, 62, 111,
    123–4, 127, 129, 159–60, 167–8,
    200, 202
  President of the Parlement 82
  revolt of the Cabochiens 117, 193,
    202
  riot of the Maillotins 193
  rising of 1356–8 191
  University of 64, 85, 167
  vicomté of 198
  see also Saints
Parlement *see* Paris
Parlements (French) 123–4, 127, 135,
  201–3
Parliament (English) 86, 97–8, 103–5,
  114, 140, 142, 161, 174, 186, 191,
  208
Passau, bishop of 166, 190
Patriotism 54–5, 166
Pavia 9, 34
Pazzi conspiracy 30

Peasants 192–4, 197
Peasants' Revolt, the 83, 193
Peasants' War, the 193
Peckham, John, archbishop of
  Canterbury 60
Penna, Lucas de 37, 39, 82–3
People, *populus* 82–4
Perigueux 133
Persians 65
Perugia 34
Petit, Jean 85
Petrarch, Francesco 3, 15
Piccolomini, Æneas Silvius, *see* Popes
Picquigny, Peace of 45
Piedmont, county of 173, 176
Pisa 13, 102–3, 107–10
Pisan, Christine de 69
Plato 38–9
Poissy, castellany of 198
Poitiers 133, 140
  battle of 30, 84, 117
Poitou, Poitevins 65, 100, 173
  Estates of 180–1, 183
Poland 3, 9–11, 49, 57, 68, 77, 84,
  87–8, 161, 183
  Boleslas Szcodry 57
  Casimir II (the Great) 49
  Casimir IV 84
  Edwige, queen of 49–50
  Mesco I 50
  see also Hungary; Polno–Lithuanian
    Union
Polenia, Poloni 50–1
Poliziano, Angelo 30
Polno–Lithuanian Union 49–50, 52,
  191
Popes:
  Alexander VI 10
  Boniface VIII 7, 10, 29, 55, 60, 182
  Clement V 78
  Clement VI 166
  Gregory the Great 38
  Innocent III 7, 10, 175
  Innocent IV 9–10
  John VIII 1–2
  John XXII 29, 53, 167
  Martin V 169

Nicholas V 145
Pius II (previously Æneas Silvius Piccolomini) 3, 9, 63
see also Papacy
Porcari, Stefano 66
Portinari, Tommaso 107
Portugal, Portuguese 9–11, 54, 74
Denis the Cultivator, king of 54
Post-Glossators, the 34, 37
Praemunire, Statute of 10
Prague 8, 150, 196
Cathedral and archbishopric of 56, 75, 167
Praguerie 88
Prato, battle of 140
Presles, Raoul de 29
Primat, monk 58
Printing 29–31
Probus, the 128
Proclus 38
Propaganda 25–31
Prophets, prophecy 44–8
Provence, county of 97, 101, 173
Estates of 180–1
Prussia 80
Public Weal, War of 48, 88

Rapondi, Dino 105, 107
Realism 32, 38, 42
Reformatio Sigismundi, the 17
Reichenhall, salt mines 150
Reims 25–6
archbishopric of 55, 166
'Miquemaque' of 193
Renaissance 18–20, 63
Representation, concept of 173–5
Retainer, retinue 141–2, 162–5
Révigny, Jacques de 7, 33, 55
Rhens, diet of 16, 182–3
Rhetoric 35–8
Rhineland, river Rhine 50–1, 53, 62, 91, 109, 125
Riccardi, company of the 106
Rienzo, Cola di 17, 25, 59, 193, 197
Roads 133–4, 150, 185
Robine, Marie 45
Rodez 93

Romans, king(s) of the 12, 183
see also Bohemia
Rome, Romans 2, 12, 16, 25, 58–61, 66–7, 99, 135, 145, 193, 197
Giles of 26, 69
Roncaglia, diet of 176
Rosier des Guerres, Le 88
Rouen 28, 51
'Hérelle' at 193
Rouergue, the 44

St Augustine, Augustinians 1, 29, 33, 38–41, 43, 53, 70
St Denis, bishop of Paris 30, 56–7
Saint-Denis, abbey, monk(s) and chronicles of 27, 54, 58, 60–1, 75, 77
St Edmund, liberty of 113
St Etheldreda, liberty of 113
St George 57, 163
St Hildegarde, Benedictine abbess 45
St Jerome 38
St Louis, *see* France
St Michael 57
Order of 57, 163
Saint-Philibert, abbey of, *see* Tournus
St Stephen 57, 74
St Thomas Aquinas, *see* Aquinas
St Wenceslas, *see* Bohemia
Saintonge 100
Saints, patron 56–7
Sallust 30
Salt 99–101, 150
Salutati, Coluccio 13, 36
Salzburg, archbishopric of 53, 150, 190
Saragossa 179
ecclesiastical province of 167
Sardinia 152
Sarnen, *White Book* of 58
Savonarola, Girolamo 47, 196
Savoy:
county of 173, 176
Amadeus VIII, duke of 13
Saxo Grammaticus 58
Saxony:
duchy of; Saxons 61–2, 110, 128
Henry (the Lion), duke of 148

Scandinavia 49
  kings of 77
Schism, the Great 169–70
Schwyz, canton of 16, 58
Scotland 60, 63, 75, 87, 131, 134
  John Balliol, king of 75
Seckau, bishop of 190
Secreta Secretorum 73
Secretaries 125–6
Selestat, *Bundschuh* of 193
Seneca 84
Serbia 95
Seyssel, Claude de 5, 38, 52
Sforza, house of 159
  see also Milan
Sibyl, Sibylline prophecy 44–7
Sicily 10, 19, 77–8, 109–10, 134, 173,
  178, 187
  Alfonso V 134
  Robert, Guiscard 9
  Roger II 6
  see also Holy Roman Empire;
    Hungary; Naples and Sicily
Sickingen, Franz von 142
Siena 12, 34, 99, 102, 193, 197
Siete Partidas 64
Smaragdus 71
Songe du Vergier, Le 29
Sovereign, sovereignty 5–11, 18, 76–8,
  82–3
Spain 3, 7–8, 10, 58, 61, 139, 149–50,
  152, 166–7, 181
  Philip II, king of 100
Spier, *Bundschuh* of 193
Staple, Company of the 98
Statute 184–5
Stockholm 192
Strasburg 14, 25
  bishop of 43
Succession, hereditary 67–9
Suetonius 30
Suffolk, county of 113
Suger, abbot of Saint-Denis 69, 83
Sweden, kingdom of 176, 192
Swiss Confederation 10, 58, 182
  192
Sylla 59

Taborites 95
Tacitus 16, 63
Tadwin, legate 52
Tarascon, lord of 100
Tarbes 133
Tax, taxes 96–105, 150, 179–82, 198–9
Tell, William 58
Temple, Order of the 182
Terre Vermeil, Jean de 88, 170
Tertullian 4
Teutonia, Teutonici 50
Teutonic Order, Teutonic State 129,
  135, 150
  Grand Master of the 79
Theocracy, papal 9–10, 40
Thuringia, margraves of 46
Toulouse 33, 102–3, 133, 135, 193
  count of 100
  Estates of 203
Tournus, abbey of Saint-Philibert 92
Tours 152
  Estates General of 28, 83
Towns 164–5, 192
Transylvania 95
Trionfo, Agostino 10
Troy; Trojans 58, 60–1, 63
Tübingen, treaty of 172
Tudeschis, Niccolo de 35
Tudors 125, 160, 162
  propaganda of the 162
Turks 2, 173
Tuscany 12
  cities of 13
Tyrant, tyranny, tyrannicide 13, 84–6
Tyrol, county of 176, 192

Unions (of states) 49–50
Universities 167, 199–200
Unterwalden, canton of 58
Uri, canton of 58
Ursins, Jean Juvenal des 9, 87–8

Valencia 173, 181, 184
Valois, house of 68, 177
  Charles, count of 8
  Philip de, *see* France
Vegetius 140

Velay 189
Vendôme, Matthew of 58
Venice, republic of 12–13, 25, 31, 46,
    76–8, 99, 107–8, 128–9, 140, 145,
    164
  Mocenigo, Doge of 128
Verona, assembly of 174
Vienna, diocese of 150, 167
Vienne, Humbert II, dauphin of 79
Villani, Giovanni and Matteo 59
Vincennes, assembly of 10, 167
Virgil, Polydore 63
Visconti 59
  court of the 36
  see also Milan
Viterbo, John of 73, 151
Vivier-en-Brie, ordinance of 124

Wales 63, 75
  Owen Glendower, prince of 44
War, warfare 137–44, 178
Wars of the Roses 44, 92, 136, 162
Weisseneck family 190
Westminster 113–4, 122, 129, 130–2,
    135, 199

Great Hall at 26, 132
  Palace of 132
Westminster Abbey 63
  see also Lytlington
Wettin, State of the 170, 184, 186
William of Ockham 32, 42, 85, 174
Wimpheling, Jacob 52, 65
Winchester 63
  Statute of 139
Wolsey, Cardinal 126
Wool 96–9, 183
Worcestershire, county of 105
Wurtemberg:
  Landtag of 172
  'poor Konrad' in 193
Wycliffe, John 196

Xanten (Klein-Troja) 60

York 130, 133–4
  house of 125
Ypres 192

Zabarella 85
Zurich 16, 192